To
Fr. George Wilson Paul
from Malind Paul
8-23-87

OUR LADY SPEAKS TO HER BELOVED PRIESTS

9th English Edition
"Pro manuscripto"

**NATIONAL HEADQUARTERS
OF THE MARIAN MOVEMENT OF PRIESTS**
IN THE UNITED STATES OF AMERICA
P.O. Box 8
St. Francis, Maine 04774-0008

". . . I obtained from God for the Church the Pope who had been prepared and formed by me.

He has consecrated himself to my Immaculate Heart and has solemnly entrusted to me the Church, of which I am Mother and Queen.

In the person and the work of the Holy Father, John Paul II, I am reflecting my great light, which will become stronger the more the darkness envelops everything."

January 1, 1979

OUR LADY SPEAKS TO HER BELOVED PRIESTS

1st English Edition: May 1974
2nd English Edition: Mar. 1977 - 10,000 copies
3rd English Edition: Oct. 1977 - 20,000 copies
4th English Edition: Apr. 1978 - 40,000 copies
5th English Edition: July 1979 - 30,000 copies
6th English Edition: June 1980 - 40,000 copies
7th English Edition: Mar. 1983 - 60,000 copies
8th English Edition: Mar. 1985 - 30,000 copies
9th English Edition: Mar. 1987 - 50,000 copies

This is a noncommercial edition in conformity with the regulations approved by Pope Paul VI on October 14, 1966. The messages it contains call for purely human credence, leaving the ultimate judgment to Holy Mother Church.

This noncommercial edition is being distributed free of charge. Therefore no one is authorized to request payment, contribution or offerings. Those who wish to make a contribution to help cover the cost of printing and distribution may send an offering to the National Headquarters of the Marian Movement of Priests in their respective country.

Imprimatur:

There is nothing contrary to faith or morals in this manuscript.

+James J. Byrne, S.T.D.
Former Archbishop of Dubuque

Feast of the Annunciation
March 25, 1987

NOTE FROM THE NEW SPIRITUAL DIRECTOR

At long last, it has been possible to prepare a new edition of the book, brought up to date with all the new messages.

What has been the reason for this long delay in the preparation of a new edition? A change in the assignment of the Spiritual Director. Indeed, he has been appointed by his superiors to a new pastoral activity and, as of April 15, 1985, has ceased to function as Don Stefano Gobbi's spiritual director.

Since the responsibility for the publication of the writings of Don Stefano, who is the initiator and promoter of the Marian Movement of Priests, devolves upon the one who directs him spiritually, it was inevitable that there would be a long delay in the publication of the book.

I gave Don Stefano Gobbi the task of tracing out, as exactly and objectively as possible, a picture of the beginning, the spread, and the spirituality of the Marian Movement of Priests and of making very clear the relationship that exists between the Movement and the present book setting out some criteria of sound spiritual theology which can certainly be of help to one who undertakes its reading.

What spurred me on to prepare the present publication was simply the desire of assisting so many brothers and sisters to walk along the way of perfect entrustment to the Immaculate Heart of Mary and of giving a helping hand to all, especially those who are more exposed to dangers and whom I urge to hasten as quickly as possible into the sure refuge of her motherly heart.

With love and trust, I confide this new edition to our heavenly Mother and I ask that she make, of such a little and poor instrument, an effective means for the triumph of her Immaculate Heart in the world.

March 30, 1986
The feast of the Resurrection

N.B.   A meditative reading of the entire introduction is recommended for an accurate and balanced interpretation of the messages contained in this book.

DON STEFANO GOBBI

PREFACE

THE MARIAN MOVEMENT OF PRIESTS
PART ONE
ORIGIN — SPREAD — SPIRITUALITY

Its Origin

On the 8th of May, 1972, Don Stefano Gobbi was taking part in a pilgrimage to Fatima and was praying in the little Chapel of the Apparitions for some priests who, besides having personally given up their own vocations, were attempting to form themselves into associations in rebellion against the Church's authority.

An interior force urged him to have confidence in the Immaculate Heart of Mary. Our Lady, making use of him as a poor and humble instrument, would gather all those priests who would accept her invitation to consecrate themselves to her Immaculate Heart, to be strongly united to the Pope and to the Church united with him, and to bring the faithful into the secure refuge of her motherly heart.

Thus a powerful cohort would be formed, spread throughout every part of the world and gathered together, not with human means of propaganda but with the supernatural power which springs from silence, from prayer, from suffering and from constant faithfulness to one's duties.

Don Stefano asked Our Lady interiorly for a little sign of confirmation. She gave it to him promptly, before the end of that same month, at the Shrine of the Annunciation in Nazareth.

The origin of the Marian Movement of Priests stems from this simple and interior inspiration which Don Stefano received in prayer at Fatima.

Concretely, what was he to do? In October of the same year, a timid attempt was made, by way of a gathering of three priests, for prayer and fraternal sharing, in the Parish of Gera Lario (Como); a notice of the Movement was given in some papers and Catholic reviews.

By March, 1973, the number of priests inscribed was about forty. In September of the same year, at San Vittorino, near Rome, the first national gathering took place, with twenty-five priests taking part, out of the eighty already enrolled.

Beginning in 1974, the first cenacles of prayer and fraternal sharing among priests and faithful took place. These gradually spread throughout Europe and every part of the world.

By the end of 1985, Don Stefano Gobbi had already many times visited the five continents to preside at the Regional Cenacles, involving a good 350 air flights and numerous journeys by car and train. He has conducted 890 cenacles, of which 482 took place in Europe, 180 in America, 97 in Africa, 51 in Asia and 80 in Oceania.

This gives evidence of how the Movement has, throughout these years, spread everywhere in an astounding way.

Its Spread

The Marian Movement of Priests has succeeded in expanding in a silent and extraordinary way. In practically all the countries of Europe, America, Asia, Africa and Oceania, national directors have at this time been appointed and entrusted with the task of gathering the membership and assisting in the formation of cenacles.

To them has been entrusted the task of appointing the various regional and diocesan directors, taking every care that all be carried out with greatest fidelity to the spirit of the Movement.

In view of the autonomy which is given to each of the national centers, it is difficult to give a precise numerical picture of the M.M.P. But this is not of great importance, as there is question of a "spirit" which escapes external controls and which becomes a reality in the measure in which each priest, who belongs to it, seeks to live daily his consecration to Mary.

If one were to judge from the letters of inscription, members would now number about three hundred bishops and more than sixty thousand priests, coming both from the diocesan clergy and from all the orders and religious congregations. As to the laity, since there is no formal inscription we cannot give even an approximate figure, although they certainly number in the millions.

Moreover, it is consoling to note the existence of a large segment of priests who are sympathetic; although they have not yet been inscribed in the Movement, they demonstrate their solidarity with it in various ways and on various occasions. I believe they are more numerous than those who have been actually inscribed. If they live the spirit of the Movement, though they are not registered, they are already doing what is essential.

Although, almost imperceptively, we have become a numerous company, it still happens that many priests do not know their confreres who live quite close to them and are also members of the Movement. This happens in areas where the M.M.P. is just beginning, but it also happens in some other places. The reasons for this are the scanty organization we make use of—and this will remain one of our traits—and secondly, a certain reserve (given that we are concerned with a spiritual choice and a commitment that is mainly interior) which makes us unwilling to hand over lists and addresses to just anyone who asks for them.

And yet, we are everywhere witnessing the following astounding phenomenon: Our Lady is seeing to it that, through cenacles of prayer and brotherhood, her priests get to know one another, help one another, love one another as brothers and become a cohesive force throughout the entire clergy.

Through the consoling reality of the communion of saints, those priests who have already preceded us into eternal life seem still active members and closer to us than ever. Among them are some cardinals (the first of whom to enroll was Cardinal Giacomo Lercaro, then Archbishop of Bologna), many bishops (we recall, among others, Bishop Joao Venancio Pereira, formerly Bishop of Leiria and Fatima, who enrolled in 1973 and died in 1985) and now more than five thousand priests who enriched their last years of intense apostolate or of sickness by accepting Our Lady's invitation and by living it in the M.M.P. Of these, it is good to recall a Servant of God, Father Gabriele Ellegra, a well-known biblical scholar and translator of the Holy Scriptures into Chinese, whose last work was a translation into Chinese of "Our Lady Speaks to Her Beloved Priests."

In its wide and rapid spread, the M.M.P. has encountered fewer difficulties than one would have feared. As its characteristic is fidelity to the Church and obedience to legitimate superiors, where these (especially at the episcopal level) have shown themselves sympathetic and encouraging, things have proceeded with greater facility. On the other hand, it has been a question of exercising patience in knowing how to wait, in those situations where Authority has been undecided or indifferent.

We are constantly aware of the watchful and enlightening presence of Our Lady, above all as she guides "her" Movement: she comforts in difficulties and restrains the enthusiastic; she teaches how to assume with courage the liberty of the children of God, while at the same time preventing from taking positions not in accordance with, or in outright rebellion to, superiors—a thing which is obviously in flat contradiction to the second fundamental principle of the Marian Movement of Priests: love for the Pope and the hierarchy united with him.

Its Spirituality

(a) What the Marian Movement of Priests Is

The M.M.P. is a little seed planted by Our Lady in the garden of the Church. Very quickly it has become a great tree which has spread its branches into every part of the world. It is a work of love which the Immaculate Heart of Mary is stirring up in the Church today, to help all her children to live, with trust and filial hope, the painful moments of the purification.

In these times of grave danger, the Mother of God and of the Church is taking action, without hesitation or uncertainty, to assist first and foremost the priests, who are the sons of her maternal predilection.

Quite naturally, this work makes use of certain instruments; and in a particular way Don Stefano Gobbi has been chosen. Why? In one passage of the book, the following explanation is given: "I have chosen you because you are the least apt instrument; thus no one will say that this is your work. The Marian Movement of Priests must be my work alone. Through your weakness I will manifest my strength; through your nothingness I will manifest my power" (July 16, 1973).

The M.M.P. is not therefore just a laudable association with a lot of statutes and directors, set in motion by some fervent priest or soul, but a "spirit," as our Holy Father John Paul II happily and intuitively perceived. It is something impalpable, but very strong and very much alive, as are the gifts of God, and it has as its main purpose the living out of the consecration to the Immaculate Heart of Mary. For priests, to entrust themselves to Mary is to become more aware of their own consecration, made to God, on the day of their baptism and their priestly ordination.

The M.M.P. becomes a reality not by numbers, or the resonance of names, or the efficiency of organization, but in the measure that one listens to Our Lady and cooperates with the work of the Holy Spirit, to the glory of the Most Holy Trinity.

He belongs to the spirit of the Movement who, whether inscribed or not, consecrates himself to the Immaculate Heart of Mary, seeking to live accordingly and to carry on his work in obedience to, and for the good of, the Church and who helps the faithful in living their entrustment to Our Lady.

It is a Movement open to all priests, diocesan or religious, without distinction of age or office. There are priests inscribed in it who are happy in their work and filled with zeal, and there are some who are embittered because of negative experiences either in their personal lives or in the apostolate.

The heart of Our Lady is open to all her sons; her arms gather and bring together her priests, without distinction or partiality. The choice of predilection is not one made on the part of Our Lady, who addresses herself resolutely to everyone: "What I communicate to you, my son, is not for you alone, but for all my priest-sons, whom I love in a special way" (August 29, 1973). The choice is made on the part of those who voluntarily accept the motherly invitation.

Whoever wishes to join the Movement and be kept informed of its activities, may send in writing his declaration of membership to the proper national or regional center or, if these do not yet exist, he may send his request to Italy to the:

> Movimento Sacerdotale Mariano
> Via Mercalli, 23
> 20122 Milano
> Italy

However, this enrollment means nothing if interior adherence is lacking. And this is all the more true of a willingness to live, and to bring others to live, the consecration to Our Lady.

It is well to remember that Our Lady is speaking not only to those who are enrolled in the Marian Movement of Priests, when she speaks to her beloved sons, but to all those bishops and priests who have entrusted themselves to her and who strive to live as her consecrated ones.

This pledge of total consecration to the Immaculate Heart of Mary gives priests a profound sense of trust and serenity. To believe, in each and every concrete situation, that Our Lady is always near, anxious to help us as much and even more than any mother, gives a feeling of security, even amid the personal sufferings and uncertainties of the days in which we live.

And so, we arrive at the very core of the evangelical message, that is, trust in the providence of God, which brings us to accept every circumstance of life with the filial confidence of little children who abandon themselves completely to his fatherly love.

Thus, the past is left to the infinite mercy of the Heart of Jesus; the future is awaited as a gift from Providence, coming to us through the hands of the mediatrix of all graces; and the present is lived with joyous zeal, like children playing or working under the eyes of their mother.

(b) The Characteristic Commitments of Its Spirituality

There are three commitments which characterise the spirituality of the Marian Movement of Priests: consecration to the Immaculate Heart of Mary, unity with the Pope and with the Church united to him, and the leading of the faithful to a life of entrustment to Our Lady.

The pages which illustrate the spirituality of the Movement are taken from Circulars 21, 23, and 24 of Don Stefano Gobbi.

-1- Consecration to the Immaculate Heart of Mary

We are living in difficult, insecure and painful times. Today the red dragon is ruling in the world and has succeeded in building up an atheistic civilization. Man, puffed up by technical and scientific progress, has put himself in the place of God and has built up a new secular civilization. This radical rejection of God is the real chastisement of modern-day society.

As God is the Savior and Jesus Christ alone the Redeemer of man, humanity of today can only be saved on the condition that it returns to the Lord. Otherwise it runs the danger of destroying itself by its own hands.

But how can it be saved if it obstinately continues to reject God who alone can lead it to salvation? It is here that Mary's role, in view of her motherhood, enters in. Mary is the mother of Jesus and has been constituted by Jesus as the true Mother of all men. And therefore Mary is also Mother of the men of today, of this rebellious humanity, so far away from God.

Her motherly task is that of saving humanity. And Our Lady, in order to be able to save it, wishes to become the way of its return to the Lord. She acts in all manner of ways and gives herself much to do in order to bring about this return. This is the reason for her many extraordinary manifestations, which have become so numerous today: she wants to make us understand that our heavenly Mother is present and is at work in the midst of her children.

She wishes to act in person, but not directly. She is able to act through those children who consecrate themselves to her Immaculate Heart, who entrust themselves to her completely, in such a way that she can live and manifest herself in them. She wants above all to work through the priests, because they are her sons of predilection.

It is typical of the spirituality of the M.M.P. not to formulate a doctrine of the consecration which is, in any case, already known in the Church, but to suggest that one learn it by the experience of everyday life. For this purpose, it sets out an itinerary which leads to the perfection of entrustment to Our Lady and which develops through four successive stages: that of accustoming oneself to living with Mary, of allowing oneself to be interiorly transformed by her, of entering with her into a communion of hearts, and lastly of reliving Mary.

The purpose of the consecration required as the first commitment for belonging to the M.M.P. is to allow Mary to live and work in us. "I want to love with your heart, to gaze with your eyes, to console and encourage with your lips, to assist with your hands, to walk with your feet, to follow your bloodied footprints and to suffer with your crucified body" (July 1, 1981).

Now we can understand why Our Lady asks for consecration to the Immaculate Heart for anyone who wishes to belong to her cohort. She herslf wants to live and act in her consecrated children, in such a way that they become an expression of her sorrow and of her motherly love, and work untiringly to lead all men back to God.

Thus present-day humanity will be able to reach salvation along the road of the motherly love of Mary, who becomes the channel through which the merciful love of Jesus can reach all people. The consecration to the Immaculate Heart of Mary is directed solely to the consecration of the world, that is to say to the complete return of the world, to the perfect glorification of the Lord.

From this we can also understand why Pope John Paul II sees, in the act of consecration or entrustment to the Immaculate Heart of Mary, the most efficacious means of obtaining the gift of divine mercy upon the Church and upon all humanity (*Dives in Misericordia*, 15).

Thus light is also shed upon the profound significance of that act, often criticized by some, which he frequently repeats with fervor and intimate joy of soul; the act, that is, of his personal consecration to Mary. We understand, then, what he is doing in every part of the world when, during his frequent apostolic pilgrimages, he goes to the most famous shrines in order to consecrate to the Immaculate Heart of Mary the local Church in which he finds himself.

The profound reason is that the Pope sees, in the consecration to the Immaculate Heart of Mary, the most powerful means of obtaining the precious gift of the merciful love of Jesus upon the world of today!

". . . Oh, *how deeply we feel the need of consecration* for humanity and for the world: for the contemporary world! . . . *Oh, how painful* therefore is everything which, in the Church and in each one of us, is opposed to holiness and consecration! . . . Blessed be all those souls who obey the call of eternal Love. Blessed be those who, day by day, with unexhausted generosity, welcome your invitation, O Mother, to do what your Jesus says, and give to the Church and the world a serene witness of a life inspired by the Gospel" (Consecration to the Immaculate Heart of Mary by John Paul II, made on March 25, 1984).

-2- *Unity with the Pope and with the Church United to Him*

The Church is both divine and human and, in its human dimension, it is fragile and sinful and thus has great need to do penance. The Church is the light of the world, "*Lumen Gentium*," but often the evils of the world in which it lives become the maladies which attack the human dimension of the Church. This has been proven by nearly two thousand years of its history.

Today the Church is living in a world which has built up a new secular civilization. The spirit of this world, or secularism, which has entered into its interior, has caused the state of great suffering and of crisis in which the Church finds itself. This is the famous "smoke of Satan" spoken of by Pope Paul VI of venerable memory.

Secularism, at the intellectual level, becomes "rationalism" and, at the level of life, it becomes "naturalism."

Because of rationalism, there is today the tendency to interpret the whole mystery of God and the deposit of revealed truth in a purely human way, and thus often the fundamental dogmas of the faith are denied and most serious errors are spread about in a hidden and ambiguous way. Sometimes these errors become taught even in Catholic schools and little or nothing survives of divine scripture or even the Gospel of Jesus.

"You have made a Gospel of your own with your own words" (September 25, 1976).

Because of naturalism, there is the practice today of giving great value to one's own personal actions, to efficiency and to the setting up of programs in the apostolic sector, forgetting the primary value of divine grace and that the interior life of union with Christ, that is of prayer, must be the soul of every apostolate.

From this originates the gradual loss of the awareness of sin as an evil and the neglect of the sacrament of reconciliation, which has now spread throughout the whole Church.

Against these errors, which are ensnaring the integrity of the faith in a subtle and dangerous way, Cardinal Joseph Ratzinger, Prefect of the Sacred Congregation for the Doctrine of the Faith, has spoken out clearly with his famous interview, publilshed in the book "The Ratzinger Report."

But the *Magisterium* of the Pope has also frequently spoken out powerfully and insistently.

So then, one spontaneously asks oneself: how is it that the Church has not yet emerged from this profound crisis of its faith? The persistence of the crisis within the Church up to the present time comes only from its interior disunity. Because of this, not everyone today is listening to and following what the Pope, together with his *Magisterium*, is pointing out.

Our Lady has obtained for the Church a great Pope, consecrated to her Immaculate Heart and whom she herself is leading along all the roads of the world, in order to spread the light of Christ and of his Gospel of salvation and to strengthen everyone in the faith, both pastors and the flocks entrusted to them. But, about the Pope, there is often a great void: his *Magisterium* is not supported by the whole Church and often his word falls upon a desert.

And yet the renewal of the Church takes place only through its interior unity. The road to be followed is still that of full union of all the bishops, priests, and faithful with the Pope.

Here we find explained the profound reason for the second commitment of the Marian Movement of Priests. Our Lady is asking of us today to be an example to everyone, in this unity. An example in loving the Pope, in praying and suffering for him, in heeding and spreading the teachings of his *Magisterium*, and especially in always obeying him in everything.

Our Lady desires that there be a return among the clergy to the humble and powerful exercise of the virtue of obedience!

Naturally obedience to the Pope, who is the point of reference and of unity with the bishops, implies the unity of obedience with the pastor of one's own diocese and with one's own superiors.

-3- Leading the Faithful to Entrustment to Our Lady

From the very beginning of this Movement there was an awareness that the religious and faithful were being called to take part in it. In fact, the third commitment on the part of a priest of the M.M.P. is that of leading the faithful, entrusted to his pastoral care, to consecration to the Immaculate Heart of Mary.

". . . But the priests must now begin to act; through them I want to return to the midst of my faithful, because it is with them, gathered about my priests, that I want to form my invincible cohort . . . " (November 1, 1973).

This explains why the M.M.P., which sprang up in the first place for priests, opens out also upon the vast world of the laity, thus giving rise to the Marian Movement.

(c) The Marian Movement

The Marian Movement is made up of all those non-clerical religious and of the faithful who have committed themselves to live a life of consecration to the Immaculate Heart of Mary, in serene union with their priests and their bishops. They are not bound together by any kind of juridical bond and can freely carry on their work within those ecclesiastical associations to which they belong.

As members of the Marian Movement, they commit themselves to the experience of a life totally entrusted to Our Lady, that they may be assisted by her to remain faithful to their own baptismal consecration and to become witnesses of communion and unity, constantly striving for conversion through prayer and penance.

-1- Living Their Baptism

In the act of consecration for the members of the Marian Movement, set out at the end of the book, we read: "By this act of consecration we intend to live, with you and through you, all the obligations assumed by our baptismal consecration." These words bring out clearly how a member of the faithful, who makes the consecration to the Immaculate Heart, is assisted by Our Lady especially in living out today the obligations assumed at the time of baptism. It is natural that, in thse times, the Christian, immersed in a world which is so secularized, finds it very difficult to live out his baptismal consecration.

Baptism brings about a radical transformation: it communicates grace and divine life itself and makes us into the image of Jesus Christ whose brothers we become and whose life we must relive in our own.

At the present time, through all the means of social communication, the Christian is easily made use of and even manipulated by the world in which he lives in such a way that often, almost without noticing it, he absorbs and shares the values which are opposed to those taught by Christ.

Thus today how many baptized persons there are who, in their everyday life, come to betray their baptismal consecration! And so Our Lady asks that the faithful consecrate themselves to her Immaculate Heart, as a specific commitment of the Marian Movement and then, as a mother, gently leads them to live out their baptism, in complete fidelity to Jesus and to his Church.

Again, it is said in the act of consecration of the laity: "We promise you to be united with the Holy Father, with the hierarchy and with our priests, in order thus to set up a barrier to the growing confrontation directed against the *Magisterium*, that threatens the very foundation of the Church."

This is a characteristic commitment, which marks every member of the faithful who belongs to the Movement, and urges him to become ever an instrument of communion, of peace and of unity.

In this period of its purification, the Church is living through times of great suffering. The M.M.P. desires above all to share fully in the sufferings of the Church, drinking together with her the chalice of much bitterness. For this reason it is never called to act by way of criticism or judgement and, much less, by way of condemnation. And therefore it has nothing to do with, and in fact totally rejects, those means taken by many today who publicly, even through the press, criticize Holy Mother Church in a bitter and mischievous way.

We must never pour vinegar on open and bleeding wounds. The only help the Movement wants to give to the Church is that of love, a filial and merciful love.

"I will bring you to love the Church very much. Today the Church is going through times of great suffering because it is loved less and less by its own children. Many would like to renovate it and purify it solely by criticism and by violent attacks on its institution. Nothing is ever renewed or purified without love" (November 9, 1975).

The specific commitment of the Marian Movement consists in leading the faithful to be witnesses of love for the Church today. A love which must become concrete in a faithful and passionate presence, to share in its sorrow and bear with it its great cross. A love which above all brings us to be, in every circumstance, instruments of coherence and of unity, and thus to contribute to healing the Church of its many deep and painful lacerations.

-3- Commitment to Conversion

In the act of consecration for the laity, it is further affirmed: "We pledge to bring about in ourselves that interior conversion so urgently demanded by the Gospel." Our Lady asks of the faithful also, who belong to the Movement, a daily commitment to conversion along the road of prayer and penance.

For this, as an attentive and concerned mother, she helps them flee from sin, to live in the grace of god, invites them to frequent confession, to an intense eucharistic life, always to observe the law of God, with a particular commitment to live the virtue of purity especially on the part of young people and those who are engaged to marry, and conjugal chastity within the sacrament of matrimony, according to the doctrine of Christ, recently reaffirmed by the *Magisterium* of the Church. And this becomes so necessary in our day in order to counteract a shameless impurity which has spread everywhere and in order to help make the world cleaner and more beautiful.

"Let the faithful be a good example by an austere manner of life, by repudiating styles which are ever increasingly provocative and indecent, by opposing in every way possible the spread of immoral literature and entertainment and this continual flooding from a sea of filth that is submerging everything. Let them be an example to all by their purity, their sobriety, and their modesty. Let them flee all those places where the sacred character of their person is defiled. Let them form about my priests my great white army" (November 1, 1973).

There are now tens of millions of lay people from every part of the world who have joined the Marian Movement and often it is from them that the priests receive good example, concrete assistance and precious encouragement.

(d) The Cenacles

It can be said that the M.M.P. is at work in all the areas of ecclesial life in which its members find themselves personally engaged: from religious houses to parishes, from the theological sector to the pastoral, and from the field of spirituality to the apostolate of the missions.

The more a priest lives the spirit of the Movement the more he commits himself enthusiastically to the initiatives of the Church and makes them his own. But at times the Movement develops within the life of the Church, with an activity proper to itself, which is that of bringing the priests and the faithful together in gatherings of prayer and fraternal sharing, called "cenacles."

-1- Regional, Diocesan, and Family Cenacles

Regional and diocesan cenacles always develop in union with the bishop of the place who either takes part personally or, at times, gives his assent and blessing. These cenacles offer an enviable opportunity of experiencing in a concrete way prayer offered together and genuine fraternity, and are a great help to all in overcoming doubts and difficulties, in order to continue with courage along the arduous road of consecration.

From among those priests who have taken on the task of bringing their confreres together, directors of the Movement have been selected at the national, regional, and diocesan level. From the Directors of each country very comforting accounts have been received. In these we find assurance that the cenacles have continued to develop increasingly.

Family cenacles are today particularly providential, in view of the serious break-up of family life. In these, one or more families of the Movement gather together in the same house. The rosary is recited. There is a meditation on the life of consecration. Also there is fraternal sharing during which mutual problems and difficulties are discussed. There is always, made as a group, the renewal of the act of entrustment to the Immaculate Heart of Mary. It has already become evident that Christian families have been helped by these family cenacles to live today as true communities of faith, prayer and love.

-2- The Structure of the Cenacles

The structure of the cenacles is quite simple. In imitation of the disciples who were gathered together with Mary in the Cenacle of Jerusalem, we come together:

- To Pray with Mary

The cenacles must, above all, be gatherings of prayer. But this prayer must be made together with Mary.

It is for this reason that one of the characteristics that is common to all the cenacles is the recitation of the holy rosary. Through it we invite Our Lady to join us in our prayer, we pray together with her, while she herslf unveils to our souls the mystery of the life of Jesus.

"Your rosary, which you recite in the cenacle in accordance with the urgent request of your heavenly Mother, is like an immense chain of love and salvation with which you are able to encircle persons and situations, and even to influence all the events of your time. Continue to recite it and multiply your cenacles of prayer" (October 7, 1979).

- *To Live the Consecration*

During the cenacles, we should help each other to live the consecration to the Immaculate Heart of Mary. This is the way we should do it: by accustoming ourselves to Our Lady's way of seeing, feeling, loving, praying, and working. The pause for meditation which is made during the cenacles must serve this purpose. There are other times and places for reflections concerning *aggiornamento* which are likewise indispensable for all.

Usually this space of time is given over to a communal meditation from the book of the Movement. It is not therefore within the spirit of the cenacle to spend this time listening to learned conferences or cultural updatings. Otherwise we would run the risk of getting away from that atmosphere of simplicity and of familiarity, which makes our gatherings so fruitful.

- *To Create Fraternity*

Lastly, in the cenacles we are all called to take part in the experience of a true fraternity. Is this not perhaps one of the most beautiful experiences, which always occurs in every cenacle? The more we pray and allow time for the action of Our Lady, the more we experience as well an increase of mutual love among ourselves.

"Why do I want you to come together in cenalces with me? To help you to love each other and to live in true brotherhood in the company of your Mother. It is necessary today that my priests know each other, that they help each other, that they truly love one another, that they be as brothers brought together by their Mother. There is today too much loneliness, too much abandonment for my priests. I do not want them to be alone: they must help each other, love each other, they must feel as – and really be – brothers" (January 17, 1974).

To the danger of loneliness, today particularly felt and dangerous for priests, here is the remedy offered by Our Lady: the cenacle, where we gather together with her to get to know, love and help each other as brothers.

(e) A Help for the Church

At the end of this first part of the preface in which we have sought above all to explain the origin, spread, and spirituality of the Marian Movement of Priests, we ask ourselves naturally this question: But what significance has this Movement in the Church today? Among the very many associations which are at work at every level, what is its function in the life of the Church? To this question it seems to me that I should give this simple response: the M.M.P. is a help which our heavenly Mother is offering to the Church today, that it may become aware of her motherly presence, be consoled in the midst of great sufferings, and feel itself ever surrounded by the love and prayer of so many of its children.

By means of the M.M.P., Our Lady wishes to offer to the Church a strong help in overcoming the painful crisis of the prufication through which it is living at this time. Because of this crisis, it can be seen that religious orders and congregations, once flourishing, are now going through times of particular difficulty.

Through her work, Our Lady wishes to assist everyone to overcome with her the present moments of suffering, and therefore invites first the priests, and then the religious and faithful to consecrate themselves to her Immaculate Heart and to be most faithful to the Pope and to the Church. The reason why the Movement does not have any juridical existence is that the aforementioned assistance can more easily be accepted by everyone. In this there lies its weakness because, not having any juridical form, it finds itself unable to seek any official approbation which could help it on its way. But this is also its strength because, as it does not impose any associative bond, it makes it easy for priests and religious to belong to it.

If we compare the Church to a great tree, I would say that the role of the M.M.P. is not to add another branch to the many which it already has, but that of infusing it with a secret strength which, coming from the Immaculate Heart of Mary, spreads through all its branches. And thus each one is assisted to develop according to its proper function and particular form, imparting to all a greater strength and beauty.

If then one wishes to know which is the most striking quality of the Marian Movement of Priests, it seems to me that I would have to say: *its essential poverty*. The Movement is so poor that it does not even have an official existence. And, not having any existence, quite naturally it cannot in any way be catalogued. Sometimes we smilingly say among ourselves: we are now more than seventy thousand priests and tens of millions of faithful, who belong to the Marian Movement of Priests, but nowhere can one find the proof that we exist.

The Movement is so poor that it cannot even own its own material resources, nor is it able to accept legacies or goods. It lives only from offerings sent to it by divine Providence to meet the heavy expenses of printing and distributing the books. But even in this matter, each national center manages its affairs autonomously in regard to the life of the Movement according to the means which divine Providence places at its disposal.

The Movement is poor in terms of human support, even in those things which could bring it comfort and joy in the midst of the inevitable difficulties which it encounters. Such could be particular recommendations on the part of superiors, praise and encouragement from ecclesiastical authority, and various other such marks of approval.

The sure support which Our Lady wishes to give us is her Immaculate Heart, and the only letter of recommendation is that which is to be found written in the life of each priest who has been consecrated to her, that he may thus be assisted in attaining holiness.

This radical poverty of the Marian Movement of Priests *must be loved, blessed and lived by each one of us*, because it is the poverty of Mary herself which is reflected in her work. It is the poverty of the Queen of Heaven who hides herself beneath the clothing of a simple housewife. It is the poverty of our Mother, immaculate and completely full of grace, which is revealed in her so simple and normal way of living in the perfect service of her spouse, Joseph, and her divine Son, Jesus.

The poverty of Mary should always be reflected in this work of hers, because the Marian Movement of Priests must also exist, spread and work *only at the service of—and as a perfect service of love for—the Church*. This is why the Movement must not even have an existence of its own: it can only live within the life of the Church and at the service of the Church.

In this way, the Church can be truly helped to carry its great cross in these bloody moments of its purification. And it is supported in its journey toward its greatest splendor, by the light which the Immaculate Heart gives to it by means of so many of her beloved children.

"And so, through you who have responded, my light spreads ever more in the Church. And thus the Church takes on vigor, confidence, power and a new impetus in the evangelization and salvation of all the peoples of the earth" (November 14, 1980).

PART TWO
THEOLOGICAL CRITERIA
FOR AN UNDERSTANDING OF THE BOOK

Some people are under the impression that the Marian Movement of Priests is identified with the book, "Our Lady Speaks to Her Beloved Priests," that is to say, the Movement and the book are one and the same thing. This is erroneous. The fact is, the M.M.P. is distinct from the book.

The Movement is a work of Our Lady and it consists essentially in calling priests to a consecration to her Immaculate Heart, to a great unity with the Pope and with the Church and to directing the faithful to a renewed Marian devotion.

As can easily be seen, it is a simple matter to set out the points which characterize the Movement, and so when one lives according to them he actually belongs to the Movement even though, hypothetically, he may never have heard of the little book. In this sense, th Marian Movement of Priests is distinct from the book.

But when one begins seriously to live out these commitments, one naturally feels the necessity to ask the question: How must I live them? Who will give me the assurance that I am living them? What is the road that I must travel? The book gives the answers to these questions, because it traces out the itinerary which one must follow in order to live out in a concrete way the consecration to the Immaculate Heart of Mary.

Then can the M.M.P. do without the book? In theory yes, but in practice absolutely no. The Movement is the work of Our Lady, and she herself has chosen the book as an indispensable instrument for its diffusion and for a genuine understanding of its spirit.

"Even the book is only a means for the spread of my Movement. It is an important means which I have chosen because it is small. It will serve to make known to many this work of my love among my priests" (June 24, 1974).

At this point it seems useful to me to pause a bit in order to explain the origin and the literary form of the book, its merits and limitations and, above all, to trace out some criteria of sound theology which are necessary for its exact understanding. In this inquiry we have made use of the considerable help provided by Circulars 16 and 18 of Don Stefano Gobbi and in particular by the introduction to the previous edition.

(a) Origin and Form of the Book

Starting in July 1973, Don Stefano began to note down some limpid and strong thoughts which sprang up in his soul. In obedience to his spiritual director, he undertook to gather them together in a little book, which numbered but a few pages and thus he managed to prepare the first edition which was presented at a gathering of priests of the Movement, which took place at the end of September of that same year. Its reception on that occasion was rather negative. Why such a rejection, despite the fact that its contents could be deemed to be in perfect conformity with what was perceived, in prayer and in discussions, to be the way of the Marian Movement of Priests? For the same reasons many find it difficult to accept the book today.

– First of all, because it lacked ecclesiastical approval. Such an approval had not been requested, as there was question then of a small publication in non-commercial manuscript form, and because writings of this nature are exempt in virtue of the "*motu proprio*" of Pope Paul VI, dated October 10, 1966.

– And then, because of the literary form in which it was presented. In fact, it provided the Movement with spiritual guidance as traced out by Our Lady herself, through the mystical phenomenon called "interior locutions," and it is with this aspect that priests are usually uncomfortable.

– And especially because, with so many messages circulating about today (of which it is permissible to think that some are pathological in origin and others of doubtful authenticity), it was feared that, by presenting a book of this nature, one would find it exposed to insurmountable obstacles and grave difficulties along the way, especially on the part of ecclesiastical authorities.

This hesitation was however gradually overcome by a great and ever-increasing acceptance of the book on the part of priests, religious and faithful and by the multiplication of translations everywhere into the principal known languages.

Everyone became aware, at first with a certain amount of surprise and then with a profound joy of soul, that it was a very small and limited means, but one chosen by Our Lady, for the spread of the Movement throughout every part of the world. The book in fact is an instrument, humanly speaking quite limited, of which our heavenly Mother has willed to make use in order to draw to herself priests and the faithful entrusted to their care. Once attracted to her motherly heart, priests and faithful will be brought by her into the intimacy of the Heart of Jesus, to live in the heart of the Church, his mystical body.

If one takes up this book with respect and meditates upon it with simplicity of heart, he will become aware of hearing a living word, sweet as honey and sharp as a sword. In it is set forth a spirituality based on Revelation and the life of the Church, by means of such luminous pillars as Saint John the Evangelist, Saint Francis of Assisi, Saint Francis de Sales, Saint Louis de Montfort, Saint John Bosco, Saint Therese of Lisieux and Saint Maximilian Kolbe. We can verify its validity only if we put it into practice; from its fruits you will know the quality of the tree.

The book is not organized into well-defined and connected chapters. However, the Marian Movement of Priests itself is understood more clearly in its demands and richness little by little as Our Lady makes it known through the writings of Don Stefano Gobbi. She herself is defining, spreading, and establishing the M.M.P., now in every part of the world, in a manner which is as discreet as it is magnificent.

(b) Merits and Limitations of the Book

The merits and limitations of the book come from the fact that it is a simple but precious instrument for the Marian Movement of Priests.

-1- It Is a Precious Means for Its Spread.

The M.M.P. has now spread into every region and it has always reached there by means of the book. It has been spontaneously translated into the principal languages and has thus been able to offer priests the possibility of knowing the urgent invitation of Our Lady to consecrate themselves to her Immaculate Heart.

From all the continents, priests, drawn by Mary's motherly invitation, have responded by joining the Movement, have entrusted themselves to her, and have began to gather together in cenacles. In this way, the work of Our Lady has succeeded in spreading everywhere and has reached even the most distant and remote parts of the earth. Whenever Don Stefano goes to even the most unknown parts of the world to take part in cenacles, he has the happy surprise of finding the Movement already spread there and thus cannot but recognize that the means of such a diffusion has always been the book. The book therefore serves, in a marvellous way, the purpose of making the Marian Movement of Priests known everywhere.

-2- It Is a Precious Means of Understanding Its Spirit

Meditation on the contents of the book often brings about a true transformation in souls. It helps one live the spirit of the consecration and sometimes gives priests the impression that it has responded to their particular needs. It encourages them to overcome difficult circumstances and leads them gradually to do everything with Mary, by means of Mary, and in Mary.

Thousands of letters of enrollment, sent in by priests to the various national centers, attest to this fact. I cite by way of confirmation some excerpts from three letters which I have received from priests.

From an Italian priest: "I have your book, which was made known to me by my bishop, now deceased. He read the book regularly and had it always in his hand. When his eyes became weak, I had the duty of reading him a few pages. They delighted him and helped greatly to bolster up his spirit. He found in them a source of joy and fervor."

From a missionary in Brazil: "My fear is that of coming to a halt, and this for a number of reasons. These can be described in brief as those simple temptations which, in one way or another, are my daily food. But then, after meditating on the contents of the book, I renew my act of abandonment to the Immaculate Heart of Mary and, little by little, my confidence is reborn. How I would like to live the awareness of being Mary's very own property."

From a country in Central America: "I am a priest who was laicized fourteen years ago. Having been swept away by a grave crisis in faith and in my moral life, I no longer prayed. I am a professor in a large university. Your book came into my hands but for many months I did not read it, thinking it to be an ordinary run-of-the-mill book of Marian devotion. But I finally felt a desire to open the book, which I had not until then touched. I don't know what happened inside of me. From the first page, there was awakened in me a growing desire to read more and more, an eagerness and a renewed love for Jesus and for his Church. I then remembered something that I had learned in the seminary: to Jesus through Mary. I prepared myself all through the month of November and, on the eighth of December, I made my act of consecration to the Immaculate Heart."

The undeniable merits of the book consist therefore in the contributions it succeeds in making to the spread and the understanding of the spirit of the Marian Movement of Priests.

-3- *The Limitations of the Book*

The limitations of the book are obvious and can be summed up in the fact that it is an undeniably humble and small instrument. Its poverty and littleness can be seen in a number of ways.

First of all in its form: it is presented to us in fact under the form of interior locutions, and this can be for many a stumbling block to its acceptance. But for whom? Generally speaking, for those who tend to reject any form of supernatural intervention, because they accept only that which passes through their own rational judgement. Such moreover can be persons who are good, well-trained and cultured but who have a mentality which is too adult and thus they stop short, scandalized, before the extreme littleness of this instrument.

It is also in its content that its littleness stands out. Indeed the book is not a treatise in either theology or Mariology, nor does it set itself forth as a complete compendium of Marian devotion. And neither does it develop, in a systematic way, the biblical and theological reasons which favor the spiritual experience of consecration to Mary. And these are however of considerable weight and value as is proven in de Montfort's *Treatise on True Devotion*.

It sets out, in extremely simple language, that which our Heavenly Mother desires today of her beloved sons, the priests. It is a matter of pages chosen from a diary, the content of which however is in accord with revealed doctrine and the teaching of the Church. It has the flavor of a colloquy between a mother and her children, in a style which, on first contact with the book, may appear to be too saccharine in some instances and too harsh in others. Some themes come back again and again with the insistence of a hammer, while others are almost ignored.

We do not have before our eyes a work which has been composed at a writing table and which develops according to a prearranged scenario. In order that disappointment may not lead to the rejection of the book, we should keep in mind that everything that each priest should know is necessarily taken for granted. Namely, for his interior life, for his apostolate and for living in communion with the whole Church and the world, the priest must draw upon Revelation and the *Magisterium* as well as the sources of sound philosophy, theology, literature, asceticism, and mysticism.

In fact the theological basis of the M.M.P. is constituted by the whole Marian doctrine contained in Sacred Scripture, illustrated by the Fathers of the Church and expounded by the *Magisterium* of the Church. The book does not seek to be a compendium of this because there already exist within the Church institutions which specialize in this task.

Nothing however is more contrary to the truth than the idea, held by some, that in the Marian Movement of Priests one finds the type of priest who is allergic to sound theological science or is sentimentalist or over-credulous. On the contrary, it can be calmly asserted that among those who have enrolled in the Movement there are priests who are outstanding in the area of culture, others who are in positions of great responsibility, and others who are assigned to more humble posts. Each of these has his own qualities and limitations, but all of them are among the most interiorly balanced of people.

A priest in Ireland has made the observation that one finds in the book a compendium of the doctrine of de Montfort concerning consecration, the way of spiritual childhood of Saint Therese of the Child Jesus and the implementation of the message of Fatima. It is for each one to verify this for himself.

It seems to me that one does indeed find here such a synthesis because, in order to live the consecration to Mary, it is necessary to offer oneself to her in a slavery of love which is fulfilled in concrete terms by living as a little child entrusted to her Immaculate Heart in such a way as to allow oneself, with utter docility, to be nourished, clothed and led by her at every moment.

At this point, if at no other, one can ask a very interesting question: Why has Our Lady wished to choose so small and limited an instrument? "You have not understood, my son, that I have chosen foolishness to confound wisdom and weakness to vanquish strength" (September 27, 1973). The whole secret is right here!

But this is the very secret of the Gospel. Jesus did not condemn the learned and the wise but He thanked his heavenly Father for having hidden from them the mysteries of his reign and for having revealed them to the little ones.

Certainly every member of the Marian Movement of Priests has the duty of reading and meditating upon what is contained in the little but precious instrument, which is the book, if he wishes to live his act of consecration to the Immaculate Heart of Mary and thus to contribute to the carrying out of her motherly plan of salvation and of mercy.

(c) Theological Criteria for Its Understanding

The Interior Locution

-1- Leaving to everyone the freedom to hold to his own convictions in this matter, it can be credibly affirmed with considered certainty that what are represented to us in this book are "interior locutions." But alas, mystical theology is too little known so that some phenomena are either under-valued to the point where they are scoffed at, *a priori*, or else they are over-valued to the extent that they are considered on a par with official Revelation.

One forgets that grace makes us true sons of God and that Mary is truly our mother. One fails to keep sufficiently in mind that prayer is not a monologue but a dialogue, the greater part of which should be left to the heavenly participants. We know that God has infinite possible ways of communicating with his children, selecting for each one the form that is most adapted to him, over and above the official means known to everyone.

-2- What is an interior locution? First of all, it is necessary to make clear that it is not something strange or sensational, but a mystical phenomenon present in the life of the Church and described in manuals of spiritual theology. It is not a sensorial communication with Jesus, Our Lady or the saints such as takes place in authentic apparitions. Here one does not see with the eyes, hear with the ears, nor does one touch anything. Nor is it simply a good inspiration, that light which the Holy Spirit normally causes to pour down into the minds and hearts of those who pray and live by faith.

In the case of an authentic phenomenon, the interior locution is that gift by which God wishes to make something known and to help someone carry something out as well as the outward clothing of this gift, in terms of human thoughts and words, according to the style and the way of writing of the person who receives the message.

The person becomes an instrument of communication, while still maintaining his full freedom, which is expressed in an act of assent to the action of the Holy Spirit. While receiving the word from the Lord, the person's intellect remains, as it were, inactive: that is to say, it does not search for thoughts or for a way to express them as, for example, would be the case when one is writing a letter or preparing a demanding discourse.

-3- Saint John of the Cross calls locutions, or formal supernatural words, those distinct words which the spirit receives not from itself but from another person, sometimes while it is recollected and sometimes when it is not. ("Ascent of Mount Carmel," Book 2, Chapter 28, note 2). Tanquerey defines locutions or supernatural words as manifestations of divine thought heard by the interior or exterior senses. ("The Spiritual Life," Book 3, Chapter 3, No. 1494).

One could therefore give interior locutions this definition: "They are very clear words perceived by the person who receives them as though they were being born from the heart and which, taken together, form a message."

The summons from heaven is almost always unforeseen: it is the Lord, or Our Lady, or the angels, or the saints, who take the initiative as regards the time and the content of the message.

-4- To discern authentic locutions from those that are spurious, or which are the fruit of deliberate deceit, or of morbid autosuggestion, or of downright satanic interference, there are norms which are fairly precise. The literature on this matter is neither rich nor up-to-date. The writings of the great mystics (Saint John of the Cross, Saint Theresa of Avila, Saint Ignatius, Saint Catherine of Genoa, Saint Catherine of Siena) are helpful as are the studies and treatises of spiritual theology of Tanquerey, Royo Marin, A. Poulin, Garrigou-Lagrange, etc.

Less easy to measure is the weight of the human element in which the ineffable Word of God becomes clothed, in order to arrive at a clear understanding of what is essential and universal in the contents of the message, in a word, what is of God.

One hears it said frequently that the messages, such as those contained in the book, are too frequent and wordy. A comparison is made with the style of the Gospel and of the apparitions which have been approved by the Church, while we forget that we are dealing here with manifestations of the Word of God which are very different, not only in the matter of authority but also of modality.

In our respect for each person and his freedom, why should we be obliged to make an exception only for God, as though He must ask permission of us and conform himself to our tastes in the choice of places, times, modes and instruments for communicating with his children?

There is need to grow in the spirit of wisdom, so as to rejoice with Jesus as He exclaims: "I thank you, O Father, because you have hidden your secrets from the learned and wise, while you have revealed them to little children," and to exult with the spirit of our heavenly Mother as she sings: "The poor He has filled with good things and the rich He has sent away empty-handed."

The Interior Locutions in the Book

In the specific case of the book, "Our Lady Speaks to Her Beloved Priests," it is good to keep in mind these theological criteria which can be of help for a deeper understanding of it.

-1- That which comes from God brings with it a profound sense of peace and inspires greater humility and confidence in our relationship with Him; it helps us detach ourselves from what is wrong and to do good in a spirit of simplicity and constancy; it respects our freedom and that of or neighbor. Whoever writes and works in the name of God edifies by his sense of balance, of humanity, of strength of soul, even within the framework of his human limitations and defects.

If some passage in this book should bring uneasiness, it would be better to put off its reading for a better occasion rather than to cause oneself to become distressed.

-2- God can and wants to communicate, at each moment of history, with his children living on earth. It is possible for us Christians to know whether something we meet up with is truly the work of God by measuring its content with Revelation which is faithfully guarded and infallibly given to us by the *Magisterium* of the Church.

In our case, the message taken as a whole, and likewise each ot its parts, is to be read and lived in the context of Christian doctrine. The purpose of these locutions is that of leading priests, more easily and steadily, to holiness of life, keeping in mind that:

a) The motherhood of Mary, with those rights and duties that follow upon it for her and for me, have to do with me personally.

b) Our Lady, who is the most humble and pure of all creatures, is not an end in herself, but she is a mother who begets and raises her adoptive children, bringing to completion the work accomplished in her Son Jesus. The goal then is solely the glorification of the Most Holy Trinity to which a priest who strives to fulfill his vocation is called.

c) As Mary is Mother of the Church, the historical context of her action and of our response is obedience and flawless unity with those who exercise the ministry of authority in the Church, namely the Pope, our respective bishops and our legitimate superiors.

d) Because the priest is a man dedicated to God for the sake of man, he feels himself duty bound to communicate to his faithful the joy, the richness and the obligations of the consecration to Our Lady which he, in the first place, has made and lived.

-3- While there is no question of age, of human gifts, of prestige and still less of past personal experience, be these positive or negative, in order to be received into the M.M.P., anyone who would want to enter it in a spirit of sectarianism would be totally ignorant of its nature. Within the Church there is an element which remains immutable and there are exterior forms with which the word and the life of the Church are clothed and which, like clothing, can change with time.

Those who are incurably nostalgic for the times that have gone confuse the ancient, which is always valid, with the old, which can be changed. So also those who search hungrily for new experiences seem to know a little more than the eternal Father. And they have an urge to solicit initiatives from the Holy Spirit, as though the salvation of each soul did not move along the one single track of prayer and penance.

-4- As the components and the expressions of doctrine and of Christian life are varied and complex, there is no intention, in these writings, of undervaluing, much less of condemning, any of them. If some expressions, for example, about contemporary theology seem strong, it must be understood that the point is not being made against theology as such but against the less than prudent way in which it is presented by some dissenting theologians and—which is still worse—against the way in which their teachings are so readily accepted by others.

Another example: some themes, such as those of a social or pastoral nature, are not treated expressly. For one thing, the book, not being an encyclopedia, cannot give answers to each and every question. And for another, those who truly entrust themselves to Our Lady do not just hold discussions in seats of learning but actually live and resolve concrete pastoral and social problems. We have only to call to mind Don Bosco, Don Orione and the present Pope himself.

-5- As regards the phenomenon of interior locutions recorded in the book, Don Stefano, in a completely normal way, neither in a trance nor in ecstasy, writes without interruption and without mental fatigue, without re-thinking or correction, that which he perceives interiorly, without paying any particular attention to it, according to the richness and the poverty of his own style and temperament, even when it is a question of bringing out truths previously unknown to the subject, or even before they were recognized as such by him.

From the writings of Don Stefano Gobbi, a preferential choice has been given to those pages which bring out best the total entrustment to Our Lady, in an atmosphere of evangelical spiritual childhood. As regards the validity of these writings, the classical and traditional criteria have been adhered to:

—correspondence with revealed truth;
—an enduring attitude of humility and obedience;
—some confirmations, humbly asked of God;
—the subject's calm availability and the peace which precedes and
  follows the divine communication.

What has been considered however as a positive sign is the enormous good which the M.M.P. has already achieved in the souls of tens of thousands of priests, many of whom were in situations of crisis, and the good that has been accomplished among very many of the faithful. From the wonderful fruits that have been produced, it can be deduced that the cause is to be found only in the spiritual light which flows from the Holy Spirit, through the intercession of the Immaculate Heart of Mary, into the minds and hearts of those who take this book into their hands.

-6- Since, in this period of considerable transformation for the Church and for the world, there is a multiplication of cases of persons who are said to be privileged with charismatic gifts such as visions, locutions, the gift of healing, etc., the M.M.P. takes this attitude:

— It does not make any bond of unity with (to the point of identifying itself with) any association, person or fact which takes on supernatural aspects. It recognizes that it has no right either to approve or to condemn because this task falls to the Church. It leaves each priest free to conduct himself, in his own personal life, in the way prudence suggests to him, always however in perfect obedience to ecclesiastical authority.

— When, on the other hand, there is question of revelations which contain doctrine not in conformity with the *Magisterium* or of persons who clearly depart from what characterizes normal human behavior and Christian balance, it must put its members on guard that they might remain completely faithful to the Church.

— When there is question of persons or events which the Church has been pleased to approve, the M.M.P. respects to the utmost the choices and tastes of each one, even though it cannot prescind from what has taken place at Fatima, which is a fact of universal importance not yet well understood and still less witnessed to, even though it has been officially accepted by the Church. We have only to recall Popes Paul VI and John Paul II, who journeyed as pilgrims to the Cova da Iria.

(d) Useful Advice for the Reader

-1- As is obvious, those who belong to the M.M.P. must accept first of all the entire patrimony of Revelation, in the light of the official *Magisterium*. On the other hand, they are free to accept, or to give no importance to, or to reject writings and happenings which are generically called, "private revelations."

Since mystical doctrine and history is little known, it is easy to fall into one of two forms of free and easy fanaticism. One is to preconceivedly deny and ridicule everything from the outset. The other is to accept naive-ly everything without any discernment.

Therefore one must avoid two extremes:

— childish credulity which does not carefully scrutinize the person or the event, in order to verify its credibility on a human plain, let alone on the supernatural. The instruments of God, even in their littleness and poverty, always exhibit a note of dignity and of purity and the signs of the Holy Spirit, which accompany every true apostle are not lacking to them.

— haughty superficiality which rejects or directly opposes that which, on the contrary, might be a work of God. In concrete situations, one loses sight of that which one respects in theory, namely, the ab-solute freedom of God and of all heaven to communicate with us, pilgrims here on earth.

-2- In reading this diary, which for many priests has already become a book for daily reflection, each sentence must be accepted with discern-ment, that is, according to the true meaning that is derived from the whole context.

Let us consider, for example, Our Lady's advice to give up newspaper and television. For some, this may be interpreted literally. For many priests, it means, rather, not wasting precious hours, following programs that are frivolous and tendentious and refraining from reading world events as interpreted in a materialistic sense, on the part of much of the present-day means of social communication.

Another example can be found in the frequent expressions, that at first sight can leave us uneasy, in which it is affirmed that the triumph of the Immaculate Heart of Mary coincides with the coming of the glorious reign of Christ. These expressions are of course to be interpreted in the light of what is taught in Sacred Scripture (Revelation 20, 1–7) and the authentic *Magisterium* of the Church. In this regard, let us keep before our eyes the frequent references which, in his first encyclical, "*Redemptor Hominis*" and in other important documents, Pope John Paul II makes concerning the Church of the second advent which awaits the second coming of Jesus.

-3- Another piece of advice lies in the invitation to accept the character of this book for what it is, a humble instrument. Our Lady wants it that way, written in a style chosen by Providence which, as Saint Paul teaches, chooses what is weak and poor in the eyes of the world, to confound earthly wisdom and diabolical strength.

-4- Because of the poisonous air we breathe, and the astuteness of the devil who can play nasty tricks on us, we ought not become hung up over the occasional sweetness of the style. Priests who have accustomed themselves to the educative action of Mary testify that she acts with sweetness but with firmness. It is with good reason that the eternal Father entrusted to her his Only-begotten Son that she might generate Him in his human nature and educate Him for Calvary. If Our Lady takes us up with gentleness it is because she loves us as a mother and that she may then place us, without any rebellion on our part, upon the wood of the cross, transforming us into the image of Jesus Crucified. This is a far cry from sentimentality!

-5- Even the numerous references to the evil times in which we are living and the painful future which awaits us must always be interpreted in their proper perspective, which is that pointed out by Sacred Scripture. How many times and in how many ways has the Lord threatened to punish his peole, precisely in the attempt to urge them along the road of conversion and of return to Him! One thinks, for example, of the preachings of the prophet Jonah, sent by God to announce the destruction of the city of Niniveh.

May have come to a halt, perplexed with the prophetic character in which some of the messages are clothed. And they have asked themselves the question: Is what is written indeed true? Will what is foretold in fact take place? And if they do not turn out to be true, what credibility can then be given to the words of the message? From an attentive reading of the book a most appropriate answer to all these questions can be found. It is this:

"Do not be delayed by the predictions I give you in the effort to make you comprehend the times in which you are living. Like a mother, I am telling you the dangers through which you are going, the imminent threats, the extent of the evil that could happen to you, only because this evil can yet be avoided by you, the dangers can be evaded, the plan of God's justice always can be changed by the force of his merciful love. Also when I predict chastisements to you, remember that everything, at any moment, can be changed by the force of your prayer and your reparative penance. Do not say therefore: how much of what you predicted to us has not come true. Instead, give thanks with me to the heavenly Father because, through your prayer and consecration, through your suffering and through the immense suffering of so many of my poor children, He alters the period of divine justice to permit that of great mercy to flower" (January 21, 1984).

-6- One must possess a solid evangelical maturity, preventing us from either disdaining or underestimating, *a priori*, a book such as this, or from overestimating it. It will give, in other words, a proper sense of respect for the experience which the message transmits to us and of the interior freedom with which it should be received. The perception that no word and no message are the Word itself, and the consciousness that in phenomena such as locutions a good deal of the subjective and human element can be introduced, should not on principle make these phenomena radically suspect. There is need to observe and evaluate, as Saint Paul says, and to retain whatever of good you can gather or extract. We should therefore take up a book of this kind with a reasonable amount of respect.

But this respect should be allied to a sense of freedom, which comes from the ability to put the "messages," which such books intend to transmit, in their proper place. It has been said and repeated: the words of Our Lady which have been made known here are neither a new Gospel nor a new faith. They lead us to discover, according to their typical resonance and outlook, the Gospel and the faith.

Hence, even a book like this can be accepted according to its measure of truth and can thus lead to the Truth which is Christ, and be a most suitable way of living, as authentic evangelical "children," this relationship with the Mother of the Lord and our Mother.

-7- This invitation to a simple and open faith in our relationship with the Mother of Christ and of the Church provides us with a sort of magnetic line of force according to which the compass of our Christian life and personality can orientate itself. This line of force must be found in the Mariological teaching of the Church which, for example, was set out for us in the Second Vatican Council (*Lumen Gentium*, Chapter VIII).

No locution, not even such as are gathered together in this book, could take the place of, or be put on a par with, an official public statement of the faith of the Church, from which the complete physiognomy of Mary and her mission will become apparent. We must also bring to the Church and show forth a childlike manner in our relationship with her, and hence in our apostolic life and mission. Mary is in the Church and leads to Christ in the Church: to that Church which has recently expressd itself in the Second Vatican Council and which has supplied us with pastoral goals which a priest must make his own. It is in this sign of the total docility of faith that Mary leads us to live the mystery of the Church, thereby accepting and disposing ourselves to accept its ministerial and apostolic dimension as well.

Even a priest, and in particular a diocesan priest, will not be able to find in this book everything that is entailed in his priestly life and mission. But sooner or later he will be able to find there a perspective, a point of view, a unifying element and a driving force for his priesthood, and above all for his personality as a Christian. And this will not be to the detriment of the attention he must give to the pastoral care of his Church, nor to the detriment of the proper attention he must give to solid theology.

-8- Finally, one last piece of advice for anyone approaching a reading of this book. One should pay more attention to its substance than to its form, and should take it up without any preconceived ideas but with humility and simplicity of heart. It should be read without presumption or avidity. One should reread it, meditating upon it calmly and lovingly. And then move on to verify it in his daily life, experiencing in a personal way what Our Lady is asking and promising.

The tens of thousands of priests who, throughout these years, have done so, have never regretted it. More than that, they are praying to Our Lady that others may follow in the same path.

Don Stefano Gobbi

Milan, February 2, 1986
Feast of the Presentation of the
Child Jesus in the Temple.

OUR LADY SPEAKS TO HER BELOVED PRIESTS

For All My Priest-Sons

"Whatever I communicate to you, my son, does not belong to you alone, but it is for all my priest-sons, whom I love with predilection.

Above all it is for the priests of the Marian Movement of Priests whom I love most tenderly, and whom I want to form and lead by the hand to prepare them for their great mission.

Therefore gather together in a booklet whatever I have told you . . . You are not to concern yourself in any way with all that has respect to its printing. Your confessor will provide for everything.

And this booklet is to be disseminated as quickly as possible among priests: it will be the means through which I will bring them together from all sides and with which I will form my invincible army.

Remain ever in my heart and trust in me, O my son!"

August 29, 1973

1973

THE MOVEMENT IS NOW BORN

1

I Will Always Be Near You

a   "Renew your consecration to my Immaculate Heart. You are mine; you belong to me.

b   At every moment you must be just as I would have you be; at every moment you must do just what I would have you do.

c   Do not be afraid. I will always be near you! I am now preparing you for great things, but little by little as a mother does with her child . . . "

2

The Movement Is Now Born

a   "Look at neither the newspapers nor television; remain ever close to my heart in prayer.

b   Nothing else should be of interest or importance to you save living with me, and for me.

c   The Marian Movement of Priests is now born, but it is so frail and small that, in order to grow, it has need of much prayer. You must live only for this. You will find relish and consolation in nothing else."

3

Your Mission Is Taking Shape

a   "Today I am really happy with you. You have remained close to my heart.

b   You see now how all the things of this world appear remote and hazy to you; how everything wearies and bores you; everything else that is not I, your Mother, who wants you whole and entire at every moment with her.

c   Learn to let yourself be possessed by me, so that in everything you do, it will be I who am doing it through you. It is no necessary now that it be the Mother who acts: and I want to act through you . . .

d   You will have to suffer more, but: courage! I will always be with you and you will delight as no one else in the sweetness of my mother's heart."

4

The Reason for My Tears

a   "(. . .) Yes, you have truly consoled me; you have changed my tears into a smile, my sorrow into joy.

b   I have smiled on you, I have blessed you.

c   The reason for my tears, for a mother's tears, is my children who, in great numbers, live unmindful of God, immersed in the pleasures of the flesh, and are hastening irreparably to their perdition.

d   For many of these my tears have fallen in the midst of indifference and have fallen in vain.

e   Above all the cause of my weeping is the priests: those beloved sons, the apple of my eye, these consecrated sons of mine.

f   Do you see how they no longer love me? How they no longer want me? Do you see how they no longer listen to the words of my Son? How they frequently betray Him? How Jesus present in the Eucharist is ignored by many, left alone in the tabernacle; often sacrilegiously offended by them, with wanton negligence?

g   You have offered me the Marian Movement of Priests; I receive it on my heart and I bless it.

h   These will all be my priests: consecrated to me, and they will do whatever I command them.

i　The time is near when I will make my voice heard by them, and when I will place myself at the head of this, my cohort, prepared for battle.

j　For the present they must be formed in great humility and at my directions: loving and being totally united with the Pope and the Church, living and preaching only the Gospel. This is so necessary today!

k　I love them, I bless them one by one."

5

July 16, 1973
Feast of Our Lady of Mount Carmel

I Will Be Your Leader

a　"You ask me why I have chosen you to spread my Movement, while you feel so inadequate and helpless.

b　Rightly do you see your nothingness and your weaknesses and you ask me: 'Why do you not choose someone more suitable and capable than me? How can you rely on me when you know very well my past infidelities?'

c　My son, I have chosen you because you are the least apt instrument; thus no one will say that this is your work.

d　The Marian Movement of Priests must be my work alone. Through your weakness I will manifest my strength; through your nothingness I will manifest my power.

e　I myself will be the leader of this army. I am now forming it in silence and in hiddenness just as, for nine months, I formed Jesus in my womb, and for many years in silence and hiddenness I brought Him up day by day.

f　This is the way it is now for the Marian Movement of Priests: like the little Jesus, I am forming it in silence and in hiddenness; this is the time of its infancy and its hidden life. What is needed now is much silence and humility, much confidence and prayer.

6

In Humility

g   I myself am now choosing the priests of the Movement and forming them according to the plan of my Immaculate Heart. They will come from everywhere: from the diocesan clergy, from the religious orders and from the various institutes. They will make up the cohort of 'my priests' which I myself will nourish and form, preparing them for the approaching battles of the kingdom of God.

h   Let there be no leader among you. *I myself will be your leader.* You must all be brothers: loving, understanding and helping each other.

i   The only thing that matters is that you let yourself be formed by me: for this it is necessary that each one of you offer himself and consecrate himself to my Immaculate Heart and entrust himself completely to me just as Jesus entrusted Himself totally to me; and then I will take care of everything.

j   I will form you to a great love for the Pope and for the Church united to him. I will prepare you for a heroic witnessing to the Gospel which, for some, will be even to the shedding of their blood.

k   And when the time comes, the Movement will then go out into the open to fight openly that cohort which the devil, ever my Adversary, is now forming for himself from among the priests. (. . .)"

6   *July 21, 1973*

Let It Be I Who Act

a   "(. . .) Why do you become troubled? Why are you worried? To be consecrated to me means to let yourself be led by me. It means to entrust yourself to me, like a child who lets itself be led by its mother.

b   You must therefore accustom yourself to a new way of thinking, to a new way of acting. It is not your place to think of what is best for you; do not be making plans or building your tomorrow, for, you see, I upset everything and then you feel bad.

c   Why do you not wish to entrust yourself to me? Let it be I who build – moment by moment – your future. It is enough for you to say just as a little child: 'Mother, I entrust myself to you, I let myself be led by you. Tell me: what must I do?'

d   And also, let it be I who act through you. For this, how necessary it is for you to die to yourself!

e   For this it is necessary that you accustom yourself to suffer, to be misunderstood, to be ignored, to be even trampled on a bit. This hurts you quite a bit, does it not?

f   But when you speak to the priests of the Movement concerning the consecration, tell them how they must rely totally on me and entrust themselves to me; then they will be able to look to your person and you yourself will be a good example for them.

g   Do not take it too hard, my son. I love you, I love you so very much!"

7

Only and Always a Mother

a   "Are you pleased with the house I have prepared for you? You never dreamed that it would be so beautiful: beneath a cliff; with your room practically in a cleft of the rock; overlooking the sea, and the little chapel where Jesus abides nearby: the Son at the side of my dearest son.

b   You had no idea of this, yet for a great while I had been preparing it for you.

c   When you were working for me, enduring the heat and the fatigue, you would say: 'How happy I am to have spent the whole evening working for Our Lady'; and at that same time I was thinking of you and preparing a place for your days of rest, and I have brought you to this place which is so dear to me.

d There is also X who loves me so dearly; and there are the little children for whom I have special love: and you are to be, for my sake, just one of them.

e Learn to see me always and at every moment as she who is truly for all a mother, only and always a mother!"

8

Watch and Pray

a "These priest-sons of mine, who have betrayed the Gospel in order to second the great satanic error of Marxism . . .

b It is especially because of them that the chastisement of Communism will soon come and will deprive everyone of all they possess. Times of great tribulation will unfold.

c Then it will be these poor sons of mine who will begin the great apostasy.

d Watch and pray, all of you, priests who are faithful to me!"

9

The Heart of My Priests

a "Be ever in my heart and, at each moment, you will find peace. Do not be worried about what you are to do!

b One who has consecrated himself to me belongs totally to me. He cannot, at any moment of the day, decide freely what he is to do with himself.

c If you remain with me, I myself will tell you at every moment what I would like you to do, and then whatever you do will always be according to my will.

d   I myself will take you by the hand and together we shall do everything. With you, I am like a mother who is teaching its child to take its first steps.

e   Now that I have snatched you definitively away from my Enemy, you are now taking the first steps along the road of love. How necessary it is that I stay with you!

f   I am so very much a mother for you; I am also very jealous of you, just as I am a good but jealous mother for all the priests of my Movement.

g   They must understand that to belong to the Movement nothing external nor any juridical act is necessary: what is indispensable however is an interior consecration of their whole selves, and the total offering of their priesthood to my Immaculate Heart.

h   Tell them that this is all I ask of them, this is what I want of them.

i   Tell them that this is the first and most important thing they must do to belong to my priestly Movement.

j   Tell them to entrust themselves to me like children, giving everything to me and renouncing all attachment to anything, — however beautiful, honorable or virtuous — that is not my very self. (. . .)

k   I will make them understand how they must be detached from everything and *live only for my Jesus*; how they must defend Him from every attack, love Him unconditionally, in living out the Gospel to the letter.

l   I will cause them to experience a great love for the Church and for the Pope, whom I love so dearly and who will be comforted, defended and saved by the cohort of my priests.

m   I will prepare them for great things and I will make them invincible in the decisive battles.

n   Let them entrust themselves completely to me; they will receive sure signs of my motherly tenderness for them!"

10

It Will Be a New Church

a   " 'O my Jesus, give me your heart because I want to love Our Lady as You have loved her.' This is the prayer, my son, which I myself have inspired in you. No one in fact has ever loved me as my Son Jesus.

b   With what tenderness He surrounded me! He has always been within me; we grew up together in his hidden life, and in his public life; we were as one during his Passion and his death on the cross.

c   The sight of the sorrow of his Mother who assisted Him in his atrocious agony shortened his life; more than his physical sufferings, his Heart-of-a-Son could not withstand this unspeakable agony.

d   'Mother!' was his last agonizing cry, the loud cry with which He expired on the cross.

e   At this present time, Jesus is greatly saddened, even angered, at seeing how numerous those priests are who have turned away from me in their hearts, who have forgotten me in their lives, who have blotted me out in the souls of so many of the faithful.

f   Through their fault, devotion to me, always such a living thing in the Church, has now become greatly weakened; in some places it is practically dead.

g   They say that I—the Mother—cast a shadow on the glory and the honor which is due to my Son alone!

h   My poor children, how senseless they are, how blind! How the devil has known how to capture them! They have reached such blindness because they have listened neither to Jesus nor to me.

i   They have allowed themselves to be led by themselves alone, by their intelligence, by their pride and thus they have allowed themselves to be made the sport of Satan, who was the one to succeed—at last—in obscuring my place in the Church and in obliterating me in souls!

j I will again have to go about searching out from among priests those who are faithful, those who listen to me, those who love me.

k Through them I will again shine more resplendently in the Church, after the great purification . . . The Mother has received from Jesus the power to bring back home the children who have gone astray.

l But I have need of humble and courageous priests: ready to let themselves be laughed at, ready to let themselves be trampled on for me.

m It will be through these priests, humble, laughed at and trampled on, that I will form the cohort that will make it possible for me to bring to Jesus an innumerable number of children, now purified by the great tribulation. (. . .)"

11

Frapiero, August 9, 1973

The Purpose of Your Life

a "How pleased I am that you are here with Y. You must love each other very much, like two little brothers.

b My two sons, whom I love so much, and whom I give as a gift, one to the other! You must have great love for one another, you must rejoice and suffer together, for the fulfillment of my plans . . .

c I have chosen you for the Movement of my priests: you must live for this; you must pray, work, suffer, you must become holy. This is the wonderful purpose, O son, that I am giving to your life! (. . .)

d How I love you, how tenderly I look out for you; how I bless you from my heart!"

12

12

Close to My Heart in Prayer

a   "Why do you not write down everything that I make known to your heart? You tell me that these things are too intimate, too beautiful. But some day it must be made known how much I have loved you, and what great things I have worked in you.

b   And this only because you have offered your nothingness totally to my heart. . . .

c   Accustom yourself to being trampled on, to being put aside, to being neither understood nor esteemed. It is necessary that this happen to you!

d   And when you feel an interior rebellion within yourself which causes you to say to yourself: 'Why? This is not right! I must claim my rights!', answer immediately: 'Get behind me, Satan! Will I not drink the chalice which the Father has prepared for me?' (. . .)

e   I myself will come to the aid of your great weakness! But as for you, remain at every instant close to my heart in prayer. Let me work ever more and more within you!"

13

The Great Goal of Sanctity

a   "Your life is so precious, son, that you must not waste it even for an instant.

b   Therefore train yourself to remain in me, in my heart, and always to act with me: to think with my mind, to see things with my eyes, to touch them with my hands, and to love them with my heart.

c   There are moments when you are particularly aware of this, and this is when you are in prayer with me. It is then that you feel that you are truly a child upon the heart of its mother and thus your soul tastes these moments of paradise, which I reserve jealously for my beloved sons.

d   When you come from prayer, it seems that everything else becomes tiresome and boring. This is another gift which I am giving to you.

e   Even when you are not at prayer, you must always be in the attitude of prayer, and you truly are if you live habitually in me. So then even when you are talking, or amusing yourself, or taking a trip, you always remain in me, because you do everything with me . . .

f   I want all the priests of the Marian Movement of Priests to be like this. They must be: my priests! I say it again: mine!

g   From the time that they are consecrated to my Immaculate Heart they can no longer belong to themselves. Their life, their soul, their mind, their heart, their possessions, even the wrong they have done and the defects they possess: all is mine, all belongs to me.

h   My Immaculate Heart is a furnace of most pure fire; it burns all, it consumes all, it transforms all.

i   Because these priests are mine, they must become accustomed to letting themselves be guided by me, with simplicity, with abandonment.

j   My joy is that of leading them, as a mother, to the great goal of sanctity. I want them to be fervent, I want them to have great love for my Son Jesus, I want them ever faithful to the Gospel.

k   They must be docile in my hands for the sake of the great plan of mercy; and through them I will save an immense number of souls.

l   They will be my joy, the most beautiful crown of my Immaculate and Sorrowful Heart which still wants to be the means of salvation for the Church and for humanity."

14

Night Has Fallen Upon the World

a   "Night has now fallen upon the world, my son. This is the time of darkness, Satan's hour; this is the time of his greatest triumph.

b   How I have accepted with great appreciation your prayer and your suffering offered in reparation for the great outrage, the most horrible blasphemy that has been directed against my Son. . . .

c   Neither during his public life, nor during his trial and the horrible carrying out of its sentence was my Son Jesus ever so denigrated.

d   Even before the Sanhedrin no accusers were found, so limpid and pure had his whole life been.

e   But now they are attempting to attack his purity; they are spreading such a horrible and satanic blasphemy that all Heaven is, as it were, dismayed and incredulous!

f   How is it possible that they could have reached such a point? What a tremendous and now inevitable storm is about to break upon poor humanity!

g   The Pope suffers and prays; he is on a cross which is consuming and killing him. This time he has again spoken but his voice falls on a desert. My Church has become more barren than a desert.

h   You priests, whom I am now gathering into my Movement to check this advance of Satan, you must, with the Pope, form a strong barrier. You must propagate his word, you must defend

15

him, because he will have to carry the cross in the midst of the greatest storm in history.

i   Yours is the duty to defend the honor of my Son which is being trampled upon, with your life, with your words, with your blood.

j   Yours is the duty to judge and to condemn the world, because more than ever this world is in the power of the Evil One. (. . .)"

15 *August 29, 1973*

For All My Priest-Sons

a   "Whatever I communicate to you, my son, does not belong to you alone, but it is for all my priest-sons, whom I love with predilection.

b   Above all it is for the priests of the Marian Movement of Priests whom I love most tenderly, and whom I want to form and lead by the hand to prepare them for their great mission.

c   Therefore gather together in a booklet whatever I have told you . . . You are not to concern yourself in any way with all that has respect to its printing: your confessor will provide for everything.

d   And this booklet is to be disseminated as quickly as possible among priests; it will be the means through which I will bring them together from all sides and with which I will form my invincible army.

e   Remain ever in my heart and trust in me, O my son!"

September 19, 1973
Feast of Our Lady of LaSalette

The Mother Must Be Loved and Lived

a   "Remain in my heart, my son, and do not think at all of what you are to say today.

b   I myself will speak, through you, to these children of mine. I will tell them all that my heart desires and I will help them to emerge from their great aridity and weariness. (. . .)

c   I will tell them, through you, that to honor me one must pray more and chatter less.

d   I want the hearts and the souls of my sons; I want to fill them with love for me. (. . .)

e   Speak to them about my priestly Movement; there are among those present here, some good priests whom I have brought here for this purpose.

f   These priests are beautiful souls whom I have been preparing for some time to enter into my Movement. They are awaiting this call as the parched land awaits a drop of dew.

g   They will welcome my invitation and join my Movement. (. . .)"

17

San Vittorino, September 23, 1973

These Are My Priests

a   "You are now at the end of these days of prayer and of union with me.

b   How many graces I have given you and how I have led you into the depths of my Immaculate Heart! How you have experienced, my son, a mother's sweetness!

c   However this is not for you alone; it is also for your brothers in my Movement who will come here tomorrow for the first gathering. I will speak to them through you, and I will tell them how much I love them.

d   Their consecration to me will be the means which will allow them to enter ever more deeply into the depths of my Immaculate Heart and I will cause them to experience a sweetness which only a mother can show to her own children.

e   Those who will come have for some time been called, chosen and prepared by me. They will quickly feel at home, and amongst themselves it will seem as though they had always known and loved each other.

f   The secret scheme, which in a hidden way I have been preparing for some time in order to realize my great plan, is now beginning to become visible: the Movement of my priests, my cohort ready for the decisive battle, and destined for victory.

g   What must they now do, these sons of mine, who for the first time find themselves gathered together?

h   They must prepare themselves; they must be ready:

i   —To obey my orders, because I will soon call them and they must be ready to respond, ready to be used by me for the ultimate defense of my Son, of me, of the Gospel and of the Church.

j   They will be the salt in a world which is completely corrupted and a shining light in the darkness which will have enveloped everything.

k   —To fight, because my Adversary will set loose his army upon them. They will be ridiculed, despised, persecuted, and some will even be killed.

l   But I will always be with them, and will protect and defend them, and will console them, wiping away every tear as only a mother knows how.

m   —To defend the Pope, who is already so very much alone in carrying the cross of the Church; there will even be a time at which, like Jesus on the way to Calvary, he will be as though abandoned by everyone.

n Then these sons of mine will be his comfort and his defense, and together with me they will be victorious in the greatest battle of the Church.

o For the present, my beloved sons, pray, love one another, be as little children: let yourselves be formed and guided by me alone. (. . .)"

18

I Will Do Everything for You

a "At the end of these spiritual exercises, which you have made
b with me, let this be your resolution: Remain always, at every moment, in my Immaculate Heart in prayer, so as to be my joy, to console me for so many sorrows caused by the sins that every day are multiplied in the world.

c Be afraid of nothing, do not be worried about anything: I will do everything for you and with you, because I love you with a greater love than you could ever imagine.

d Offer me the most beautiful fruit: the Marian Movement of Priests! I accept it, I bless it, I guard it jealously.

e Do not be worried about the first meeting tomorrow: I will arrange everything; the priests whom I want here (. . .) are already on their way and the meeting will be a wonderful occasion for all, and I will give so very much joy to each one. My priests will receive a special grace which will transform their whole lives. (. . .)"

19

Foolishness to Confound Wisdom

a "You have not understood, my son, that I have chosen foolishness to confound wisdom, and weakness to vanquish strength.

b It is my will that this little book be distributed just as it is. It will be the means through which I will call many priests into my Movement and form my invincible cohort. . . .

c Your weak faith and your lack of confidence in me grieve me, my son. What is it you dread? Whom are you afraid of? Pray and abandon yourself to me. Let it be really I alone who act."

20

October 13, 1973
Anniversary of the final apparition at Fatima

A Way of Acting Different from Yours

a "Do not be concerned about the spread of the Marian Movement of Priests. Let me act; trust in me. Offer me your prayers and sufferings for this intention.

b Do not look at the results. My way of acting and of evaluating is so different from yours.

c You do not have to be numerous, but you must be holy.

d And I will lead you all to great holiness, if you all truly entrust yourselves completely to me."

21

October 16, 1973

I Want to Save Them

a "You are now having a time of quiet and I invite you to enter into the intimacy of my Immaculate Heart to see what an abyss of love and of sorrow it contains.

b My heart is the heart of a mother, a real living heart of a mother who is real and living for all her children.

c   All men redeemed by my Son are also my children; they are my children in the fullest sense of the word.

d   Even those who are far away, even the sinners, even the atheists, even those who reject God, those who fight against Him and hate Him: they are all my children.

e   And I am a mother to them. For many of them I am the only mother they have, the only person who is taking care of them, who truly loves them.

f   And so my heart is continually consumed with sorrow and with a greater love for these children of mine.

g   I want to help them, I want to save them because I am their Mother. Because of this I suffer for them, I suffer for their sins, I suffer because they are so far from God, I suffer because they do wrong, I suffer because of all the harm they are doing to themselves.

h   But how to help them? How to save them?

i   I have need of much prayer, I have need of much suffering. Only through the prayer and the suffering of others, of the good and the generous, will I be able to save these children of mine.

j   And so there is then the Movement of my priests. It is desired by me to make reparation for the immense harm caused in souls by atheism, to restore in so many desecrated hearts the image of God, the merciful countenance of my Son Jesus.

k   My priests are my restorers; they will restore in so many souls the face of God, and thus they will bring back many of my children from death to life.

l   And in this way they will be the true consolers of my sorrowful heart.

I Will Give Them a New Purity

m   But mine is also an immaculate heart, that is to say, a motherly

21

heart that has never been tarnished by any shadow, by any sin, limpid as a spring, clear as light.

n And now, it is itself, as it were, submerged in all the mire that has submerged the hearts and the souls of so many of my children.

o Truly the Demon of Corruption, the Spirit of Lust has seduced all the nations of the world! Not one of them is any longer preserved.

p This veil of death is spread out over the world and souls are being defiled, even before they awaken to the knowledge of life.

q The priests of my Movement must restore purity in souls and fight firmly against the Demon of Lust in all its manifestations.

r They must combat styles that are more and more indecent and provocative; they must combat the press that publicizes evil and entertainment which ruins morals. They must struggle against the prevalent mentality that legitimizes and justifies everything, and against current morality that permits everything.

s Above all, my priests will have to be pure, very pure! I myself will cover them with my immaculate mantle and I will make them new men, priests who are upright and spotless.

t To those who have fallen I will give a new purity; I will call them to a second and more beautiful innocence of repentance and love.

u I want it to be the Movement of my priests which will bring back the fragrance of purity to the world: for it is only on the billow of this perfume that my Son Jesus will once again become the King of hearts and of souls.

v This, my beloved priests, is what it means to be consecrated to me. It means to live for me, it means to perceive things as I do, to love and to suffer with me in preparation for the great moments that are awaiting you."

22

The Light of the Gospel

a   "You see how everything wearies you and leaves you with a certain emptiness when you do not do everything with me.

b   And you ask yourself: 'But why does this strange thing happen to me? Are not these perchance the very things that used to so captivate me and completely absorb me? What has now happened to me?'

c   What has happened to you, my son, is the great and decisive fact of your consecration to me. This act has been taken seriously by me and it has in itself the capacity of truly changing and transforming your whole life.

d   With the act of consecration you have put your life in my hands. Now it belongs to me, it is mine. I have taken possession of it and now, bit by bit, I am transforming it according to my will.

e   Gently will I lead you to that perfection which is pleasing to my heart and little by little I will transform you into a very faithful image of my Son Jesus.

f   **I will give you a new way of seeing things:** you will see with my own eyes. Everything that is of the world will no longer be able to interest you; it will even leave within you a profound sadness. You will say of these things: 'How vain they are, how useless!'

g   Yet how many of your brothers let themselves be led and dominated by them. They look on things as the world does, they live for the world, thereby uselessly wasting the gift of their life.

h   **I will also give you a new way of feeling:** you will feel according to my heart. Thus your capacity to love and to suffer will become extraordinarily more powerful, because you will feel, my son, as the heart of your Mother feels!

i What grief you will feel for so many who today render vain the redemption of my Son: all those who, through no fault of their own, are straying because they are unsuspecting victims of these errors.

j What boundless apprehension you will have for so many of your brother-priests who, abandoning Jesus and me, are no longer faithful to the Gospel. They become propagators of many errors; they feel and judge as the world feels and judges. They have already apostatized in their hearts, but they can still be saved. They can still be saved by me.

k **I will also give you a new way of thinking:** you will think according to the heart of Jesus and my motherly heart, seeing everything in God and as God sees, according to the Spirit of Wisdom. I will give you wisdom of heart.

l Well now: the priests of my Movement must all be like this. Because they have consecrated themselves to me, they must feel, see and think as I do, together with me, because I want to take complete possession of their life. I want to transform it, and make of it an image of my Son Jesus, the First Born of so many other sons of mine.

m They must let themselves be formed by me, as little children, with much trust and abandonment!

n Then through them the light of the Gospel will shine anew in this world so filled with darkness. (. . .)"

23 October 30, 1973

The Hours of Agony

a "This evening, my son, I want to tell you of the tenderness which my motherly heart feels for the Vicar of my son, the Pope.

b   In these so very painful moments for the Church, the Pope finds himself alone, like my Son Jesus in the Garden of Gethsemane, to live through his hours of agony and dereliction.

c   These are for him moments of profound anguish. His heart is as it were oppressed with mortal sadness, and a cross of unspeakable sufferings marks the hours of his day.

d   As a mother, I am at his side to comfort and sustain him.

e   All the suffering and the rebellion in the world leave a deep wound in the heart of the Pope, just as all the sins of the world were accumulated in the heart of my Son during his atrocious agony.

f   That which causes the heart of the Pope to suffer is this world which is so far away from God, the denial of God on the part of so many, this wave of rebellion and of filth which is constantly increasing as though it would inundate everything.

g   That which causes the heart of the Pope to suffer is the solitude and the dereliction in which he has been left. My Son's deepest and greatest suffering during the hours of his agony was the betrayal by Judas and the desertion of his dearest friends when He had, humanly speaking, most need of them.

h   At the present time the Pope suffers from the betrayal and the desertion of many. Even some of his closest collaborators often disobey him and thwart him. Many priests, whom he loves so much, oppose him; many of my sons, victims of Satan, deride and condemn him.

i   How many, who even call themselves Christians and Catholics, daily criticize, oppose and judge him. Truly for my Church this is the hour of the power of darkness.

Always with the Pope

j   You, O my son who are consecrated to me, who desire to be the joy and the comfort of my sorrowful heart, become the powerful interpreter of this profound apprehension of mine, and of my motherly lament.

k   Console the Pope's heart with your filial affection, with your prayer; share his suffering, help him to carry his cross, which is now too heavy for him.

l   This is what I want the priests of my Movement to be in the Church: they must be friends, consolers and defenders of the Pope.

m   —**Friends**, because they will fill his solitude with much love and prayer.

n   They will always stand by him even at that time when he will be greatly abandoned; they will carry the cross with him even when, as did my Son, he will have to climb the road of Calvary.

o   Near the Pope on the cross and with me, the Mother, I want to find his dearest friends: the priests of my Movement.

p   —**Comforters**, because they will alleviate his abandonment and his suffering and will not be afraid to share with him the same fate that today awaits those whom I have prepared for the ultimate sacrifice for the salvation of the world.

q   —**Defenders**, because they will always be faithful to him and will combat all those who challenge and calumniate him.

r   At Fatima I foretold of these moments which would come upon the Holy Father, but I also promised him my special assistance and my protection. I will defend him and assist him through you, my priests.

s   You must be my cohort, ready to fight for the Church and the Pope. Thus you will remain faithful to the Gospel and through you I will gain my great victory."

24

From the Hands of My Adversary

a "(. . .) By means of my Movement, I will snatch many of my priest-sons from the hands of my Adversary.

b Many of them are in darkness and in the greatest of desolation because they have betrayed Jesus and the Gospel.

c But I will bring them to see my light and to hear my voice, and they will once again become my dearest sons. I myself will bind up their wounds, I will heal them, and I will make them invulnerable to any further falls.

d I am a mother and I want to save them because they are my children.

e Therefore no one should feel lost; no one should despair. My Immaculate Heart is preparing this great return of my dearest sons."

25

My Faithful Cohort

a "I want every priest of my Movement and every priest who has consecrated himself to me to pray, suffer and work in order to bring me back once again into the midst of my faithful.

b Today more than ever, he who finds me will have found life and will receive salvation from the Lord.

c My Adversary fears only this. He will make every effort to remove me even further from the hearts of my faithful, in order to keep me even more obscured in the Church. He is now engaging in his greatest battle against me, the decisive one, in which one of us two will be defeated forever.

d   At the moment, from many indications, it seems as though my Adversary is the victor; but the time of my greatest return and of my total victory is at hand.

e   In the decisive battle, I want my priest-sons to be with me. They will be led by me, they will be docile to my orders, obedient to my wishes, responsive to my requests. (. . .)

f   I will manifest myself in them and through them I will act to strike at the heart of my enemy and to crush his head with my heel.

g   But these priests must now begin to act; through them I want to return to the midst of my faithful, because it is with them, gathered about my priests, that I want to form my invincible cohort.

h   Of the faithful, who are supporters of my Movement, I ask:

i   **—That they consecrate themselves** in a special way to my Immaculate Heart, without being concerned for external or juridical bonds, but only for giving themselves completely to me, so that I may dispose freely of their whole being and arrange their whole life according to my plans.

j   They must let themselves be led by me, like little children. They must begin again to pray more, to love Jesus more, to adore Him more in the mystery of the Eucharist, so that He becomes the Sun which illuminates their whole life. What joy and what a gift of love will Jesus in the Eucharist communicate to these faithful who are consecrated to me!

k   Let them recite the holy rosary every day so as to hasten my great return.

l   **—That they be faithful to the Pope and to the Church united with him,** by a total obedience to his commands, anticipating and seconding his desires, spreading his teachings, defending him from every attack, ready to fight even to the shedding of their blood in order to remain united to him and faithful to the Gospel.

m   There will soon come a time when only those who are with the Pope will succeed in keeping the faith of my Son and being preserved from the great apostasy that will be spread everywhere.

n   **—That they must observe the commandments of God** and carry out everything that my Son Jesus has taught so that they may be his true disciples. Thus they will be a good example to all.

o   Let them be just that especially by an austere manner of life, by repudiating styles which are ever increasingly provocative and indecent, by opposing in every way possible the spread of immoral literature and entertainment and this continual flooding from a sea of filth that is submerging everything.

p   Let them be a good example to all by their purity, their sobriety and their modesty.

q   Let them flee all those places where the sacred character of their person is defiled. Let them form about the priests my faithful cohort, my great '*White Army*.' Through them my light will once again shine in the midst of the great darkness, and my immaculate whiteness in the midst of so much corruption of death.

r   These faithful children of mine will be called by me and formed for this great task: to prepare this world for the great purification which awaits it, so that at last a new world may be born, completely renewed by the light and the love of my Son Jesus, who will reign over all."

26   *November 14, 1973*

The Demon Fears and Hates Them

a   "(. . .) I am for you a mother, kind and jealous, vigilant and terrible against the Evil One who wants to do you harm. I will send my angels to guard and protect you from every danger and from every snare which the Evil One sets for you (. . .).

b   Let all the priests of my Movement know how much the devil dreads them and hates them, and how much they will have to suffer because of his plots.

c   Now the Evil One is beginning to suspect something. (. . .) And he will rage about with ever increasing fury. But I will be with my priests to protect and defend them.

d   They will not be touched, not even a hair of their head, because they are my beloved sons and I am now forming them and bringing them up; I am preparing them so that they will be strong and invincible at the hour of the decisive battle.

e   I love them, I keep them in my heart, one by one; I protect them, I bless them."

27
November 27, 1973
Apparition of the Blessed Virgin Mary to St. Catherine Labouré

Only for My Son Jesus

a   "I want all the priests of my Movement to rely on me as little children. They must no longer think of themselves; I want to take care of them myself. I will grant all their requests and satisfy their deepest desires.

b   They must no longer live for themselves, not even as regards their priestly activity, which absorbs them so much, tires them, and consumes them, but leaves them empty and far from me.

c   On the contrary, they must live only for my Son Jesus, carrying out the Gospel to the letter. For this, they must live only for me, with me. I alone will be able to form them to an ever greater unity of mind and of heart with my Son Jesus; I will have them act solely for Him, as though led by the hand by me and under the sweet influence of my inspiration.

d   They will then be still doing the same things, but in how different a manner! And because these same things will be done by them in union with me, I will manifest myself in them, and through them I will be able to carry out my great plan of salvation.

e   But it is necessary for me that these priests become ever increasingly *mine*: in silence, in prayer, in humility, in equanimity. How beautiful it is when they speak of me, but it is even more pleasing to my heart when they live me.

f   I want to live again in them so as to be once again as a mother in the midst of my children. Let them be docile, humble, and kind toward all, especially toward those who are furthest away, who are lost, who are despairing.

g   I want to give them my heart; for this they must accustom themselves to live always in my motherly heart. Let them worry about nothing. For the rest, for all the rest, I myself will provide so that my great and loving plan may be realized."

28

December 1, 1973
First Saturday of the Month

The Spirit of Rebellion against God

a   "Begin this new liturgical year with much prayer.
b   In my heart you will find the safe refuge from the many troubles of the life of today.

c   Troubles, anguish and tribulation are bound to increase from day to day, because humanity, redeemed by my Son, is withdrawing ever more and more from God, and transgressing his laws.

d   The Demon of Lust has contaminated everything. My poor children, how sick and stricken you are!

e   The Spirit of Rebellion against God has seduced humanity; *atheism* has entered into so many souls and has completely extinguished the light of faith and love.

f   This is the Red Dragon spoken of in the Bible. Read it, my sons, because the present times are those of its realization! How many of my children are already victims of this error of Satan!

g   Even among my priests how many there are who no longer believe; and yet they still remain in my Church, true wolves in sheep's clothing, and they are bringing to ruin a countless number of souls!

h   Nothing can now hold back the hand of God's justice, which will soon be roused against Satan and his followers, as a result of the love, the prayer and the suffering of the elect.

i   Times of great indescribable tribulation are in preparation. If men only knew, perhaps they would repent!

j   But who has listened to my messages, who has understood the meaning of my tears, of my motherly requests? Almost no one, but a few unknown souls thanks to whom the chastisement has again been put off.

k   But this year will not end before a great sign is accomplished. Pray, pray, pray, O you souls chosen by me and prepared so maternally by me.

l   Above all, you, my priests: forsake vain and superfluous things. These are times of emergency; you must live only with me, in me, for me.

m   Be vigilant, be ready. Soon I will have need of you, because the time of my triumph has arrived."

The Triumph of My Immaculate Heart

a   "This morning, my son, you came with your mother to my sanctuary, before the image of Our Lady of the Tears. (. . .)

b   I have chosen you from your infancy and have always led you by the hand. Never have I ever abandoned you, even when my Adversary attacked you and snatched you from me, and was then sure of having conquered once for all.

c   Because of this you have had to suffer much; you have had to walk often in darkness and abandonment, almost despairing that I had heard your wails and your cries for help.

d   But all this was part of my great plan; you seem now to have some glimpse of it, and your heart is filled with joy. But that which is most beautiful, most important, my son, is yet to come.

e   I have chosen you and prepared you for the triumph of my Immaculate Heart in the world, and these are the years when I will bring my plan to completion.

f   It will be a cause of amazement even to the angels of God; a joy to the saints in heaven; a consolation and great comfort for all the just on earth. Mercy and salvation for a great number of my straying children; a severe and definitive condemnation of Satan and his many followers.

g   In fact at the very moment when Satan will be enthroned as lord of the world and will think himself now the sure victor, I myself will snatch the prey from his hands. As if by magic he will find himself empty-handed and in the end the victory will be exclusively my Son's and mine. This will be *the triumph of my Immaculate Heart in the world.*

The Wisdom of the Heart

h   If all the priests of my Movement only knew with what care they have been chosen and molded by me to prepare them for this great task!

i   Every detail of their life—even the most insignificant—has a precise and profound meaning. Therefore let each one become accustomed to read with me in the stupendous book of their own existence.

j   I will give them the gift of wisdom of heart, and they will understand with me the reason for all that concerns them: the reason

k   for much of their lack of understanding; the reason for their sufferings, the reason for those times when they were abandoned, and even the reason for their falls. Oh, how many moments of darkness and of agony they must have had to experience in their lives, these beloved sons of mine!

l   But these have been for them necessary and fruitful moments: because I was thus able to take greater possession of them; because I could detach them from their way of seeing, from their way of feeling, from their easy attachment to things, to results, to goods, to success, so that they would learn to be mine, to live only for me by carrying out my wishes.

m   I have wanted them to have, as it were, the impression that they were good for nothing, to be considered of little value. I have given them the great gift of humility of heart, of childlikeness of spirit, so that they might feel themselves as mine alone and thus lose their dependence and reliance on everything else but me alone.

n   Yet it will be with these poor children of mine, mocked and trampled on, that I will realize my great plan.

o   That is why each one must entrust himself totally to me at every moment. I will speak to them and tell them my desires.

p   Do not be afraid of the difficulties and the misunderstandings you will encounter along the way. I will always be with you and you, in spite of everything, will always be joyous.

q   To win the battle which is approaching I want to give you a weapon: *prayer*.

r   Forget everything else and form the habit of using nothing but this weapon. The crucial times have come and there is no longer any time for certain vain and superfluous things. There is no more time for useless discussions, there is no more time for chatter and projects: *this is the time for prayer!*

s   Priests of my Movement, offer yourselves to me so that I myself, in you and with you, may always pray and intercede with my Son for the salvation of the world.

t   I have need of you and of your prayer to realize the great plan of the triumph of my Immaculate Heart.

30

December 26, 1973
Feast of Saint Stephen

The Caress of a Mother

a   "(. . .) How I love you, my son, and what love of predilection I have for you! You must accustom yourself to understand this in so many little things; in so many circumstances which are hardly noticed, such as today: the splendid bright day which I have given you, the blue of the clear skies, the luminous brightness of the snow caressed by the sun, the color of my heavenly mantle under which I ever protect you; the white of my most pure robe with which I wish to cover you.

b   These simple things are like the caress of a mother for you . . . Entrust yourself more and more to me; do you not see that now I alone am your life?

c   Pray now for your brothers: for the priests of my Movement. Today, whatever you ask for them I will grant you.

d   Pray; profit from this time of rest to enter more deeply into my

35

heart. Transform every moment of your day into a colloquy with me. I want to hear your voice, my son! Turn everything into a prayer."

31

My Church Will Be Renewed

a   "My son, you must be the comforter of my Immaculate Heart. For this you must live each moment outside of yourself, indifferent to all your personal problems.

b   If you love me, if you are all mine, if you are my consoler, how can you still have problems of your own? How can you still want or desire anything?

c   I have given you the dimensions of my heart, and what is mine must be yours; my desires must be your desires, my concerns and sufferings must be yours as well!

d   Henceforth, you will be happy only if you remain always and at every moment in my Immaculate Heart.

e   How many thorns afflict my heart: the souls which stray from my Son, even from among the faithful, become more numerous every day. Those who only yesterday were good and generous souls, swept away by the general confusion, become timorous, insecure and as though paralyzed.

f   The most painful thorns are those caused me by the most loved and especially chosen of my children, the priests.

g   Along with these who, like Judas, daily betray my Son Jesus and his Church, how numerous now are the wavering, the doubting, the unfaithful! They celebrate Holy Mass, they administer the sacraments and they no longer believe . . .

h   Their sacrileges have now reached that limit which cannot any longer be exceeded without abusing the very justice of God.

i   If these unfaithful sons of mine only knew the horrible trials which await them, oh, perhaps they would repent! . . . On the contrary, they go heedlessly to meet their great chastisement and at the decisive moment they will be taken unprepared.

They Will Love Him Alone

j   And so you understand, O my son, why I am now so active among the faithful souls from among my priests.

k   I will call them and they will answer me; I will cover them with my immaculate mantle and they will be invincible. Jesus will pour out upon them the Spirit that filled my soul, and they will be transformed.

l   I will give them, as only a mother can, my Son Jesus and they will listen to Him alone, they will love Him alone, they will faithfully announce Him according to the Gospel. And through them my Church will be entirely renewed.

m   What must I do—you ask me—to spread this Movement of priests throughout the world?

n   Remain solely in me, always, at each moment in prayer. I will do everything myself, O my son, because this is my hour.

o   I ask you only to believe, to pray, to suffer, to let yourself be led by me by the hand and you will soon see my marvels. Even now you are able to learn many things from the year that is about to end.

p   With me you will make no mistake in reading the true signs of the times, of these times which are so very distressful, and yet so blessed by me!"

32

December 31, 1973
Last night of the year

They Become Intoxicated with Emptiness

a   "Begin this new year with me, in prayer.

b   At this moment how many there are who are celebrating the arrival of the new year with amusements which are for the most part empty and offensive to the great dignity of creatures who are loved and redeemed by my Son!

c   They become intoxicated with emptiness, these poor children of mine, and how unhappy they are!

d   As for you, keep watch; pray also for them. With the new year, the decisive moments draw near; great events await you. And so begin the new year on your knees, praying with me, O my son.

e   With the coming year, my Movement will develop beyond all expectations. Will this be enough for your little faith so that you may come to believe more and to entrust yourself to me? (. . .)"

1974

CENACLES OF LIFE WITH ME

My Heart Will Be Your Refuge

a   "Today, I want to lead you by the hand like a mother; I want to lead you ever deeper into the depths of my Immaculate Heart. My heart must be as a refuge for you, in which you ought to live and from which you ought to contemplate all the events of this world.

b   If you live each moment in this refuge, you will always be kept warm by my love and that of my Son Jesus.

c   Every day that passes, this world will plummet deeper and deeper into the coldness of egoism, of sensuality, of hatred, of violence, of unhappiness.

d   Before the great darkness, the night of atheism which will envelop everything will descend upon the world.

e   It is especially then that my Immaculate Heart will be your refuge and your brightness. Fear neither the cold nor the darkness, because you will be in the heart of your Mother, and from there you will point out the way to a great multitude of my poor wandering children.

f   But my heart is still a refuge which protects you from all these events which are following one upon another. You will remain serene, you will not let yourself be troubled, you will have no fear. You will see all these things as from afar, without allowing yourself to be in the least affected by them.

g   'But how?,' you ask me. You will live in time, and yet you will be, as it were, outside of time. My Immaculate Heart, O my son, is like a part of paradise in which I want to enclose my beloved sons in order that they may be preserved from the great events which await you, so that they may be consoled by me, prepared by me, directed by me for the great and approaching moment of my triumph!

Remain therefore always in this refuge of mine!"

34

Cenacles of Life with Me

a " 'When two or three are gathered in my name, I am there in the midst of them,' thus spoke my Son Jesus.

b When two or more priests of my Movement are gathered together on my account, I also am in the midst of them. I manifest myself to them and through them, especially when these priests are joined in prayer.

c It is therefore necessary that these priests of my Movement begin to meet each other and to gather together. It is not necessary that they come together in great numbers: even two or three are enough. These gatherings must constitute real and true cenacles.

d Now that my Movement of priests is spreading everywhere, these cenacles must be multiplied.

e There is no need of organization. Everything should be simple, spontaneous, quiet and fraternal. Where two or more priests of my Movement come together because of me, *there is the cenacle.*

f In the Cenacle, there were the Apostles with Mary, the Mother of Jesus. In these cenacles, I want the priests of my Movement to be gathered with me, the Mother of Jesus, and a mother most especially for them.

The Purpose of the Cenacles

g Why do I want them to come together in cenacles with me?

h **—To remain with me**, so that I myself can nourish and form them, and cause them to grow in perfect consecration to me; so that they may truly be my priests alone, and in them and through them I may once again manifest myself.

i   **—Above all to pray with me**: when my priests pray, united with each other and with me, how efficacious is their prayer!

j   For it is then that I myself accomplish in them my maternal task of interceding before God for all my children.

k   Let them be united among themselves and with me in the celebration of Holy Mass, in the recitation of the Liturgy of the Hours, and in praying the holy rosary.

l   This is my prayer! The rosary is the weapon that I give to these children of mine to fight the great approaching battles which await them.

m   **—To love each other** and to live in true brotherhood in the company of their Mother. It is necessary today that my priests know each other, that they help each other, that they truly love one another, that they be as brothers brought together by their Mother.

n   There is today too much loneliness, too much abandonment for my priests! . . .

o   I do not want them to be alone: they must help each other, love each other, they must all feel as—and really be—brothers.

p   **—To await the decisive moments** which are drawing ever closer. The time is near when some of my poor priest-sons, tricked and seduced by Satan, will come out in the open and set themselves against my Son, against me, against the Church and the Gospel.

q   Then the cohort of my priests, prepared and led by me, are to come forth into the open to proclaim with courage and before everyone the divinity of my Son, the reality of all my privileges, the necessity of the hierarchical Church united to, and under the leadership of, the Pope, and all the truths contained in the Gospel!

r   Many priests, uncertain and, as it were, overwhelmed by the tempest, will follow your example and return along the road of salvation. For the present, prepare yourself with me during this time of waiting.

Let your gatherings be *true cenacles* of life with me, of prayer, of brotherhood, and of waiting. . . ."

35

The Sign That I Will Give to Each One

a   "Do not be concerned about all that is necessary for the spread of the Movement. I myself will provide for everything.

b   I want my priests to live always and only in the greatest trust in me. They must expect everything from me, even whatever concerns their life and their means of sustenance.

c   My priests will have to be poor in imitation of my Son Jesus; but they will never lack whatever is necessary to live, and to live with dignity.

d   I am the Mother and I will take care even of this. I will do great and extraordinary things, even miracles, when it is necessary.

e   But my priests must be neither eager nor preoccupied about what concerns food and clothing. As little children, they should leave it up to their Mother to provide!

f   On the other hand, let them be solely and always concerned about the salvation of so many of my children who, more and more each day, are being lost and falling into the hands of Satan. Do they not feel my great motherly sorrow which is growing ever greater?

g   Let them live solely with me, to console the heart of my Son Jesus. Jesus, at this time, *must be consoled.* Let it be my priests who will be the consolers of his Most Sacred Heart!

h   Let them live solely and always looking to me, remaining with me, loving with me, praying through me. From the way they allow themselves to be possessed by me they will be recognized as priests of my Movement.

i This will be the sign that I will give to each one, so that the life of each one may be truly transformed!"

36

What a Mother Can Do

a "How happy I am, my son, with the gathering which took place here with the twelve priests of my Movement! It is a little seed which soon will become a tree and from here, my beloved city, it will spread out its branches over the whole Church, throughout the whole world.

b Have you not noticed how, through you, I myself spoke to the hearts of my priests? They have received an extraordinary grace which will transform their whole life. They will now be apostles of my Movement. (. . .)

c Oh, always let yourself be led by me; then you will see what a mother can do for her sons."

37

February 10, 1974

Rely on Me Alone

a "You must be more attentive, O my son, in order to remain always in my Immaculate Heart, and not let yourself be taken up or discouraged by things, especially when these are independent of your will.

b You are in a hurry. You would like my Movement to spread more rapidly, and that the booklet would not encounter so many difficulties in its reprinting.

c How much of the human there is in your desires! It is necessary that I, as a mother, purify you, if you want me to lead you to that perfection which is pleasing to my heart.

d   Rely only on me and not on human means; entrust yourself only to me. There is one thing that you can always do, and which is the only thing that I want you to do at each moment, because it is so useful to me for the Movement: your prayer, your suffering, your trust in me.

e   This is what I ask of you: that you let yourself instead be divested of all other preoccupations. This is not one of many movements, but it is *my Movement*, my son. So then let me act!

f   All my priests must act this way. I will make them understand by causing every human means in which they had placed their trust to come tumbling down. They must entrust themselves to me alone. I know that this asks much of human nature. But I want the priests of my Movement to be *mine alone!*

g   If they do not accustom themselves now to seek me alone, to listen to me alone, and to entrust themselves to me alone, how are they going to find me at the moment of the great tempest when everything will be plunged in darkness? Let them accustom themselves as of now to see me as the light of their every action!"

38

February 11, 1974
Feast of Our Lady of Lourdes

Let Them Live Out the Trust of the Present Moment

a   "How I am present, O my son, each moment of your day . . . You are no longer alone. You always have with you the Mother who leads you by the hand, who clasps you to her Immaculate Heart.

b   Everything that happens to you has been prearranged by me for your good. Learn to entrust yourself to me ever more and more.

c   Even the moments of obscurity, of suffering and of misunder-standing are prearranged so that you may grow and become strong along the way of perfect consecration.

d   Learn to see me even in obscurity; learn to feel my presence even in abandonment, O my son; learn to do everything with me, in me. Give me your whole self completely, at each moment.

e   Your past does not exist. I now see you only in my heart; *you are mine.* Do give me the present moment with generosity: for me this is all that matters, because I can make use of it for my designs.

f   Oh, if all the priests of my Movement only knew how much I have need of them! Let them offer me each moment of their exis-tence with perfect surrender, so that I can make use of them ac-cording to my wishes!

g   Since they have consecrated themselves to me, they belong to me; they are mine. If they are mine, they can no longer belong to themselves, they can no longer possess anything that is not my very self.

h   So then why do they still think of the past? Why do they still make plans for the future? (. . .)"

39

It Is Time that I Myself Gather Them Together

a   "Let yourself be led by me, my son, and you will see marvels happening around you: one of these is that which you are living through today. (. . .) N. is an example of all the priests of my Movement. What love he has for me and for my Son Jesus! How he lives for souls; how many he saves!

b   This is a humble place, a place of little things, almost unnoticed by most. And yet it is here and no place else that today my presence is to be found.

c   Even today I like to reveal myself to my children in places similar to those in which I lived with my Son Jesus: Bethlehem, Nazareth. Yes, even today I choose poverty, simplicity, littleness, and the ordinary in order to manifest myself.

d   I know this can be a difficulty for many; and yet this is necessary for those who wish to encounter me. It is necessary to be little, and that all feel themselves to be just what they are before me: *just little children.*

e   The little child never looks at himself, but gazes intently at his mother! And it is the mother who looks at her little child. She is the one who, looking at him, can say to him: 'Oh, how beautiful you are, how precious you are, how good you are!'

f   (. . .) Today for you, here in this very place, something is really being born. It is like a small seed, but it will spread itself out, grow and become a great tree. For you, there has been a meeting here today: you have found a brother. But for a long time he has been made ready by me! You see, from long ago I have been fashioning this priest; through suffering, through misunderstandings, through solitude; oh, how I have accustomed him to that interior humility and to that childlikeness of spirit which is so pleasing to my Immaculate Heart.

g   Now I look upon him with satisfaction; he is only a little child in my arms, and I can carry him and make use of him as I wish. Such is one of my priests; such are all my priests.

h   Called by me long ago, long ago they have answered. Nourished by me, fashioned and guided by me, now they let themselves be led with docility.

i   It is time that I myself gather these children of mine from all sides. With them I must form for myself an invincible cohort.

j   They meet each other, they look at each other, and it seems as though they had always known each other; they feel themselves to be really brothers. I give you as gifts, one to the other.

k   Love one another, my beloved sons, be united, look after each other, help each other! Oh, how happy the Mother is when she sees you all gathered together as good brothers in her house . . ."

40   February 23, 1974

It Will Begin with My Priests

a   "You ask me if I am pleased. Oh, you do not know, my son, the joy that you give me! It is a mother's joy to be with her children. My paradise is that of being close to each one of you. The priests are children whom I love in a special way because, by their vocation, they are called to be Jesus.

b   It is my duty to form the image of my Son in them. I never abandon them, I never leave them alone.

c   Let them not become discouraged because of their defects or their falls, because even though they are very frail, I am mother. My greatest delight is to forgive because — in that case — I can show an even greater love.

d   These children of mine should not be afraid to give themselves to me completely. They are now living in times of great confusion; in many of them faith in my Son and trust in me is diminishing. Bad example is everywhere increasing, and how discouraged are many of them becoming. . . This is the time to call on me, to yearn for me; this is all I am waiting for in order to reveal myself to them.

e   That which most touches my heart is to hear them cry like little children. Can a mother not be moved before her little child who is crying?

f   Behold: when everything will have come tumbling down, all that will remain will be the strength of their tears that will compel me to intervene in an amazing and terrible way. And my triumph will begin with these beloved sons, my priests.

g　(. . .) You will have to become accustomed to seeing ever greater and greater things. My Immaculate Heart is an inexhaustible channel of mercy and forgiveness, and can no longer hold back the flood of this fire. Soon God will begin to cause torrents of pardon and mercy for these poor children of mine to gush through the whole world."

41

Great in Love

a　"Today you had something like a sign: a confirmation of how much I love you, my son. I permitted that up to the last moment everything would be contrary to what I had told you beforehand; and then, in an almost miraculous manner, it turned out just as I had promised.

b　This is because I want you to grow in *trust* in me. You must let yourself be led by this trust without ever offering resistance, but rather being, as it were, carried and guided by it every moment of your day. Raise yourself up ever higher and higher, until you live habitually in my Immaculate Heart.

c　Then this being habitually in me will be for your soul like the air which will permit you to breathe and to live.

d　Every priest who is consecrated to my Immaculate Heart and who belongs to my Movement is called to live this way.

e　My heart is sometimes saddened to see that some childen who are consecrated to me are not *totally mine*. They do not give me everything. Why do they still keep something back? From now on they must possess nothing, nothing at all: they must simply be little children, the smallest of my children.

f   Because I call them to be great in love, in holiness, in heroism, they must become the smallest of all. (. . .)

g   When they are perfect in spiritual childhood, when their only concern is to let themselves be led by trust in me, then they will be ready for my great plan.

h   My children, let yourselves be formed and fashioned by me. Without you or others being aware of it, I will transform you completely, I will give you great gifts of love, I will call you to an ever deeper union with God and with me.

i   This is why I ask you to entrust yourselves to me: if this giving of yourself is not perfect, you bind my hands and I will not be able to act according to my wishes. (. . .)"

42   March 23, 1974

I Give You the Joy of the Cross

a   "Let yourself be led by me at every moment, my son, and you will find peace. (. . .) Even in sorrow, even in abandonment, even in contradictions, even when you seem to feel that you are powerless to do good.

b   You would like to and you cannot, because this does not depend on you; you would like to and yet you cannot, because you meet with difficulties which you cannot overcome alone. You would like to and yet you cannot, because, one by one, all those human supports on which you counted so much fail you.

c   Even for me and for my Movement, how many times you would have liked to do something and you cannot . . . Oh, this inability to act, this experience of your own fragility, and the patience which you must exercise, and this waiting— how much this costs you at times, how it makes you suffer, how it purifies you!

d   Indeed, you will know joy in your every sorrow; moreover, you will offer for my joy each of your sufferings, even the smallest, and I will accept it as a gift which the little child makes to its Mother, and I will change it immediately into joy for you.

e　However, the joy that I give you is deep, it is not superficial; it is peaceful, it never brings agitation. It is for you, my son, *the joy of the cross*. The joy of remaining always in my sorrowful heart to experience all its indescribable motherly bitterness.

f　I want to bring all the priests of my Movement to this joy. They must know how I completely change and transform their existence, taking literally the gift which they made to me by their consecration.

g　I will lead them, these little children of mine, very far in love, in suffering, in the joy of the cross!

h　Those moments are approaching when I will be able to act, for the salvation of the world, through the sufferings of my priest-sons. (. . .) From them I want trust, prayer, simplicity, silence. . .".

43　　　　　　　　　　　　　　March 27, 1974

Place Them in My Maternal Heart

a　"Gather these sons of mine together. This is the time for them to get to know each other, to meet each other, to love each other.

b　You are in me and when you speak in these gatherings I am *truly present* in the midst of you. Even though you do not see me, I am not only spiritually but really and truly present. And I will give you sure signs of this presence of mine.

c　Each one will be aware of it and his life will be gently changed and his soul will be delicately touched with my motherly caress. Therefore, my son, you should not seek anything else; you should not be concerned about anything but remaining ever in my Immaculate Heart.

d What joy and comfort you give to your Mother, O my son! Bring to me all these beloved sons of mine. Gather them into my cohort; place them all in my maternal heart."

44

Let Them Offer Me Their Sufferings

a "The road on which I lead you is difficult, my son, but it is the one that I have ever been preparing for you.

b With what difficulties and what sorrows it is strewn! But you must not be discouraged. Why do you feel so frightened? What are you afraid of? Let yourself be led by me, remain always in my heart.

c Give me all the difficulties which you encounter, all the sufferings and the abandonment which you experience. Nothing comforts my immaculate and sorrowful heart more than a suffering which is offered to me out of love by my priest-sons.

d Even Jesus willed to offer to the Father all his sufferings through and with me. And it was thus that, offering my Son freely to the Father, I became true co-redemptrix.

e Let these children of mine offer me all their sufferings, all their misunderstandings, all their difficulties. This is the greatest gift that they can make to me, because thus they allow me to carry out in time—in this, your time!—my task as Mother and Co-Redemptrix. I will save many souls redeemed by Jesus, but at present so far away from Him, because my sons, together with me, will pay for them.

f Oh, all I want of them is prayer and suffering. This is how they will really comfort my heart and respond to the great plan of mercy which I am about to realize through them."

45 *April 18, 1974*

I Will Give Them This Water

a   "Do you not understand that, as the parched earth cries out for a drop of dew, so also my Church has long been awaiting this work of mine which I am carrying out among my priests?

b   Indeed the priests of my Church are today the most prepared, the most desirous of accepting it. The confusion and the numerous defections of these recent times have, as it were, parched the souls of my sons. They have so much need now of pure water, crystal-clear water, to quench their great thirst!

c   I myself will give them this water.

d   For this reason you must become more and more available in my hands; let yourself be led completely by me, who have great plans. From now on you must free yourself from all other obligations (. . .) for the sake of my Movement.

e   My son, gather together from all sides my beloved sons. They need so very much to know each other, to meet each other, to love each other deeply as brothers, to help one another, to encourage one another in walking always in simplicity and abandonment along the difficult and painful path of these times.

f   I will be with you; do not fear. As a mother, I will provide everything for you: home, clothing, and food, as only a Mother knows how.

g   I will lead you to a complete emptiness of all human support and to a more total abandonment, so that you may at last learn to do that which pleases me most and that which I am always asking of you: entrust yourself to me alone, let yourself be always led by me, expect everything and ask everything of me.

h What joy my motherly heart feels when you ask me for something. Ask me for everything for your brother-priests, these sons so loved by me, and you will obtain everything, because my Immaculate Heart has already begun its great triumph in them!"

46   *Lourdes, April 30, 1974*

My Beloved Priests

a "You have become aware of the great tenderness my motherly heart feels for all these children of mine! Especially do I reveal myself to the little and the innocent.

b If you only knew how much my heart loves and cherishes *purity*. This is a virtue which makes souls open to receive a special influx of my love, which enables them to see me, to feel my presence with them.

c This is the time when I am drawing all these privileged souls to myself, so that they may be protected and kept unharmed, by me and by my Son Jesus.

d All the sick and the suffering whom you see everywhere, these too are my privileged children. They remind you of the value of suffering, of the necessity to suffer.

e But, more than all others, my beloved children are *the priests*. In striking them, my Enemy has truly struck at my heart.

f This has been permitted by God for the sake of his great designs which are as yet unknown to you; however, this wounded and sorrowful heart of mine is preparing the greatest return of my straying and wavering priest-sons.

g For this I bless in a special way all you priests of my Movement. You are the soothing balm for this wound of mine, my comfort in this great sorrow; you are the instruments personally chosen by me for my great triumph!"

47

The Prayer of My Priests

a   "As each day passes, I want you to be ever closer to my heart: far from human vicissitudes and the events which so convulse the world and disturb my Church, so that you will remain with me alone.

b   I want you with me *in prayer*. These present moments are so important and grave that they demand much, very much prayer on the part of my priests. The prayer of my priests is necessary for the salvation of the world.

c   Holy Mass must be celebrated well, and it must be lived by my priests. The Liturgy of the Hours must be for them a summons to consecrate every moment of their day to me.

d   The Rosary should be a time of conversation with me. Oh, they must speak to me and listen to me, because I speak softly to them, as a mother does to her little children.

e   But even every action of their day can become a prayer. And this happens when they let the Spirit within them—which still today laments with ineffable groanings—cry out invoking God as a Father.

f   Seek the Father, cry out to the Father, yearn for the Father! For yourselves and for all my children.

g   The sufferings of your day will dispose you to be prompt to enter into continuous prayer.

h   The moments which are approaching are more serious than

you can possibly imagine. And so I want to prepare you so that at the opportune moment you will all be ready.

i   This is why I cry out to you, *'To prayer!'* "

48   *May 27, 1974*

The Work I Am Accomplishing

a   "For all that pertains to my Movement, let yourself be led only by me. You will receive light little by little; this will be assured you through your confessor and spiritual director.

b   At the present time you do not see, my son, all that my Immaculate Heart wants to do through you and through my Movement.

c   I want things this way for many reasons. First of all, you must remain always poor, humble and simple, considering yourself as the least of my children. Then you must become accustomed to letting yourself be led by the hand, and always by me. At *every moment you must expect everything from me.* This is the way I want the consecration which you have made to me to be truly lived out.

d   Do not rely on other charisms or on other confirmations; do not look to other works or other plans. This is the work which I am carrying out in the Church through you.

e   For this you will receive everything from me; walk in simplicity and total abandonment. Never let your heart be troubled.

f   No external interference will ever be able to harm this work of mine which I am jealously bringing to birth for the salvation of my Church.

g   In this, consider yourself as *a nothing*, truly incapable of anything, because that, O son, is just what you are. But in the measure you offer your utter nothingness to me, I will be able to act and operate according to my plans.

h Prepare yourself now to also suffer a bit; I want you to be always more and more my own, and soon I will purify you. But this will be in order to give you a greater love than you could ever imagine, O my son . . ."

49

I Want to Make Jesus Live Again

a "You must remain more attentive to my voice, my son, and let yourself be led by me with much docility. It is also good that you form the habit of writing all that I cause you to hear in your heart.

b I know that this costs you much, yet it is thus that you please me, because you are more and more obedient to your confessor and spiritual director. He will receive from me the gift of understanding what should be made known, since this will be beneficial to many of my sons. He will also know what should be kept secret. For your part, write an account of everything in all simplicity . . .

c I will accustom you to depend on me at each moment; oh, but in a manner so simple and spontaneous, as a child does in the arms of its own mother.

d At every moment I will tell you what I want of you; thus it will be I myself who will do everything in you and with you. You will always act, as it were, under my sweet motherly inspiration.

e And thus you will grow continually in a life united with me. My life will be your life. It will become painful and insupportable for you to live even for a moment outside of me.

All Your Nothingness

f My son, you see how I have accepted with pleasure and taken at your word the gift of your consecration which you have made to me!

g   Certainly you are small, you do not have great qualities, you get frightened over nothing, you are almost afraid of your own shadow! And yet, I have considered the intensity and the love of your total gift.

h   Your nothingness, which you have offered completely to me, will be transformed and made great by my motherly heart.

i   My beloved priests, give me all your nothingness; give me your whole selves!

j   Oh, do not look to yourselves any longer. I want even your miseries, your defects and your failures!

k   Give me everything with great love and I will transform it all in the burning furnace of the most pure love of my Immaculate Heart. I myself will transform you into most faithful replicas of my Son Jesus.

l   It is Jesus whom I want to make live again in these priests who are consecrated to me, these priests of my Movement. It is Jesus living in these priests of mine who will again save my Church at the very moment when it will seem to be sinking.

m   If you only knew, my sons, the designs which I have upon you, you would leap for joy! This is why I say to you: Give yourselves to me completely, your whole Priesthood, without fear. Abandon yourselves to me . . ."

50

June 21, 1974
Feast of the Sacred Heart of Jesus

In the Furnace of the Heart of Jesus

a   "Before leaving this place where I have wanted you to be for a time of rest and of prayer and to give you graces which you will understand later, I want to manifest to you once more all the benevolence and the predilection of my motherly heart.

b   Here you have been very closely united with the one whom I love and hold especially dear, and whom I myself give to you as an elder brother for the sake of my Movement.

c How he loves you, this beloved son of mine! He is one of the greatest gifts that I give you; and you will understand this later on . . . He will be called upon to wear himself out on a cross of true martyrdom, a martyrdom of love and of pain, which will make him into a living copy of my Crucified Son.

d Let him not be troubled over the difficulties that surround him. They are allowed by God for his sanctification. Let him always pronounce his generous and total 'yes.' This is so necessary and pleasing to me.

e And thus I will have him live always in my motherly heart, and there he will taste such great, such very great sweetness.

f Oh, my sons, if the Mother has thus kept you together for so long it is because she has great designs upon you.

g I place you in the burning furnace of the Heart of my Son. I press you both to my own Mother's heart and I bless you."

51
June 24, 1974
Feast of Saint John the Baptist

I Have No Need of Human Means

a ". . . The Movement goes forward when you offer me your prayer and your suffering.

b I have no need of human means. Even the little book is only a means for the spread of my Movement. It is an important means which I have chosen because it is small. It will serve to make known to many this work of my love among the priests.

c But to adhere to it depends entirely on correspondence to a special grace which I will grant to each one. And this you can obtain through your prayer, my son, through your love, through your suffering, and even through your inability to act.

d Remain with me always."

I Accept Your Crown of Love

a   ". . . Now I have made known to you the dimensions of my Mother's heart. Every instant of your existence has been prepared by me so that through you I can manifest myself more and more.

b   You have at last found your post: my heart. Rest, my son, on this heart. Pray, console; and then let me do everything for you.

c   My heart is surrounded by a crown of thorns. Oh, my son, how sharp and painful these thorns have become in these recent times! I am continually being pierced by them.

d   Now you ask me for this crown of thorns. How can a mother offer the crown of her great suffering to her little child? Nevertheless, I accept your desire, the gift of your love.

e   And so now, I will have you share in my great sufferings. For this, very gently, I will make you more and more capable of suffering and I will make you resemble more and more my Crucified Son.

f   I accept the *crown of love*, the Movement of my priests. They form about my Immaculate Heart a triple crown, as it were, which truly brings about a soothing of all its wounds.

g   **—A crown of lilies**, by their purity. Oh, I know that many of these sons of mine have had to undergo the violent attacks of my Adversary and that often they have fallen, and that many have lost their innocence.

h   They must not become discouraged, these sons of mine. I myself will clothe them with my purity, giving them back their innocence. My innocence will be theirs and, as the fruit of my special predilection, they will be made like me, immaculate.

i   **—A crown of roses**. What is the rose if not the most beautiful symbol of love? That is why, from among all the flowers, I am called upon by you as the 'mystical rose.' Oh, these priest-sons of mine must have only one great love: Jesus and souls!

j   They cannot love anything else. They must live and let themselves by consumed only by this great love. For this, I myself will purify them through great sufferings, I will detach them from everything, and I will lead them by the hand along the road of my motherly predilection.

k   **—A crown of cyclamens:** these are tiny and fragrant flowers, which grow only in the coolness of the woods; it is necessary to climb up high to find them.

l   They signify the love that my sons must have for me. They must truly be all mine, my little children who always expect everything from me.

m   But they will not be completely my little children if they do not climb the summit of spiritual childhood, a gift which I make to my priest-sons who consecrate themselves to my Immaculate Heart.

n   In this way my Immaculate and Sorrowful Heart will be truly consoled and the many thorns will cause me less pain because of the great joy you give me.

o   For the rest I myself will provide because this is my hour, and I have prepared you all for this hour . . ."

53

My Triumph and That of My Children

a   "Walk in simplicity. I am leading you by the hand and you should follow me always. Let yourself be led by me; let yourself be nourished and cradled by me like a little child in my arms.

b   Since Satan has today deceived the greater part of humanity by pride and by the spirit of rebellion against God, it is only through humility and littleness that it can now encounter and look upon the Lord.

c   Caused by the rebellion against God and this pride of Satan, the flood tide of the denial of God and of atheism truly threatens to seduce a great part of humanity.

d   This spirit of pride and rebellion has likewise contaminated part of my Church. Even those who should be a light for others have been deceived and seduced by Satan and are now nothing more than shadows walking in the darkness of doubt, of uncertainty and of lack of faith.

e   They now doubt everything. My poor children, the more you search for light by your own selves and through your own strength, the deeper you will plunge into darkness!

f   You must return today to simplicity, to humility, to the confidence of little children, in order to see God. For this, I myself am preparing this cohort: my priests, whom I will cause to become littler, ever littler, so that they may be filled with the light and the love of God.

g   Humble, small, abandoned and trusting, they will all let themselves be led by me. Their weak voice will one day be changed into the roar of a hurricane and, joining the victorious cry of the angels, it will resound in a powerful cry throughout the world: 'Who is like God? Who is like God?'

h   Then will come the conclusive defeat of the proud, and my triumph and that of my little children."

54   *July 30, 1974*

I Will Lead You by the Hand

a   "Continue, my son, your life of simple and filial abandonment. Live always in greatest confidence in my motherly action.

b   Do not let yourself be caught up with things; do not become anxious. I tell you once again: no outside interference will be able to harm his work of mine.

c   I am making known to you how I want this work done and I myself will lead you by the hand to realize this plan of mine. Bit

by bit, I will detach those who are to help you from everything—even from what they consider good and useful for my
Movement—and I will lead them along the road of perfect abandonment and of the accomplishment of my will.

d   They will be personally called by me to this detachment; from
them I expect total submission.

e   O my son, if you only knew with what care I am molding my
priests, just as I am molding you yourself! Entrust yourself ever
more completely to me, let yourself be led by me. You will see how
the Mother knows how to do all things well in your place!"

55

August 15, 1974
Feast of the Assumption of Mary into Heaven

In Heaven to Be More a Mother

a   "Today is my feast: all Paradise exults and the Most Holy Trinity rejoices at the reflection in me of its most pure light.

b   Even with my body, I am in heaven so that I can be more a
Mother: the Mother of all.

c   Today I want you with me at Fatima. You have not returned
there since the time when, through you, my Movement was born.
Bring me all these priests of mine in order to make with them a
crown of love which you will place about my Immaculate Heart.
(. . .)

d   Continue to walk deprived of all assistance and in this abandonment. Do not be afraid; I myself am leading you by the hand
and clasping you to my heart. In this way, I can now make use
of you as I wish and, never before as now, are you the instrument
chosen by me for the spread of my Movement."

My Reign

a   ". . . You will soon see in all its splendor the great design which the Mother has upon you. You will be always her little child who does not know how to say anything or to do anything other than to remain with me, speak with me, and let yourself be used by me.

b   I will manifest myself in you. You will also have to suffer because many—in good faith—will place obstacles in the way of my motherly action. But in the end they will understand and will become my most docile sons.

c   Today the Church and all Heaven acclaim me as Queen. My Son Jesus has given me this crown of glory.

d   If you only knew, my son, what great glory and what comfort is given to me when I reign as sovereign in your heart! The hearts of all my priests must be the kingdom where I may reign. Thus, very soon, my motherly heart will triumph in all my children!"

57

Pray for the Holy Father

a   "Spend these days in continuous prayer; make your Spiritual Exercises with me . . . Upon your descent from this mountain, I myself will lead you here and there, that you may gather my priests into my Movement.

b   Pray also for the Holy Father. There are grave and painful moments approaching for him, and I myself want to give him the comfort of your filial affection and of your prayer."

No One Passes beyond This Point

a   " 'I want to bring you to a detachment from everything and to an absolutely total abandonment.' These words of mine, my son, I repeat to you today so that in the present difficulties you will not become discouraged. (. . .)

b   There are many ways, but there is only one path for my beloved priests: that of my Immaculate and Sorrowful Heart.

c   Here I want them all to be like little children. For this they must learn to be silent, not to become agitated, not to organize themselves, not to act. They must be little children who pray and love, little children who suffer with me, for me and in me for the salvation of all my children.

d   Oh, this is for my Church the hour of greatest confusion. The Pope speaks and points out the faith with assurance, and he is left alone and unheeded by almost everyone.

e   There are also speaking today false prophets, who announce the Gospel by betraying it, and these are listened to and followed! And they bring disorder and confusion among the most faithful children of my Church.

f   You priests consecrated to me, set up once again a strong barrier of defense *together with the Pope.* Do not leave him alone; form with him the last line of defense, the last trench for the defense of my Son and of my Church.

g   I am with you and no one passes beyond this point; and from here I will begin my battle for my greatest triumph!"

59

Prayer and Docility to My Voice

a   ". . . I have already told you many times what you must do, and I now repeat it: just pray and remain always in my heart in prayer. I will look after the Movement myself.

b   You are not to let yourself become worried about any preoccupations. (. . .) I myself am calling together and uniting the priests from all sides, and they, these beloved sons of mine who have been nourished and formed by me, they are all heeding my call.

c   Have you not seen how the declarations of membership are now coming from all parts of the world?

d   Tell X that there will be more and more for him to do for my Movement. Therefore he must accustom himself to do less and less on his own, and to leave the action to me alone. He must pray, pray much and I myself will be his light. (. . .)

e   The booklet should be the only means of spreading [the Movement]. Do not look at its weakness because it is willed by me.

f   I do not want any propaganda, but only prayer and docility to my voice. I am pressed for time. The decisive times have come and my army is now ready and awaiting my orders.

g   I bless you all from my heart."

60

How Much You Have Need of a Mother!

a   "I am always near you; let yourself be led by me, without looking to anyone or anything.

b   As I have said to your heart many a time, human events are constantly getting worse and worse. Men have forgotten God; many obstinately deny Him. How many there are now who ignore HIm in practice!

c   This poor poor generation whose sorry lot it is to be so polluted and corrupted by the Evil Spirit, who has risen up against God to repeat again his challenge: '*Non serviam*: I will not serve, I will not acknowledge God!'

d   My sons, how much you have need of a mother! She alone can understand and help you. She alone can heal you. She alone can, by divine plan, snatch you from the hands of Satan and *save you*. Have recourse to me still, and I will be your salvation.

e   To realize my plan of salvation for all poor humanity, I am gathering together *my priests* from all parts of the world . . . They must be docile to my voice and respond, each and all, to the gentle invitation of my motherly heart.

f   I who have triumphed over all errors and heresies, everywhere, will again, with the cohort of my beloved sons, triumph over the greatest error which history has ever known: *the error of atheism* which has now drawn away from my Son almost all humanity.

g   Write this, my beloved son: these are now the years when I will realize my greatest triumph.

h   Humanity, renewed by much suffering and by a great purification, will re-consecrate itself completely to the worship and the triumph of God, through the triumph of my Immaculate Heart."

61 *November 19, 1974*

The Altar on Which They Will Be Immolated

a   "(. . .) And yet, how I am molding you and transforming you, my son! Are you not now aware of how completely I live and act in you? (. . .)

b   Consider how formerly you longed for success; and now it seems that even life is burdensome to you. How you used to make plans and projects for tomorrow; and now it seems that the future does not interest you at all. How often, even unconsciously, you have sought yourself . . .

c   Now something is really changing: it is I who am living and working in you. Your heart beats in unison with mine; your mind follows my thoughts; your words repeat my voice; your hands repeat my gestures: you are, as it were, born again in me.

d   Oh! . . as for one, so also for all the priests of my Movement. All little children, nourished, kissed, caressed and cradled by me.

e   So that I may place them all, with much love, on the wood of the cross, I must prepare them for this ineffable and painful moment. They, like my Son Jesus, will have to be immolated on the cross for the salvation of the world.

f   Let them entrust themselves therefore to me like little children. The heart of their Mother will be the altar on which they will be immolated, victims acceptable to God, for his triumph."

62   *November 30, 1974*
                          Last day of the liturgical year

The Sign Which God Gives

a   "My beloved sons, do not let your hearts be troubled. Why do you doubt? Why do you look with uncertainty at the present and the future in search of the sign which I have predicted to you?

b   There is only one sign which God gives to the world and to the Church of this day: *I myself.*

c   I alone am announced as a great sign in the heavens: this Woman, clothed in the sun, with the moon as a carpet under her feet and twelve stars as a luminous crown about her head.

d   My victory over the Red Dragon has been foretold and over atheism which is triumphing and apparently victorious today. This victory will be obtained through the triumph of my Immaculate Heart in the world, and I will achieve this victory through the priests of my Movement.

e   For the present, do not look for any other prodigies in the heavens: this will be the only prodigy! (. . .)"

63

Revealed to the Little Ones

a   "You have come, my son, before my image, which you have venerated with special love since your childhood and which even then was a sign of my special predilection.

b   You have celebrated Holy Mass to console my Immaculate and Sorrowful Heart and for all the priests of the Marian Movement of Priests.

c   Have no fear. I myself am gathering these sons from all parts of the world into *my cohort*; all are now responding to my call!

d   If now and then you meet up with some obstacles, with difficulties or with misunderstandings, offer everything to my heart.

e   I have already told you, and I repeat again, that no external interference will be able to harm this work of mine. It is the sign that I am today giving to my Church.

f   At the moment of its greatest confusion, on the very eve of events which will upset the faith of so many of my children, this is the sign which I will give: *My very self!*

g   I, the Mother of the Church, am personally intervening and initiating my work of salvation. I am initiating it thus: with simplicity, in hiddenness, and in such a humble manner that most people will not even be aware of it. But this, my son, has always been the way your Mother has acted.

h   Therefore, in order to recognize this action of mine, you must have the eyes of a little child, the mind of a little child, the heart of a little child. You must again become simple, humble, recollected, poor, innocent. You must truly become once again *those little children* to whom alone will be revealed the plans of God, the mysteries of the kingdom of God.

i   Thus the interior space of your souls will be brightened, and your hearts will be truly transfigured because I myself will imprint my image upon them.

j   Your hearts will be my kingdom and through you, the priests of my Movement, I will give the Church of today a sign – which will become clearer and clearer and perceived by all – of my presence, of my assistance and of my action which is destined for the victory and the triumph of my Immaculate Heart."

64

Moments of Anxiety

a   "Spend these hours of vigil with me, my son. Forget everything else and do not let yourself be taken up with any other person. (. . .)

b   Relive with me these moments of anxiety and painful apprehension when my spouse received a refusal at each request he made for hospitality for *this night*.

c   Pain and apprehension not for ourselves, but for my Son Jesus who was about to be born. Every refusal given to us was a refusal given to Him.

d   Many times during the day He had, so to speak, knocked at the door of my heart. The time had come for his birth and I, the Virgin, was, as a Mother, to give Him to all humanity.

e   But humanity had no place to receive Him. Every door which closed opened a new wound in my heart which opened itself more and more to beget in love and pain – in this pain – my Son Jesus.

f   And thus there was no welcome for Him but the poverty of a cave and the warmth of an ox and the young donkey which had carried us throughout the day.

g   Relive with me these hours of vigil, my son, that you may understand that it is *your poverty* alone that has drawn down upon you the predilection of my Son Jesus who has given you the gift of being a priest especially beloved of my Immaculate Heart.

h   Your poverty which makes you only and always such a little child; your *total poverty*: of goods, of attachments, of ideas, of sentiments. To be poor means precisely to possess this nothingness. It is this nothingness which attracts God's pleasure and which is alone capable of receiving it.

All Poor in This Way

i   Priests whom I cherish, you must all be poor in this way. This is why I ask you to be as little children.

j   Then I will always be able to lead you by the hand; and you will let yourselves be led with docility. You will listen only to my voice, because you will not be filled with other voices and other ideas.

k   And the voice and the ideas which I will communicate to you will be those of my Son. How clear then for you will all the Gospel be! The Gospel of my Son will be your only light and you, in a Church filled with darkness, will give the full light of the Gospel.

l   You will not be rich in other affections. Your only affection will be *mine*, that of your Mother. And I, as your Mother, will bring you to love my Son Jesus with a total love. I will lead you to such a degree of love that you will not be able to live without Him. I will make love for Him your very life, and He will truly be able to live again in you!

m   My beloved sons, this is why I need your poverty, your humility, your docility.

n   Do not be afraid if the world does not understand you and does not accept you; there is always the heart of your Mother which will be your home and your refuge."

65

The Power of the Spirit

a   "(. . .) Saint Stephen was truly a little child. What candor illuminated his soul, what purity his unshakeable faith in my Son, and what strength his whole person!

b   He conquered everyone with his glance, with the purity of his faith, with the power of his love. After Jesus, he was my first child whom many times I clapsed to my heart (. . .). I knew that he had to be the first one to die, after my Son Jesus. And with what tenderness did I encourage him so that he would become stronger and stronger.

c   And when he fell, killed, they brought him to me and I again clasped him to my heart . . . Oh, it was, as it were, the same scene as at Calvary!

d   (. . .) You too are called to be a *crown*: the crown of my Immaculate and Sorrowful Heart.

e   As upon him, so also upon you I pour out the fullness of my Son's love so that no one will be able to resist this grace. The Holy Spirit will sweep you along like a little feather on the wave of his fullness.

f   Each of the priests of my Movement will be this *crown of love* for me. A crown of lilies, of roses and of cyclamens, all these little children of mine. But no one will be able to resist the power of the Spirit which I will obtain for them.

g   Oh, and even they—in great part—will be called to the ultimate testimony. But their blood will wash and purify this world, so that from it a new world may be born, renewed in love and consecrated anew to the triumph of God! (. . .)"

66

Your Only Light

a   "End this year and begin the new year with me, my son, close to my Immaculate Heart, in prayer.

b   *Prayer of thanksgiving* for all that I have done this year for my Movement, accepting that which was most precious of those things which you offered me on their behalf: your prayer, your suffering, your complete trust in me.

c   It is in this way that the invitation, sent out by me, has now reached all my chosen ones throughout the world. Thus the seed has been sown and is already beginning to germinate.

d   With the coming year it will mature and blossom into so marvellous a spring that it will be a great joy and comfort for all my children.

e   *Prayer of propitiation* for so many of your brothers who await this new year amidst amusements, simply straining to forget things and to enjoy themselves, and often they offend the Heart of my Son and my motherly heart.

f   With the new year, the decisive events will begin: at a moment when a great part of humanity will least expect them.

g   Now my cohort is ready for the battle and soon the entire Church will witness this struggle between me and him who has always been my adversary: Satan, who has seduced a great part of humanity and who has corrupted and led astray so many children of my Church. (. . .)"

1975

LIVE IN JOY

67

Faithful to My Voice and That of the Pope

a   "(. . .) How I appreciated the holy Mass in honor of my Immaculate and Sorrowful Heart which you celebrated this morning in my venerated Sanctuary!

b   You came as on a pilgrimage of prayer, reciting the rosary and singing hymns in my honor.

c   I have already manifested to you how delighted I am and you are aware of this: especially at the moment when I stopped you and, through you, blessed all the priests of my Movement, in particular those who are the farthest away geographically: those of the German, the French and the English language, those in far-away America, and those in the missions of Africa and Asia.

d   At that moment, in every part of the world, all my priests felt me close to them: my sons who on this first Saturday of the month and of the year are spiritually united in honoring my Immaculate Heart.

e   My beloved sons, what joy and what comfort you give to my mother's heart! You are at last answering with your generous *yes* to what I asked at Fatima for the salvation of the world.

f   Your *yes*, O priests consecrated to my heart, was the one thing I was waiting for in order to begin to act. Now, with you, I will begin my work!

g   First of all, this Movement of mine will spread everywhere. I will bring together from every part of the world my beloved priests who, as it were, impelled by the irresistible force of the Holy Spirit, will respond and will gather together in the cohort of my priests who are called to remain *faithful* solely to the Gospel and to the Church.

h   When the time comes for the terrible encounter with those priests who are bearers of error and who will range themselves against the Pope and my Church, dragging a great number of my poor children toward their perdition, you will be my faithful priests.

i   In the darkness which the Evil Spirit will spread everywhere, in the midst of the many false ideas which, propagated by the Spirit of Pride, will be asserted and followed by almost everyone, at that moment when everything in the Church will be called into question, and when even the Gospel of my Son will be proclaimed by some as a legend, you, my consecrated priests, will be my *faithful*

j *sons*: faithful to the Gospel, faithful to the Church. And the strength of your fidelity will come from your habit of entrusting yourselves to me alone, and of remaining docile and obedient solely to my voice.

k   Hence, it will not be the voice of this or that theologian, nor the teaching of this or that person—even though he gain widespread approbation—but my voice alone which you will listen to, O my sons.

The Voice of the Church

l   And my voice will repeat to you gently only that which the Pope and the Church united to him will proclaim.

m   Faithful to my voice and that of the Pope, you will be the cohort prepared by me to defend his person, to disseminate his unheeded teachings, to comfort him in his abandonment and his solitude.

n   You also will be persecuted: the time will come when you will be the only light left burning and thus, through your fidelity to the Gospel and your sufferings, you will be able to point out the way of salvation to a vast number of souls. And through my intervention, this light of yours will never be completely extinguished.

o   My specially loved ones, be aware of my presence as a mother at the side of each one of you. Now the days are passing and the great moment is approaching. This is the hour when I am gather-

ing you together from each part of the world to enfold you all in
my Immaculate Heart. (. . .)"

68

The Time Left to You

a "Prepare, my son, to bring together again these sons of mine.
Follow the directives which I have already made known to you.
b I must hasten and I desire that the priests of my Movement be
once again reunited before the great tempest.

c —**To pray together**: as in the Cenacle, I, the Mother, gather
you together in prayer. O priests specially chosen by me, return
to prayer. I *have need* of your prayer.
d Pray with me and through me, with that prayer which is so
simple and yet so efficacious and which is the prayer I asked of
you: *the holy rosary.*
e Pray well: with humility, with simplicity, with abandonment,
with trust. Do not be any longer concerned about other things;
you must no longer become troubled by other disturbing problems . . .
f In great numbers, souls are straying far from God and rushing
down the road of depravity which is daily becoming more violent
and inhuman. Now any action of yours, or any action undertaken
by you alone, to restrain them, is no longer sufficient. They are
one step from their eternal damnation. I alone, through a motherly
and miraculous intervention, will be able to save them at the last
moment.
g This is why *I need* your prayer!
h My priests must be, at every moment, in this priestly attitude:
close to my heart in prayer for the salvation of the world.
i Discussions, feverish activity, taking on the problems and the
ways of acting that are in vogue at this time but which dissipate
and waste your energies, these are all the disturbing tactics of my

Adversary who today succeeds in ensnaring everything and everybody.

j You my beloved sons, you will never be seduced by him, because you are consecrated to my Immaculate Heart. Therefore you will always be *my priests* alone, who pray with me without ceasing so that the great apostasy will be in part contained and the great and imminent chastisements be at least mitigated.

k **—To love each other as brothers,** gathered about your own Mother. What grief my motherly heart experiences every day in seeing that even amongst themselves priests today no longer love each other, nor do they help each other! Egotism has smothered every impulse of fraternal charity and in the souls of many of my sons there is only coldness and darkness.

l Love one another, my beloved sons! Seek out each other, be united with each other, help each other to be faithful priests: faithful to the Pope, to the Gospel and to the Church.

m Do not be worried if at present everything concerning the faith seems to be in ruin. Not one word of the Gospel of my Son is to be denied. All must be taken in its intended sense if you wish to remain in the truth.

n You yourselves must be the living Gospel in order to oppose with your light the great darkness which is growing ever denser throughout my Church.

o **—To remain with me:** in these gatherings all will experience my special presence. And because time is pressing, I will make myself perceptible to each one in an extraordinary way. (. . .)

p There must be many more of these gatherings. The time left at your disposal is now short. Everything must be done well, so that the spirit of my beloved sons be prepared, but without their becoming fearful."

79

The Joy of Making You Grow

a   "My dearly beloved son, why are you troubled? Why do you sometimes lose your peace of mind?

b   All that has happened to you these past days was arranged by me in order that you would really detach yourself from *everyone*, even from those persons who are especially loved by me and by my Son Jesus.

c   You are so little that, without your noticing it, you end up by attaching yourself to them and depending on them. And your attachment becomes all the stronger, the closer these souls are to me.

d   You have no need of anything but their prayers and their sufferings: and this is what I ask of them for you and for my Movement. And you should reciprocate with your prayer and your great brotherly love. This is sufficient. Anything else is not from me; for you, anything else is vain and superfluous: it is truly a waste of time. (. . .)

e   My beloved sons, let yourselves be truly detached from everything! See: it is not your defects, your falls or your great limitations that prevent you from being totally mine and available for my great plan. Oh, no! On the contrary, these are a great gift to you because they help you to realize how little you are, and to remain little. They give you, so to speak, measure of your littleness.

f   It is your attachments which make up the only obstacle which prevents you from being totally mine. How many ties you still have, my sons! Ties to your own self, to other persons however good and holy they be, to your activities, to your ideas, to your feelings. And I will break them, one by one, so that you will be mine alone. (. . .)

g   Then I will be able to act in you and carry out my work as a Mother, which is that of making each one of you into a living copy of my Son Jesus. Entrust yourselves to me without fear. Every pain that you feel because of a new detachment will be soothed by me with a new gift of love. Each time that you detach yourself from a creature, you will feel your Mother closer to you.

h   My little children, let me have the joy of making you grow!"

70 March 15, 1975

Without Thinking of Tomorrow

a   "(. . .) Live each moment in me, without thinking of tomorrow, without ever worrying about what you must do. I will guide you by the hand at each moment. (. . .)

b   For a little while yet you will walk in light: but soon everything will be plunged in darkness. Then I myself will be your light and will guide you in carrying out that which my Immaculate Heart desires.

c   To do this, beloved sons, I must ask of you that which your human nature finds most costly: I ask you to live without thinking of tomorrow, without being preoccupied about the future.

d   Do not ask me: 'What shall we do? How should we conduct ourselves? Is the great purification near? What will be the outcome for us?'

e   Live, with perfect love and perfect abandonment, the present which I — moment by moment — arrange for you, my little babes.

f   For this, accustom yourselves not to look at things but to me alone. Do not consider what is awaiting you, the deeply distressing events of these times of yours. Do not consider what many are doing today against my Son and against me and what they are preparing to do against you.

g   The hour of darkness is approaching, the hour when you must drink the chalice which my Son has prepared for each one of you. But do not even think of this hour, that you may not be caught up in fear and anxiety.

h   Look only to my Immaculate Heart: take refuge and warm yourselves here, strengthen yourselves here. Feel yourselves in safety here! (. . .)"

71

The Way of the Cross

a   "The reason why I have wanted you here today, far from all preoccupations and activities, is that you might remain alone with my Son Jesus. (. . .)

b   The path along which I wish to lead my beloved sons, the priests who are consecrated to my Immaculate Heart and who belong to the Movement, is *that of the cross.*

c   I want them all on the cross with my Son, in prayer and in suffering. This is the road that Jesus took to carry out the work of redemption and to save all men.

d   This is the road which the priests called to form my cohort must follow, in order that men redeemed by my Son, but snatched from Him by Satan, may yet be saved today through a special intervention of this motherly heart of mine.

e   *The way of the cross,* my little children, is the only way that I have traced out for you because it is that which your Mother has first travelled, together with her Son Jesus.

f   Journey along it without fear, because you will be led by the hand, by me, enheartened by my motherly tenderness.

g   Journey along it with me, in my Immaculate Heart; near your cross you will thus feel the presence of your Mother who will comfort and help you.

h   This road *must be travelled* by you, because only in this way can you become similar to my Son Jesus in all things. My duty is that of making you *in every way* similar to Him.

i   Now that I have detached you from everything to make you ready to do the will of the Father, and formed you once again into little children to make you priests according to the Heart of Jesus, the time has come when you are being called to climb Calvary with Him.

j   This is the hour of Calvary for my Church, for the Holy Father, and for all the priests who want to be faithful to my Son and to the Gospel.

k   But it is also, beloved sons, your most beautiful hour for which I have prepared each one of you for a long time. Say with me: 'Yes, Father, your will be done!'

l   Even if this hour is one of darkness, you are called by me to reflect the light of the will and the plan of the Father. You will be called to bear witness to the fatherhood and the merciful love of God. (. . .)"

72

April 25, 1975
Feast of Saint Mark the Evangelist

Do Not Grieve Me by Your Doubts

a   "My most beloved son, you have now almost completed the work which I have entrusted to you.

b   Take refuge now in my Immaculate Heart: I want you here to strengthen you and to protect you at the time of the terrible trial.

c   My beloved sons, priests consecrated to my heart, listen again to the voice of your Mother who is gently admonishing you that you may be prepared for the great events which are now weighing upon the world.

d   Be truly and *only mine*; give yourselves to me without reserve. (. . .)

e   Think no longer of your past.

f   There are some among you who are still dwelling upon their past, feeling again the pain of the many wounds which I have healed, and they are, as it were, impeded from giving themselves totally to me. They are impeded by this thought: 'Is it possible that I – after all my shortcomings and infidelities – could be truly chosen and especially loved by my heavenly Mother?'

g   O my children! My heart overflows with tenderness for you precisely because you are small and weak, because you have sometimes fallen, because you feel yourself to be so frail.

h   By yourselves, my little children, you would never be able to surmount that which is awaiting you: and this is why I want to enfold you in my Immaculate Heart. I myself will be your security and your defense.

Prayer and Trust

i   There are some among you who are still caught up in the temptation of doubt and criticism. After all I have done for you! . . .

j   Do not grieve my heart by your doubts, by your incredulity. Have you not yet learned to let yourselves be guided by me? Overcome this temptation by prayer.

k   From my priests, I want only prayer and confidence in me. Every moment which is not spent by them with me in the most complete abandonment is, as it were, lost to them and taken away from me: and this deeply grieves my motherly heart.

l   The time has come when some of my priest-sons are preparing to openly oppose my Son, myself, the Pope and the Church.

m   I will then be no longer able to recognize them as my children; I myself will come down from heaven to place myself at the head of the cohort of my beloved sons, and I will crush their plots.

n   After a great upheaval and the purification of the earth, my Immaculate Heart will sing of its victory in the greatest triumph of God.

o   It is for this moment, my beloved priests, that I have called you one by one from all parts of the world and have made you ready.

p   This is no longer a time for doubt and uncertainty: this is the time of battle!

84

^q Each one of you should let himself be enfolded by me in my Immaculate Heart."

73

Respond to My Supreme Call

a "Once again write what I will dictate to your childlike heart, chosen by my Immaculate Heart.

b Be ever more docile and obedient to your spiritual director. Entrust yourself to him completely. I will give him the necessary light to understand what I want of him for the realization of my plans.

c Do not fear, my most beloved son. Why do you become troubled and sometimes lose your peace of mind?

d You are in my heart; live habitually enfolded in my mother's heart. Feel all its serenity, and all the tenderness it has for you!

e Live, my son, so that I may pour out on you *all the tenderness* of my Immaculate and Sorrowful Heart. (. . .)

f Whoever looks at you, listens to you or passes by you should be able to sense in his soul a touch of this supernatural perfume of mine and the tenderness which my Mother's heart has *for all her children.*

g And so I want you to be truly detached from everyone. Do not seek other voices or other supports. Do you not see that I myself am speaking to you and leading you? My Immaculate Heart will be your only comfort, and from this heart will come all your encouragement.

h As for the rest, leave it to me. This is my work alone and no one will touch it, because I am jealous of it with the very jealousy of God. This work is willed by me for the great triumph of God and the conclusive defeat of Satan.

Each Thing in Its Place

i   Do not become uneasy if you find that movements inspired by souls to whom I have revealed myself are springing up here and there: on the contrary, all is part of my great plan. And so each thing must be in its place.

j   Your place is the Marian Movement of Priests. Through my priests, an immense number of the laity will again be consecrated to my heart, and entrust themselves completely to me. With simplicity and without organization, let them give themselves to me as a little child gives himself *completely* to his own mother.

k   My children, the battle has already begun and I ask you only to respond to my supreme call.

l   Be my priests; be solely priests of prayer. Do not waste any more time, because the time left to you is far too precious. Pray the holy rosary continually and well. Live and spread the Gospel of my Son Jesus.

m   Pray for, help and defend the Vicar of Christ: the Pope. Be poor, be little, be humble: be nothing other than my little children who form a crown of love about my Immaculate and Sorrowful Heart.

n   Today, one by one, I bless you, I embrace you and I enfold you in this heart of mine.

o   Never, even for an instant, feel yourselves alone and without me. Sons consecrated to my heart, I am *your Mother* who today gives you the gift of her habitual presence at the side of each one of you."

74

July 9, 1975

Your Heaviest Cross

a   "How often I tell you: remain always in my heart and fear nothing. Never become preoccupied, even concerning my Movement; all I want of you is prayer, suffering and a most complete surrender to me.

b At this time, I have not wanted to put you to the test. You are so little and so completely mine that your Mother cannot leave you alone, not even for an instant. . .

c I have wanted you to taste just a *little drop* of the great bitterness which overwhelms my heart because of so many of my poor priest-sons of whom Satan has now taken complete possession. . .

d My poor sons, what anguish they cause me!

e Priests of my Son, they no longer believe in my Son and continually betray Him; priests called to be ministers of grace, they now live habitually in sin: their life is an uninterrupted succession of sacrileges. Priests sent to proclaim the Gospel of salvation, they have now become propagators of error. Priests chosen to save many souls, they lead so very many souls along the road of perdition.

f This is the hour when the abomination of desolation is truly entering into the holy temple of God.

g They are no longer the salt of the earth, but a salt without savour, corrupted and nauseating, good only to be strewn on the ground and trampled under foot by everyone. They are no longer the light on the candlestick, but darkness which makes the night even more obscure.

h They are all poor ailing priest-sons of mine, because they have fallen under the dominion of Satan. . .

i My beloved son, how can my heart not be submerged in an infinite sea of sorrow?

For the Salvation of All

j Priests of my Movement, beloved sons of my sorrowful heart, what must you do in order to save all these priests who are so ill and so much in need of my motherly help?

k **Help them**, without ever judging them. Love them always. Do not condemn them; this is not your role. Love them by your suffering, by your witnessing, by your good example.

l Be an example to them by defending, even exteriorly, your dignity. You should never abandon the ecclesiastical garb, thus obeying the will, time and time again expressed, of the Vicar of my Son, the Pope.

m **Pray for them**. Much prayer is needed to obtain from the Heart of Jesus the conversion and repentance of these poor sons of mine. You have been chosen by me for the triumph of my Immaculate Heart in the world. But this triumph will begin with the salvation of many of these poor priest-sons of mine who have gone astray.
n Form an unbroken chain of prayer and of love to ask for their salvation and that my Immaculate Heart may become, especially for them, the most secure refuge.

o **Suffer** with the Pope, with the Bishops, with the faithful priests.
p This is the cross which Jesus now asks you to carry: to live side by side with brother-priests who no longer believe, who spiritually are no longer alive, who betray the Gospel, who are *unfaithful servants* and yet remain in the Church to be ministers of this infidelity. (. . .)

q This scandal will become even greater and more serious. You will be called upon to suffer more and more, because this veritable apostasy from the Gospel will one day become general in the Church, before the great liberating purification.
r Therefore, no longer fix your attention on time; do not be even reckoning on the time of my triumph. Live simply in surrender and trust, like my little children, in my Immaculate Heart."

75   *July 24, 1975*

Serene in This Time of Your Repose

a "Enter, my dearly beloved son, into my Immaculate Heart: this is the place of your repose.

b   Spend these days constantly with me, in my company. I wanted you here again this year: in the midst of these little children of mine, humanly speaking a little frail and more needy, and therefore dearer to my heart.

c   Be only and ever my little child, in need of everything, rejoicing to receive everything from me in all simplicity. . .

d   This way I have of talking to you may astonish the grown-ups, but it is very natural and simple for my little children.

e   The sun, the sea, nature: all is a gift to you from the heavenly Father; all is made holy by the presence and the joy of my son Jesus.

f   In times of anguish, how comforting for the Heart of my Son was this nature, prostrate, as it were, at his feet: the sun with its light, the charming countryside of Galilee with its flowers, with its songs,with its warm and golden harvest and the lovely mirror of the great lake.

g   Everything spoke in harmony, as it were, with the great prayer of my Son Jesus, with his ardent thirst for solitude, with his natural desire of living in the company of his Father.

h   How many today, on these same shores, live forgetful of God, submerged in a new paganism, and offend Him, ungrateful for this great gift of his.

i   But here, in these same places, many of my little children love and console Him.

j   Your presence, my son, should be like an *act of reparation*. It must therefore be a presence of love and of prayer, a presence of life with me.

A Sign of Reparation

k   So also is the presence of the priests of my Movement in the world of today: consecrated to my Immaculate Heart, they are offered by me to the Father as *a sign of reparation*.

l   For this reason, the more sin will increase the more their love for God will grow; the more filth will submerge everything the more their purity will become limpid and shining; the more apostasy will spread the more heroic will be the witness of their faith, even to blood.

m   In this way they will be a sign of reparation: by their love, by their fidelity, by their purity.

n   And it will be due to these little children of mine, consecrated to my heart, that evil will not prevail. And thus in the end it will be defeated.

o   For this purpose they have been all chosen and prepared by me for this great purification of the earth.

p   From this place I bless you all with an abundance of graces, including your spiritual director whom I have placed at your side and whom I am making an increasingly docile instrument in my hands for the realization of my plans, and including also these little children of mine who are keeping you company.

q   Pray, rest, work, love: even these days of yours form part of the great plan which I have in your regard. So then, enter serenely into this time of rest."

76   *July 29, 1975*

Behold the Handmaid of the Lord

a   "Consider, my son, the good that this Mother wants for you.

b   You are now becoming accustomed to doing everything with me; you are coming to realize how at each moment I lead you to do what I desire of you. It is the Mother's heart which is carrying you; here you now experience how all your anxieties cease.

c   Priests so dearly beloved by me, I want you all to abandon yourselves to me in this way.

d   Do not think about yourselves any longer; do not be worried about anything; let yourselves be carried by me, one and all.

e   I need only your trust; I want only your complete abandonment to me.

f   Satan fears only this: an army of priests consecrated to my Immaculate Heart and completely abandoned to me.

g   He knows that through them I myself have accepted the challenge which he has again dared to hurl at my Son, and he now senses that his defeat is at hand.

h   To his renewed gesture of pride and rebellion by which he has now seduced the whole of humanity, I will again repeat through my little children: *'Behold the handmaid of the Lord; be it done unto me according to your word.'*

i   And then will come the final defeat of Satan and of his many followers, through the triumph of my little children in my Immaculate Heart.

j   Do not ask me when this will take place, because I have already initiated this triumph."

77

August 5, 1975
Feast of Our Lady of the Snows

The Priests Are Responding to Me

a   "Remain serene; have confidence in me, even for what pertains to the spread of my Movement.

b   Do not be anxious over the many requests for the little book over these past months, to which, through no negligence on your part, it has been impossible to answer.

c   Let us suppose that with a perfect organization we could send out immediately all the booklets requested. Do you think that this would be sufficient for the spread of my Movement? No, my son, because the booklets, once they had arrived at their destination, could very well just lie there; or else, even if they were distributed, they could be put away in a drawer by those who receive them, without being read; or even if read, they could leave the reader completely indifferent.

d   My *motherly action is the only thing necessary* for the spread of my Movement. It is my action alone that prepares souls to receive this gift of mine; that determines for each one the moment when this will be given; that gives a special grace by which my words can be understood and can produce in souls that marvellous reality which they express.

Your Prayer

e   This is why I ask you insistently to support my action with *your prayer*. This is what I am always asking of you because this, and not technical perfection, is what is necessary for me.

f   Tell X that I look upon him with delight when he is working for my Movement, as I know that he is already taken up by so many other occupations.

g   But in order that my sorrowful heart might be consoled by him and that he himself might live in the intimacy of this heart, I ask his generous soul for *more prayer*, more moments of silence and of living with me. . .

h   Of you, my dearest son, I ask prayer, suffering and silence.

i   *Silence*, above all, concerning our intimacy.

j   Do not speak about what I am doing for you, so as not to curb my action and delay the plan of my Immaculate Heart. Tell everything only to your confessor and spiritual director.

k   You see how I myself have brought you to a great intimacy with me; but your brothers are still on the way. Therefore they are not yet able to understand.

l   Of you I always expect *prayer and suffering*.

m   The announcement of my Movement has now reached all parts of the world and those priests consecrated to my Immaculate Heart are all responding to me.

n   However it is necessary that these sons of mine walk under my guidance, without ever halting. Not one of them must be mediocre. I want to lead them all, in my Immaculate Heart, to the summit of sanctity.

o   If you only knew how much Satan tempts and obstructs them, torments and discourages them.

p   Remain always in my heart and on the cross for their sakes: your prayer and your suffering will help them to grow in holiness.

q   On the cross and in my Immaculate Heart, at my side, you will then be constantly helping those who are your brothers and my beloved sons."

78

Satan Breaks Loose

a   ". . . You are aware that I am always near; sometimes my motherly action absorbs, as it were, your own activity, and you live habitually recollected in my Immaculate Heart.

b   You are here in this place where my Son Jesus resides, and where I also am present . . .

c   Why have I wanted you up here?

d   To help you climb your cross, my little one. I will give you great gifts of love and of pain. Only in this way will you be able to help your brother-priests to grow in holiness and to become priests after the Heart of Jesus.

e   It is true, you have consecrated them all to my Immaculate Heart; they are now mine, they belong to me, and it is my duty to form them as the priests that Jesus wants them to be.

f   But if you only knew, my son, how human they still are: attached to themselves, to pleasures, to the esteem of others, to the goods of this world, to their own way of looking at things. They still distrust me, my son; and they distrust you and the mission that I myself have confided to you.

g   Satan torments them, sifts them violently, seduces them with pride and greatly discourages them! He bites furiously at my heel; he hurls himself with rage at my little children; he knows that soon it will be the faithful priests, and I with them, who will crush his head forever.

h   I have wanted you up here because it is here that your Calvary begins. (. . .)"

79

You Will Have Them Walk toward Me

a   "Be at peace once again in my Immaculate Heart. How much you have suffered these past days: the darkness, the obscurity, the doubt. In a certain sense, you have tasted even the bitterness of being abandoned!

b   At these moments it seems to you that you have lost your way; you call on me and it seems to you that I am far away, that all is an illusion. On the contrary, never as in these moments, never as at this very moment, my son, am I so close to you and do I clasp you so close to my Immaculate Heart and gaze on you with such tenderness and love.

c   I need this suffering of yours: all I want of you is prayer and suffering. And then I will give you new light and new serenity; you will rejoice and be strengthened and thus made even more ready to be placed again upon your cross.

d   Only when you will be lifted up on your cross will you be able to help all the priests of my Movement to be that which my Immaculate Heart wants them to be.

e   What a long road these sons of mine must still travel and you will give them your hand and have them walk toward me. . . (. . .)"

September 12, 1975
Feast of the Holy Name of Mary and
anniversary of the victory of the
Blessed Virgin Mary at Vienna (1683)

Little to Others, Great to Me

a   "I have chosen you precisely because of your littleness, your poverty. Jesus looks with pleasure and with predilection on the small, the pure of heart, the simple.

b   Be ever thus!

c   And so never look at yourself, because I will make you the gift of leaving you with your faults.

d   My Son Jesus does not love you for what you can do, but for yourself. He loves you just as you are. It is not your merits but only his love which draws Him strongly to you.

e   I also, your Mother, love you just as you are: even with your defects, as long as you are always striving to correct them. And if they give you a true measure of your littleness, even they will help me to make your more my own.

f   Priests of my Movement, do not fear if you sometimes feel far away from the ideal which I am proposing to you. Your humility, your trust and your good will suffice for me.

g   I am forming a cohort of priests who will perhaps never be perfect, but they will certainly be *all mine*.

h   The perfection which I will build in them will be interior and hidden: little to others, great to me. They will even be despised and persecuted by many, but in their soul they will always have my joy.

i   I want you to offer me these flowers, my son, on this feastday of mine.

j   I bless you, I bless you all with gratitude and thankfulness."

Offer and Suffer with Me

a   "My very dear sons, through the entreaty and wish of my dying Son, I became your true Mother.

b   I am the Mother of all.

c   By the privilege of my bodily assumption into heaven, my Immaculate heart never ceases to beat with love for you.

d   Thus it has never ceased to be saddened and pained by so many of my children who continue to do evil and who walk on the road of perdition, making useless all the suffering of my Son Jesus and mine.

e   To be sure, I am in heaven: I am perfectly happy close to my Son, in the light of the Most Holy Trinity, in the eternal joy of the angels and saints. But my duty as a Mother still binds me to you, and keeps me close to you on this earth.

f   If I am your Mother, all your pain is mine as well.

g   And so it is that in my heart I truly feel the repercussions of all the bitterness, all the misery and all the great suffering of the world.

h   If I am the Mother, I cannot help but suffer for my children. For all, especially those who are farthest away, who are most in need, and above all for my poor children who are in sin.

i   If I am the Mother, I cannot help but suffer for those who are sinners; for all of them, because I desire that they all return to the Heart of my Son Jesus and to my mother's heart.

j   I who am happy in heaven am grieving on earth, close to you, my poor afflicted children.

Live in the Present Instant

k   Priests of my Movement, beloved sons of my sorrowful heart, do you wish to accept my gentle invitation to suffer with me?

l Often I am, as it were, surprised to see with what anxiety – and sometimes even with such great human curiosity – you scrutinize the future. You often on occasion ask yourself: 'But when will this purification take place?'

m There are even some who, in my name, believe that they can indicate the dates of events and exact occurrences, and they forget that the hour and the moment is a secret hidden in the merciful and fatherly Heart of God.

n The Mother cannot put time limits on her motherly admonition or her merciful expectation.

o And so I say to you, beloved sons, do not scrutinize the future; and thus neither anxiety nor discouragement will take hold of you! Live only in the present instant, in complete abandonment, close to my Immaculate Heart, the present instant which the love of the heavenly Father puts at your disposal, my little children . . .

p Before the Father – the omnipresent Father – only the present moment counts: not the past nor the future because this time is not yours.

q Share my suffering, privileged sons of mine. At the time when the whole world was once for all redeemed and purified, the Father accepted the Son's divine suffering together with my human suffering as a mother.

r Your suffering, my sons, is truly contributing to the purification of the earth.

s If the chastisement comes, it will be only as an ultimate and solemn demand for suffering to bring about the renewal of the world and the salvation of so many poor children of mine.

t But nothing contributes so much to the triumph of my Immaculate Heart as a priestly heart which suffers. In you, my sons, it is Jesus who continues his mission of purification. Only his blood can wash away all the evil, all the hatred and all the sin of the world.

u And so, now that the moment of the purification is here, you will be called upon to suffer more and more. For you, my sons, this is the hour of the cross. But you will suffer with me, with your Mother who begot you under the Cross.

v   Be ever with me, in the present moment which the Father gives you: to offer and to suffer in the heart of your sorrowful Mother."

82

October 7, 1975
Feast of Our Lady of the Rosary
Anniversary of the victory
of the Blessed Virgin Mary at Lepanto

What it Means to Be a Mother

a   "My son, you have come here only because I wanted you here, and you have seen my marvels.

b   You have seen where my special favor is always directed: upon the little ones, the poor, the suffering, the sinners.

c   Wherever there is suffering, there also is my predilection.

d   If you knew what it means to be a Mother! . . .

e   If you could but succeed in understanding this, you would no longer fear anything: it is my maternity that saves you.

f   The justice of the Father has determined that the sufferings and the death of the Son are to pay for your redemption. The love of the Heart of the Son has determined that his Mother is to bring you to salvation.

g   Priests so dearly loved by me, it is for this reason that I say to you: *Do not be afraid; it is your Mother who is preparing each thing for you.* Do not be anxious; leave all your worries in my heart. (. . .)

h   Be prepared to see my greatest marvels. Today you recall one of my victories, but soon you will all be witnesses of my greatest triumph.

i   My cohort is now ready and the time has come. With the weapon of prayer, of the rosary and of your trust, it is now the time to enter into battle.

j   Soon, my sons, a new date will be celebrated. The entire

Church will flourish anew under the most pure mantle of your Mother."

83

Be Joyous

a   "I have chosen you, my son, for this simple reason: because you are the poorest, the smallest and the most limited. Humanly speaking, you are the most destitute.

b   I have chosen you because in your past life my Adversary had almost succeeded in claiming a victory. In your life, I have had you live, as if by anticipation, the experience of what I myself will do at the moment of my great triumph.

c   My Adversary will one day think that he is celebrating a complete victory: over the world, over the Church, over souls.

d   It will be only then that I will intervene—terrible and victorious—that his defeat may be all the greater when he is certain in his conviction that he has conquered once for all.

e   What is in preparation is so extraordinary that its like has never happened since the creation of the world. That is why everything has already been predicted in the Bible.

f   The terrible struggle between me, 'the Woman Clothed in the Sun,' and the Red Dragon, Satan, who has now succeeded in seducing many even with the error of Marxist atheism, has already been foretold to you. The struggle between the angels together with my children and the followers of the dragon led by the rebellious angels has already been foretold to you. Above all, my complete victory has already been clearly foretold.

g   You, my sons, have been called to live through these events.

h   It is now the time for you to know this, that you may be consciously prepared for the battle. This is now the time for me to begin disclosing part of my plan.

i   First of all, it is necessary that my Enemy have the impression of having conquered everything, of having everything now in his hands. This is why he will be permitted to penetrate even into the interior of my Church and he will succeed in plunging the sanctuary of God into darkness. He will reap the greatest number of victims from among the Ministers of the Sanctuary.

j   This will in fact be a time of great falls on the part of my beloved sons, my Priests.

k   Satan will seduce some of them by pride, others by love of the flesh, others by doubts, others by unbelief, and still others by discouragement and loneliness.

l   How many will have doubts about my Son and about Me and will believe that this is the end of my Church!

It is not the end!

m   Priests consecrated to my Immaculate Heart, my beloved sons whom I am gathering together for this great battle: the first weapon that you must make use of is *trust in Me*. It is *your complete abandonment to me*.

n   Conquer the temptation of fear, of discouragement, of sadness. Distrust paralyzes your activity and greatly benefits my Adversary.

o   Be serene, be joyful!

p   This is not the end of my Church; what is in preparation is the beginning of its total and marvellous renewal!

q   The Vicar of my Son, in virtue of a gift I grant to him, is already able to foresee this and, though living in the present moment of sadness, he invites you to *be joyous*.

r   'To be joyous?' you ask me, all surprised.

s   Yes, my sons, in the joy of my Immaculate heart where I enfold you all. My mother's heart will be for you the place of your peace, while outside the most violent storm is raging.

t   Even if you have been wounded, even if you have fallen many times, even if you have doubted, even if at certain times you have been unfaithful, do not become discouraged, because *I love you!*

u   The more my Adversary will have sought to rage about you, the greater will be my love for you.

v   I am a Mother and I love you all the more, my sons, for your having been snatched away from me.

w   And my joy is to make each one of you, priests beloved of my Immaculate Heart, sons so purified and strengthened that from now on no one will ever again succeed in snatching you from the love of my Son Jesus.

x   I will make of you living copies of my Son Jesus.

y   And so be content, be confident and be totally abandoned to me. Remain always in prayer with me.

z   The weapons that I will use to fight and win this battle will be your prayer and your suffering.

A   And so then, yes, you too will be on the cross with me and with my Son Jesus, close to his Mother and yours. (. . .)"

84

Your Silence

a   "How many times I repeat to you: you will meet with sufferings and misunderstandings, but never obstacles! This is my work; no one will touch it.

b   My angels have already begun the battle; at my orders they are bringing these sons of mine together from all parts of the world. My heart knows what means to use to reach them; I find my greatest joy when they answer 'yes' to me.

c   Many feel so small and unworthy; they are conscious of so many past infidelities and weaknesses and they are rather perplexed in taking this step.

d   The 'yes' which they say to me makes my heart leap for joy.

e   Count now how many of these yeses there are; calculate how much joy is given to my Immaculate Heart!

f   This complete offering of yours is the only thing I ask of you, my sons: the offering of yourselves with your limitations, your weaknesses and your inabilities.

g I need this in my plan.

h If I have asked for no juridical structure for the Movement, it is precisely because I want it to be spread in silence and hiddenness.

i The second weapon which you must use, after your trust and abandonment of yourself to me, is your prayer and your silence.

j **Interior silence**: let it be the Mother who speaks within you.

k She will repeat softly to your childlike heart all the Gospel of Jesus. She will give you once again a taste for his word.

l You will not listen to other voices or other words: you will hunger and thirst for his alone and thus you will be formed in the school of the word (*Parola*) of God.

m **Exterior Silence**: let it be the Mother who speaks through you. I am so eager to do this, if you will let me act freely within you.

n In order that I may speak, I need your silence. Some of you find it difficult to understand this. Yet this silence is so necessary, even for your own word.

o Some of you believe that even for my Movement it is necessary to do, to write, to act. Yet your silence is so necessary for the spread of my Movement, according to the plan which has already been clearly outlined by my Immaculate Heart.

p Speak always through your manner of living. Let your life be your word. Then it will be I myself who will speak in you and through you. Then your words will be understood and received into the hearts of your listeners.

q Today when the spoken word is the weapon used by my Adversary to seduce all humanity, I ask you to oppose him with your silence.

r Thus it will again be the Spirit who will speak in you, and by means of the Spirit, making use of you, the whole world will be completely renewed."

85

I Am Calling Them All

a   "Have you seen how I place in your path the priests called by me to consecrate themselves to my Immaculate Heart? Your task, my son, is to gather them together and to entrust them all to me.

b   These sons of mine have now such great need to be consoled and encouraged. And this is why I am always present in these gatherings. The souls of these sons of mine will thereby rejoice and they shall all be consoled.

c   The time has come when I will make myself more manifest in the Church, through increasingly greater signs.

d   My *tears* are shed in many places to call everyone back to the sorrowful heart of their Mother.

e   The tears of a mother succeed in moving the most hardened hearts. But now my tears, even tears of blood, leave many of my children completely indifferent.

f   My *messages* which will become all the more frequent the more the voice of the ministers refuses to proclaim the truth.

g   Because so many priests have abandoned their trust, how many of my children are now suffering from a true spiritual famine of the word of God.

h   The truths which are most important for your life today are no longer preached: heaven which awaits you; the Cross of my Son which saves you; sin which wounds the Heart of Jesus and mine; hell into which innumerable souls are falling every day; the urgent necessity of prayer and penance.

i   The more sin spreads like a pestilence and causes the death of souls, the less it is talked about. Today some of my priests even deny its existence.

j   It is my duty as a Mother to give nourishment to the souls of my children; if the voice of the ministers is stilled, the heart of their Mother will open up more and more.

Present in Person

k Following now upon my interventions, the time has come *when I must make myself present in person and act in the Church whose Mother I am.*

l I want to act through you, O priests consecrated to my Immaculate Heart. This too is part of my plan.

m The Evil One, my adversary from the beginning, is now in the process of seducing a great number of priests and he is working among them and gathering them together against my Son, against me and against the Church.

n I am personally intervening and calling together into my cohort the priests who are determined to remain faithful. *I call them all* to consecrate themselves to my Immaculate Heart and to take refuge in me.

o The struggle will be especially between me and the ancient Serpent whose head I will, in the end, crush. And so I now ask of you only those things which, according to your human way of looking at things, seem small and insignificant.

p As day by day propaganda increases, as well as the clamor of the enemies of God who are succeeding in winning everything over to themselves, all I ask of you is to respond with your *trust* and total *abandonment*, with *prayer*, with *suffering* and with your *silence*.

q However, whatever you offer to my heart will become in my hands a terrible weapon with which to fight and to win this battle.

r To the haughty cohort of the arrogant who rebel against God, I will reply with the cohort of my little, humble, despised and persecuted sons.

s And through you the victory will belong, in the end, to the humble 'handmaid of the Lord.' "

Live Your Consecration

a   "(. . .) You were chosen by me to make everyone – and especially your brother-priests – understand the wealth and the wonders of my heart.

b   At Fatima, I gave my Immaculate heart as a means for the salvation of all humanity. I pointed out the way of return to God. But I was not listened to.

c   Now I want to offer you my Immaculate Heart as your only refuge in the very painful moments that await you.

d   Day by day your sufferings will increase. The crisis, now under way within my Church, will grow deeper to the point of open rebellion especially on the part of many of my sons who share in the priesthood of my Son Jesus. The darkness, which is indeed already growing denser, will deepen into night throughout the world.

e   Marxist atheism will contaminate everything; like a poisonous fog it will penetrate everywhere and will bring many of my children to death of faith.

f   It will subvert the truth contained in the Gospel. It will deny the divinity of my Son and the divine origin of the Church. Above all, it will threaten its hierarchical structure and attempt to break down the Rock upon which the edifice of the Church is built.

Totally at My Disposal

g   This is the time when I want to pour out the mercy of my heart upon all my children, to save them through my motherly love which always understands, helps and pardons.

h   I want to act through you, O priests especially chosen by me.

i   In order that I may do this, you must be totally at my disposal. I will be able to act in you to the extent that you allow yourselves to be possessed by my gentle motherly action.

j You do this through your consecration to my Immaculate Heart: it is the only thing necessary for you to do in order to belong to my priestly Movement.

k Make it, renew it often and especially, my sons, *live this consecration of yours!*

l How much comfort you give to my sorrowful heart when, in your gatherings, coming together for concelebration, you renew all together the act of consecration to my heart!

m If you live your consecration, your life will be truly transformed: I will accustom you to my way of seeing, of thinking, of praying, of loving.

n I will communicate my spirit to you and will make you ever littler, more simple and more humble.

o I will bring you to trust always and only in God. And the more that doubt and denial increase, the more you will find your certainty in Him and you will bear witness to this.

p I will bring you to love the Church very much. Today the Church is going through times of great suffering because it is loved less and less by its own children.

q Many would like to renovate it and purify it solely by criticism and by violent attacks on its institution. Nothing is ever renewed or purified without love!

r I will bring you to love the Pope with a deep filial love; the Mother will lead you to carry his cross with him and to share his sufferings.

s Where are they now, those priests who are close to the first priest, to this first son whom the Mother loves with special tenderness?

t Let it be you, O priests consecrated to my Immaculate Heart, who are closest to the heart of the Pope.

u Pray for him, suffer with him, be always with him! Listen to him, put his instructions into practice, spread his unheeded teachings!

v When the night is at its darkest, he will be the only light left burning. You will be illumined by this light and, led by me, you will spread it throughout the world, so full of darkness.

w   It will also be with the weapon *of your fidelity* that I will fight and win the battle.

x   For this reason, my sons, I invite you to take refuge completely in my Immaculate Heart."

87

This Time Will Be Shortened

a   "My plan, O son, is now being accomplished.

b   The decisive events have begun and you will be called to suffer more and more.

c   I have need of *all your sufferings*: this is the most precious weapon that can be used in this battle of mine. So I ask you to be prepared to suffer, to get ready to climb Calvary with Jesus and me, to offer yourselves to the Father as victims chosen by me and long prepared with motherly care.

d   In fact, as your Mother, I have gathered you all into my Immaculate Heart. Here is your refuge, the altar on which you will be immolated for the salvation of the world.

e   Do not let your hearts be troubled, my sons. Give yourselves to me at every moment! The time of desolation and abandonment of my Church has come. It will be abandoned especially by many of its ministers and its own children.

f   It will be scoffed at, betrayed and given into the hands of him who is its enemy and who wishes to destroy it. It will be some of its own ministers who will hand it over to its executioners.

g   Prepare yourselves with me to live out these moments. Everything has already been arranged by the Father. This is the chalice which you must drink to the dregs.

h   You too will be scoffed at, betrayed and persecuted with the Vicar of my Son, the Pope. Many will have to give their lives and shed their blood. The others will remain to be consumed as a holocaust, by living through these moments of great suffering which are in preparation for the purification of the earth. Thus you will be my light in the great darkness.

i   But this most severe trial, my beloved sons, will be of short duration. Through my special intercession, these hours will be shortened. (. . .)"

88   *December 8, 1975*
Feast of the Immaculate Conception

I Will Be Victorious

a   "I am the Immaculate Conception!

b   I came from heaven, my sons, and at Lourdes I recalled that truth which the Church had but a short time before officially defined.

c   By a privilege I am exempt from all sin whatsoever, even from that original sin which each one of you contracts at the moment of conception.

d   I was preserved from sin because, in this humble creature, the Most Holy Trinity wanted its wondrous plan to be reflected, whole and entire.

e   I was preserved from sin and filled with grace because I was chosen to become the Mother of the Word and destined to give you my Son Jesus. And my Son Jesus has given me to each one of you as your true Mother.

f   Therefore my motherly plan for you is to clothe you in my own immaculateness. I want above all to heal you from the evil that makes you so ugly: sin.

g   My beloved sons, priests consecrated to my Immaculate Heart: from the beginning I have been announced as the enemy, the antagonist and the conqueror of Satan, the father and the first artificer of all sin.

h   My mission is to fight and defeat Satan, to crush his head with my heel.

i I conquered in the beginning when the Trinity proclaimed me as the sign of sure victory, at the moment when all humanity had fallen under the bondage of sin. 'I will put enmity between you and the Woman; between your offspring and hers. She will crush your head as you make an attempt on her heel.'

j I conquered when, by my *yes*, the Word was made flesh in my most pure womb and when on Calvary my Son Jesus offered himself on the altar of the Cross.

k In Him, who has redeemed you all, my total victory was accomplished.

l I have continued my battle throughout the long years of the Church's pilgrimage on earth: its greatest victories have been due to my special motherly action.

m But when, in this last century, my Adversary wanted to challenge me and begin a struggle which, through *the error of atheism*, would have seduced and deceived all humanity, from heaven I appeared upon earth as the Immaculate One to comfort you, because it is, above all, my duty to fight and to conquer the Evil One.

My Heart Will Triumph

n And in this century, while atheism has organized itself as a force spread out for the conquest of the whole world and the complete destruction of my Church, I again appeared from heaven to tell you not to fear, because in this terrible struggle I will be the victress: 'In the end my Immaculate Heart will triumph!'

o You, my poor sons, are the ones most knocked about in a struggle which is, above all, between me and my Adversary, the Ancient Serpent, Satan, the seducer and the artificer of all evil.

p For this reason, before telling you of the battle, I have, like a good Mother, invited you to seek a safe refuge. Take refuge in me; entrust yourselves completely to my heart.

q *My Immaculate Heart*: now you understand, my sons, why it is the greatest gift which the heavenly Father offers you.

r   My *Immaculate Heart*: it is your safest refuge and the means of salvation which, at this time, God gives to the Church and to humanity.

s   The special intervention of this heart of mine is the work which I am carrying out in my Church to call all priests, my beloved ones, to take refuge in me.

t   Do you see how Satan has now entered into the interior of the Church? How he deceives, corrupts and drags off so many of my poor priest-sons?

u   This is then the hour when I will personally intervene.

v   I have called you to trust, to complete abandonment and to consecrate yourselves totally to my Immaculate Heart. I have revealed my plan to you and I have indicated the arms which I have selected for this battle.

w   Now, my sons, I reaffirm to you that I *alone will be the victress.* (. . .)"

89

Do Not Fear

a   "This is the holy night, my most beloved son, and so live it in my heart.

b   I want to have you share completely in my love, in my motherly anxiety at the moment when, caught up in a light from heaven, my Son Jesus is born into this world. He is born of me, his Mother in a virginal and miraculous manner.

c   It was deep night. Deeper still was the night which enveloped humanity, enslaved in sin and beyond hope of salvation. The night also enveloped the Chosen People, who no longer responded to the spirit of their election and were not ready to receive their Messiah.

d   On this night so deep, the Light appeared, my little Infant was born. At a time when no one was looking for his coming, when there was no place open to receive Him . . .

e   Unexpected, unwelcomed, rejected by humanity,—and yet, at this moment redemption begins for humanity,—my Jesus is born to redeem all men from their sins.

f   Thus the light rises in the midst of such great darkness and my little Child comes to save the world.

g   He is born in poverty and in the pain of this rejection, and his first cries are but tears of mourning: he feels the rigor of the chill, as the whole world envelops Him in its cold.

h   My Immaculate Heart gathered the first tears of the divine Child. They were mingled with those of my own heart and I wiped them away with my mother's kisses.

i   On this holy night, as I again give you my Son, I say once more: *Do not fear*; Jesus is your Savior.

j   Now, more than ever, the world is plunged in darkness; the coldness of hatred, of pride and of unbelief envelops the hearts of men. Even the Church is disrupted by a profound crisis: and even many of its priests have doubts about my little Child.

k   O my Church, receive with joy the coming of your Jesus: He is living in you because He wants to save all these poor children of mine!

Jesus Is Your Savior!

l   Priests consecrated to my Immaculate Heart, *do not fear*. Today I announce to you great tidings of joy for all: my Son Jesus is your Savior. You were all redeemed by Him; now you can all be saved by Him.

m   *Do not fear*: as my heart has given you the Savior, so now in these times my Immaculate Heart gives you the joy of his salvation.

n   Soon the whole world, which is pervaded with darkness and which has been snatched from my Son, will at last rejoice over the fruit of this holy night.

o   The triumph of my Immaculate Heart will be realized through a new birth of Jesus in the hearts and the souls of my poor wandering children.

p   Only have confidence and do not let anxiety or discouragement take hold of you. The future that awaits you will be a new dawn of light for the whole world, now at last made clean.

q   On this night, close by the humble crib of my Child, I feel the loving presence of these dear sons of mine, these priests consecrated to me and, together with my Son Jesus whom I clasp to my heart, I thank and bless you all."

90

December 31, 1975
Last night of the year

The Gift Which I Give to the Church

a   "Spend the last hours of this year close to my Immaculate Heart in a prayer.

b   So closes a year which has been a year of grace and of mercy: the Holy Year, 1975.

c   Many of my children have accepted the invitation of the Vicar of Christ and have come from all parts of the world to receive the great pardon.

d   Other children of mine have passed this year in complete indifference, immersed only in their earthly interests.

e   A great many others have not heard this invitation; on the contrary, they have deliberately closed their souls to the great mercy of my Son Jesus.

f   Among these, alas, are also many priests.

g   This is the sign of the truth of what I have often caused you to perceive in your heart.

h   Satan is maneuvering more and more openly in my Church.

He has now associated many of my priest-sons with himself, deluding them with the false mirage that Marxism proposes to all: exclusive interest in the poor; a Christianity engaged solely in the building up of a more equitable human society; a Church which would be more evangelical and therefore disengaged from its hierarchical institutions!

i   This real division within the Church, this real apostasy on the part of so many of my priest-sons, will become accentuated and thus develop into a violent and open rebellion.

I Will Gather Up All the Good

j   This is why, my dearly beloved sons, I have now completed my work in the course of this past year. As I foretold to you a year ago, my Movement has spread everywhere and has blossomed into a wonderful spring for the whole Church. My work has expanded throughout the whole world; the cohort of my priests is now ready.

k   I will still continue this motherly action of mine, which will become daily more apparent and strong, for the triumph of my Immaculate Heart.

l   And so spend the last hours of this year in prayer. Unite your prayer to that of all my beloved sons. In every part of the world, they will hear during these hours my invitation to gather in prayer with me and to draw close — all of them — to my Immaculate Heart.

m   What now awaits you, my most beloved sons, is nothing less than your complete sacrifice for the salvation of the world and the purification of the earth.

n   The time which the Father still leaves at your disposal is too precious: do not waste it! You should live every moment with me, in my heart.

o   Do not look to the future; live only the present which your Mother prepares for you.

p   May the evil which is increasing ever more and more and appearing to submerge everything neither disturb nor discourage you. Very soon, I myself will gather up all the good that is to be found in the whole world and I will lay it up in my heart to offer to the justice of God.

q   Begin the new year with me, my beloved sons. Let yourselves become the warp and the woof of your Mother's loving plan, the gift that I give to the Church, to comfort her in the passion and apparent death that awaits her, before her wondrous renewal through the triumph of my Immaculate Heart in the world!"

1976

YOU MUST BE LITTLE

91

A Sign of Contradiction

a   "Do not be troubled, my sons, if you are not understood by some and if on the contrary you are openly criticized and persecuted. My heart permits this to accustom you not to rely on any creature, but on me alone. Beloved sons, lean on my Immaculate Heart alone.

b   Let yourselves be carried just as the baby Jesus let himself be carried in my arms to the house of the Father. He presented himself in the Temple to be offered to the Lord on this Mother's heart of mine.

c   At the moment when I entrusted Him into the hands of the priest, the old prophet Simeon revealed that the Mother had been chosen by God for this offering; 'He is destined to be a sign of contradiction and a sword, O Mother, will pierce your soul.'

d   You also, my little children consecrated to my Immaculate Heart, you will be called today to be *this sign of contradiction*.

e   **By your life**, which will be, purely and simply, a living Gospel. Today the Gospel of my Son Jesus is believed in less and less, and even in the Church there are some who tend to interpret it in a human and symbolic manner.

f   You will live out the Gospel to the letter: you will be poor, simple, pure, little and totally given over to the Father.

g   **By your word**, which will repeat ever more loudly and clearly the truth which my Son Jesus has come to reveal to you.

h   Do you see how many of your brother-priests betray this truth, in the attempt to adapt it to the mentality of the world, impelled by a false illusion of being better understood, listened to by more people and more easily followed? No illusion is more dangerous than this.

i   Always announce the Gospel that you live with fidelity and clarity! Your speech must be: 'Yes, Yes—No, No'; everything else comes from the Evil One. Therefore let yourselves be guided and led with docility by the Church.

j   See how the Pope is now announcing this truth with power and how his voice falls more and more on barren soil!

k   My mother's heart is again pierced by a sword as I see how the Holy Father, this first of my beloved sons, is abandoned even by his brother-priests and left more and more alone.

l   You, O priests consecrated to my Immaculate Heart, must be the voice which spreads throughout the whole world whatever the Vicar of my Son announces again today with firmness, for the salvation of my poor misguided children.

m   **By your witness**, which must be a light and example for all the Church. It has been ordained by the Father that yours be a witness which will become more and more painful. I repeat, my sons; the road upon which I am leading you is that of the cross.

n   Do not fear if you become increasingly the target of misunderstandings, criticisms and persecutions. It is necessary that this happen to you because, as was my Son Jesus, so also are you being called today to be a sign of contradiction.

o   The more you are followed, the more you will be rejected and persecuted.

p   When they attack your person or my Movement, answer with *prayer*, with *silence* and with *forgiveness*.

q   You will soon be called upon to struggle openly when my Son Jesus, myself, the Church and the Gospel are attacked.

r   Then only, led by me by the hand, should you come out in the open to at last give your public witness. For now, continue to live with simplicity, by entrusting yourselves, each and all, to the care of my motherly heart."

92

The Perfume of Your Purity

a   "Today, my beloved sons, I receive with joy the perfume of your purity and I place it on my Immaculate Heart to offer it to God as a sign of reparation.

b   How much filth submerges this poor humanity, urged by me to set itself free from sin: 'Come and drink of this water I give you; come and wash at the fountain!'

c   Do you see how, every day, many of my children remain defiled with this filth which is spreading more and more and dragging countless numbers of souls to their death? How can even many of my poor priest-sons escape from this tide of filth?

d   I am the Immaculate One: I am purity.

e   Take refuge in my Immaculate Heart.

f   Even though the surroundings in which you live become more and more submerged in this impurity, you must breathe in only my heavenly perfume.

g   I have come down from heaven to make of you, sons consecrated to my heart, my heaven on earth. In you my light is reflected. Thus through you many souls will again be drawn by my candor, and they will spread the perfume of my virtue.

h   The Pope has given you the signal for turning the tide of this moral battle.

i   *Listen to him! Defend him! Console him!*

j   The outrage which was recently perpetrated against his person and the insults which are increasingly being hurled against him deeply pain my mother's heart.

k   This tide of filth has finally reached to his very feet! But you must set up an embankment about the feet of this angelic Pastor, of the gentle 'Christ on earth.'

l By a special intervention on my part, carried out through you, this diabolical wave of rebellion and of filth, unleashed against the Pope, will stop at his feet. And the greatness of his innocent person will appear intact to all."

93

The Perfect Consolers

a "My sons, be the perfect consolers of my Son Jesus. Never as at the present time has his divine lament been so often repeated: 'I looked for comforters and I found none!' Why does my Son ask if there is anyone who is able to console his Heart?

b Jesus is God, but He is also man. He is perfect man. His Heart beats with divine and human love: in Him is all the fullness of love. His is the Heart which has loved most, which has suffered most, which is sensitive to the delicacies and the manifestations of affection, as it is to outrages and offenses.

c The Heart of my Son is now, as it were, submerged in the great sea of human ingratitude.

d How much it still loves you! It continues to beat with love for you, and it receives only offenses and sins.

e To you He has revealed the secret of the Father, and He has led you back to Him. And now humanity has rebelled by the very rejection of God.

f The flood of atheism is the thorn which now makes the Heart of my Son Jesus bleed continuously.

g And you, O priests, are all my privileged sons because you are the most painful and loving fruit of the predilection of my Son Jesus.

h You are called by divine plan to be his ministers, his apostles, his consolers.

i Why then do so many of you again betray Him today?

j Why do many of you again flee today and leave Jesus and the

Church all alone?

k Why are so many of you again sleeping today? And that sleeping is often the very work in which you allow yourselves to be caught up and overwhelmed.

l That sleeping is also the way in which you seek to adapt yourselves to the world, and to succeed in being agreeable to, as well as accepted and understood by, this world. That sleeping is everything which humanly weighs you down.

m Where are my sons who again today are willing to keep watch? In prayer: 'Watch and pray lest you give in to temptation!' In the suffering of this new hour of agony for my Church: 'The spirit is willing but the flesh is weak!'

n I am now calling you, my beloved sons; I am gathering you together from all parts of the world, as a mother hen does her chicks. I am gathering you all into my Immaculate Heart.

o Can a Mother remain indifferent to the great abandonment and the great sorrow of her Son?

p And so then, understand that my duty is above all to console Him.

q Therefore I want you all consecrated to my heart to make you all into perfect consolers of the Heart of my Son Jesus."

94

Mother of Jesus, and Yours

a "Priests consecrated to me, my sons, this is the reason why *you have need of me* to become perfect consolers of my Son Jesus.

b At the moment when, overshadowed by the light of the Spirit, I uttered my 'yes' to the will of the Lord, the Word of the Father, the Second Person of the Most Holy Trinity, descended into my most pure womb, in the expectation of my maternal collaboration, to receive from me his human nature and thus become also man in the divine Person of my Son Jesus.

c   Do you see how God entrusted himself completely to this human creature of his? The reason is to be found in the mystery of the love of God.

d   What moved God to stoop down to me was the profound sense I had of my littleness and of my poverty, as well as my perfect availability for the accomplishment of the will of the Lord.

e   God could have chosen many other ways to come to you: but He chose to select mine.

f   And therefore, this way now becomes necessary for you to reach God.

Your True Mother

g   The first thing that I ask of you, sons, is your unconditional 'yes': and you say this by your consecration to my Immaculate Heart.

h   And then I ask you to entrust yourselves to me with the greatest confidence and most complete abandonment.

i   Your 'yes' and your complete availability will allow your Mother to act.

j   As with great love I formed the human nature of the Word, so too I will form in you, my sons, that image which corresponds more and more to the plan which the Father has for each one of you. The plan which God has for you, my beloved sons, is that you be priests according to the Heart of Jesus.

k   I am the Mother of God because I was chosen to bring God to men; I am your Mother because I have the duty of bringing to God those men redeemed by my Son and entrusted, each and all, by Him to me.

l   I am therefore the true Mother of Jesus, and your true Mother as well.

m   On this day, when all heaven exults in the contemplation of

121

the mystery of the Incarnation of the Word, you too must rejoice while meditating on this mystery of the love of your Mother.

n   It is not given to everyone to understand this mystery of love: it is given only to the pure of heart, to the simple, to the little, to the poor. (. . .)"

95

Your Light Will Shine Resplendently

a   "My beloved sons, today I accept with joy the homage that you give to my Immaculate Heart.

b   Let your hearts never become troubled.

c   Obscurity is descending ever more and more upon the world wrapped in the chill of the denial of God, of hatred, of egoism, of rebellion against God, of impiety.

d   The cup of iniquity is almost full and the justice of God demands atonement.

e   I need you, my beloved sons, to form you into victims worthy of being offered to the divine justice.

f   And so you will be called more and more to suffer. The hours of agony and passion are drawing closer to you.

g   Do you see, sons, what is happening even in the Church? Errors are being spread more and more and have taken hold of even the good; infidelity is spreading increasingly among the ministers of God and the souls consecrated to Him; even the hierarchy is impaired in the bond of charity and in its unity.

h   Above all, the Vicar of my Son Jesus is left more and more alone! He is calumniated, even in a most vulgar and blasphemous way; he is criticized and challenged and left more and more alone by my own sons.

i   You must share his lot with him: this is for him and for you the hour of Gethsemane.

j Live it with me, in my Immaculate Heart.

k You are the crown of love woven by me to place, as a source of comfort, about the Heart of my Son Jesus and of his Vicar on earth.

l Therefore I ask you again for prayer, suffering and silence.

m But your light must shine ever more and more brightly as the darkness envelops everything.

n And yours will be the light of my presence in this most severe trial. (. . .)"

96

April 13, 1976
Holy Tuesday

Look at My Crucified Son!

a "Beloved sons, look at my Crucified Son.

b Look at his face stained with blood; his head crowned with thorns; his hands and his feet pierced by nails; his body which has been made an open wound by the scourges; his Heart pierced by a lance.

c My beloved ones, look at my Crucified Son and *you will be faithful priests.*

d How many of you have gone no further than to merely consider his word. They have wanted to penetrate and understand it only with their own human intelligence and have thus inadvertently fallen into most serious errors.

e It is not with human intelligence alone that the word of my Son is to be read. He thanked the Father for having hidden the mysteries of his kingdom from the wise and prudent of this world in order to reveal them to the little ones.

f It is above all with interior humility and full docility of the soul that his word is to be read and understood.

g   For this reason, my Son has entrusted its authentic interpretation only to the *Magisterium* of the Church. And this, to accustom you to this difficult, and yet so necessary, attitude of humility and interior docility.

h   If you remain united to the *Magisterium* of the Church, and if you remain humble and attentive to what the Church points out to you, you will always keep within the truth of the word of Jesus.

i   Today error is being spread more and more within the Church and it seems that there is no longer any barrier that can contain it. It is spread about especially by many theologians; it is propagated by many of my poor priest-sons.

j   How can you now, in the Church, be sure of being preserved from error?

k   Look at my Crucified Son and you will be faithful.

l   My Son who, God though He was, became obedient even to the death of the cross.

m   Look at his thorns; look at his blood; look at his wounds: they are flowers blossoming from the pain of his obedience.

n   My beloved sons, now that darkness covers all things, you are being called to bear witness to the light of complete obedience to the Church: to the Pope and to the bishops united with him.

o   And the more you witness to this complete obedience to the Church, the more you will be criticized, ridiculed and persecuted.

p   But it is necessary that yours be an increasingly painful and crucifying witness in order to help many of my poor children to remain, even today, in truth and in fidelity."

97

April 16, 1976
Good Friday

See if There Is a Greater Sorrow

a   "Beloved sons, behold my sorrow. See if there is a greater sorrow than mine!

b   My Son Jesus, abandoned by all, scourged, crowned with thorns, climbs Calvary with difficulty, carrying the heavy cross on his poor shoulders.

c   He is unable to walk: He totters. There is not one gesture of pity: only hatred, hostility and indifference surround Him.

d   It is at this moment that the Father gives Him the comfort of his Mother. Think, my beloved sons, of the comfort and of the pain of this encounter.

e   Oh, the glance of my son at that moment! . . . In my heart there opened a wound which has never healed.

f   See the sorrow of your Mother as she contemplates her crucified Son, agonizing and slain.

g   Sorrow for Him who was dying; sorrow for you.

h   Now my Son continues his Passion in his mystical body which is the Church.

i   Today I think again of the villainous gesture made by *Judas in betraying Jesus.* I feel again the same pain at the betrayal which so many of my priest-sons perpetrate every day.

j   O priests, my beloved sons, why do you still betray? Why do you still persist in your treason? Why do you not repent? Why do you not return?

k   And *Peter, who three times denies* my Son out of fear . . .

l   How many of you, for fear of not being understood, appreciated or esteemed, still deny the truth of the Gospel: 'I do not know that Man!'?

m   And *the apostles who run away* and leave Jesus alone for the whole of this long Friday! . . .

n   How many of you run away and abandon my Church. Some leave the Church to follow the world; others remain in the Church and, to please the world, abandon it in their minds and hearts.

o   The Church is not loved by many of you. The Vicar of my Son finds himself in a state of isolation which grows ever greater.

p   The bishops united with the Pope feel in their souls the thorn of this solitude: they are increasingly criticized, challenged and abandoned by their priests.

q   John remains. He stays with the Mother.

r   Priests of my Movement, you at least stay with the Church and with me, your Mother.

s   Look well at my sorrow and suffer with me. In this hour of Calvary for the Church, you will thus be the sign of my presence. (. . .)"

98

May 3, 1976

You Will Be Capable of Loving

a   "Beloved sons, let your hearts never be disturbed by the attacks against my Movement, which are becoming increasingly frequent.

b   This is my work alone and it corresponds to a special plan of my Immaculate Heart.

c   Difficulties, misunderstandings and sufferings are permitted by me that this work of mine may be purified.

d   I want it to be purified of every human element that it may thus reflect only my most pure light.

e   I want to cover all my beloved sons, the priests consecrated to my Immaculate Heart, with this most pure light.

f   This is why I ask you for complete detachment from all persons, that I may give you true purity of heart. Every human attachment to yourselves, to creatures and to the world beclouds your interior purity.

g   Of course I cannot ask you to live apart from the world. It is in accord with the will of my Son that you live in the world, but without being of the world.

h   You should live in the world in such a way as to belong solely to my Son Jesus.

i   You must belong solely to my Son Jesus to bring the whole world to Him and thus lead souls to salvation.

j   This is the kind of sympathy that you should have for the world: the only kind desired by my Son and still proposed to you by the Church today.

k   Many of my sons are today being drawn into numerous errors, and becoming alienated from my Son and from me, by this false way of understanding how you should live in the world.

l   How many of my poor priest-sons have ended up by being totally of the world and have become its prisoners.

m   My Jesus saved this world above all when, to be faithful to the will of the Father, He detached himself from everyone to be raised up from the earth and hung upon the cross.

n   You will begin to bring back many souls to my Son when, like Him, you also will be raised up from the earth. You must become accustomed to being raised up even now, spiritually speaking, by interior detachment from everyone.

o   Thus you will possess true purity of heart. And you will be truly capable of loving. Even to the supreme test.

p   You will always be carried by your Mother, who knows where and how to lead you, that in each one of you the design of the Father's will may be realized."

99

May 13, 1976
Anniversary of the First Apparition at Fatima

Consecrate Yourselves to My Immaculate Heart

a   "Today, my beloved sons, recall my coming down upon this earth, in the poor Cova da Iria in Fatima. I came from heaven to ask you for the consecration to my Immaculate Heart.

b   Through you, priests of my Movement, what I had then asked

127

is now being realized. You are consecrating yourselves to my Immaculate Heart and leading souls entrusted to you to this consecration which I desire.

c Since that day how much time has passed! It is now fifty-nine years.

d The second world war, foretold by me as a punishment allowed by God for a humanity which alas did not repent, has also taken place.

e Now you are living in that period of time when the Red Dragon, that is to say Marxist atheism, is spreading throughout the whole world and is increasingly bringing about the ruin of souls.

f He is indeed succeeding in seducing and casting down a third of the stars of heaven.

g These stars, in the firmament of the Church, are the pastors: they are yourselves, my poor priest-sons.

h Has not perchance even the Vicar of my Son affirmed to you that it is the dearest friends, even the confreres of the same table, the priests and the religious, who are today betraying and setting themselves against the Church?

i This is then the hour to have recourse to the great remedy that the Father offers you to resist the seductions of the Evil One and to oppose the real apostasy which is spreading more and more among my poor children. *Consecrate yourselves to my Immaculate Heart.*

j To everyone who consecrates himself to me I in return promise salvation: safety from error in this world and eternal salvation.

k You will obtain this through a special motherly intervention on my part. Thus I will prevent you from falling into the enticements of Satan. You will be protected and defended by me personally; you will be consoled and strengthened by me.

l Now is the time when my call must be answered by all priests who want to remain faithful.

m *Each one must consecrate himself to my Immaculate Heart*, and through you priests many of my children will make this consecration.

This is like a vaccine which, like a good Mother, I give you to preserve you from the epidemic of atheism, which is contaminating so many of my childen and leading them to the death of the spirit.

o These are the times that I myself foretold; this is the hour of the purification. (. . .)"

100   *May 28, 1976*

Follow Me on the Path of My Son

a "Beloved sons, listen to the voice of your Mother who calls you gently to follow her.

Follow Me Along the Path of Prayer.

b Many of my children are on the point of being eternally lost in these decisive moments, because there is no one to pray and sacrifice himself for them.

c You must pray for them. Help me to save your brothers!

d This is the hour of error, which is succeeding in entering everywhere and especially in seducing many of my priest-sons.

e Do not be astonished if you see fall those who, still only yesterday, seemed the most faithful and most secure.

f You will see fall even those who set themselves up as teachers of others.

g Do not be surprised if, in this battle, those fall who did not want or did not know how to use the weapon that I myself gave you: my prayer, the simple and humble prayer of the holy rosary.

h It is a simple and humble prayer and therefore it is most efficacious in combatting Satan who today is leading you astray especially by ostentation and pride.

i   It is my prayer because it is offered with me and through me. It has always been recommended to you by the Church and also by the first of my beloved sons, the Vicar of Jesus, with words that moved my motherly heart.

Follow Me Along the Path of Suffering.

j   You have now arrived at the moment of your immolation; you are being called to suffer more and more.

k   Give me all your suffering. Today it is the misunderstandings, the attacks, the calumnies of your brothers. Tomorrow it will be persecutions, imprisonment, condemnations on the part of atheists and enemies of God who will see in you the obstacles that must be eliminated.

l   Walk with me and follow me along the path of my Son Jesus. Along the way of Calvary, along the way of the cross.

m   Never as in these moments will you have to live so profoundly that which is the vocation of every Christian: 'He who wishes to come after Me must deny himself, take up his cross and follow Me!'

n   Follow me, beloved sons: today it is necessary to follow your Mother if you want to travel without fear the path of my Son Jesus."

101   *June 19, 1976*

Say with Me Your "Yes"

a   There is another thing I ask of you, beloved sons: your life. These are times, my sons, when I must ask of some of you the gift of your very lives.

b   The hour of martyrdom is in preparation, and the Mother is gently leading you to the moment of your immolation.

c   *Do not look any longer at this world:* look to me, look upon the face of your heavenly Mother.

d   I am reflecting upon you the light of paradise which awaits you and, at the hour of trial, you will be strengthened and encouraged.

e   *Do not look to creatures* who, misled and corrupted by Satan, will hurl themselves upon you with hatred and violence.

f   And yet, my beloved sons, you have always loved and done good to all; you have always sought to help everyone.

g   And now the chill of hatred and ingratitude is spreading all about you.

h   Do not be afraid. This is the hour of Satan and of the power of darkness.

i   Do not fear: take refuge in my Immaculate Heart.

j   In this motherly heart you will be warmed and consoled. Here is the source of your joy and the secret of your confidence.

k   In this heart you are little children whom I am forming in interior meekness so that, at the invitation of my Son who is associating you in his Sacrifice, you may respond with a 'yes.'

l   Say it with me, my beloved sons, this 'yes' of yours to the will of the Father. Then very soon you will see appearing the dawn of a new world, washed and purified by your reparative offering."

102

Lourdes, July 3, 1976
First Saturday of the Month

Your Necessary Witness

a   "Be ever more docile in my hands, beloved sons.

b   Your life will be truly mine alone, if at every moment you offer me your interior docility.

c   How many priests there are today who do not obey, who are in rebellion, who no longer observe any kind of discipline!

d   Your interior docility will bring you to a more complete discipline in respect to the norms and directives of the Church.

e   You suffered today when you saw, in this place consecrated to me, what a great number of profanations there are, and how many sorrows are inflicted on my mother's heart. Children who come to me dressed so indecently and who manage to pass freely at the very feet of my venerated image . . .

f   Share in my sorrow and make reparation for these true profanations that are being committed every day in this place consecrated to me.

The Ecclesiastical Garb

g   Unfortunately the most responsible are the priests. You see how they themselves dress in all sorts of ways, sometimes in ways that are so shocking that they even scandalize the faithful themselves.

h   And yet the existing discipline of the Church obliges these sons of mine to wear the ecclesiastical garb. But who any longer observes this discipline? Few, and they are for this reason all the more thought of as backward and old-fashioned.

i   This question of garb is just a small example, but it is indicative of a sad reality: today lack of discipline, disobedience and intolerance of any norms is spreading among priests, who are nevertheless still the sons of my maternal predilection.

j   You at least, O priests consecrated to my Immaculate Heart, be an example by your interior docility and your obedience to the discipline of the Church.

k   This is today the most urgent and necessary witness that you can give.

l   Only thus can you spread about you the example and the fragrance of my Son Jesus. You will be chosen instruments for the return of many priests to their duty of giving that good example, which is one of the most important exigencies of your own ministry."

103

In the Spirit of Filial Surrender

a "Son of my maternal predilection, do not let yourself be distracted by things and by human vicissitudes. Remain always close to my heart in prayer!

b I am arranging everything for you as your real Mother: the persons you are to meet, the circumstances in which you find yourself and what you are to do. And so accustom yourself to live trustfully in the present moment which the Father gives you and the Mother prepares for you.

c Sons consecrated to my Immaculate Heart, you should all live in the spirit of filial surrender, with the most complete confidence in your Mother's action.

d A priest who consecrates himself to my heart, draws upon himself this predilection on my part, which becomes stronger and more evident, and which the soul comes to perceive with greater and greater clarity.

e It is I myself who, with you, am enabled to carry out in a more complete manner my function as Mother. I am thus able to act through you because, by your consecration to my Immaculate Heart, you truly place yourselves like little children in my arms.

f Thus I speak to you and you can hear my voice. I lead you and you let yourselves be guided by me, with docility.

g I clothe you with my own virtues; I nourish you with my food. You are more and more interiorly drawn by the perfume of this motherly action of mine which makes you little, poor, humble, simple and chaste.

h Above all, I bring you gently before the divine Person of my Son Jesus present, as in heaven, in the sacrament of the Eucharist. You acquire from me a taste for prayer. Prayer of adoration, prayer of thanksgiving, prayer of reparation.

The Coldness of Desertion

i   The more the coldness of desertion and silence surrounds my Son Jesus, present among you in the Eucharist, the more I myself gather the voices of my beloved sons so that, united with my voice, there may be composed even here on earth a melody of love to be offered to the Heart of my Son for his consolation.

j   This is the army that I am preparing; this is the cohort of my priests that I am now gathering from all parts of the world. A hidden cohort of little children consecrated to my Immaculate Heart, whom I am making more and more like myself, that Jesus may offer them to the Father as a sign of reparation and atonement.

k   Therefore I say to you again: pay no attention to all the evil which is spreading more and more and flooding everywhere. Disregard also the great evil which Satan is succeeding in spreading even in the Church.

l   Turn your gaze to me alone and consider the great good which, in silence, your Mother is accomplishing by drawing an ever-increasing number of priest-sons to her heart. (. . .)"

104

July 26, 1976
Feast of Saints Joachim and Ann

My Time

a   "My time, beloved sons, is not measured by days. My time is measured only by the beating of my mother's heart. Each beat of this heart marks a new day of salvation and of mercy for you, my poor children.

b   And so I invite you to live only in trust.

c   Your time must be measured by trust in the merciful love of the Father and in the action of your heavenly Mother.

d   My parents Ann and Joachim, whom the Church calls to mind today and holds up to you as examples, lived in this trust.

e   All the saints and the friends of God lived in this trust.

f   The Almighty, in carrying out his plan in every age, always made use of this trust alone.

g   Often He realized it even against everyone's expectation, at a moment when no one thought it possible. This is how the great plan of God was accomplished through these two poor and humble creatures, whom He called to prepare for the birth of your heavenly Mother.

h   And your Mother was called to hope against the very evidence of things and to place her complete trust only in the word *(Parola)* of God. Thus she became the Mother of the Word *(Verbo)* and gave you her Son Jesus.

i   Now I have announced to you the triumph of my Immaculate Heart and the necessary and painful purification which must precede it.

j   I have also told you that this is the time of the purification and that these are the years of my triumph. But do not search out the moment, scrutinizing the future and counting the years, the months and the days. In this way you would be caught up by anxiety and agitation and would truly waste your time, which is so precious.

k   My beloved sons, my time is not to be measured in this way, but only *by your trust in me*, who am preparing you to be instruments chosen and formed by me to bring about at this time the triumph of my Immaculate Heart."

105   *July 31, 1976*

Your Difficulties

a   "Follow me, beloved sons, in complete trust and do not let yourselves be troubled by the difficulties which you encounter on your way.

b   These difficulties are permitted by God to help you grow in your life of perfect consecration to my Immaculate Heart.

c   They detach you from your way of seeing and thinking, from your tastes and attachments and, little by little, they bring you to see and think according to the Heart of my Son Jesus.

d   After each difficulty I see the life of Jesus increase in you: and it is this that gives such great comfort to my mother's heart.

e   Have you not become aware, my sons, of how, under my personal influence, your life is truly changing?

f   It is the **interior difficulties** of the soul which cause you most pain.

g   You are mine and yet you feel attracted to the world; you are clothed in my own purity and yet you experience the affliction of temptations of the flesh. Some of you complain and would like to be free of this.

h   And yet, my beloved sons, how much this interior difficulty which you are experiencing makes you grow in detachment from your own selves!

i   Never look at yourselves. The less beautiful you look to yourselves the more beautiful you will look to me and my Son Jesus.

j   It is my mantle that covers you. It is my own purity which causes you to shine.

k   Then there are the **exterior difficulties**. These are the ones in the midst of which you find yourselves: misunderstandings, criticism. Sometimes I permit even scorn and calumny.

l   My Adversary makes special use of this last mentioned, above all, to strike at you and discourage you.

m   And you, how are you to respond? As Jesus did: by silence, by prayer, by living in intimate union with the Father.

n   In the light of the Father, all that is not true, all that is not good, all deceit and all calumny dissolve of themselves like mist in the sun.

o   And since you are in my Immaculate heart, there is nothing that can touch you.

p   Anyone who would intentionally do you harm will not succeed in striking you; anyone who acts in good faith will see the light even before the evil reaches you.

q   And you will walk in peace, even in the midst of the tempest of the present moment.

r   Then there are also the **difficulties of your time**. Beloved sons, with what care you have been formed and prepared by me for your time!

s   These difficulties are also permitted by me that they may make you ever more docile instruments in my hands for the plan which I am realizing at this time.

t   Atheism which is spreading throughout the world, the crises which continue to expand within the Church, error which is being disseminated everywhere: these are the waves of the great tempest.

u   You are being called to be my peace in this storm.

v   And so walk in serenity, walk in tranquility, walk in trust. (. . .)"

106

Only with the Pope

a   "Today from every part of the world comes that homage which is so pleasing to my Immaculate Heart, the homage of those priests who are consecrated to me, of you, sons of my maternal predilection.

b   Let yourselves be led by me, and you will not feel the weight of your daily difficulties.

c   I want you in my arms, all of you given over to my Immaculate Heart, that you may thus walk toward the goal which I have set for each one of you.

d   I have already pointed out what this goal is: to make of you priests according to the Heart of Jesus.

e   You must be truly Jesus today, for the men of your time.

f   **Jesus who speaks**, and thus you will speak only the truth. The truth contained in the Gospel and guaranteed by the *Magisterium* of the Church.

g   Today, as darkness descends upon everything and error spreads more and more in the Church, you should direct all people to that fount from which Jesus causes his words of truth to issue forth: the Gospel entrusted to the hierarchical Church, that is to say, the Pope and the bishops united to him.

h   Not to individual priests, not to individual bishops; but only to those priests and bishops who are united with the Pope.

i   Today, as Mother of the Church, how deeply the scandal, even of bishops who do not obey the Vicar of my Son and who sweep a great number of my poor children along the path of error, wounds and pains my heart.

j   And therefore you should at this time proclaim to all by your words that Jesus has made Peter alone the foundation of his Church and the infallible guardian of truth.

k   Today whoever is not with the Pope will not succeed in remaining in the truth.

l   The seductions of the Evil One have become so insidious and dangerous that they are succeeding in deceiving almost anyone.

m   Here even the good can fall.

n   Here even the masters and the wise ones can fall.

o   Here even the priests and the bishops can fall.

p   Those will never fall *who are always with the Pope*.

q   This is why I want to make you a disciplined and attentive cohort, obedient and docile even to the desires of this first of my beloved sons, the Vicar of my Jesus.

r   **Jesus who acts**: you must above all re-live Jesus in your life and be a living Gospel.

s   For this I will make you ever poorer, ever more humble, ever purer, ever smaller.

t   Do not be afraid of entrusting yourselves completely to me. I am his Mother and yours and I know how to do only one thing for you, and that is to help you to be born and to grow up like other little Jesuses for the salvation of all my children.

138

When this cohort of priests is ready; then it will be the time for me to crush the head of my Adversary and the renewed world will experience the joy of the triumph of my heart."

107

August 15, 1976
Feast of the Assumption
of the Blessed Virgin Mary into Heaven

Live in Paradise with Me

a "Live, my beloved sons, there where I am: in paradise, assumed body and soul, to share fully in the glory of my Son Jesus.

b Always associated with Him through my role as Mother on this earth, I am now in paradise associated in the glory of the Son, who wants his Mother at his side, having given me a glorified body like his own.

c Here is the reason for this extraordinary privilege of mine.

d As by my 'yes' I made it possible for the Word of God to assume his human nature in my virginal womb, so also by my 'yes' I entrusted myself to the action of my Son Jesus, who assumed your Mother into the glory of heaven, body and soul.

e Mine is a transfigured and glorified body, but a real body, my beloved sons. Mother and Son are now together in paradise forerver.

f But I am also your real Mother; and thus I can love you not only with my soul, but also with my glorified body.

g I love you with this Mother's heart of mine which has never ceased to beat with love for you.

h Beloved sons, you also should be living there where I am: *live in paradise with me.*

i It is true, you are still on this earth of sorrows and often you experience all its weight and suffering.

Do Not Let Yourselves Be Imprisoned

j But why, while still living in this land of exile, do you not also live, even now, there where your Mother is? Live in paradise with me and do not let yourselves be attracted by the world, nor imprisoned by this earth.

k   Today there is a tendency which is extremely false and dangerous. That of looking only at this earth. It is as though we are afraid that, if we look at paradise, we will be drawn away from the duties of daily life. Live in paradise with me, and then you will live well, even on this earth!

l   Carry out here below the plan of the heavenly Father and you will create true happiness all about you.

m   The more you look to the Father and live with me, the more will you labor on this earth for your own good and the good of all.

n   Paradise—that is, the real one—can never be found on this earth.

o   How he deceives and seduces you, this Adversary of mine who in his fury tries to prevent you from coming up here to be with my Son and with me!

p   Paradise is found only in the light of the Most Holy Trinity, with my Son Jesus and with me.

q   The angels and the saints are illumined by this light and they rejoice in it. All paradise is resplendent with this light.

r   Live then while searching for, cherishing and gazing upon this paradise which awaits you, my beloved sons.

s   And here below, *live in the paradise of my Immaculate Heart.*

t   Then you will be serene and deeply happy.

u   You will always be littler and more abandoned, poorer and more chaste.

v   And the littler, poorer and more chaste you become, the more you will be able to enter into the paradise of my Immaculate Heart, where time is now marked by the beating of a heart which knows no stopping."

108

Your Queen and Your Leader

a "I am your queen.

b The power of the Father, the wisdom of the Son and the love of the Holy Spirit, in the light of the Most Holy Trinity, have confirmed me forever in my function of maternal royalty.

c This is my crowning glory.

d It is my universal royalty: Mother of the Son, Queen with the Son.

e I am your leader.

f I am calling you, my beloved sons, to gather you all into my cohort, of which I myself am the Queen and the Leader.

g Therefore *there should be no leader* among you: you are all brothers, united in love that must grow ever more and more.

h If anyone wishes to become the greatest let him become truly the least.

i Only he who loves the most, who serves the most, who listens to me the most, who becomes ever smaller to the point of disappearing in my Immaculate Heart is the one whom I myself will make ever greater.

j I am your leader.

k You therefore, my beloved ones, must listen to my voice, be docile to my teachings and above all be prompt and obedient to my orders.

l I want to make of you sons who want to obey, who always know how to obey.

m Obedience and docility: this is the livery in which I wish to attire you.

n I will give my orders through the voice of him whom my Son has appointed to govern his Church: the Pope with the hierarchy united to him.

o How my motherly heart is wounded and saddened today to see that some priests and even some bishops no longer obey the orders of the Vicar of my Son Jesus!

p   Every kingdom divided against itself is destined to defeat and ruin.

q   These poor sons of mine who do not obey and who rebel are already victims of the most subtle and insidious kind of pride and are walking towards their death.

r   How Satan, my adversary from the beginning, is succeeding today in deceiving and seducing you!

s   He makes you believe that you are guardians of tradition and defenders of the faith, while he causes you to be the first to make shipwreck of your faith and leads you, all unaware, into error.

t   He makes you believe that the Pope is denying the truth, and thus Satan demolishes the foundation on which the Church is built and through which the truth is kept intact throughout the ages.

u   He goes so far as to make you think that I myself have nothing to do with the Holy Father's way of acting. And so, in my name, sharp criticisms aimed at his person and actions are spread about.

v   Priests, sons of my maternal predilection, be prudent, be attentive, be enlightened because the darkness is invading everything.

w   How can the Mother publicly criticize the decisions of the Pope, when he alone has the special grace for the exercise of this sublime ministry?

x   I was silent at my Son's voice; I was silent at the voice of the apostles. I am now lovingly silent at the voice of the Pope: that it might be disseminated more and more, that it might be heard by all, that it might be received into souls.

y   And so I am very close to the person of this first of my beloved sons, the Vicar of my Son Jesus.

z   By my silence, I am helping him to speak.

A   By my silence, I am lending strength to his own words.

B   Return, return, my priest-sons, to love, obedience and communion with the Pope!

C   Only in this way can you belong to my cohort, of which I am the Queen and Leader.

D   Only in this way can you hear my orders, which I will give through the very voice of the Pope.

E   Only in this way can you fight along with me for the assured victory; otherwise you are already marching toward defeat. (. . .)

F   I will clothe you with my interior docility and you will be ever obedient; I will thus make you instruments fit for this battle of mine and you will see in the end my queenly victory."

109

You Must Be Little

a   "Look, O sons, at this Mother of yours, as a little infant. Because I was little, I was pleasing to the Most High.

b   The exemption from all stain of sin whatsoever which I enjoyed, by privilege, from the first instant of my conception, gave me the true measure of my littleness.

c   Little, because a creature of God and chosen beforehand to be the Mother of the Word.

d   Little, because I received everything from God.

e   Little, because I was overshadowed by the power of God who covered me with his greatness.

f   My richness is therefore only that of the little and poor: humility, faith, abandonment, hope.

g   Today the Church invites you to contemplate your heavenly Mother at the moment of her birth.

h   Look, my beloved ones, at this infant Mother of yours and learn to be little.

i   You must be little because you are my children, and therefore you should live the same life as I.

j   You must be little to become docile instruments in my plan and to draw upon yourselves the good pleasure of my Son Jesus.

k   How Jesus loves you, my dear sons! Indeed He loves you because you want to be little, poor, simple and humble.

l   You must be little to oppose Satan who is succeeding in leading people astray by pride and arrogance.

m   Do you not understand that he will never succeed in leading you astray or in deceiving you if you remain humble?

n   You must be ever littler because your Mother wants you entirely for herself: she wants to feed you, to clothe you, to carry you in her arms.

o   You must be little because in this way you will always say *yes* to the will of the Father.

p   Say with me your *yes*. Thus in you I will repeat the *yes* of my perfect docility to the will of God.

q   And lastly, you must be little to form this humble heel which Satan will try to bite, but with which I will crush his head.

r   You must therefore be ever littler if you wish to prepare for the greatest triumph of my Immaculate Heart."

110

September 25, 1976

This Is Why I Speak to You

a   "If you are little, you will always hear my voice.

b   My beloved sons, do not let yourselves be misled by the many voices which are heard today. My Adversary deceives you with ideas and confuses you with words.

c   You are, as it were, being submerged by a sea of words which grows ever greater and covers everything. The event of the Tower of Babel described in the Bible is now being repeated. You are now reliving the drama of the confusion of tongues.

d   Your own words confuse you. Your own voices hinder you from understanding.

e   It is now more than ever necessary to listen to my voice. *This is why I speak to you.*

f   *I speak to you* to help you recover from the confusion, created

144

today by your own words. Hence, as a Mother, I gently lead you to listen only to the Word of the Father. This Word was made flesh and life in my most pure womb. My heart opened to welcome it, and guarded it as a precious treasure.

g   *I speak to you* because today it is necessary to listen to his word. It is necessary to welcome it and to guard it jealously.

h   It is only the word of my Son that I want you to hear. Today his voice has become, as it were, drowned out: it is the Word of the Father, it is my Son Jesus who is no longer heard.

i   His word, so clearly contained in the Gospel, is, as it were, submerged by so many other human voices. You have made a gospel of your own with your own words. You, my beloved sons, should listen to and announce only the word of my Son, just as it is set down in his Gospel.

j   The Church speaks to you. But each one wants to have his own say as to what she is telling you, and thus insecurity and confusion spreads about. And the Church is more than ever torn by this real confusion of tongues.

Little Children Understand Their Mother

k   *I speak to you* to tell you what sort of word you should listen to today in the Church: that of the Pope, and that of the bishops united with him.

l   The darkness grows ever deeper and I speak to you to be your light. Error spreads and I speak to you, my beloved sons, because you are called to remain in the truth, you the ministers of the word, you the heralds of the truth.

m   The future looks distressing and I speak to you to urge you to be confident and completely abandoned, in my motherly heart.

n   A deafening uproar of voices brings greater and greater confusion to everything. And I speak to you to implore silence, suffering and prayer.

o   I speak to you to ask of you today those things which are most precious to me. Each day I gather up your prayer and your suffering and they are deposited by me in the chalice of my Immaculate Heart and are offered to the justice of God which seeks to be appeased.

p   Hence today everything can still be saved: *and this is why I speak to you!*

q   Beloved sons, do not close your hearts to my words.

r   The plan of the Father has made much of what awaits you depend on whether my words are harkened to or rejected.

s   The purification can still be set back or shortened. Much suffering can still be spared you.

t   Listen to me, sons, with simplicity. If you are little, then you will hear me and heed me. Little children understand very well the voice of their Mother.

u   Happy those who still listen to me. They will now receive the light of the truth and will obtain from the Lord the gift of salvation."

111

Look at Your Mother!

a   "Look, son, at your heavenly Mother. See how beautiful she is!

b   She is the Father's masterpiece of beauty. She is the cradle of the Son. She is the delicate tapestry of the Holy Spirit. She is the enclosed garden in full bloom, where the delight of the Most Holy Trinity has grown ever greater.

c   Look only at your Mother! Thus my beauty will cover you. I want to clothe you in my heavenly mantle; I want to clothe you with my purity; I want to surround you with my own light.

d   You feel little, and this is true. You feel poor and you see yourself full of defects; it seems to you that you have nothing to give me.

e   Oh, your love is enough for me! I do not want anything else of you . . .

f   You cannot understand at this time: but in heaven you will contemplate, in yourself, the glory of your Mother and the summit of love to which Jesus, with her, has brought you.

g   It seems to you as though Jesus is hiding himself to put his Mother before Him. But this is because He wants it to be she who loves Him in you!

h   It seems to you that you always have the Mother before you. I see that it is Jesus himself who leads you to me, because in this way you will give to his Heart that joy which others cannot give Him.

i   Do not talk; be more and more silent with everyone. Do not become discouraged because of your defects. I love you so much, son; I look at your heart, not at your character. And when by impulse you make mistakes, how great is the joy you give me if immediately you humble yourself and ask forgiveness. Offer me your wounds. Give me always a 'yes' and no longer think anything of yourself. I want to be the one who thinks of everything . . ."

112

The Time of the Purification

a   "Listen to my voice and let yourselves be led by me, beloved sons. Thus my own life will increase in you and my light will shine all about you.

b   It is now becoming ever more necessary and urgent to spread the gentle invitation of your Mother throughout the world.

c   This world is constantly drawing further and further from God and no longer pays any attention to the word of my Son Jesus. Thus does it fall into the darkness of denial of God, and into the deceitful mirage of being able to do without Him.

d   It is as if you have even succeeded in building a purely human civilization, obstinately closed against any divine influence whatsoever.

e   God, in his infinite majesty, cannot but hold in disdain this humanity which has gathered itself together in opposition to Him.

f   Thus the cold of egoism and pride spreads ever more and more. Hatred prevails over love and daily claims its countless victims, victims known and unknown, violence against innocent and defenseless creatures who, at every moment, cry out for terrible vengeance before the throne of God.

g   And more and more, sin continues to pervade everything.

Satan Is Seducing You

h   Where today is there a place where sin does not exist? Even those houses consecrated to the worship of God are profaned by the sins that are committed in them. It is the persons who are consecrated, the very priests and religious, who have lost even the sense of sin. Some of them, in their thoughts, their words and their way of life sacrilegiously allow themselves to be led by Satan.

i   Never before as today has the Devil succeeded so well in seducing you.

j   He seduces you through pride and thus brings you to justify and legitimize moral disorder. And after you have fallen he succeeds in smothering within you the voice of remorse which is a true gift of the Spirit, which calls you to conversion. How numerous now are my poor children who for years have stopped going to confession!

k   They are rotting in sin and are eaten up with impurity, with a devouring attachment to money, and with pride.

l   Satan has now pitched his tents even among the ministers of the sanctuary and has brought the abomination of desolation into the holy temple of God.

m   It is necessary, then, that the Mother speak to you and lead you by the hand. Her duty is above all that of guiding you in the struggle against the infernal dragon.

148

n   So I say to you: these are the times of the purification, these are the times when the justice of God will chastise this rebellious and perverted world, for its salvation.

o   The purification has already begun within the Church: pervaded with error, darkened by Satan, covered with sin, betrayed and violated by some of its own pastors.

p   Satan sifts you like wheat; how much chaff will soon be blown away by the wind of persecution!

q   From now on, my presence among you will become more continuous and more apparent. (. . .)"

113

December 4, 1976
First Saturday of the Month

What Are You Afraid Of?

a   "My beloved sons, be ever more docile and allow yourselves to be led by me with complete confidence.

b   In the darkness of this hour of trial for the Church, you are called by me to walk in the light.

c   The light shines forth from my Immaculate Heart and comes to you to envelop you and illumine your path.

d   Stand firm; never again must you doubt! Your road is safe because it has been marked out for you by your heavenly Mother. How much my mother's heart is saddened by the doubt and mistrust which is taking more and more hold of the souls of so many of my priest-sons! Why do you doubt? What are you afraid of?

e   Jesus redeemed you from the Evil One at the very hour of his triumph: 'This is the hour of Satan and of the power of darkness.'

f   My Son Jesus gave you life for ever at the very hour when He was slain on the Cross.

g   At the moment of his death He set you all free form death.

h   My Church, of which I am the Mother, lives again the life of Christ and is now called to tread the same path He trod.

In Serenity of Spirit

i   Of what, then, are you afraid?

j   Of a world that has hurled itself with violent hatred against you? Of Satan who has succeeded in making his way into the heart of the Church and of reaping his victims from among its very pastors? Or of the error which menaces it, or the sin which darkens it more and more, or the infidelity which floods it?

k   This, my beloved sons, is for my Church still the hour of Satan and of the power of darkness.

l   It will be also immolated like Christ on the cross, and be called to die for the salvation and the renewal of the world.

m   And since this is the hour of your purification, it is above all the hour of your suffering.

n   Could it perhaps be this that you fear?

o   But what if the Father has called you, one by one, from all eternity for this hour? And what if your heavenly Mother has long since chosen you and prepared you for this hour? . . .

p   Live then in serenity of spirit and without fear, even in the midst of the anxieties and threats of your time.

q   And so I say again: do not be always peering into the future to see what is going to happen. Live only the present moment with trust and complete abandonment, in this heart of mine."

114

December 24, 1976
The Holy Night

I Ask the Gift of Your Love

a   "Beloved son of my Immaculate Heart, spend these hours of vigil with me: in prayer, in silence, in attentiveness to your heavenly Mother.

b   Today, as of old, is the birthday of my Son Jesus; today, as of old, my dear sons, you should prepare for his coming.

c   With my spouse, Joseph, a just and chaste man, humble and strong, chosen by the Father to be of precious assistance to me especially during these moments, I completed the last stage of a most fatiguing journey.

d   I felt the fatigue of the journey, the sharpness of the cold, the uncertainty of the arrival, the insecurity of what might be lying ahead of us.

e   And yet I dwelt, as it were, far from the world and the things of the world, all absorbed in a continual ecstasy with my Child, Jesus, whom I was about to give you.

f   My sole support was trust in the Father; the sweet expectation of the Son lulled me; in the Spirit, I was filled only with the fullness of love.

g   As a Mother I thought of a house, and the Father prepared us a shelter; I dreamt of a cradle for my little baby, and even then the manger was ready; on that night all paradise was contained within a cave.

h   And when fatigue had seized upon us and the continual refusal to receive us had worn out our human endurance, then the cave was ready for the light. And in the light of a heaven which opened to receive the great prayer of the Mother, my virginal bud opened in the divine gift of the Son.

i   With me, my beloved sons, give to his Heart the first kiss. Feel with me its first beat. Be the first to look into his eyes.

j   Hear his first cry of weeping, of joy, of love.

k   He wants only your comfort.

l   He asks for your gift of love.

m   Enwrap his little limbs in love; He has so much need of warmth! All the coldness of the world surrounds Him. Only the warmth of love comforts Him.

n   Since that time, each year the Church renews this mystery. Since that time, my Son is ever being born again in hearts.

o   And today, also, there is a world which rejects Him and, in great part, closes its door to Him. Just as in those days, the great ones ignore Him.

p   But the hearts of the little ones open to Him. The longing of the simple is appeased. The life of the pure is enlightened.

q   On this holy night, my beloved sons, I want to entrust my Child to you.

r   I lay Him down in the cradle of your hearts. Let the great fire of your love increase. With Him I must enkindle all the love of the world."

115

True Poverty of Spirit

a   "Spend the last hours of this year, which the Immaculate Heart of your heavenly Mother has made extraordinary for you by its graces and gifts, in prayer and interior recollection.

b   I myself have wanted you here and have led you to this house which I have been preparing for you for some time. You are here in silence and in prayer: listen to me, speak to me, call upon the Father with me. You have close to you this brother of yours who loves you so much and who, in my heart, deeply cherishes you.

c   Your heavenly Mother sees with eyes that are different from yours: hers is a regard of light and of love. For me, that person is great who is considered a nobody and of no value in the eyes of men.

d   This house which is hidden and unknown and attracts no attention, is now the place of my presence and it is here, and nowhere else, that I have wanted you to spend these holydays with me.

e   Accustom yourself to see everything with the same eyes as your Mother. Always regard with pleasure and very special love those whom the world ignores and disdains.

f   May your heart always consider those to be greater whom men consider as nobodies and of no worth: the poor, the small, the humble, the suffering, the unknown.

g   Even among your brother-priests you should feel closer to those who are overlooked and considered as nothing. Oh, if you only knew what precious treasures to my mother's heart are all these beloved sons of mine whom no one esteems.

h   Give them to me on this last night of the year: offer them to me, one by one. What comfort their love brings to my Immaculate Heart! How their hidden beauty makes amends for the sorrow caused to my heart by those who consider themselves great and esteemed, and who spend their lives seeking every kind of human recognition.

i   True poverty of spirit is the gift I make to him whom I call. It is emptiness which draws my love. It is the wave-length on which my voice can be heard and understood.

j   Be always poor in this way, that you may see each new day through my eyes and give me to him who, in poverty, has awaited me for so long."

1977

IN EVERY PART OF THE WORLD

January 1, 1977
Feast of the Blessed Virgin Mary, Mother of God
First Saturday of the Month and Year

Walk in My Light

a   "Begin the new year with me, my beloved sons, on this day when the Church invites you to comtemplate my divine maternity.

b   As my Son Jesus entrusted himself totally to me, to find in his Mother a safeguard and protection, so too should you let yourselves be led in security by your heavenly Mother.

c   What will this year be like? What events await you?

d   My beloved sons, you should not have to trouble yourselves over what awaits you, if you accustom yourselves to live each moment in my motherly heart.

e   Each day, humanity is drawing further and further away from God, and men in ever growing numbers persist in turning away from his law.

f   Because of this, with the new year the darkness will become more dense and the calamities and sufferings that await you will become greater.

g   Even in my Church the crisis will become more acute because my most urgent call to prayer, to conversion and to penance will be listened to less and less.

h   Unfortunately, there will be many priests among those who do not heed my voice.

i   Consequently, the pastors will have less light and the flock will be scattered along the roads of insecurity and division, of error and apostasy.

j   Pastors of the Church, become once again that which my Son Jesus wishes you to be!

k   Once again, be zealous and ardent only for the salvation of souls; once again, be strict guardians of the truth of the Gospel!

l   Once again, follow Jesus to calvary, and do not let yourselves be misled or distracted by the world to which you often conform your life!

It Is Good Which Triumphs

m My beloved sons, the more this darkness will descend upon the world and into the Church, the clearer will be the light which will shine forth from my Immaculate Heart to show you the way.

n Walk in this light. Thus you will always be filled with light.

o In you who are following me, my Immaculate Heart has already today achieved its triumph.

p The triumph of the heart of the Mother is won in the souls and the lives of her faithful children.

q In them it is good which triumphs at the very moment when evil is spreading everywhere. While sin tries to pervade everything, the grace and the love of God triumph in them; if error succeeds more and more in corrupting minds, they bear witness to the truth.

r If division tears the Church, they love her and live for her unity; if the Vicar of my Son is more and more left alone and abandoned, they draw close to him with greater love to become his constant comfort and defense.

s Yes, at this very moment when my Adversary is now triumphing everywhere, my Immaculate Heart also has its triumph in the lives of my beloved sons.

t So do not fear if you are beginning a year which will be even more difficult and painful: the more you see darkness enveloping everything, the more brilliant will be the light of my presence among you.

u Consequently, I ask you to begin this new year with me confidently and without fear. My Son Jesus will always be with you, and with Him, in your company, will be his Mother and yours."

I Will Teach You to Love

a   "My very dear son, I love you. I love you so much! It pleases you to hear this said to you; it pleases my mother's heart to say it to you more and more often.

b   From now on, it should be love alone that guides you at every moment and in each of your actions.

c   Love for the Father, for the Son and for the Holy Spirit; love for this divine and Most Holy Trinity which, dwelling within your soul, impels your heart towards an ever greater love for your heavenly Mother as well.

d   It is in my Immaculate Heart that your Mother will form you to an ever greater and purer love for God.

e   No creature has ever been able to love the Lord as has your Mother in heaven.

f   The Spirit of the Father and of the Son begets in you a great thirst for perfect love, and thus your soul is inclined spontaneously to seek the heart of the Mother.

g   I will teach you to love God and your neighbor ever more and more. I will give to your heart my own capacity to love. I will help you to divest yourself of every other yearning, to bring you to a simple, continuous and pure act of love.

h   And thus you will realize your vocation. (. . .)

i   My only joy is to bring you to love, so that my own heart may love, within yours, the Most Holy and Divine Trinity."

You Will Be Completely Renewed

a   "My Church, beloved son of mine, has become now more than ever the target at which my Adversary directs his rage in an increasingly violent manner.

b   The Vicar of my Son Jesus has had a foreboding of this decisive hour of combat, and so he has solemnly proclaimed me to be Mother of the Church.

c   As I am the true Mother of Jesus, so also am I the true Mother of the Church which is his Mystical Body. And as a Mother I look today upon this daughter of mine with apprehension and with a sorrow that is constantly growing.

d   My heart is again pierced by a sword to see the Church more and more violated by my Adversary.

e   Satan has truly penetrated within it and every day he is harvesting his victims, even from among its very pastors. He has succeeded in obscuring its light with the darkness of error which endeavors to pervade everything.

f   The Vicar of my Son is at times cut off, as it were, from his own children whom he must nevertheless guide, and the cross of this suffering of his becomes daily greater.

g   Among those who surround him there are those who sometimes do not act out of love for him, but who are moved rather by a spirit of pride and a thirst to dominate.

h   Satan is trying to strike even the hierarchy in its bond of love and unity.

i   How many pastors are there today who do not love and help each other?

j   Many of them criticize and often obstruct each other, seeking only to get further ahead more quickly, trampling under foot at times the most elementary demands of justice.

k   Even in the case of important problems which regard the life of the Church and souls, how many are there who, in their love for truth, demonstrate unanimity of thought and action?

l   And as a consequence these priests, these sons of my maternal predilection, find themselves left to their own resources.

m   Thus an increasing number are led astray by the general confusion, become the victims of error and wander far from my Son Jesus and the truth of his Gospel.

n Thus their light becomes extinguished and the faithful walk in darkness. How many there are among them who now live habitually in sin, and who turn a deaf ear to my pressing invitations to conversion! They even try to justify themselves, adapting themselves to the mentality of the world which today legitimizes even the most serious moral disorders.

o How many of my priest-sons no longer pray? They are swallowed up in activities and no longer have a moment to pray.

You Will Be More Beautiful

p This poor Church of mine! As a Mother I draw near, my daughter, and I find you so sick! It would seem as though you are close to death . . .

q How profound is your affliction and your abandonment! More and more each day, my Adversary strikes at you in those pastors who betray you and those priests who become unfaithful servants.

r This grave malady of yours, this apparent victory of my Adversary over you, is not however unto your death! It is for the greater glorification of God.

s I myself, as your Mother, am helping you in this agony of your most painful purification. I take you into my motherly arms and press you to my Immaculate Heart.

t As a Mother, I pour balm on your wounds and await the hour of your complete healing. I myself—when the time comes—will heal you.

u You will be more beautiful! You will be totally renewed and completely purified at the moment when, through the new life that will be yours, the triumph of the Heart of Jesus and of my Immaculate Heart will shine forth throughout the whole world."

I Am Carrying You in My Arms

a   "Behold the mystery of love of my divine motherhood: as Mother, I entrust my Child to the hands of the priest, and in Him I adore my God who enters into the glory of his house.

b   Every provision of the law is fulfilled: the offering, the sacrifice, the ransom. A Child is confided to the priest: for him He is only one among many.

c   But to him who possesses the heart of a child is revealed the mystery of the Father. The Holy Spirit comes down upon a poor old man lost in the crowd. The arms of the old man reach out to embrace with love the promised Messiah, the awaited Savior of Israel.

d   My spouse, Joseph, and I look on in astonishment.

e   For the first time, the mystery is made manifest and a human voice proclaims it.

f   It is not revealed to the doctors and the priests.

g   It is manifested to an old man, and to a woman, to folk who are humble and poor in spirit. Thus is the future design anticipated: 'this Child will be set as a sign of contradiction, for the salvation and the ruin of many.' And for me, the Mother, 'a sword will pierce your soul.'

h   And, surprisingly, when He will begin his mission, this same fact will be repeated.

i   He is driven out of the Synagogue and obliged to flee; his message is rejected by the great ones: the doctors of the law, the scribes, the priests.

j   This official rejection, like a sword, pierces my mother's heart.

k   But Jesus is welcomed by the poor, the sick and the sinners. His voice reaches down into the hearts of the simple. And my motherly sorrow is assuaged by the response which the littlest ones know how to give my Son.

l   The little ones are for Him the gift of the Father. The little ones are his thanks which He returns to the Father, the little ones who alone understand the mysteries of the kingdom of heaven.

The Action of the Spirit

m   My beloved sons, become today my little children. My Church must open itself to the action of the Holy Spirit.

n   This edifice is built on columns that defy the centuries and against which hell cannot prevail: the college of the apostles founded upon Peter, which is perpetuated till the end of the world through the bishops in union with the Pope.

o   But today, such profound darkness seems to pervade this edifice: it is necessary that the Spirit make it all resplendent again with a totally new light. For this I am gathering together from every part of the world the cohort of my beloved sons: that the Holy Spirit may transform them and prepare them to carry out today the great plan of the Father.

p   Again this design is entrusted to the sorrow and the love of my Immaculate Heart; and so I ask you to consecrate yourselves to my heart. I ask you to become little children, so that I may carry you all in my arms.

q   As I did with my child Jesus, so too with you I present myself in the holy temple of God and I offer you as a holocaust to the Father to satisfy his divine justice.

r   Do not be troubled if again today I receive the rejection of the great ones. For nonetheless, my voice is being welcomed more and more by the little ones. It will be only with these children of mine that I will achieve my triumph of love."

Pure of Mind, of Heart, of Body

a   "Look, beloved sons, at your heavenly Mother who appears on earth in the lowly grotto of Massabielle.

b   You should look more to your immaculate Mother. You should have a firmer belief in my apparition.

c   I come from heaven to show you the road to follow: that of prayer and of penance. I come from heaven to give you, my sick children, the medicine you need in order to be healed: go and wash at the fountain!

d   Wash yourselves at the spring of living water which flows from the pierced Heart of my Son Jesus and which the Church still gives you today through the sacraments, especially that of reconciliation.

e   Wash yourselves often at this fountain because you have need of it to be purified of sin and to heal the wounds which evil leaves in your lives.

f   Wash yourselves at this fountain that you may become always purer. Your immaculate Mother, dear children, casts about you her heavenly mantle and gently helps you to live the virtue of purity.

g   I want you pure in mind, heart and body.

h   **You must first of all be pure in mind.**

i   In thought, you should seek and do only the will of the Lord. Your mind should be completely open to receive his light. Do not defile it by attachment to your way of thinking, to the way in which the majority of men think today. Do not obscure truth with error.

j   My Adversary, today more than ever, leads you astray by pride in order to corrupt that purity of your mind which alone permits you to receive the word of God with humility and to live it.

k   And then by means of the widespread corruption and immorality which is everywhere propagated and glorified, he attempts to corrupt your chastity of thought.

l   Close the eyes of your body to this evil and your soul will open itself to receive my most pure light.

m   Only the chaste in mind can continue to keep themselves upright and strong in the faith. And so, walk along the road of this corrupted world to spread only my light from heaven, and to the multitudes which each day are seduced by error, give the good example of remaining firm in the truth of the faith.

n   **I want you pure of heart** to be truly capable of loving. Your love should be supernatural and divine. All inordinate attachment to yourselves or to creatures bedims its interior purity.

o   You ought to love my Son Jesus, and souls for love of Him. Can one love one's neighbor and not love God? Today there is this tendency, so false and so widespread even among many of my children: to seek to love one's neighbor while ignoring God.

p   You can always do good, and help your neighbor. But for your love to be supernatural and perfect, it must begin with God. Love the Most Holy Trinity with the Heart of my Son Jesus, and among yourselves love each other as He has loved you. In this way your love will always be more pure and you will be capable of truly loving your brothers.

q   Only he who is pure of heart can open himself to a great capacity for loving, and can live the virtue of charity.

r   Today still, it is the pure of heart who can see God and, in his light, understand and love all men.

s   **I want you pure in body**.

t   You have made the offering of your chastity to God. This is a virtue which you should live with particular consciousness. Today this is done only with difficulty because of the errors which are becoming constantly more widespread, and which tend to diminish the value of your true consecration.

u   How many of my beloved sons have given up living their priesthood, because the Holy Father has required that celibacy still be maintained today!

v   But how many others remain and no longer observe it because either they believe it to be outmoded, or they believe it to be something transitory; or they even feel interiorly that is is unjustified and no longer obilgatory . . .

w   And thus, how numerous today are my priest-sons who live
     habitually in impurity!

x   Begin anew, my beloved sons, to relive, in your bodies, the vir-
     ginity of my Son Jesus, and the stigmata of his Passion: your priestly
     body should be a crucified body. Crucified to the world and to
     its seductions.
y   Be, once again, pure of body because one day it will rise again,
     spiritual and purified, to enjoy the light and the life of God.
z   Your body is not destined for the sepulchre, where it will be laid
     to corrupt, but for paradise into which it will enter, risen again,
     that it may live forever.
A   It is, above all, through your chastity that you are able today
     to bear witness to your hope for the paradise which awaits you.

B   Today, your immaculate Mother calls all of you to be chaste
     in mind, heart and body in order to live the virtues of faith, charity
     and hope.
C   Thus it will be Jesus in you who again loves and saves his brothers
     and yours."

121

Mexico, February 18, 1977

In Every Part of the World

a   "If you are pure, my beloved sons, you can see my light. In the
     darkness which daily becomes deeper, a ray of light shines forth
     from my Immaculate Heart and comes right to you. Look at my
     light; it is the light given you by your Mother!
b   How much you have need to it, especially today!
c   No one listens to you any longer; few still understand you and
     help you. Many, having become victims of atheism, hate and
     disparage you; even among the faithful many criticize you and will
     not accept you; and more and more, you remain alone.
d   Who can understand you and help you? Who can console you?
     Your heavenly Mother.

e   For you I leave heaven again; for you I set out on the roads of the world; for you I pray and ask help of many generous souls.

f   And when you come together among yourselves, I join in your prayer as in the Cenacle: your souls open to the light of the Spirit and to your Mother's consolation.

g   This happens in every part of the world. And today I have again given you proof of this in this new continent, to which I have led you to gather together my beloved sons. Have you seen with what joy they opened their hearts? (. . .)"

122

Your Martyrdom of the Heart

a   "The confusion grows greater even within the Church and now spreads to every part of the world. The first to be stricken are the priests. Each day, the number of those who allow themselves to be misled by the error which leads to infidelity grows greater and greater.

b   In the name of progress, some priests have become nothing but ministers of the world and live according to the world.

c   For prayer they have substituted a feverish activity; for mortification, the constant seeking after comfort and pleasures; for holiness, a progressive yielding to sin, especially impurity, which is becoming more and more committed and justified.

d   They have become walking corpses, whitened sepulchres who still call themselves priests, but whom my Son Jesus no longer recognizes as such.

e   And these are indeed sometimes the most esteemed, those who have succeeded in achieving success and those who have been placed in positions of responsibility.

f   Those who have remained faithful are generally the most persecuted, the most ignored, and sometimes intentionally ostracized.

g   Thus the darkness spreads and the smoke of Satan seeks to cover everything; each day the apostasy grows greater.

h   How great is your suffering, beloved sons; how great is your suffering, O priests consecrated to my Immaculate Heart!

i   Your suffering will of necessity grow greater as the great apostasy spreads more and more.

j   This is your martyrdom of heart for which I am preparing you all. Upon my mother's heart, let each one offer his interior immolation to the Father.

k   Accept, to its very dregs, this hour of darkness. Live this martyrdom of the entire Church, invaded by the night. Remain faithful and confident, now that infidelity becomes more widespread and extolled.

l   Say *yes* to the Father and to your heavenly Mother, who is gently preparing you to live without fear. (. . .)"

123

The Angel of Consolation

a   "Never become discouraged.

b   As Jesus in the Garden of Gethsemane, you too are being assailed by the temptation of fear. Offer this to the Father and continue trustful.

c   At every moment, your heavenly Mother is close to each one of you. She is at your side to help you suffer, and to comfort you in your great abandonment.

d   With you, the whole Church is living through this hour of trial.

e   The Holy Father, the Vicar of my Son Jesus, who never before has received so many blows from all sides and been so abandoned, even by some of his own, is today living through this hour.

f   I, the Mother, am, for the Pope, the angel of consolation.

f   I am such, through you. I offer him the chalice of my Immaculate Heart, and in it is all the love of his priests, my beloved sons.

h   Thus, through me, you are his comfort before the great trial which is awaiting you all and for which I have long been preparing you."

124

With Me Beneath the Cross

a   "Today, beloved sons, I am bringing you with me to Calvary; with me beneath the Cross of my Son, where I became your Mother.

b   *Here I want to teach you to love.*

c   There is no greater love than to give one's life for those whom one loves. Look at my Son Jesus who is dying on the Cross for you. He is dying because He is giving his life. He is giving his life out of love.

d   My mother's heart feels Him dying and it is pierced by all his horrible agony.

e   My mother's love unites with his in loving you; my sons, learn from us always to love thus!

f   *Here I want to teach you to suffer.*

g   My son Jesus has become nothing other than the Man of Sorrows. He no longer bears resemblance to a man; He is crushed under the weight of suffering, cruelly beaten, outraged, humiliated. He suffers without complaint; as gentle as a little lamb, He is nailed to the cross.

h   Behold the path along which I am calling you today: that of Calvary which you must tread with docility and meekness.

i   Do not seek to escape this trial; do not beg for human consolation. You will always find the heart of your Mother who will help you to say *yes* to the will of the Father.

j *Here I want to teach you to be silent.*

k The word of my Son is silent in these final moments. Now He speaks with his life. This is the supreme witness to the will of God.

l Thus the last word of his life comes forth: a word of pardon for all and of complete abandonment to the Father.

m Learn today especially to be silent. Create a silence within yourself in order to hear only his divine word.

n Create silence about yourself. Do not reply to the criticisms and the calumnies of him who does not accept you.

o Give no answer to the sneers and the offenses of him who persecutes you. Judge no one.

p In the moments that await you, you will be called upon more and more to keep silent. You will speak by your life. And for you too, from this life of yours beneath the cross, will come forth the word of love for all men and of complete abandonment to the will of the Father."

125

April 23, 1977

Do Not Let Yourselves Be Led Astray

a "My beloved sons, do not let yourselves be led astray by the world in which you live.

b *It misleads you by word.*

c Never before as today has the word become an instrument of truly diabolical seduction. Speech is used to ensnare. Speech is used to spread error. Speech is used to hide the truth.

d Thus things which are real transgressions of the natural law and the law of God are proposed as values and conquests of the human mind.

e   Errors are propagated as new ways of understanding the truth.

f   Even in the explanation of the word of God the most serious errors are propagated. The Pope speaks and is no longer listened to. People continue along the same road and plunge deeper and deeper into the darkness of error which is spreading everywhere.

g   Today my Adversary is seducing you especially through the mind.

h   Answer with your humility, your docility and your obedience. Look only to my Son Jesus, who is the truth.

i   **It misleads you with images.**

j   Never have immorality and obscenity been so widespread and so extolled as in your days.

k   In the name of this false way of understanding the value of freedom, every moral aberration is justified.

l   Indeed they begin with the little ones, betraying the innocence of so many souls. And thus many end by being infected almost without noticing it.

m   As for you, answer by looking to me alone. Thus you will see the evil which surrounds you without gazing upon it. And you will go forward keeping your eyes on my Son Jesus who alone is your way.

n   **It misleads you by works.**

o   The works of the world have never been so evil as in these times. It has rejected God and walks in the darkness of this refusal. There is no longer the capacity to love, no longer the capacity to walk in the light.

p   Where are those who still manage to live as true children of God?

q   How it seduces you, above all today, this world in which you live!

r   Because of this, I ask you to follow only my Son Jesus, who is your life. He ascended into heaven to help you to live here below while nevertheless keeping your eyes on paradise. He ascended into heaven to help you to be in the world, while not being of the world.

s   You will not let yourselves be misled by this world if, led by me by the hand, you follow at every moment Jesus, your truth, your way and your life."

126

My Plan

a   "This is my hour. No one will be able to obstruct my plan, which I have long since been preparing for the salvation of the Church.

b   It is you, O priests, sons of my maternal predilection, who are the strategic elements of this plan.

c   My plan can be carried out only through you.

d   Nevertheless, it is not for you to know it in detail. It is enough that it is known by me, as I am your leader. You must all obey my orders with docility and let yourselves be led by me. Do not ask me where I am leading you.

e   I shall place each one of you at his proper post. Each one must look only to doing his own part well. For the rest, do not concern yourself to be preoccupied about it.

f   It is for me to arrange everything according to the plan prepared long ago by my Immaculate Heart, in the light of the wisdom of God.

g   Some of you will be called to stand **in the line of action**.

h   They will be given the light and the strength to overcome the attacks of those who will endeavour to destroy all the truth contained in the Gospel of my Son Jesus. In your mouth will be found the two-edged sword with which to unmask error and defend the truth.

i   In one hand you will have the crown of the rosary and in the other, the cross of my Son to whom you will draw souls in increasingly large numbers in the measure that the battle becomes more intense and more decisive.

j   You will be clad in the fire of the most pure light of the Holy Spirit with which to burn away all the darkness of error; through you, the truth will in the end conquer.

k   Others will be called to stand **in the line of support.**

l   They will have to pray and suffer much. From many of these I will have to ask a suffering so great that it will culminate in the offering of their own lives.

m   I will grant them the comfort of my habitual and extraordinary presence. My Immaculate Heart will be the altar on which they will be immolated for the salvation of the world.

n   My priest-sons, I am now calling you from every part of the world. And each one of you has been assigned to his post. (. . .)"

127   *May 18, 1977*

My Battle

a   "Let yourselves be led by me, beloved sons. My battle has now already begun.

b   I will begin to strike at the heart of my Adversary, and I will act especially there where he now feels that victory is assured.

c   He has succeeded in seducing you through pride. He has managed to pre-arrange everything in a most clever fashion. He has bent to his design every sector of human science and technique, arranging everything for rebellion against God. The greater part of humanity is now in his hands. He has managed by guile to draw to himself scientists, artists, philosophers, scholars, the powerful. Enticed by him, they have now put themselves at his service to act without God and against God.

d   But this is his weak point.

e   I shall attack him by using the strength of the little, the poor, the humble, the weak.

f   I, 'the little handmaid of the Lord,' shall place myself at the head of a great company of the humble to attack the stronghold manned by the proud.

g   The only thing I ask of all these sons of mine is that they consecrate themselves to my Immaculate Heart, and let themselves be possessed by me. Thus in them it will be I myself who will act.

h   And my victory, through them, has already begun.

i   Even in my Church, Satan seems to have now succeeded in winning everything over.

j   He feels secure because he has succeeded in tricking you and misleading you:

k   —by error which has spread everywhere and is even proclamied by many of my poor priest-sons;

l   —by infidelity which is dressed up as culture and modernization, in an endeavor to make evangelization more up-to-date and acceptable. Thus the gospel which some preach today is no longer the Gospel of my Son Jesus;

m   —by sin, which is more and more committed and justified. Often it is precisely priestly and religious lives which have become veritable cesspools of impurity.

n   Over this Church, which seems about to sink, Satan desires to dominate as the decisive victor. I shall strike him to the heart by turning his own victory to the cause of the triumph of my Immaculate Heart.

o   I shall avail myself of the darkness which he has spread everywhere, to choose the souls of the littlest of my sons and I shall give them my own light.

p   Thus everyone will be led by this very obscurity to seek salvation in the light which issues from my Immaculate Heart. And all the triumph of my Adversary will have only served to help many souls to take refuge in my mother's heart.

q   I will call upon my priests to give witness to their faith, even to the point of heroism. By their example they will help the souls of many of my poor wandering children to return to the path of fidelity.

r   I will bring my beloved sons to great holiness so that, through them, reparation may again be made for all the sins of the world. And thus it will be still possible to save many of my lost children.

s   This is why Satan has now such great fear of me!

t   But I have now moved into action with the cohort of my little children. Nothing will be able to stop me until my victory is complete in every detail. Thus, at the very moment when everything will seem lost, Providence will bring about the triumph of my Immaculate Heart in the world."

128   *July 8, 1977*

The Snares of My Adversary

a   "Allow yourselves to be led by me, beloved sons, with the greatest trust in my Immaculate Heart.

b   To be submissive to my commands, to form my invincible cohort, you must resist the snares of my Adversary who never as in these times has unleashed such attacks upon you.

c   He desires to bring you to want of confidence, to discouragement. He causes you to suffer from his deceitful and cunning tactics.

d   He even brings you to doubt that you have been really chosen by me and loved by me, so effectively does he convince you of your wretchedness and make you feel the extent of your human fragility.

e   To bring you to this paralysis of mind and thus render you ineffective, he will turn upon you with every kind of temptation.

f   Be attentive, my beloved sons; these are the snares of my Adversary.

g   This is the secret weapon which he uses against you. This is the venomous bite with which he strives to wound my little heel.

h   Your Mother desires now to lay bare his plot and to put you on your guard against his snares.

i   **You are my lilies** and for this reason my Adversary often torments you with impure images, fantasies and tempations.

j   Remain serene and confident! Never, as in these moments, has all your purity shone so dazzlingly and inviolate before God and your heavenly Mother, because it is born of a gift which you renew by an act of your will, in the midst of the greater suffering of your entire being.

k   From every snare which Satan sets for you, you will emerge purer, more beautiful and more renewed. And the suffering which you undergo is used by me as a terrible weapon to snatch from my Adversary many of your brother-priests whom, for years and years, he has held prisoners and slaves.

l   **You are my roses** which should give off the fragrance of love only for my Son Jesus and for me.

m   Because of this, he will lay snares for you by presenting to your heart creatures to which, imperceptibly, he will seek to bind you. Here again, his action is always deceptive. Often he presents you with creatures that are good, even virtuous, even endowed with extraordinary gifts, but which can nevertheless constitute an obstacle to your act of love for my Son Jesus, an act I would like to make ever more pure, unceasing and perfect.

n   Even the slightest attachment to any creature is enough to prevent your act of love from being that which my Immaculate Heart desires it to be! And in this way your souls become darkened by shadows which prevent you from receiving and understanding all the light that I give you and which you need in order to make up my crown of love.

o   Oh, my beloved sons! Come to me, all of you, because you are so little, so insecure, so helpless! Come, because you are my little babes, because you have such need of me to walk along the way of perfect love!

p   **You are my cyclamens** by reason of your interior littleness, by the childlikeness of your spirit.

q   Satan ensnares you by causing you to feel like adults, sure of yourselves, and by causing you to set the basis of your security in your own selves, in your own ideas, your own actions. And because confidence and self-abandonment are qualities of the humble, he tempts you more and more with doubt and lack of confidence in my action in your regard.

r   He tries to convince you that it is you who should do, you who should organize, you who should act, that everything depends upon you alone.

s   And you constantly toil all the harder and you do not let me act.

t   And so I cannot lead you any further because you are thus no longer capable of being docile.

u   If you do not remain little in this way, my designs cannot be realized.

v   Therefore, my beloved sons, I wanted to expose for you the traps with which my Adversary will constantly seek to trick you and lead you astray.

w   Respond always and only with heroic trust in me. That is all I need from you, my little children, to crush the head of my Adversary, while he will attempt to bite my heel, by laying snares for you, my dearest sons."

129   Hermitage of Montegiove, July 14, 1977

United in Love

a   "You are here, my beloved sons, on this mountain with me in prayer. This is a continuous cenacle, as was the one in Jerusalem, after the return of my Son Jesus to his Father.

b   Here too, I am always in your midst. I am united with you in prayer to help you to pray well, to encourage you to intercede unceasingly for all my poor children, straying but not yet lost. I will save them too, through you; for this, your prayer is necessary to me.

c   I am here to help you love one another always more and more.

It is the Mother who kindles in you the desire to know one another, who impels you to love one another, who invites you to unite; it is the Mother who each day builds up an ever greater unity among you.

d   I am here to form you to a life of union with me. Because, through your consecration, you have entrused yourselves to me, I can now truly live and manifest myself in you, especially when, as priests, you speak to my children.

e   It is the Holy Spirit who suggests everything to you. But it is the Mother who gives word and form to all that the Spirit prompts you to say, so that you may reach the hearts and minds of those who listen to you, according to their capacity to receive and their spiritual need.

f   Now you are here with me, and I watch over you with a love that is ever more motherly. I have truly great plans for you.

g   I am entrusting many of my priest-sons to you. Help me to make them grow in this life, by your prayers, by your generous and apostolic activity, and by your suffering which will increase.

h   Gather them together in cenacles of life with me: they are awaiting you as the parched earth groans and awaits a drop of dew.

i   Walk united in love, led by the hand of your heavenly Mother, of whose close presence you will become strongly aware, as you go down from this mountain. I now enfold you in my Immaculate Heart. And I bless you, one by one."

130

Your Docility

a   "(. . .) With your consecration to my Immaculate Heart, you have entrusted your priesthood to me. You have put it in a safe place.

b   But in so doing, however, you have only taken the first step, even though it is a very important one. Now I myself, as Mother, am committed to make each one of you just what my Son Jesus desires you to be.

c   The second thing you must do is to allow yourselves to be formed by me, in a way which is different for each one of you.

d   It is my duty as Mother to form you in a very particular and personal way. Even the paths along which I am leading you differ among themselves, but they all bring you to the same goal, that set for each of you by my Son Jesus.

e   Pay no attention to how I am forming you; do not ask me where I am leading you; do not seek to know beforehand the path which I have marked out for you. Your duty is to second my action with your docility.

f   **An interior docility** which leads you always to say 'yes' to me, and to seek only to carry out my will in whatever you do. You now know the will of your heavenly Mother:

g   —I want you humble, silent, recollected and burning with love for Jesus and souls. Only thus will you become great in my eyes;

h   —I want you trustful, abandoned to me and without human preoccupations. Even wanting to 'act' for my Movement can become a human preoccupation. Only thus can your mind see the great work which I am doing in you and through you;

i   —I want mortified in your senses, persevering in prayer, and gathered about Jesus in the Eucharist like living lamps of love. Only thus will you feel me close to you;

j   —I want you ever purer; thus you will finally be able to see me. You will see me with the eyes of the soul, if you close the eyes of the body to the vanity of this world.

k   Your life will be transformed by me, as gently and firmly I lead you to sanctity. Only if you cooperate with my action will you be able to escape the danger of coming to a halt or of allowing your fervor to grow tepid, after your act of consecration to me.

l   **An exterior docility** which now leads you to be examples of obedience which is lived out and witnessed.

m   Obedient to your Mother who speaks to you and who brings you, by her word, to obedience to the Pope and the Church united with him. Every day my motherly heart is wounded anew by acts, even public, of real disobedience to, and rebellion against, the Pope.

n   Your obedience ought to be like mine: humble, conscious, perfect. In this way you will cooperate with my action, as a second phase, so to speak, begins for my Movement.

o   Now that in all parts of the world you are responding to me by allowing yourselves to be enclosed in my Immaculate Heart, I must as quickly as possible make you into faithful copies of Jesus Crucified.

p   You have answered me with a *yes*; now I ask you to respond to my action with your exterior and interior docility. Only in this way can you resist the ambushes which my Adversary lays for you and respond to my great plan of love."

131 *July 29, 1977*

Enter My Garden

a   "Let yourselves be led, beloved sons, into the depths of my Immaculate Heart. Enter my garden. In it is reflected the most pure light of the divine Trinity.

b   **The Father** finds herein his design intact and perfectly realized. Here therefore all creation is resumed and contained, to sing with me the eternal praise of its Lord and Creator. It is the place where the heavenly Father receives his greatest glory from his creature.

c   **The Son** finds here his habitual dwelling place. My heart is the house where the Word was formed in his human life; it is the refuge where Jesus withdrew to find aid and comfort.

d   Here He also brought his first disciples, that they might be strengthened and receive, each and all, his very own imprint. In this garden they grew, little by little, according to his divine plan;

they became more humble, purer, more generous, stronger. Here they were well cultivated until each one attained that resemblance to Jesus which He himself desired.

e   [My heart] was also the altar on which my Son was immolated; the chalice which received his blood, which opened itself to the moaning of his wounds, which was opened wide to the great gift of his dying heart.

f   He desired that this garden of his should also become yours; and so, He gave you his Mother.

g   **The Holy Spirit** is the only Gardener within my enclosure. He has overshadowed me with his light of love; He has filled me with all his gifts; He has embellished me with his grandeur and has made me his spouse.

h   In my Immaculate Heart this divine prodigy has taken place.

i   My garden is his exclusive property: it is the Holy Spirit who waters it and gives it light; it is He who causes the most beautiful flowers to spring up; it is He who gives them their color and fragrance; it is He who brings therein whom He wills.

j   No one can enter unless He himself opens to them: no one walks therein unless He leads them forward.

k   If you but knew, my beloved sons, the gift you have received by consecrating yourselves to my Immaculate Heart!

l   It is the Holy Spirit who has brought you into my garden. And through your heavenly Mother, He is now cultivating you, embelleshing you with his gifts, and enriching you with all the virtues.

m   This is how you are growing in holiness, becoming more and more priests according to my design, and moving foward that you may be introduced by Him into the depths of my Immaculate Heart, wherein shines brilliantly all the glory of the Most Holy Trinity.

n   Remain, then forever in my garden."

132

Love Always!

a   "Remain in my Immaculate Heart. Always. Then at each moment, I myself will accomplish everything in you.

b   Never consider yourselves. Accept your littleness with humility and meekness. Say to the Lord: 'I am your smallest child. I know my poverty and I thank you.'

c   And then, love. You can love more if you are truly the littlest.

d   Love always! All that Jesus and I desire of you is love. Nothing else is yours; but the beating of your heart is yours.

e   Hearts of my beloved sons, beat with love only for my Son Jesus, for me and for souls! Then you will be, even here on earth, my perfect joy."

133

My Property

a   "If you remain in the garden of my Immaculate Heart you become my property. And so no one can any longer take you away from me, because I myself am your defense; you should always feel safe.

b   You must no longer fear either Satan, or the world, or the frailty of your nature.

c   Certainly you will experience that seduction and that temptation which the Lord permits as a test to allow you to experience the extent of your weakness.

d   But I will defend you from the Evil One, who can do nothing to harm those who are part of my property.

e   Then gently I cultivate you till each one of you becomes that kind of garden in which, as in mine, the divine splendor of the Trinity can be reflected.

f   I form you with maternal solicitude. With my own hands, I root out from you whatever might, in any way, be displeasing to the Lord.

g   The Spirit in whom I am clothed is like a fire which consumes everything within you, so that there remain not even a shadow which might bedim that beauty to which your heavenly Mother wishes to bring you. I want to make you a most pure transparency of God.

h   And then, I am strengthening in you those virtues which are like roots on which depends any possibility of your growth: faith, hope and charity. Round about these, I am giving you, as ornaments, all those other virtues which have made your Mother beautiful in the sight of God.

i   And in the measure that you open yourself more and more to the light of God, I am sprinkling upon you the balm of my perfume: humility, confidence, self-abandonment.

j   Grow thus, O flowers cultivated by me in my garden, that you may receive the beauty and the perfume of your Mother.

k   Then, accompanied by the angels and the saints of paradise, and with the prayer of the souls in purgatory, I present myself each day before the throne of God to offer Him ever larger bouquets of these flowers from my garden.

l   When you have become like this, then all the Church will become my garden, in which the divine Trinity will take delight in being reflected.

m   The Father will rejoice to see the design of his creation perfectly realized in it. The Son will dwell with you, into whose midst the reign of the Father has already come. The Holy Spirit will be life itself, in a world reconsecrated to the glory of God.

n   This will be the triumph of my Immaculate Heart."

The Decisive Move

a   "My beloved sons, look with my eyes at the world in which you live.

b   See how my Adversary has taken possession of everything: never before as in these present times has the world become so completely his kingdom over which he exercises his power as ruler.

c   And souls, the victims of his enticement, are daily being lost in ever greater numbers.

d   I want to save them through an extraordinary intervention of my maternal love. For this, I need you; I need your love.

e   Love, with my own heart, these poor children whom Satan and sin have already led to their death. Love above all those who have strayed the furthest: even those who deny God and who reject and oppose you; even those who are victims of vice, hatred and violence.

f   They have become docile instruments in the hands of Satan, who is using them as he wishes; and often they act only under the impulse of his malevolent influence.

g   But even these have been redeemed by Jesus; even these are my children. They are the sickest children, and therefore have the greatest need of me.

h   You are the ones who must love them, in me and for me. Let your love be pure and without reserve; let it be my very own love.

i   Even if it seems that they do not respond to you, such is really not the case; your love is already a force which is drawing them from the dominion of Satan! It is already a light which cuts through the darkness in which they find themselves; it is the most precious help that you can give them to lead them to salvation.

j   You must be mine, and I shall use you to bring back home all those children whom my Adversary has snatched away from me to make them subjects of his dominion.

k   I want all these lost children of mine to come back, through you, and enter the enclosure of my garden: thus they will again be saved!

l   I am in a hurry, beloved sons, because the times are critical. I am pressed for time because the battle, already under way, has a plan which is in the process of being fully realized.

m   My decisive move, which will bring about the victory, is you, beloved sons: I need all your love to snatch from the hands of my Adversary all those children whom he has taken for himself.

n   Only when they all have entered into the garden of my Immaculate Heart will it be understood that my triumph is nothing more than the triumph of love in the world."

135

September 8, 1977
The Nativity of the Blessed Virgin Mary

I Have Been Pointing Out the Way to You

a   "Remain ever in my Immaculate Heart, beloved sons. I must, as quickly as possible, form you to be such as Jesus wishes. I am pressed for time and I am asking ever greater things of you.

b   Let yourselves be led by me. Never become afraid: let all of you answer with a *yes*. For years I have followed you, day by day. For years I have been pointing out the way to you.

c   Travel this road with me. I am leading you along it that, at the moment of greatest darkness, you may find there my light. Do not let yourselves be drawn aside by vain curiosity; do not look for other confirmations.

d   This way which I have pointed out to you will be your only confirmation. Journey ever along it, and never allow yourselves to become wearied. Live whatever I have told you. I have spoken in order to be listened to.

e   You are listening to me when you put into practice all the things that I have told you.

f   Keep them in your heart, against him who tries to suggest doubts and uncertainties to you.

g   Put them into practice if you wish to prove to yourself and to others the truth of my words. (. . .)"

136

Nijmegen (Holland), October 1, 1977
Feast of Saint Therese of the Child Jesus
First Saturday of the Month

It Is Not Given to All

a   "It is not given to all to understand my plan, but only to those whom I call.

b   My beloved sons, for how long have I been forming you, following you and leading you to prepare yourselves to answer this call! From your very mother's womb I have received you into my Immaculate Heart and, in life, I myself have arranged everything for you.

c   Your whole life has been a tapestry of my love. And now this design must be completed as quickly as possible for the good of all.

d   Few have been called to this: but through them, the Mother wants to offer the possibility of salvation to all her children.

e   See how many of them are hurrying along the road to perdition! Who is there to help them? Who is there to hold them back?

f   You see how so very many of them, while still young, are already reaping the works of death, almost before they are able to sow. The world in which they live has poisoned and killed them.

g   How many generous souls today have been swept away by this darkness which has pervaded the whole Church!

h   You are experiencing again my own sorrow by your having also met here some brother-priests who no longer believe. They continue to exercise their ministry. They are teachers who teach error; they are the blind who lead others into blindness.

i   Share my own sorrow in this place from which progressivism and apostasy are spreading throughout this country and many parts of the world.

j   It is from here that my Adversary has gone into action; but it is also here that, as a sign of reparation, I have wanted to bring together today with me in prayer the priests of my Movement.

k   It is not given to everyone to understand my great plan. This is the hour when all who are called should respond to me.

l   Soon you will have no more time, because the number which the heavenly Father has determined will have been completed."

137

Fatima, October 13, 1977
Sixtieth Anniversay of the Last Apparition

The Miracle of the Sun

a   "Beloved sons, walk in trust.

b   Today you recall with joy the sign which, sixty years ago, I gave in this place chosen by me to manifest myself. You call it the miracle of the sun.

c   Yes, sons, even the sun, like all creation, obeys the laws established by its Creator. But sometimes it can act otherwise when God requires this.

d   Even the sun, like all the beings in creation, behaves in obedience to the laws of God.

e   Through this miracle, I have desired to indicate to you that my victory will consist in leading men back to a docile obedience to the will of our God.

f   But the sun is the source of light. The earth blossoms and opens to its warmth; you live on this earth by the light which it gives you. Your activity begins with its rising; and with its setting your work comes to a stop.

g   I have thus wanted to indicate to you that my victory will consist, especially, in making the light shine again upon the world and the Church. The world will be enlightened anew because it will offer itself completely to the adoration and the glorification of God.

h   In the Church, once the darkness of error, infidelity and sin by which it is presently eclipsed has been dissipated, the light of truth, of grace and of holiness will shine forth once again. Jesus will be so resplendent in the life of the Church that she herself will be the very greatest light for all the nations of the earth.

i   But the greatest victory of my motherly and Immaculate Heart will be to cause Jesus to shine in the souls of all my children.

j   Some of those present in this place today are thinking: 'What a great marvel it would be if the miracle of the sun were to be repeated!'

k   But every day I repeat it for each one of you: When I lead you along the pathway of my Son; when I help you to be healed of sin; when I lead you to prayer, and when I form you to holiness, it is the light of this sun that I cause to shine every more brightly in your souls and your lives: the sun of *my Son Jesus*.

l   And so the miracle of the sun which took place here was but a sign. The eyes of those present perceived this extraordinary phenomenon which caused many to believe in the action of your Mother whose duty it is to set burning in the hearts of all men the light of Jesus, the true Sun of the world."

138

Doubts and Perplexity

a   "Do not be surprised, beloved sons, that my Adversary does everything he can to obstruct this work of mine.

b   His favorite weapon is to sow doubts and perplexity about what I am doing in the Church. He tries to base these doubts on reasons which are seemingly solid and justifiable. Thus he instils a critical attitude toward whatever I tell you, even before you have received and understood my words.

c   You happen to hear of certain brothers of yours who are cultured men and often even experts and masters in theology, who reject those things I tell you, because they sift all my words with their minds, which have already been filled with the richness of their culture. And so they find insurmountable difficulties precisely in those phrases which are so clear to the simple and small.

d My words can be understood and accepted only by one whose mind is humble and well-disposed, who has a simple heart, and whose eyes are clear and pure. When the Mother speaks to her children, they listen to her because they love her. They do whatever she tells them, and thus they grow in knowledge and life.

e Those who criticize her even before they have listened to her, and those who reject what she says before putting it into practice cannot be her children. These people, even though they increase in learning, cannot grow in wisdom and life. (. . .)"

139

Everything Is About to Be Accomplished

a "Everything is about to be accomplished according to the plan of God. Your Mother wants to enfold you in her Immaculate Heart in order to make you fit for the perfect fulfillment of the divine plan.

b In it shines forth the triumph of the mercy *of the Father* who wants to lead all his wandering children along the path leading back to himself who so eagerly awaits them.

c Through it there is actualized the great hour of the merciful love *of the Son* who desires to purify completely with his blood this world, which was redeemed by Him on the Cross.

d With it comes the time *of the Holy Spirit*, who will be given you by the Father and the Son in ever increasing superabundance, to lead the whole Church to its new Pentecost.

e All is about to be accomplished that the Church may issue forth from the great suffering of its purification more beautiful and luminous in a renewed world.

f   Let everything that happens to you be viewed in this light. Let every single detail of the time in which you live be placed in the context of this wonderful design.

g   Do not stop to consider the ever thickening darkness, the sin which has been set up as the norm of human action, the suffering which is mounting to its peak and th chastisement which this humanity is preparing with his own hands. (. . .)"

140

December 8, 1977
Feast of the Immaculate Conception

The Immaculate One at Your Side

a   "I am your Immaculate Mother.

b   Let all of you, in every part of the world, today lift their gaze towards me to contemplate me in the glory where, through a singular privilege, the Most Holy Trinity has placed me.

c   *I have never known sin.*

d   My Son Jesus willed to make the first and most beautiful fruit of his redemption shine forth thus in me.

e   As his blood makes it possible for you to be washed from every stain of sin, so too has He given me the privilege of never being contaminated by it from the first instant of my conception.

f   He has wanted me to be 'all fair' that He might find in me a worthy gateway through which to come to you.

g   My beloved sons, let yourselves be drawn always more and more by your heavenly Mother, if you wish me to help you be set free from sin, which is the only true evil which can befall you, and which distorts the image of my Son Jesus, which alone should shine in each one of you.

h   It is on this day that I draw close and say to you: 'Do not be afraid; fear nothing, because you have your Immaculate Mother at your side!'

i I have pointed out to you the goal to which I wish to lead you.
j I have marked out the road.
k I have called you from every part of the world and I have enfolded you in this Immaculate Heart of mine.
l I have even foretold to you what is to happen.
m And now, on this day, I am inviting you to entrust yourselves completely to me, without fear and without apprehension.

n If I have told you that, in the greatest darkness, the light will come to you from my Immaculate Heart, I have wanted in this way to inform you that, at the decisive moments, I myself will suggest everything to you.
o I will tell you whom you must follow in order to be faithful to the Vicar of my Son Jesus and to my Church.
p I will confirm you in what you must say to remain in the truth. I will point out to you those whom you ought to fear, and what roads you can follow to avoid dangers, while for him whom I will lead up Calvary to be immolated, I myself will arrange everything beforehand.

q *I am the Immaculate One who is at your side*: in these moments of your purification I will make my presence felt in an extraordinary way, because great indeed is this battle which we must fight against Satan, sin and all the great army of evil. (. . .)"

141

December 24, 1977
The Holy Night

You Too Beget My Son

a "My beloved sons, bend with me over this manger where my Son, just born, is still shivering from the cold and uttering plaintive cries.
b Let us together adore Him, for He is the true Son of God!
c You are especially dear to me because you are his priests. You have received a power which makes you very much like your

heavenly Mother.

d　When you celebrate holy Mass, *you too beget my Son.* Jesus truly makes himself present in the consecrated host by means of the words of the priests.

e　Were it not for you, my beloved sons, my Son could not become present in the sacrament of the Eucharist.

f　In the Eucharist Jesus is truly present with his body, with his blood, with his soul, with his divinity.

g　You priests renew the reality of his birth in time.

h　Again today, as then, this coming of his is wrapped in mystery.

i　Then, a cave received Him; now, it is the stone of an altar. The tender features of a baby veiled his divinity; now the white appearance of bread hides Him.

j　But just as then, in the little baby, so too now in the consecrated host, the real presence of the Son of God is to be found.

k　On this hallowed night, my mother's heart is once again torn to see how widespread, even among priests, are the doubts concerning the divine presence of my Son Jesus in the mystery of the Eucharist.

l　And thus indifference towards the sacrament of the Eucharist spreads, adoration and prayer are snuffed out, and the sacrileges of those who approach it in a state of mortal sin increase day by day.

They No Longer Believe

m　Alas, even among priests the number of those who celebrate the Eucharist without any longer believing in it is increasing. Some of these deny the real presence of my Son Jesus; others would restrict it to the time of the celebration of holy Mass; and still others reduce it to a presence that is merely spiritual and symbolic.

n　These errors continue to spread despite the fact that the doctrine has been clearly reaffirmed by the *Magisterium*, especially the Pope.

o　The time will come when, unfortunely, this error will have even more supporters; and in the Church, the perfume of adoration and of the Holy Sacrifice will be, as it were, extinguished. And thus the abomination fo desolation which has already made its way into the holy Temple of God, will reach its culmination.

p   It is for this reason that, on this holy night, I want to gather together in my Immaculate Heart all my beloved sons scattered throughout the world.

q   I invite you to bend with me over the altar where you too will beget Jesus in the Eucharistic mystery. Adore Him with me; heap love upon Him with me; console Him with me; thank Him with me; with me, make reparation for the offenses, the coldness and the great indifference with which He is surrounded. Together with me, defend Him with your life, ever ready to shed your blood for Him.

r   And so, in this night so dark, Jesus will once again, through you, cast his light upon this world which his merciful love still wants saved!"

142

The End of a Period

a   "Most dearly beloved son, spend with me the last hours of this year which has been for my Movement truly extraordinary in view of its graces.

b   Sixty years have passed since I appeared in the poor Cova da Iria in Fatima to bring my important message to men.

c   My message is now more urgent and timely than ever.

d   *Timely*, because never as in these moments has humanity found itself so close to the brink of its own destruction; and *urgent*, because that which the justice of God has decreed is now in the process of being quickly realized.

e   Beloved sons, let all of you heed the anguished appeal of your

Mother: turn back along the road which leads to God through prayer and conversion.

f   Today I offer you again the means which the Father is giving you to help you return to Him: my Immaculate Heart. All of you must consecrate yourselves to this heart, and entrust yourselves to the arms of your heavenly Mother.

g   During this year which is about to end, I have been able to hold back the chastisement because of the prayers and sufferings of many of my children. Your 'yes' has enabled me to add strength to my action of maternal intercession on your behalf.

h   Jesus has again willed to entrust to his Mother and yours the ultimate possibility of interventing to lead you to salvation and to alleviate the great suffering that awaits you. (. . .)"

1978

YOUR PUBLIC MISSION

143

It Will Begin with the Church

a   "Today the whole Church looks with great hope to its heavenly Mother.

b   With filial tenderness and unlimited confidence, the Vicar of Jesus, the Pope, this victim who is offering himself more and more on the cross for the salvation of the world, is praying to me. Today he is invoking me for the peace of all humanity. Turning to me with incessant prayer, he is especially asking this peace for the Church of which he himself has solemnly proclaimed me to be the Mother.

c   All my children scattered throughout the world are invoking me: the innocent little ones, the young who as never before are suffering from this uncertainty and darkness; the poor, the sinners, the sick, the aged, the exiled, the straying.

d   And you my beloved sons, priests consecrated to my Immaculate Heart, are calling upon me with special fervour.

e   Today I want to tell you that I welcome your prayers and am placing them on the altar of the justice of God.

f   In this new year I will carry out even more vigorously my work of maternal mediation between you and my Son Jesus. (. . .)"

144

You Can Love Us This Way Too

a   "My dearly beloved son, turn with serenity to the Heart of Jesus.

b   If you knew how much He loves you, how He looks on you with predilection! Do you know why? Because you continue to be so small, so poor, so full of defects. . .

c Cast everything into the burning furnace of his Heart and everything will be burned up in his merciful love: your sins, your weaknesses, your defects.

d In the end, nothing of yourself will remain: the good you do will be our work alone. You will offer us that gift which is, to us, the most precious and which we always want from you: your love.

e *You can love us this way too:* in littleness, in poverty, in your truly great misery.

f Do not become discouraged when you find that you promise me something and then do not keep it. . .

g You have however offered me your sorrow and regret for your error and my motherly heart leaps for joy because of this.

h Nevertheless you should also strive to observe whatever I ask of you and to keep to what you promise me.

i *Silence with everyone,* prayer, suffering and the greatest confidence in me.

j These intimate sufferings, these secret humiliations of yours, make your similar to my crucified Son. Let yourself be made more and more like Him by your heavenly Mother, who wants to adjust you well upon the cross, that cross which my Son Jesus has prepared for you. . ."

145

Rome, January 21, 1978
Feast of Saint Agnes

Help Me, O Sons

a "With each day that passes, beloved sons, your numbers increase. My action for the renewal of the Church and for the salvation of the world is becoming stronger and more evident.

b Never as in the present time has your heavenly Mother been so concerned and, as it were, anguished. I draw close to the hearts of my beloved sons and ask each of you with maternal insistence to come to my aid.

c   *Help me, O sons!*

d   Your Mother has now need of your help.

e   Are you not aware of how I am summoning you from all sides, gathering you together and pleading with you? I am imploring you with signs which are becoming greater and more numerous: my tears, my apparitions, my messages.

f   I am now no longer able to restrain this poor world from plunging itself to the bottom of the abyss. And this is its greatest punishment, for if it touches the bottom it will destroy itself.

g   It will indeed be destroyed and consumed by the fire of unbridled egoism and by the hatred which will drive one person against the other. Brother will kill brother; one nation will destroy another in a war of unheard-of violence which will claim countless victims. Blood will flow everywhere.

h   *Help me, my beloved sons,* to keep this world from falling into the abyss! Help me yet save many of my poor lost children.

i   With your little hands give strength to the merciful hands of your heavenly Mother. For this I ask you all to heed my anguished appeal.

j   Each new priest who unites himself to my Immaculate Heart gives your Mother new strength to lead you all to salvation. And so let your only concern be always to answer with a yes to whatever I ask of you.

k   I will be asking greater and greater things of you, as the need for my extraordinary intervention on your behalf grows more pressing."

146

You Will Be Immolated in the Temple

a   "I am carrying you in my arms, beloved sons, and you should simply let yourselves be carried by me. And so I ask you to become little children. You are my tiniest babes.

b   And this is the measure of your littleness: that of Jesus who, forty days after his birth, is carried to the Temple in the arms of his Mother. His eyes look into mine and He feels at peace. He sees nothing else and He sleeps, cradled on my heart, while the joy of giving peace, repose and love to the Child grows within me.

c   *Beloved sons, you too should let yourselves be carried by me.* Thus will you become my perfect joy. Only in this way can you feel secure.

d   And so in the cold, which more and more is chilling everything, you feel the warmth of my motherly affection; midst the insecurity which is now taking hold of everyone, you feel the shelter which my arms offer you. In the darkness which is becoming deeper, here for you is my light.

e   You too should look into my eyes, at the light which God gives your through your Mother.

f   I carry you in my arms to the temple of God; you, the ministers of the Lord, you, the guardians of his temple.

g   It is a temple that is now profaned, that appears to be crumbling.

h   The columns of truth seem to be cracking, and many pastors are victims of the gravest errors!

i   Everything is contaminated by sin which seeks to cover even the altar. Sacrileges are increasing and the cup of divine justice is now full.

j   *You will be immolated in the temple.* Blood can still wash away every stain; with it my Church will be purified.

k   It is for this that the Mother is at your side.

l   With complete abandonment, let yourselves be carried by me. Do not look about you; do not search for shelter or protection. In my Immaculate Heart, all is about to be fulfilled in regard to each one of you."

Only Then Will You Understand

a   "How pleased I am that you have come on a pilgrimage of love and prayer to my famous shrine, where you have begun the gatherings for my beloved sons of Sicily! You have come to console the sorrowful heart of your Immaculate Mother.

b   I have accepted the gift of your love and have wrapped it around my heart as a splendid crown which you are making for me with the priests whom you are gathering from all parts of the world. Thank you for the joy which you give me!

c   You have also had a sign. This is its meaning: the light will now be going out everywhere. Those whom I have called are now taking refuge in my Immaculate Heart. This is where you will still be able to see; this is the shelter where you will be able to gather together; this is the path which will lead you to God.

d   Darkness will descend upon the Church and will become even more dense after your heavenly Mother has come to get the soul of the first of her beloved sons, Pope Paul VI, who is consummating on the cross his supreme sacrifice.

e   As long as he lives, thanks to his grievous martyrdom, I can still hold back the arm of God's justice. But after his death, all will come crashing down.

f   The Church will be, as it were, submerged in error which will be embraced and propagated, and thus apostasy, which already long since has been spreading like an oil stain, will reach its peak.

The Hour of the Martyrs

g   The pastors and the flock entrusted to them will be struck; for a short while, the Lord will permit it to appear as though the Church had been abandoned by Him.

h   The darkness will grow deeper over the world, which will reach the extremes of its perversion. The more perverted it becomes the more obstinately it will advance along the roads of rebellion against God, of idolatry, of blasphemy and of impiety.

i   Thus by its own hand it will draw down upon itself all that which divine justice has decreed for its total purification through darkness, through fire and through blood.

j   This will be the hour of the martyrs who, in great numbers, will shed their blood, and of the remnant who will envy those they see persecuted and slain.

k   Only then will you understand all that I have done for you . . ."

148

February 11, 1978
Feast of Our Lady of Lourdes

You Must Prepare Yourselves Now

a   "From every part of the world, beloved sons, I gather you together today in my Immaculate Heart.

b   With humility, you have accepted the invitation to entrust your lives to me, and now at every moment I myself will be your defense.

c   You have also consecrated your priesthood to me: I take upon myself the duty of making it daily more and more conformable to the loving design of the Eucharistic Heart of Jesus.

d   You have given me your hearts. I will put in the place of your hearts, filled with sin, my Immaculate Heart, and thus I will draw down upon you the power of God which will form in each one of you my Son Jesus in all his fullness.

e   To this end, accede to whatever your immaculate Mother now asks of you.

f   I ask of you docility, prayer and suffering.

g   *Be, first of all, more and more docile.* Only thus can I nourish, clothe, lead and form you.

h   These are the times when I am working the greatest wonders in hiddenness and silence. I am working my greatest miracles in the

201

hearts and the souls of my beloved sons.

i   Without you or others noticing it, I am leading you to great holiness.

j   I am giving you my own spirit, and thus the Spirit of the Father and the Son will be irresistibly drawn to descend upon you as He descended upon me, and He will transfrom you completely. You will become great in love, in virtue, in sacrifice and in heroism.

k   And thus you will be ready for my plan.

l   *Pray more, beloved sons.*

m   Never give up the prayer of the Liturgy of the Hours, your daily meditation, and your frequent visits to Jesus present in the Eucharist.

n   The sacrifice of the holy Mass must be lived interiorly by you, in your life and at the moment of its celebration. It is above all at the altar that each of you comes to be like Jesus Crucified.

o   Never neglect the recitation of the holy rosary, this prayer which I hold so dear and which I came down from heaven to ask of you. I taught you to recite it well, by passing the beads of the rosary through my fingers, as I joined in the prayer of my little daughter to whom I appeared in the grotto of Massabielle.

p   When you recite the rosary you invite me to pray with you and, each time, I truly join in your prayer. And so you are children who pray together with your heavenly Mother. And it is for this reason that the rosary becomes a most powerful weapon to be wielded in the terrible battle which you are called to wage against Satan and his army of evil.

q   *Offer me also your sufferings:*

r   —your interior sufferings, which are so humiliating to you, because they come from the experience of your limitations, your defects and your numerous attachments. The smaller and the more hidden the sufferings which you offer me, the greater is the joy which my Immaculate Heart experiences.

s   —your exterior sufferings, which my Adversary often provides for you, as he hurls himself at you with rage and fury, all the more violently because he foresees that you will be used by me for his definitive defeat.

t He torments some of you with temptations of all kinds, some with doubt and mistrust, others with aridity and weariness, others with criticism and derision, and others with even the most serious calumnies.

u Respond in only one way: by offering me the suffering you experience; and have confidence, confidence, confidence in you heavenly Mother.

v If I have always been near you, I am especially so at times such as these, with all the tenderness of my motherly love.

w Do not be afraid! I repeat: be mine and Satan will not touch you. You are in my garden and no one will be able to snatch you from my Immaculate Heart. (. . .)"

149

March 3, 1978
First Saturday of the Month

You Will Be Consoled

a "Beloved sons, look to your Mother. Enter into the refuge which her love has prepared for you. Rest in my Immaculate Heart.

b How great is the toilsome work which you must complete! You are treading a path which, from day to day, becomes rougher and more difficult.

c Often you are tempted to stop because of weariness, aridity and the obstacles you encounter. Never must you stop. Let yourselves be led always by the hand of your heavenly Mother.

d You are journeying today along the difficult path of purification.

e Is there still a long way to go? When will it end? Must we suffer much? What will happen to each of us, and who will reach the finish-line?

f These are the questions you often ponder.

g   Yes, sons, the most painful part of the journey is still ahead of you, and it will still be some time before all is accomplished.

h   To avoid becoming exhausted, take refuge in my Immaculate Heart. It is the garden which the Trinity has prepared for Itself and for you. For Itself, because in it is reflected its most pure light, and it is the place where God is most glorified. For you, because you have need of this delightful garden, especially in these times in which you are living.

i   You have need of it:

j   *for your rest.* Beloved sons, enter into this rest. I myself will then bind up your wounds, mend your tattered garments, prepare you the food that will restore you, and help you to grow stronger;

k   *for your consolation.* You are the littlest of children whom I am now gathering from all parts of the world and who, with great generosity, are answering my call to suffering and to the cross. Do not become sad if your suffering has to become even greater. In my arms and in my Immaculate Heart you will be consoled. And you will be given by me that which others will not be able to understand or taste;

l   *for your immolation.* Grow each day according to my motherly plan, as I heap my tendernesses upon you and embellish you with my own virtues.

m   My work is silent and hidden, but it is transforming you interiorly and drawing down upon you the good pleasure of the Lord.

n   When you are ready, I will then gather you up and bring you to adorn the garden of God with the angels and the saints. How many of you I have already brought up here to paradise, and they form a most beautiful crown of glory about my Immaculate Heart! (. . .)"

150

The Hour of Darkness!

a   "My beloved sons, remain in my Immaculate Heart and live with me the moments of your painful passion, which has now begun. You too are to live it as did my Son Jesus.

b   You are entering into that time which the Father has prepared that his design might be realized.

c   Today, at the beginning of this Holy Week, you too should say your 'yes' to the will of the Father. Say it with Jesus, his Son and your Brother, who still offers himself each day for you.

d   This is the hour of Satan and of his great power.

e   *It is the hour of darkness!*

f   The darkness has spread to every part of the world and, just when men are deluding themselves of having reached the peak of progress, they are walking the deepest darkness. Thus all is darkened by the shadow of death which is slaying you, of sin which is imprisoning you, and of hatred which is destroying you.

g   The darkness has pervaded even the Church. It is spreading more and more, and each day it is reaping victims from among its very chosen sons.

h   Seduced by Satan, how many of them have lost the light which enables them to walk along the way of justice: that of truth, of fidelity, of the life of grace, of love, of prayer, of good example, of holinesss!

i   How many of these poor sons of mine are even now abandoning the Church, either criticizing and challenging it, or even going so far as to betray it and deliver it into the hands of its Adversary!

j   'Is it with a kiss, Judas, that you betray the Son of Man?'

With a Kiss. . .

k   Even you, today, are betraying with a kiss the Church, the daughter of your heavenly Mother! . . .

l   You still belong to her and you have your life from her; you exercise her ministries, and you are often even her pastors.

m   Each day you renew the Eucharistic sacrifice, administer the sacraments, and proclaim her message of salvation. . .

n   And yet some of you are selling her to her Adversary and striking her to the heart by corrupting the truth with error, by justifying sin and living according to the spirit of the world, which thus through you enters into her interior, threatening her very life.

o   Yes, with a kiss, you, my very own poor sons, are again today betraying my Church and delivering her over into the hands of her enemies.

p   And so she too will soon be dragged by you before him who will do all he can to exterminate her. She will once again be condemned and persecuted. She will again have to shed her blood.

q   Priests consecrated to my Immaculate Heart, beloved sons whom I am gathering together from all parts of the world to form you into my cohort, if this is the hour of darkness, *this must also be your hour!*

r   The hour of you light, which ought to shine more and more brightly.

s   The hour of my great light, which I am giving to you in an extraordinary manner, that you may all walk together to meet my Son Jesus, the king of love and of peace who is now about to arrive."

151

March 24, 1978
Good Friday

How Much Blood!

a   "Beloved sons, today live with me on Calvary.

b   Stay with me beneath the Cross.

c   How much my Son Jesus suffers: He is pierced with nails; He is hung upon the gibbet; He is completely covered with wounds and blood. His body is shaken by spasms of excruciating agony, while all about Him the abuse and mockery grows louder.

d   Yet He utters no word of complaint: He prays, He suffers, He listens, He is silent, He offers himself up.

e   With the life which He is giving, He is saying his perfect 'yes', to the will of the Father.

f   My mother's heart is called to repeat with Him this 'yes', which I already gave at the moment when the Word was placed in my most pure womb.

g   Thus my Son becomes, himself, the victim and the priest, the altar and the offering by this bloody sacrifice of the new and eternal covenant. Kiss, with me, his bleeding wounds.

h   How much blood my eyes have seen today! His hair is soaked with it, his face is bathed in it; his hands and feet are torn, and his whole body is marked with deep wounds.

i   Now his blood runs down the wood of the Cross and waters the earth. This is the blood of my Son which washes away all the sin of the world. This is the blood of the true Lamb of God who is being immolated for your salvation.

His Blood and Yours

j   Today his blood can again purify this world.

k   His blood and yours, my beloved sons! Because through you Jesus truly lives again. With you He renews his sacrifice of the eternal covenant. In you He immolates himself again each day, as victim and priest, altar and offering.

l   By his blood and yours the Church will be purified. By his blood and yours the whole world will be renewed.

m   Do not be afraid if today I want you all with me on Calvary: you are in my motherly heart and here you too must learn to pray, to suffer, to be silent, to offer yourselves up.

n   Thus am I preparing you for your priestly immolation.

o   Say your yes to the will of the Father.
p   Say it with me, your heavenly Mother, who have long been
preparing you in the same way that I prepared my Son Jesus.
(. . .)"

152

You Will Be the Witnesses

a   "Your heavenly Mother is in paradise, taken up in glory even
with her body, now transfigured. She is now sharing, in a way
which is for the present unique and not granted to any other
creature, in that which my Son has prepared for you.

b   Close to the Father, Jesus has already prepared a place for each
one of you. Walk each day on this earth looking to Jesus, who is
now sitting at the right hand of the Father.

c   The love of the Father and the Son has been given you by
them that you may fulfill here below the plan which God, in his
eternal wisdom, has already determined for you.

d   The place which Jesus has prepared for you in heaven corresponds to the plan which each of you must realize here on earth,
under the powerful influence of the Holy Spirit.

e   And that which the Holy Spirit accomplishes in you, O sons
consecrated to my Immaculate Heart, *is my own plan.*

f   Therefore Jesus, while preparing a place for you in heaven near
the Father, has completely entrusted you on this earth to the
action of his Mother and yours.

g   You are fulfilling the plan of God only if you correspond to my
maternal action which is gently transforming you.

h   In fact I want to bring you all to reproduce in your life the perfect image of your heavenly Mother.

I Will Live Again in You

i   For this, I am causing you to become little, and to become ever littler, till each of you reaches the point of utter nothingness of his own self. I turn all your misery to great advantage, because it is this alone which irresistibly draws down upon you all the merciful predilection of my Immaculate Heart.

j   I am leading you to docility, to trust and filial abandonment by causing everything in you and about you in which you might put your trust and collapse.

k   I am nourishing and clothing you; I am caressing you and leading you with firmness toward the perfect realization of my motherly plan.

l   When I see my image reproduced in you, I will be able to give each of you my spirit and fill you with the fullness of my love. I will clothe you in my immaculate garment and embellish you with all my virtues.

m   Then all that is mine will also be yours and I will, at last, be able to live again in you.

n   It will be I myself, living in these littlest children of mine, who will bring to completion the work which the Most Holy Trinity has entrusted to me, that its greatest glory may shine forth over the world.

o   And you will be witnesses of all that the Immaculate Heart of a Mother, who is nothing other than merciful, can do in these years to lead all her poor wandering children to salvation."

153

Florida (United States), May 13, 1978
Anniversary of the First Apparition at Fatima

My Hour Has Come

a   "See my marvels everywhere in the world! My beloved sons are responding with ever increasing generosity and I am bringing them together in my cohort, which is now drawn up for battle.

b   In this great nation too, you are daily meeting with priests in cenacles of prayer and brotherly sharing.

c   You have accepted my invitation and are gathering together.

d   My duty is to bring you together, to form you and to prepare you.

e   *The hour of the great battle has come!*

f   At my orders you must now give evidence by word and example of your fidelity to Jesus, to the Gospel and to the Church.

g   Soon all will see the Church flourishing again and being renewed under the action of your heavenly Mother.

h   You must continue in docility, humility and confidence.

i   *My hour is come!*

j   I will give my spirit to all my little children so that I myself, through you, may again today live and work.

k   Thus all the world will see the loving plan which the Immaculate Heart of your heavenly Mother is carrying out for the coming of the reign of my Son Jesus."

154

Nagasaki (Japan), June 3, 1978
Feast of the Immaculate Heart of Mary

The Whole Church in My Refuge

a   "I have brought you here today to this great nation of a new continent to celebrate the feast of my Immaculate Heart.

b   You are in the city that was bathed with the blood of the first Japanese martyrs, and you find yourself in the very place where a terrible weapon, in one single instant, killed thousands and thousands of my poor children.

c   Near you is the church over which the atomic bomb exploded.

d   My little child, this place and this day are for you a sign and, through you, I want to pass it on today from this place to all my beloved children.

e   What happened in this place could soon happen in every part of the world if my children do not accept my invitation to return to God.

f   *Look at my Immaculate Heart*: it trembles and is anguished at the fate that now awaits you if you do not accede to the urgent request of your Mother.

g   Return, my children, never before so threatened and in such great need, return to your God who awaits you with the mercy and the love of a Father!

h   Observe his law; do not let yourselves be seduced by sin. Do not offend my Son Jesus any more; He has already been too much offended!

i   The time now left you is short: my hour has come and I myself am intervening to save you.

The Small Remnant

j   *Enter into my Immaculate Heart*: it is the refuge which the Mother gives you. In it you will find all that I have prepared for you in order to pass through the terrible hours of purification through which you are now living.

k   The whole Church must now enter into my refuge: with the Pope, the bishops, the priests and all the faithful.

l   It is for this reason that I am leading you to all parts of the world. The time has come when the small remnant, who will remain faithful and with whom Jesus will bring about the realization of his reign, must enter, in its entirety, into my Immaculate Heart.

m   Whoever does not enter into this refuge will be carried away by the great tempest which has already begun to rage.

n   *Comfort my Immaculate Heart.*

o   Never as in these present times has my heart been so pierced by a crown of thorns: these are the sins, the ingratitude, the sacrileges, the desertions and the betrayals, especially on the part of my beloved sons and of consecrated souls.

p   Often I cannot enter some of their houses because they

close the door on me and do not want me.

q   From being gardens of God some of them have become swamps in which Satan covers and corrupts everything with filth.

r   *Beloved sons, console me in my great sorrow!* Thus you will draw out the thorns, pour balm on my wounds, and form about my sorrowful heart a most beautiful crown of love.

s   Through you, your heavenly Mother again today wants to save all her lost children.

t   And so, what you are experiencing here is a sign which I am giving you. From it you will be able to understand how, through the death and sacrifice of a few, your Mother is preparing a new life for all."

155

Hong Kong, June 12, 1978

This Immense Nation

a   "Look at this immense nation from which the very idea of God has been officially expunged.

b   Hundreds of millions of my poor children have thus been educated from childhood to do without God. And often they are good and generous children, though deprived of the true light which alone can give joy and hope to their lives.

c   Think of all the great suffering that covers this immense land . . .

d   I assure you that what I already foretold you at Fatima has truly come to pass: Russia has spread its errors throughout the whole world. The Lord has made use of godless nations to chastise the Christian peoples who have left the path marked out by my Son Jesus.

e   Now that you are living through those events of which I have foretold you, what must you do, my poor children, to run for shelter?

212

f *First of all, have recourse to prayer.* Pray more, pray with greater confidence, pray with humility and absolute self-abandonment.

g Especially, recite the holy rosary every day.

h By your prayer, you prevent error from becoming even more widespread; you hold in check the action of the Evil One; you move to the counter-attack and you limit, more and more, his capacity to act.

i And in the end, through your prayer, you are able to gain the victory: it will be God alone who will conquer, through you.

j *Offer up the holocaust of your suffering.* The hours through which you are living are truly difficult and painful. That which is awaiting you is suffering such as the world has never known.

k Yet, through this holocaust, you are able to save those who are seeking your ruin, and you are able to do good to those who are, for you, a scourge.

l Thus, even these great nations which have openly rebelled against God and have become a veritable scourge for all humanity can, in the end, be saved."

156

Rome, July 13, 1978
Anniversary of the third apparition at Fatima

Your Public Mission

a "My beloved sons, you are gathered here with me in a cenacle of prayer and love.

b I have called you from many parts of the world, and you have come. Now you are making your spiritual exercises that during these days I may form you and prepare you for what awaits you.

c All that I have for some time now foretold you is about to come to pass.

d Therefore, the plan that I have for each of you must be carried out as quickly as possible.

e You have consecrated yourselves to the Immaculate Heart of your heavenly Mother. So you have a part to play in my own plan which is that of defeating Satan, the first artisan of sin and of every evil that has spread throughout the world.

f Walk with me, and thus you yourselves will be, in the world, the immaculate light which will conquer the darkness of evil and sin.

g That is why I have summoned you all to enter into the intimacy of my heart in order to work this veritable transformation in you.

The Final Stage

h You are also here in the city where the Vicar of Jesus, the first of my beloved sons, the Pope, lives, suffers and is offering himself in sacrifice.

i I wanted you near him to help him now in the final and most painful stage of his journey.

j In you and through you, I myself am present beneath the cross on which the Holy Father is living out the hours of his agony.

k It is for this reason that the Immaculate Heart of your heavenly Mother, in the cenacle, has always directed you, through prayer and love, towards his white-clad person.

l You have ever before you my Son Jesus who looks upon you with special favor. It is Jesus who is present under the white appearance of the Eucharist bread.

m Yours is a true Eucharistic cenacle: your prayer, your love and your life are directed to Jesus in the Eucharist.

n You are being called more and more to become the apostles and new martyrs of Jesus, present in the Eucharist.

o And so you must increase your reparation, your adoration and your life of piety.

p The Eucharistic Heart of Jesus will work great things in each of you.

q Be docile: this is what pleases me more, and costs you more.

r Be docile: this is what you often do not succeed in being, and your heavenly Mother is saddened when so much good will is met, in practice, with so little docility.

s I have chosen your for a plan which you will fully understand later on.

t Just as for the apostles the cenacle preceded the fullness of their mission even to martyrdom, so also it will be for you.

u The time for your public mission has now arrived. Gather together, my beloved sons; advance together with me in the life I have traced out for you.

v *This is the hour of your witness!*

w In the Immaculate Heart of your heavenly Mother, go now into all parts of the world to carry out the mission which my Son Jesus has entrusted to each one of you."

157   *Częstochowa (Poland), July 28, 1978*

A Sign for All

a "I have brought you to this country which has been consecrated many times to my Immaculate Heart and of which I have been officially proclaimed Queen. From my Sanctuary I am watching over it; I am protecting it, consoling it, strengthening it and defending it.

b It has become my property because it has been entrusted to me through the consecration of each one to my Immaculate Heart. Its sons are conscious of this, because they renew it often and live it.

c See how the Church here is alive and flourishing, although it has been persecuted for many years and in many ways! The seminaries have not enough space for all the young men who wish to become priests; the churches are filled with faithful; the priests wear the ecclesiastical garb. All prayer is centered about Jesus in the Eucharist, which is venerated, loved and exposed for public adoration.

d　　What is happening in this country is a sign for the whole Church. If the request I made at Fatima for all to consecrate themselves to my Immaculate Heart had been accepted, what has taken place here would also have taken place everywhere in the world. I would have obtained peace for the world and, for the Church, its greatest sancification.

e　　On the contrary, the world is plunged into a desert of hatred and violence, and the Church is living through a period of great desolation.

f　　But, my beloved sons, this is my hour!

g　　Through you, my priests, I now call all to consecrate themselves to my Immaculate Heart. In this way, you give your heavenly Mother the opportunity of intervening to bring the Church to its greatest splendor and to prepare the world for the coming of the reign of my Son Jesus."

158

August 5, 1978
First Saturday of the Month
Feast of Our Lady of the Snows

In the Heart of the Church

a　　"My beloved sons, look with my eyes and you will see how the Church is being renewed interiorly, under the powerful action of the Spirit of God.

b　　This does not yet appear externally because of the great coldness which covers her and the great darkness which pervades her. She is now living through the most painful moments of her purification.

c　　Assisted and comforted by her Mother, the Church is now climbing the arduous road to calvary, where she must again be crucified and immolated for the good of many of my children.

d　　But enter with me into the heart of the Church! Here the triumph of my heart has already taken place.

e It has taken place in the person and the life of the Holy Father, who is being led by me to the summit of sanctity through his daily immolation which will bring him to a veritable martyrdom.

f It has taken place in the lives of my beloved sons who are consecrated to my Immaculate Heart. Their number increases from day to day. See, the light increases within them, as does love, faithfulness, holiness and heroic witnessing to the Gospel.

g Even in their littleness, my light shines forth in them. Led and formed by me, they will be the new apostles for the renewal of the whole Church. They are in the heart of the Church and of your heavenly Mother.

h This triumph has taken place in the lives of many consecrated souls who, drawn by my gentle and powerful action, have again come to live their religious vocation with generosity, following and imitating Jesus, chaste, poor and obedient even to the death of the cross.

i It has taken place in the souls and lives of many of the faithful who have responded with exemplary enthusiasm to the invitation of your Mother, and have now become good examples to all.

j In all these children of mine, the triumph of my Immaculate Heart has already taken place: and they thus form, as it were, the heart of the renewed Church.

k Through them my action has begun, and but a short time remains before my complete victory, because when this vitality has been sent out by the heart into all parts of the organism, then the whole Church will flourish anew.

l Under the powerful action of the Spirit of God, its soil will open up to put forth its greatest growth, and there will be in the Church a greater splendor than has ever existed. She will become a light to all the nations of the earth who will turn to her, to the glory of God!"

159

The Death of the Pope

a "Tomorrow, my very dear son, you will end this brief period of repose.

b I wanted you here again with your spiritual director and these children, so weak and limited, humanly speaking, but whom my heart loves in a special way.

c It is only littleness and weakness that draw upon you my motherly predilection. You have lived with them in great simplicity.

d You have spent this time in prayer, in interior recollection and in union with me.

e With me, you have also spent these moments of sorrow which the Church is going through because of the death of its supreme pastor, the Vicar of my Son Jesus, Pope Paul VI.

f He was, in truth, a great gift made by the Heart of Jesus to the Church.

g His mission has been accomplished. As on this earth you have been very close to him through prayer and through your love, so now from paradise he will be close to you to help you carry out your mission through the powerful assistance of his intercession. . ."

160

Your New Birth

a "Share, beloved children, in the joy of all the Church which today venerates that mystery of love which is the birth of your heavenly Mother. With it, the plan of your salvation begins to take form.

b Life is given to me that it might be given by me to Him who is life, to the Word of the Father, who assumes human nature in my virginal womb in order to be born of me in time.

c   All heaven exults in this mystery; the angels and saints share in your joy, my children who are still pilgrims on this earth.

d   Look to your heavenly Mother. I am at your side at every moment. From my Immaculate Heart rays of light and of grace are ever issuing forth and showering upon you in every part of the world.

e   Thus I enlighten and beget you, nourish and form you, guide and sustain you. Each day, you too share in the mystery of love which is your new birth given you by your Mother.

f   Come to me, all of you, my beloved children, because you have need of me.

g   The Church too is now living through her great trial, and what is awaiting her is something she has never known before.

h   I am watching over her and arranging everything for her good. And now the Heart of my Son Jesus has given her a new chief pastor in the person of Pope John Paul I. Love him, listen to him, defend him, follow him, because he will have to suffer for the Church.

i   The days of her trial are all numbered, and in my Immaculate Heart I am preparing for her as well the moment of her new birth in time. She will be more beautiful and radiant, holier and more godlike, after the great trial of purification.

j   And so I am calling you all today to gather about the cradle of your infant Mother. Learn from me to grow in littleness and trust, in humility and greater abandonment to the love of the Father."

The Hour of the Apostles of Light

a "I am your Immaculate Mother, who am at the side of each one of you, my beloved sons.

b My plan is about to be fulfilled because the triumph of my Immaculate Heart has now come to pass.

c You are being prepared by me to be the apostles of this time. You are therefore the apostles of light in this hour when darkness is enveloping all things.

d Live in the light.

e Walk in the light. Spread the light which comes from my Immaculate Heart.

f As your heavenly Mother, I have been preparing you for years in silence and leading you by the hand.

g Thus, while my Adversary was casting darkness over the Church and reaping victims from among many of her very pastors, I was preparing secretly, in my heart, the new Church, all of light.

h It is the the same Church, but a renewed Church in which the glory of the Most Holy Trinity will shine forth resplendently, and in which Jesus will be adored, honored, listened to and followed by all.

i Thus the Church will shine gloriously with a great light such as has never been known since the time of the Cenacle to this very day.

j Today you are commemorating my coming down to earth in the humble Cova da Iria, and the miracle of the sun which, prostrate at my feet, so to speak, testified to you that this is my hour, the hour of your Mother clothed in light.

k Today I am announcing to you that this is also your hour.

l The hour of your witness.

m The hour of your public life.

n The hour of the apostles of light.

o   With vigor and courage, spread everywhere the light of truth, the light of grace, the light of holiness.

p   It is the light of my Son Jesus, who has shown you the way to reach the Father through perfect docility to the action of his Spirit of Love.

q   Soon, nothing more will remain of the great darkness which has obscured the Church. After her great suffering, she will, at last, be ready for her rebirth: the new Church of light. (. . .)"

162   *October 17, 1978*

The New Pope, John Paul II

a   ". . .Have more confidence and trust in your heavenly Mother: pray and live with her; never again be fearful!

b   I am leading and protecting you, I am at your side at each moment; what I ask of you is silence, prayer and confidence. I ask little and humble things of you because you must walk along the path of littleness and humiliations.

c   Today you have prayed for the new Pope whom my Immaculate Heart has obtained from Jesus for the good of his Church. He is a son especially loved by me because he has consecrated himself to my heart from the beginning of his priesthood.

d   Unite yourself, through love and prayer, with all the priests of my Movement, whom I myself am bringing to an ever greater love for the Pope and for the Church united with him.

e   You must support him with prayer, with your love and with your fidelity. You must follow him, carrying out to perfection whatever he determines for the good of the Church. In this, be a good example to all.

f   You must defend him at those times when my Adversary lets loose his fury upon him, deceiving those of my poor children who oppose him.

g   With the Holy Father whom Providence has today given you, I bless you, my beloved sons throughout the whole world, chosen by my Immaculate Heart for the hour of its great triumph."

163

Do Not Feel You Are Alone

a "Do not feel you are alone!

b In the battle to which I am calling you, many of your brother priests whom I have already brought up here to paradise, are also taking part.

c This is the lot which awaits my beloved sons: my Immaculate Heart, about which they will, for all eternity, form its most beautiful crown of glory.

d Do not feel you are alone! There also belong to my cohort the saints of heaven and your brothers who are still being purified in purgatory, offering to me their prayers and sufferings.

e All those priests who, during their earthly life, responded to my invitation, listened to my voice and consecrated themselves to my heart are now in paradise as lights which shine resplendently about your immaculate Mother.

f They are still very close to you; they are helping you to carry out my plan, they are supporting you by their invisible presence, defending you from evil and protecting you against the many perils in the midst of which you live.

g Do not feel you are alone! Along with these brother priests of yours, your heavenly Mother's angels of light are also at your side. They are preparing you for your perfect offering, just as they prepared my heart to say yes to the will of the Lord.

h They encourage you at the moment of your priestly immolation.

i For you also, my little ones, the hour has come. And so, heaven and earth are united today in this extraordinary communion of love, of prayer and of action at the orders of your heavenly Leader.

j   The plan of my Immaculate Heart is now being carried out, because my Son Jesus is on the point of achieving his greatest victory through the coming into this world of his glorious reign."

164

My Motherly Action

a   "Beloved sons, let yourselves be led by me at each moment, and always second the desires of my Immaculate Heart.

b   In silence and hiddenness your heavenly Mother is now carrying out her great loving plan.

c   This is the hour of my battle. With you, I have now begun to attack my Adversary precisely where he seems to have, for the moment, won a victory.

d   Where Satan has demolished, I am building.

e   Where Satan has wounded, I am healing.

f   Where Satan has conquered, I am achieving the greatest triumph.

g   In this, my motherly action becomes visible to all.

h   I am Mother, and my action comes from the depths of my Immaculate Heart to help all those children who are at present in great difficulties.

i   Above all, my love wishes to manifest itself in an extraordinary manner to those who have strayed and who are in grave danger of being eternally lost.

j   It is in this motherly action of mine that there shines forth all the love of God, who wishes to let pour out upon the world the torrents of his merciful love.

k   The time has come when the desert of this world will be renewed by the merciful love of the Father who, in the Holy Spirit, desires to draw all to the divine Heart of the Son so that his reign of truth and grace, of love, of justice and peace may at last shine in the world.

l   The Church and the world will thus be able to attain a splendor which they have never before known.

m   And that his mercy might shine forth all the more, God has entrusted the preparation of this renewal to my motherly action.

n   It is my desire that the time be shortened, because each day many souls are being eternally lost!

o   How many souls are going to hell. . . because people no longer pray, because sin increases and reparation for it is no longer made, because error is followed with such ease!

p   I can shorten the time of the great purification through you, the apostles of light of my Immaculate Heart. (. . .)"

165

Mother of the Church

a   "I am the Immaculate Conception!

b   My beloved sons, I am your Mother, all fair. Today the Most Holy Trinity causes its most pure light to be reflected in me so that, through me, all paradise, with the choir of angels and saints, may sing to God his very greatest glory.

c   And the whole Church, also, looks to its Immaculate Mother with tremendous hope.

d   *I am the Mother of the Church.*

e   Today there shine forth from my Immaculate Heart luminous rays of love and grace which I am pouring out upon my children:

upon the Pope, the bishops, the priests, the religious and all the faithful.

f   Have great confidence in the special action of your Immaculate Mother. I gaze upon you with that tenderness with which a mother looks at her sick children who are therefore so much more in need of her.

g   Your real malady is sin. Each day it brings many of my poor children to eternal death. . .

h   It is sin which obscures the face of my beloved daughter, the Church, whom I want to be resplendent, without wrinkle and all fair in imitation of her Mother. Today sin is spreading like a mysterious illness, and with the force of a plague it has caused many of my poor children to fall into the deepest darkness.

i   This is a time of suffering for the Church because infidelity is spreading and compromise with the spirit of the world has succeeded in misleading even some of those who carry great responsibilities.

j   *I am the Immaculate Mother of the Church.*

k   I myself have begun my work of maternal assistance through those who are answering my urgent appeal to fight sin, to pray, to suffer, to love and to make reparation.

l   Through them I am able to heal many of my sick children and to lead them back to true love for Jesus, who was born of me for the salvation of all.

m   Every day there are many who are answering me with a yes, especially among my beloved priests.

n   *I am victorious Mother of the Church.*

o   Through the cohort of my priests I have already begun my victorious action, which will cause my Immaculate Heart to shine resplendently over the entire world.

p   This will be the triumph of mercy and of pardon.

q   I am bringing together my good and docile children, that they may build up with me that which the Evil One and his followers are tearing down.

It is in this way that the renewal of the Church and the world has alread begun. It is taking place in silence, because noise is not becoming to the action of your heavenly Mother. It is taking place in hiddeness and humility.

s But with each day that passes, it will become more apparent and complete. The more my children respond to the gentle invitation of their Immaculate Mother, the shorter the time of the battle will be and the sooner the hour of the great victory will come.

t And so today I bless all those priests, scattered throughout the world, who have responded with a yes to my invitation and have thus begun to form part of my loving plan."

166

His Second Coming

a "My beloved sons, I am gathering you here with me, close to the poor manger, waiting to place in it my new-born Child.

b This is the holy night. You are spending it in prayer and recollection. You are spending it with me.

c In this night, darkness covers everything, and silence has now dimmed every sound, when suddenly a new light pours forth from heaven and the festive voices of angels resound along the deserted roadways of the world.

d The desert of the world opens to receive its God who is born of me in his human life.

e His second coming, beloved sons, will be like the first. As was his birth on this night, so also will be the return of Jesus in glory, before his final coming for the last judgement, the hour of which is still hidden in the secrets of the Father.

f The world will be completely covered in the darkness of the denial of God, of its obstinate rejection of Him and of rebellion against his law of love. The coldness of hatred will still cause the roadways of this world to be deserted. Almost no one will be ready to receive Him.

g   The great ones will not even remember Him, the rich will close their doors on Him, while his own will be too busy with seeking and affirming themselves. . .

h   'When the Son of Man comes, will He still find faith on the earth?' He will come suddenly and the world will not be ready for his coming. He will come for a judgment for which man will find himself unprepared. He will come to establish his kingdom in the world, after having defeated and annihilated his enemies.

i   Even in this second coming, the Son will come to you through his Mother. As the Word of the Father made use of my virginal womb to come to you, so also will Jesus make use of my Immaculate Heart to come and reign in your midst.

j   This is the hour of my Immaculate Heart, because the coming of Jesus' glorious reign of love is now in preparation.

k   Beloved sons, just as I did, you too must prepare yourselves to receive Him!

l   This holy night is a sign and a grace for you. I am gathering you together close to his poor manger to fill the vast emptiness which humanity has made for Him. (. . .)"

1979

THE SIGNS OF THE PURIFICATION

The Plan of Merciful Love

a   "Beloved sons, I am close to you at the beginning of this new year. Have confidence in my Immaculate Heart!

b   Enclosed within my heart is the plan of the merciful love of my Son Jesus, who wants to lead the world back to the Father for the perfect glorification of God.

c   The world is not lost, even though it is now walking along the road of perdition and of its own destruction. Through a trial which I have foretold to you many times, it will in the end be saved by an act of the merciful love of Jesus, who has entrusted you to the action of your heavenly Mother.

d   Sin still covers the earth; hatred and violence are erupting everywhere; the greatest crimes are crying out daily for vengeance in the sight of God.

e   You are beginning a year during which all will be particularly aware of the powerful hand of God, which will be stretched out over the world to help it through the irresistible force of his merciful love.

f   And so, my sons, events which you cannot imagine are awaiting you.

g   But there are also the prayers of the good, the sorrows of the innocent, the hidden sufferings of many, the tears and supplications of numerous victims scattered throughout the world. Through them, I have hastened the time of my extraordinary intervention.

h   The Church, my beloved daughter, is now emerging from a great trial because the battle between me and my Adversary has been waged, even at her very summit. Satan has attempted to infiltrate to the very point of threatening the rock on which the Church is founded, but I have prevented him from doing so.

i   Precisely when Satan was under the illusion that he had conquered, after God had accepted the sacrifice of Pope Paul VI and of John Paul I, I obtained from God for the Church the Pope who had been prepared and formed by me.

j   He has consecrated himself to my Immaculate Heart, and has solemnly entrusted to me the Church of which I am the Mother and Queen.

k   In the person and the work of the Holy Father, John Paul II, I am reflecting my great light which will become stronger the more the darkness envelops everything.

Obey Him in Everything

l   "Priests and faithful consecrated to my Immaculate Heart, children whom I have gathered from all parts of the world into my cohort for the great battle which awaits you, unite, all of you, about the Pope, and you will be clothed in my own strength and in my marvelous light!

m   Love him, pray for him, listen to him! Obey him in all things, even to wearing the ecclesiastical dress according to the desire of my heart and his will which he has already made known to you. Offer me the suffering you may experience if, because of this, you are sometimes ridiculed by your own confreres.

n   For the Church too, which has a sure guide in the person of the Pope, the time of purification will be shortened, in accordance with my loving plan.

o   This then is your hour, the hour of the apostles of my Immaculate Heart.

p   Spread courageously the Gospel of Jesus, defend the truth, love the Church; help all to flee sin and to live in the grace and the love of God.

q   Pray, suffer, make reparation! (. . .)"

231

The First Sign: Confusion

a "Beloved sons, take refuge in my Immaculate Heart.

b The glorious reign of Christ will be preceded by a great suffering which will serve to purify the Church and the world and to lead them to their complete renewal.

c Jesus has already begun his merciful work of renewal with the Church, his spouse.

d Various signs indicate to you that the time of purification has come for the Church: the first of these is the confusion which reigns there. This in fact is the time of its greatest confusion.

e Confusion is spreading within the Church, where everything in the field of dogma, liturgy and discipline is being subverted.

f These include truths revealed by my Son and which the Church has defined once and for all, through her divine and infallible authority.

g These truths are unchangeable, as the very truth of God is unchangeable. Many of these form part of real mysteries in the strict sense of the word, because they are not and never can be understood by human intelligence.

h Man must accept them with humility, by an act of pure faith and firm trust in God who has revealed them and proposed them to men of all times, through the *Magisterium* of the Church.

i But now there is spread abroad a most dangerous tendency of wanting to penetrate and understand everything—even mysteries —to such a point that only that part of the truth is accepted which can be understood by human intelligence. There is a desire to unveil the very mystery of God.

j Any truth which is not understood by reason is rejected. There is an inclination to propose all revealed truth in a new and rationalistic way, under the illusion of making it acceptable to all.

There Is No Longer Any Belief

k   Thus truth is being corrupted with error. Error is being spread in a most dangerous way, namely, as a new and modern way of understanding the truth; and it ends by subverting the very truths which are the foundation of the Catholic faith.

l   They are not denied openly, but they are accepted in such an equivocal way that doctrine is most seriously compromised by error in an unprecedented manner.

m   As a result, talk and discussion go on and on, but there is no longer any belief, and the darkness of error spreads.

n   The confusion which tends to prevail within the Church and to subvert its truths is the first sign which indicates to you with certainty that the time of her purification has come.

o   The Church is in fact Christ who is living mystically in your midst.

p   Christ is the Truth. The Church must therefore always shine with the light of Christ who is the Truth.

q   But at present, its Adversary has succeeded, through his subtle and deceitful works, in bringing much darkness into its interior.

r   And today the Church is darkened by the smoke of Satan.

s   Satan has first of all bedimmed the understanding and the thinking of many of my children, seducing them through vain-glory and pride, and through them he has darkened the Church.

t   You, beloved sons of your heavenly Mother, you, the apostles of my Immaculate Heart, are being called today for this purpose: to fight by word and example that the truth may be more and more accepted by all. Thus the darkness of confusion will be defeated by the light.

u   For this reason, you must live the Gospel of my Son Jesus to the letter.

v   You must be, purely and simply, the living Gospel. Then you must proclaim to all, with strength and courage, the Gospel which you live. Your words will have the power of the Holy Spirit who will fill you, and the light of the wisdom given you by your heavenly Mother. (. . .)"

169

The Second Sign: Lack of Discipline

a   "Contemplate your heavenly Mother as she presents herself at the Temple to offer her little Child.

b   He is the Word of the Father, made man; He is the Son of God through whom the universe was created; He is the awaited Messiah to whom Prophecy and Law have been directed.

c   And yet, from the very moment of his human conception, He becomes obedient in all things to the will of the Father: 'Behold, I come to do your will, O God.' And from his very birth, He submits himself to all the prescriptions of the Law: after eight days, the circumcision and today, after forty days, the presentation in the Temple.

d   Just as every other first-born, mine also belongs to God, and He is ransomed by the prescribed sacrifice. From the priest, He returns to my arms that He might be offered anew by me through the wound of my Immaculate Heart, already pierced by a sword; and thus our 'yes' to the will of the Father is pronounced together.

e   Beloved sons, when I appeal to you to become littler, in my arms, it is to make you like my child, Jesus, through docile and perfect obedience to the divine will.

f   Today my heart is wounded anew by seeing so many of my beloved sons who live without docility to the will of God, because they do not observe and often openly disdain the laws proper to their priestly state.

g   Thus lack of discipline is spreading in the Church and reaping victims, even from among her very pastors.

h   This is the second sign which indicates to you that the Church has reached the final time of her purifications: a lack of discipline which has spread throughout all levels, especailly among the clergy.

i   *It is lack of discipline* to be wanting in interior docility to the will of God, a lack of discipline which is manifested by the flouting of those obligations which are proper to your state of life: the obligation to pray, to give good example, to lead a holy and apostolic life. How many there are, among the priests, who allow themselves to become absorbed in excessive activity and who no longer pray! They habitually neglect the Liturgy of the Hours, meditation and the recitation of the holy rosary. They limit their prayer to a hurried celebration of Holy Mass.

j   And so my poor sons become interiorly empty and no longer have the light and strength to resist the many snares amidst which they live. They thus become contaminated by the spirit of the world and accept its way of life, share its values, take part in its profane manifestations, allow themselves to be conditioned by its methods of propaganda and, in the end, come to adopt its very mentality. And so they end up by living as ministers of the world, according to its spirit which they justify and propagate, thus provoking scandal amongst many of the faithful.

k   From this springs the growing rebellion against canonical norms which regulate the life of priests, and the recurring objection to the obligation of sacred celibacy, desired by Jesus as expresed by his Church, and which has at this time been once again strongly reaffirmed by the Pope.

l   *It is lack of discipline* to disregard with ease the norms which the Church has laid down for the regulation of liturgical and ecclesiastical life.

m   Today each one tends to direct himself according to his own tastes or free choice, and with what scandalous facility are violated the norms of the Church, which have been reaffirmed again and again by the Holy Father, such as the obligations for priests to wear the ecclesiastical dress!

n   Alas, sometimes the first to continue disobeying this prescription are the pastors themselves, and it is their bad example which then fosters lack of discipline in all sectors of the Church.

o   This disorder, which is spreading in the Church, indicates to you with clarity that the final moment of her purification has come.

p   What must you do, beloved sons of your heavenly Mother, apostles of light of my Immaculate Heart?

q   Let yourselves be carried in my arms, as my tiniest babes, and I will make you perfectly docile to the will of the Father.

r   Thus to everyone you will give a good example of perfect obedience to the laws of the Church, and your heavenly Mother will be able to make use of you to restore order in her house so that after the suffering, the triumph of her Immaculate Heart may shine forth in the Church."

170

The Third Sign: Division

a   "I am your Immaculate Mother.

b   I appeared on earth, in the poor grotto of Massabielle, in order to point out to you the road you must walk in these difficult times.

c   It is my road: that of purity, of grace, of prayer, of penance.

d   It is the road which my Son Jesus has already pointed out to you, to lead you all to the Father in his Spirit of Love. You have within you his own Spirit which causes you to cry out to God as Father because He has shared his divine nature with you.

e   Walk the road of love. Make place within you for the Spirit of Love which is bringing you, in life, to be more and more united.

f   Love one another as Jesus has loved you, and you will become truly one. Unity is the perfection of love.

g   And so Jesus has desired that his Church be one, to make of her the sacrament of God's love for men.

h   Today my Immaculate Heart trembles and is anguished to see the division within the Church.

i   This division, which has penetrated the Church, is the third sign which indicates to you with certainty that the final moment of her painful purification has come.

j If, in the course of the centuries, the Church has many times been torn by division which has led many of my children to separate themselves from her, I nevertheless obtained from Jesus the singular privilege of her interior unity.

k But in these times, my Adversary has, with his smoke, suceeded in darkening even the light of this divine prerogative of the Church.

l *This interior division* is manifesting itself even among the faithful who often set themselves one against the other, in an attempt to defend and better promote the truth. Thus the truth is betrayed by even them, as the Gospel of my Son cannot be divided.

m This interior division sometimes even leads priests to set themselves against priests, bishops against bishops, and cardinals against cardinals, for never before as in these times has Satan so succeeded in finding his way into their midst, rending asunder the precious bond of their mutual love.

n *This interior division* is expressed by the tendency to leave to himself and to abandon, so to speak, the very Vicar of Jesus, the Pope, who is a son particularly loved and enlightened by me.

o My Mother's Heart is wounded to see how the silence and neglect of my children often envelop the words and actions of the Holy Father, while he is increasingly struck and impeded by his adversaries.

p Because of this interior division, his very ministry is not sufficiently supported and furthered by the whole Church whom Jesus has wanted to be united about the successor of Peter.

q My motherly heart grieves to see how even some pastors refuse to let themselves be guided by his enlightening and trustworthy words.

r The first way of being separated from the Pope is that of open rebellion. But there is also another way, more subtle and dangerous. It is that of proclaiming one's unity openly, but of dissenting from him interiorly, letting his teaching fall into a void and, in practice, doing the contrary of what he says.

s Oh, Church, mystical body of my Jesus, in your painful journey to Calvary, you have reached the eleventh station and you see yourself wrenched and torn in your members, which are again nailed to the cross!

t   What must you do, my sons, apostles of my Immaculate and Sorrowful Heart? You must become a hidden seed, ready even to die for the internal unity of the Church.

u   And so I am leading you each day to a very great love for, and fidelity to, the Pope and the Church united to him. For this reason I am now letting you share in the anxiety of my motherly heart; for this reason I am forming you in the heroism of sanctity and leading you with me up calvary. Through you also, I wil be able to help the Church emerge from her painful purification, so that in her all the splendor of her restored unity may be manifest to the world."

171

March 3, 1979
First Saturday of the Month

The Fourth Sign: Persecution

a   "Remain, all of you, in the refuge of my Immaculate Heart and you will find your peace and interior serenity.

b   My beloved sons, the storm which I foretold at Fatima has now unleashed its fury for the purification of the Church and all the world. This is the hour of the Father's mercy which, through the love of the Son's divine Heart, is made manifest at the moment when everyone's suffering is at its greatest.

c   The fourth sign which indicates to you that the culminating period of the Church's painful purification has come, is persecution. The Church is in fact being persecuted in various ways.

d   *She is being persecuted by the world* in which she lives and journeys, pointing out to all the way to salvation. The real enemies of God are those who set themselves deliberately against God, in order to lead all humanity to live without Him; it is they who are persecuting the Church more and more.

238

e   Sometimes she is persecuted in an open and violent manner; she is despoiled of everything and prevented from preaching the Gospel of Jesus.

f   But in these times, the Church is often subjected to an even greater ordeal; she is persecuted in a subtle and imperceptible manner, by being deprived bit by bit of the oxygen which she needs to live. Then an attempt is made to bring her to compromise with the spirit of the world, which thus enters into her and affects and paralyzes her vitality.

g   Collaboration is often brought about through a most subtle form of persecution; an outward show of respect for her has become the surest way to strike her.

h   A new technique has been discovered by which she can be put to death with no outcry and without shedding blood.

i   The Church *is being persecuted also from within*, especially at the hands of those sons of hers who have reached a compromise with her Adversary. He has succeeded in seducing even some of her very pastors. Some of these are even knowingly collaborating in this plan of interior and hidden persecution of my Church.

j   My beloved sons are being called to the trial of finding themselves sometimes obstructed, pushed aside and persecuted by some of their own confreres, while those who are unfaithful have free scope for their action.

k   The same hours of suffering that my Son Jesus lived through are awaiting you too, beloved sons: the hours of Gethsemane, when He experienced the interior agony of being abandoned, betrayed and denied by his own. . .

l   If this is the road trodden by the Master, it is also the road which you too must tread, you his faithful disciples, as the purification of the entire Church becomes more painful.

m   Have confidence, beloved sons, apostles of my Immaculate Heart!

n   No other trial will serve so much to bring about the complete renewal of the Church as this interior persecution. In fact she will emerge from this suffering purer, more humble, more enlightened, stronger.

o You must be ready to suffer more and more, the closer the final moment of purification comes. And so I have wished to prepare a safe refuge for you.

p In my Immaculate Heart you will be consoled and formed in the virtue of fortitude, as you become more and more aware of the presence of your heavenly Mother at your side. She will gather up all your sufferings, as beneath the cross she did those of Jesus, because she must now carry out once again for the Church her maternal function as co-redemptrix, and lead back to the Father all the children who have gone astray."

172

Your Liberation Is Near

a "Beloved sons, consider with me the signs of the times in which you are living. The hearts of men have grown cold and the world has become a desert.

b But you should have all the more confidence in your heavenly Mother! Look, with me, at the times in which you are living and you will see the signs of my extraordinary intervention.

c When the first buds appear on the trees, you reflect that winter is now coming to an end and that a new spring is near.

d I have pointed out to you the signs of the cruel winter through which the Church is now passing, by way of a purification which has now reached its most painful peak. The spouse of my Jesus appears again covered with wounds and obscured by my Adversary, who appears to be celebrating his complete victory.

e He is certain that he has won the victory in the Church, by the confusion which has subverted many of her truths, by the lack of discipline which has caused disorder to spread, by the division which has attacked her internal unity and by the insidious and hidden persecution which has crucified her anew.

f But see how, in this most cruel winter of hers, the buds of a renewed life are already appearing. They tell you that *the hour of your liberation is near!*

A New Spring

g "For the Church, a new spring of the triumph of my Immaculate Heart is about to burst forth. She will still be the very same Church, but renewed and enlightened, made humbler and stronger, poorer and more evangelical through her purification, so that in her the glorious reign of my Son Jesus may shine forth for all.

h She will be the new Church of light, and even now her branches can be seen sprouting with many new buds: these are all they who have entrusted themselves to their heavenly Mother; you also are among them, you apostles of my Immaculate Heart.

i All of you are these buds, my little children, who have consecrated yourselves to me and who live by my own spirit.

j You are these buds, you faithful disciples of Jesus, who are desirous of living a life of contempt for the world and for yourselves, in poverty, in humility, in silence, in prayer and mortification, in charity and in union with God, while at the same time being unknown and scorned by the world.

k The time has now come for you to emerge from your hiddenness and to go out and enlighten the earth. Present yourselves to all as my sons, for I am always with you. Let faith be the light which illumines you in these days of darkness, and let it be zeal alone for the honor and glory of my Son Jesus which consumes you.

l Fight, sons of light, few though you still be! Many will follow in your footsteps and will become part of my cohort, because the hour of my battle has now come.

m In this most cruel of winters, it is you who are the buds which are burgeoning forth from my Immaculate Heart, and which I am placing on the branches of the Church, to tell you that her most beautiful springtime is at hand.

n   This will be for her like a new Pentecost.

o   Beloved sons, look with my eyes at the times in which you are living.
p   Persevere in prayer, in suffering and in hope because the hour of your liberation is near."

173

Your Interior Equilibrium

a   "I am the Mother of the Incarnate Word.
b   By my 'yes' I offered to the Father my personal co-operation in his plan of salvation.
c   From the bosom of the Father the Word was placed in my maternal womb to assume from me his human nature. I became the true Mother of Jesus.
d   This 'yes' to the will of the Father blossomed in my soul as the fruit of a long and silent preparation.
e   Behold the road your Mother travelled to reach this ineffable moment: that of humility, of trust, of filial abandonment, of silence, of intimate and profound union with God.
f   Already from my childhood, I offered myself completely to the Lord, putting myself as a slave at his service in perfect virginity, in hiddenness and in prayer.
g   My soul opened itself to an ever greater light, and my life was formed in detachment from all creatures in order to love the Lord perfectly, by fulfilling his will and listening to his Word. I fostered within myself a relish for seeking, for gathering in and for treasuring only the Word of God.
h   When the Father decided to place his Word in my virginal womb, He found your Mother ready to welcome Him with love and joy, being only intent upon the perfect fulfillment of the divine will.

i   My beloved sons, contemplate your Mother at the moment of her annunciation, as with her heart and her lips she says her 'yes' to the will of the Lord.

j   You too should learn always to say 'yes' to whatever the Lord now asks of you through the voice that comes to you from the Immaculate Heart of your heavenly Mother. You must no longer doubt! Do not seek elsewhere. Do not beg for confirmations or encouragement.

k   I have arranged, through this work of mine, that your support should be founded solely in my Immaculate Heart. I will cause every support to collapse about you and I will not allow you to put your trust in purely human encouragement or approval.

l   My sons, from you too I desire littleness, humility, hiddenness, silence and trust.

Filial Abandonment

m   You must tread the same road as your heavenly Mother: that of intimate union with God, of detachment from all creatures and of perfect service to the Lord. I am bringing you to say 'yes' always to whatever Jesus asks of you. How few there are, even among those specially chosen by me, who know how to say 'yes' to Jesus! . . .

n   Tread with me the road which I am pointing out to you and along which I am leading you, letting yourselves be guided with docility and filial abandonment. I am training you to listen to the Word of God that it may be received, understood, loved and treasured by you, and put into practice.

o   In these times of purification, many are led astray by other words. In fact, my Adversary succeeds in seducing even the good by false manifestations of the supernatural in order to bring about deception and confusion on all sides. He will succeed in working many prodigies which will beguile the minds of even the good.

p   As for you, remain within the refuge of my Immaculate Heart, and there listen to the Word of God which the Church guards, interprets and proclaims. Never before as at the present time has the Pope had such light with which to lead you along the road of clarity and truth.

q   Within my Immaculate Heart I will build up your interior equilibrium, my beloved sons, because today you have need of being ever more prudent and well-balanced.

r   This equilibrium will be a sign to all of what your heavenly Mother is doing in you and will assure the Church of finding in you faithful and wise sons. . ."

174

April 13, 1979
Good Friday

Near My Son and My Sons

a   "Today my place is here: near my Son who is suffering.

b   The will of the Father so disposed that I would not be near Jesus during his interior agony in Gethsemane, because the very absence of his Mother would make his abandonment more complete.

c   'If it is possible, let this chalice pass from me.' But in my soul, during the night, I remained ever near my Son.

d   Through prayer and suffering, I truly shared in all his agony in order to comfort and help Him, by uniting my 'yes' to his in saying: 'Father, not my will but yours be done.' And when the angel was sent to Him from heaven to comfort Him, he passed by me also, in order that I might place in his chalice all the love of my motherly heart.

e   Today my place is here: near my Son who is dying.

f   The meeting takes place on the road to Calvary, after Jesus has been betrayed, denied and abandoned by his own. Of the twelve, there remains only one, whom I take by the hand to encourage him and to give him strength to remain with us. The condemnation is written on the scourged body of Jesus and the thorns cover his eyes with blood.

g   It is here that I meet my Son: I am at his side to help Him die. I feel the nails which pierce his flesh, the tearing of his body hung on the gibbet, his labored breathing; I hear his voice as it grows weaker with words of prayer and pardon, and He appears to me to be dying.

h   But I continue to live, beneath the Cross, with a pierced heart and a wounded soul, still miraculously alive because, as a mother, I must help my Son to die. No one will ever understand the hidden mystery of this moment.

i   *Today my place is here: near my buried Son.*

j   And now my sorrow bursts forth as a flooding river bursts through all its embankments. My tears bathe his face, my laments cradle his body and with my hands I close the deep wounds, while my Immaculate Heart becomes his first sepulchre.

k   Then when night casts a veil over all things, the vigil begins for the mother. I am here, recollected in the faith which has never deserted me, in the hope which completely illumines me and in prayer which has become continual and unceasing as though to mark the passing of time which for me no longer has either day or night.

l   The fervent prayer of the mother penetrates heaven and is accepted by the Father who, to shorten my anguished wait, anticipates the moment of the resurrection of the Son.

m   *My place is here: near my risen Son.*

n   When Jesus comes to me in the light of his glorified body, receives me in his divine arms and bends down to kiss the wounds of my great sorrow, I understand that my mission on his behalf has been accomplished.

o   I am beginning my maternal mission for you, for the Church which has been born of his great suffering and mine.

p   *Today my place is again here: near all my sons.*

q   Till the end of the world, I will always be close to you, sons begotten of the death of my only Son.

r   Above all, I am with you during these moments of darkness and suffering, when you are being called to live out what Jesus endured during his redemptive passion.

s   I am always near you to help you to suffer, to die and to rise again, that the plan of the Father to be fulfilled and that, with Jesus, you too may rejoice in the glory of his kingdom of life."

175

The Woman Clothed in the Sun

a   "I have come from heaven to reveal to you my plan in this struggle which involves everyone, marshalled together at the orders of two opposing leaders: the Woman Clothed in the Sun and the Red Dragon.

b   I have shown you the road you must take: that of prayer and penance. I have called you to the interior conversion of your life.

c   I have also prepared a refuge for you that you may be brought together, protected and strengthened during the present tempest which will become even more violent. The refuge is my Immaculate Heart.

d   I am now announcing to you that this is the time of the decisive battle. During these years, I myself am intervening, as the Woman Clothed in the Sun, in order to bring to fulfillment the triumph of my Immculate Heart which I have already begun through you, my beloved sons.

e   Sufferings will be asked of you but, in my Immaculate Heart, you will be called to taste as well the intimate joy of my motherly love.

f   The darkness will grow deeper, but the ray of light which comes from my heart to show you the way will become even stronger. Sin will cover everything, but you will be helped by me to clothe yourselves in divine grace which must become ever more resplendent within you that you may give a witness of holiness to all.

g   Listen to my voice with humility and docility. (. . .)"

176

Jesus in the Eucharist

a   "My beloved sons, continue to walk trustingly along the road on which your heavenly Mother is leading you. My plan is about to be fulfilled through you who have responded to my motherly invitation.

b   Second my action, the purpose of which is to transform you interiorly, in order to make you all priests according to the Eucharistic Heart of Jesus. The triumph of my Immaculate Heart cannot take place except in the triumph of my Son Jesus, who will reign once again in the hearts, the souls and the lives of each person and nation: in all humanity.

c   But as Jesus is truly in heaven, so also is He truly present on earth in the Eucharist: with his body, his blood, his soul and his divinity.

d   His glorious reign will shine forth above all in the triumph of his Eucharistic person, because the Eucharist will once again be the heart and center of the whole life of the Church.

e   Jesus in the Eucharist will become the focal point of all your prayer, which should be a prayer of adoration, of thanksgiving, of praise and of propitiation.

f   Jesus in the Eucharist will once again be the center of all liturgical action, which will unfold itself as a hymn to the Most Holy Trinity, through the continual priestly action of Christ which will be carried out in the Eucharistic · mystery.

g   Jesus in the Eucharist will once again be the center of your ecclesial gatherings, because the Church is his temple, his house which has been built above all that his divine presence may shine forth in your midst.

h   Beloved sons, in these present times the darkness has alas obscured even the tabernacle; around it there is so much emptiness, so much indifference, so much negligence. Each day, doubts, denials and sacrileges increase. The Eucharistic Heart of Jesus is wounded anew by his own, in his own house, in the very place where He has taken up his divine dwelling in your midst.

i   Become again perfect adorers and fervent ministers of Jesus in the Eucharist who, through you, makes himself again present, immolates himself anew and gives himself to souls.

j   Bring everyone to Jesus in the Eucharist: by adoration, by communion and by a greater love.

k   Help everyone to approach the Eucharistic Jesus in a worthy manner, by cultivating in the faithful an awareness of sin, by inviting them to present themselves for the sacrament of Holy Communion in the state of grace, by educating them in the practice of frequent confession, which becomes necessary before receiving the Eucharist for those who are in mortal sin.

l   Beloved sons, build a dam to hold back the flood of sacrileges. Never before as in these present times have so many communions been made in such an unworthy manner.

m   The Church is deeply wounded by the muliplication of sacrilegious communions! The time has come when your heavenly Mother says: enough!

n   I myself will fill up the great void about my Son Jesus, present in the Eucharist. I will form a barrier of love about his divine presence. I myself will do this through you, beloved sons, whom I wish to set up as a guard of love round about all the tabernacles of the earth."

177

San Miguel (Azores), June 23, 1979
Feast of the Immaculate Heart of Mary

In My Immaculate Heart

a   "Even in this remote archipelago you see my wonders. Today, from every part of the world, I am gathering you all into my Immaculate Heart. It is the refuge which your heavenly Mother has prepared for you.

b   Here, you will be safe from every danger and, at the moment of the storm, you will find your peace.

c   Here, you will be formed by me according to the plan which the Heart of my Son Jesus has entrusted to me. Thus each one of you will be helped by me to carry out in a perfect manner the divine will alone.

d   Here, I will give your hearts the capacity of love of my Immaculate Heart, and thus you will be formed in pure love for God and neighbor.

e   Here, each day I beget you to your true life: that of the divine Grace with which my Son has filled me, in view also of my motherly function on your behalf.

f   I am nourishing you, my beloved children, with this most pure milk, and clothing you with all my virtues. I am forming you interiorly and transforming you, because I am sharing with you my beauty and reproducing in you my image.

g   Thus your life is becoming daily more conformable to my motherly plan, and the Most Holy Trinity can reflect its light in you and receive greater glory.

h   My time has now come: this extraordinary intervention of mine must be clearly recognized by all.

i   Therefore it is my desire that the feast of my Immaculate Heart be once again celebrated throughout the Church, with the devotion and liturgical solemnity that had once been determined by the Vicar of my Son when times were very tempestuous.

j   Today everything is becoming worse and plunging headlong toward a most painful ending.

k   And so it must be apparent to the Church what that refuge is which I, the Mother, have prepared for all: my Immaculate Heart.

l   With the Holy Father, this beloved son of mine who is shedding upon the Church the light which comes from my heart, I encourage you all and bless you."

Fatima, July 1–7, 1979
International cenacle of priests of the M.M.P.,
coming from the five continents

In This Cova Da Iria

a   "I have called you from every part of the world and you, beloved sons, have replied with generosity to my maternal invitation.

b   You have come here in great numbers to this Cova da Iria, where I manifested myself from heaven, to give you a message of assurance and of salvation for these difficult days in which you are living.

c   United with you spiritually are all my beloved sons now scattered throughout all the parts of the earth.

d   Why have I wanted you here this year?

e   To press yo all to my Immaculate Heart.

f   What can a mother do when a great danger menaces her children? She can gather them in her arms and shut them up in a safe place, where they will be defended and protected.

g   And here is the shelter that I am giving you, the protection that you need: *my Immaculate Heart.*

h   In these days, I want to enclose you and all my beloved sons in the refuge of my heart, to give your filial hearts the same dimensions as mine, and thus to transform you into an every more perfect image of your heavenly Mother.

i   The time has come when all of you must live, without doubts or reservations, the consecration which you have made to me.

j   For this reason, I wish to put in the place of your little hearts, filled with sin, my Immaculate Heart, so as to give you my own capacity to love and thus transform the life of each one of you.

k   And finally I have wanted you here to give each of you my spirit, in such a way that I might truly live and work in you. The time has come when I wish to manifest myself through you to the whole Church, because the time of the triumph of my Immaculate Heart has come.

l   I am your heavenly leader.

m   I have wanted you here to gather you into my cohort, drawn up for battle, because now is the hour to go with me into combat.

n   Do not be afraid, apsotles of my Immaculate Heart, beloved sons of your heavenly Mother.

o   At the orders of the Vicar of Jesus, go into every part of the earth and spread the light which comes from my heart.

p   Soon you will understand fully the great gift which I have given to each one of you during these days; then you will all come to know why I have wanted you all here this year at Fatima, in a cenacle which has been full of extraordinary graces for you and for all my sons scattered throughout every part of the world."

179

July 29, 1979

Your Response

a   "Beloved sons, each moment I look at you with the eyes of a mother, because I want from all of you an ever more perfect response to the desires which I have already made known to you in many ways.

b   Only thus can you be ready for my great plan of love.

c   Only thus can you be made use of by me for the battle which has begun.

d   Only thus can you really form part of my cohort of which I am the queen and the leader.

e   In order that my plan may be carried out, I must also be able to count on the response of each one of you.

f   Let your response be generous, persevering and without reserve.

g   You must respond to the great gift which I have given you, letting yourselves be nourished, formed and led docilely by me.

h   Respond to my pressing invitation to be priests of prayer, focusing your every action on giving souls the light of the divine life of which you are ministers and dispensers. All your priestly prayer should be offered with me, on the altar of my Immaculate Heart.

i   Respond to my motherly invitation to suffer. It is thus that I make you ever more similar to my crucified Son that you may cooperate personally in his work of redemption. It is through your sufferings, my beloved sons, that I can intervene in order to spare much suffering on the part of many of my poor wandering children.

j   Respond to my invitation to walk towards that holiness to which I want to lead each one of you, because only thus can you be apostles of my Immaculate Heart, called to illumine the earth with the light of Christ, which must shine forth in your persons, in your lives and in all your apostolic actions.

k   It is in this way, beloved sons, that the whole Church can be renewed. And then, through you, my great plan of love can be accomplished for the triumph of my Immaculate Heart, which is the triumph of the merciful love of God in the world.

Each at His Post

l   On your response depends whether I will be able to count on you in the great battle against Satan and his powerful army, which has already begun.

m   I have told you that each of you has his post, prepared by me, a post which is unique and irreplaceable.

n   Do not ask me what your post is, or how I am making use of you, or where I am leading you, because the particular role which each one must carry out has, through my motherly love, been assigned to each and all of you. And in silence and humility, each one must carry out this role to perfection.

o   And so you must entrust yourselves to me with absolute confidence, you must believe in me, and you must let yourselves be led by me with docility and filial abandonment, without allowing yourselves to be stopped by doubts, or by the disbelief of those who surround you, or by your own desires, sometimes excessive, or by your curiosity which makes you want to know that which, for the present, you ought not to know.

p   I am your queen and your heavenly leader and I am bringing you together in my cohort, as I clothe you in my own invincible strength, terrible against my enemies.

q   So now, you must obey my orders.

r   Some are, however, still uncertain and insecure. They stop to ask confirmation and encouragement, and thus their response is neither prompt nor complete.

s   This is now the time for you to be confident, because the time to go into combat has come. Soon each one of you will understand the great task to which you have been assigned, by the special predilection of my Immaculate Heart. For now, beloved sons, I ask of each one a response without reserve, so that my great plan of love may be accomplished, and your battle waged according to my orders."

180

The Five First Saturdays

a   "Beloved sons, I look on you with motherly predilection and from all parts of the world I am enclosing you more and more in my Immaculate Heart.

b   These are the hours of battle, and therefore those weapons which I have prepared especially for you must be made use of: the consecration to my Immaculate Heart, the frequent recitation of the Holy Rosary, and the practice of the five first Saturdays of the month in reparation for the offenses committed against my motherly heart.

c   During these Saturdays, I invite you to unite yourselves with me in the prayer of the rosary, in the meditation of its mysteries, in confession, in taking part in Holy Mass and in a Communion of reparation.

d   To my daughter, Sister Lucy, I promised special protection at the moment of death and to obtain the graces necessary for salvation for all my children who, harking to my requests, will have devoutly carried out the practice of the five first Saturdays.

e   At this time, when the danger of being eternally lost is so grave, bring souls to safety by entrusting them to the particular protection of your heavenly Mother.

f   Today, reparation on the part of my children must also increase, because there is an ever increasing number of offenses committed against my Immaculate Heart, by insults against my Immaculate Conception, against my perpetual virginity, against my divine and universal motherhood and against my images and because, above all, the souls of the little ones are being alienated from me.

g   Through you, this filial and loving crusade of reparation must spread and grow.

h   Let the first Saturdays of every month be for you real encounters of reparative prayer and a generous response to the request which I have made of you. Above all, the religious and the faithful consecrated to my Immaculate Heart should, on these days, gather in cenacles of life with me.

i   Now, as the battle grows more violent, I must provide moments of spiritual peace and repose for all. In these cenacles you will enter into my repose because, by praying and making reparation with your heavenly Mother, you will be consoled and strengthened by me.

j   Thus, I will receive greater reparation from you, and you will receive new strength and light from your Mother, to walk along the difficult road of these times of yours."

Faithful, Prompt and Obedient

a   "I am your Queen.

b   I am calling you, my beloved sons, to become, each and all, faithful, prompt and obedient subjects.

c   You are being faithful when you always do what I ask of you, when you listen to my voice, and when you let yourselves be led by me with docility.

d   Your faithfulness should increase each day, by your perfect fidelity to the duties of your particular state.

e   In this you should be a good example to all.

f   Whoever is faithful to me, makes of his life a mirror in which I can reflect my image, and he spreads about him the perfume of all my virtues.

g   Whoever is faithful, moves ahead with confidence and abandonment along the road which I have pointed out, without looking to any creature, without waiting for human approval, without seeking support or encouragement, but entering more and more into the depths of my Immacualte Heart, he allows himself to be led by me along the way of the Cross until he reaches the summit of Calvary.

h   The degree of your fidelity, which I desire to bring to the point of heroism, will be able to be measured by how you know how to suffer, to be silent and to offer things up.

i   You are being prompt when you carry out my orders readily and without hesitation.

j   During these years, I have pointed out to you the road you must take. Why do you not follow it with confidence and trust? Why do some of you come to a halt, still uncertain and insecure?

k   My Adversary succeeds in bringing you to a halt with doubts, and paralyzes you with mistrust. I have already shown you my battle-plan, as I have formed you and led you by the hand to prepare you for the great battle which awaits you.

l   You are being prompt when you make use of the weapons which I have given you: prayer, your priestly prayer, the frequent recitation of the holy rosary, suffering, and your priestly immolation.

m   You must now be prompt to answer to the orders of your Queen, because you are about to enter into a most painful and decisive period.

n   Very soon all could come to pass. You will be called to live through serious moments, following him whom God has placed at the head of my cohort, the Vicar of my Son Jesus who, with strength and courage, is advancing toward his perfect immolation for which I have long been preparing him, ready to give his very life for me and for you.

o   You are being obedient when you give to all a witness of perfect docility to the norms which the Church prescribes for priests.

p   This is your livery, and I want you all to be clothed in it to make you invulnerable in combat: your silent, humble and perfect obedience.

q   Obedient to the Pope, to the bishops united with him and to the norms which regulate your priestly life.

r   I want you to be disciplined in everything, even in the smallest things. Say always and with promptness your 'yes' to the Father who calls you to follow his son Jesus who, for your sake, made himself a perfect example of obedience even to death on a cross.

s   If all are faithful, prompt and obedient, I will be able truly to reign in each one of you. And through you I will be able to reign also in the whole world, preparing the way on which Christ the King is about to come to restore in your midst his glorious reign of love."

An Anguished Appeal

a   "In the most venerated sanctuary of this great nation, so exposed to dangers, I have wanted you today to celebrate the feast of the birth of your heavenly Mother.

b   In your person, I bless all my beloved sons scattered throughout the whole world. I have led you everywhere to gather into the refuge of my Immaculate Heart all those priests who, swept away by the tempest which has now been unleashed, are running the great danger of being lost.

c   How many of my beloved sons are now responding with ever greater generosity, and are consecrating themselves to my Immaculate Heart!

d   All of you must hasten to entrust yourselves to me! Follow the example and the pressing invitation given you by the Vicar of my Son Jesus, who knows all and who perceives that the painful event, of which for years now I have been foretelling you, is now close at hand.

e   Yes, a little longer, until the time which the Father has ordained will be complete, and then the battle between me and my Adversary will break out in all its fury and enter its final phase.

f   I have prepared many of you for the supreme test. In my arms you will be immolated like little lambs so that, with the blood of Jesus, yours too may serve to purify the Church and to renew the world.

g   Others will have to undergo persecutions and sufferings such as you cannot now imagine. But have confidence because I will be at the side of each one of you, in an extraordinary way, to help you to fulfill my plan to the very last detail.

h   I must hasten, and I am making to you now, as it were, a last and anguished appeal.

i   Answer, each one of you, and entrust yourselves to me.

j   Be little, docile, humble, poor.

k   Be the most beautiful flowers about the crib of your infant

Mother, who smiles on you and blesses you all."

183

Nijmegen (Holland), September 29, 1979
Feast of the Holy Archangels

The Angels of the Lord

a   "You have just ended a cenacle with these sons of mine, so dear to me, who are suffering because of the torn and confused situation in which my Church here finds herself.

b   Unite your anguish with mine, and be the expression of the maternal benevolence with which I look upon them, receive them, comfort and lead them.

c   Pay no attention to the fact that they are few in number and, for the most part, frail because of age or poor health. They are nevertheless so faithful and generous that they console the great sorrow of my Immaculate Heart.

d   To me they are very precious treasures. And through them, even here, how numerous are the children who are responding to my invitation, entering into the refuge of my heart and are now being formed by me, in heroic fidelity to Jesus and his Church.

e   Thus in this very place where my Adversary has begun his work of subtle destruction of the Church, I am replying to the challenge and forming my cohort.

f   It is a cohort of the little, the poor and the humble whom I am gathering into my Immaculate Heart to give them my spirit of wisdom, that the pride of those who allow themselves to be seduced by false knowledge and the spirit of loftiness and vain-glory may be defeated.

g   Once again today, by means of this, my work, out of the mouths of babes and sucklings the Lord is receiving perfect praise.

h   With you also, are the angels of the Lord; I am their Queen and they are ready to follow my orders, because the Most Holy

Trinity has entrusted the work of the renewal of the Church and the world to my Immaculate Heart.

i Saint Michael is at the head of my entire heavenly and earthly cohort, which is now drawn up for battle. Saint Gabriel is at your side to give each one of you the very invincible strength of God, and Saint Raphael is healing you of the numerous wounds which you often receive in the great struggle in which you are engaged.

j Be ever aware of the angels of God who are at your side and invoke their help and protection often. They have great power to defend you and to rescue you from all the snares which Satan, my Adversary and yours, sets for you.

k Their protection will now intensify and will be particularly experienced by you, because the time of the great trial has come and you are about to enter upon a period of greater anguish than you have ever before experienced.

l At my orders, you will become aware of the angels of the Lord at your side. They will be your defense and your guide so that each of you will be able to carry out what I have determined for the triumph of my Immaculate Heart."

184

Lourdes (France), October 7, 1979
Feast of Our Lady of the Rosary

Your Rosary

a "Here also, I have brought you to gather many priests, religious and faithful into cenacles of prayer and life with me.

b I am truly present in these cenacles and I am joining in your prayer.

c By this prayer, you offer your heavenly Mother a powerful force in intervening for the salvation of many of my poor straying children and in disposing the painful events of your time according to the motherly plan of my Immaculate Heart.

d Your entire rosary, which you recite in the cenacle in accordance with the urgent request of your Mother, is like an immense chain of love and salvation with which you are able to encircle persons and situations, and even to influence all the events of your time.

e   Continue to recite it, and multiply your cenacles of prayer, thus responding to the invitation which the first of my beloved sons, the Vicar of Jesus, has so urgently made to you.

f   I am now able to make use of the power that comes to me from your prayer and I want to intervene as a Mother to shorten the time of the trial and to comfort you in the sufferings which await you.

g   Everything can still be changed if you, my children, listen to my voice and unite yourselves, through prayer, with the unceasing intercession of your heavenly Mother.

h   For this reason, here, where I appeared as the Immaculate One, I ask you again to continue with greater generosity and perserverance in the recitation of the holy rosary.

i   The rosary is the prayer which I myself came down from heaven to ask of you.

j   By it you are able to lay bare the plots of my Adversary; you escape from many of his deceits; you defend yourselves from many dangers which he puts in your way; it preserves you from evil and brings you ever closer to me, because I am able to be truly your guide and your protection.

k   As has already happened in other critical situations, so also today, the Church will be defended and saved by its victorious Mother, through the power which comes to me from you, my little children, by means of the frequent recitation of the holy rosary.

l   *Take courage, beloved sons!* Pray, have confidence and enter into the refuge of my Immaculate Heart, that you may form part of my victorious cohort.

m   This is my hour and soon the whole Church will be brought to a new splendor by her whom you invoke as Queen of Victories."

185

November 21, 1979
Feast of the Presentation of the
Blessed Virgin Mary in the Temple

In the Temple of My Heart

a   "Beloved sons, comtemplate your heavenly Mother as she is being brought to the Temple to offer herself in the perfect service of the Lord.

b   Although, from the very moment of my conception, I was already prepared for the sublime mission which had been entrusted to me, yet even for me a time of silence and more intense prayer was necessary.

c   In the Temple my soul opened itself to the light of the Spirit, who led me to the love and the understanding of his word. Thus, I was brought interiorly to participate in the most hidden mysteries, while the true meaning of divine Scripture became ever clearer to me.

d   In the Temple my body was offered in an act of continual holocaust to the service of God, which was carried out by me in prayer and in the joy of fulfilling perfectly the humble tasks that were entrusted to me.

e   In the Temple my heart opened itself to an act of pure and uninterrupted love of the Lord, while detachment from the world and creatures prepared me, each day more and more, to pronounce my perfect yes to his divine will.

Intense Recollection

f   Priests whom I so love, today you too must enter into the temple of my Immaculate Heart!

g   Now that my time has come, it is necessary for you also to enter into a time of more intense recollection and fervent prayer, which will prepare you to carry out your important mission.

h   In the temple of my heart, your soul will be filled with divine wisdom, which I am now giving you in greater abundance, that you may shine forth ever more brightly and shed your light in these days of darkness. Thus, you will help many of my poor wandering children to return to the arms of their Mother.

i   In the temple of my heart, your body will be purified in the fire of innumerable trials, in such a way that it may be conformable in everything to that of my Son and your brother, Jesus.

j   Jesus wants to live once again in you, in order to realize at this time the great plan of his merciful love, and to prepare for the coming of his glorious reign.

k   For this, He assimilates your mortal body into his glorious body, so that you in Him might participate ever more fully in his glory, and that He in you might share in your sufferings by means of your human frailty.

l   Once again, through you, Jesus returns to act, to work, to love, to suffer and to immolate himself for the salvation of all.

m   In the temple of my Immaculate Heart, your heart too will be purified, to be formed by me to a pure and incessant act of love for the Lord. I am leading you on the road of perfect love, that you too may follow your Mother in saying your yes to the divine will.

n   For this, you must enter into the temple of my heart. You have need of silence and of prayer, of detachment and of renunciation. Thus the design that God has on you will be revealed to you, and you will be free and ready to accomplish it to the end.

o   Only in this way can the great mission which I have entrusted to you be accomplished by you.

p   Take courage, my little children! My time has now come. And so, today, in the temple of my heart, I want to offer you all to the Most Holy Trinity, in an act of supreme reparation and of maternal supplication."

The Desert Will Blossom

a   "You are on the eve of your departure for Africa, for this great continent which I love with such a special love, because so many of my children live in great want and therefore have need of my motherly tenderness.

b   Go, and give to all the light which comes from my Immaculate Heart. Go forth with me in prayer, in love and in trust.

c   Each day, your Mother will cause torrents of grace and mercy to gush forth from the Heart of her Son, torrents which will water the earth and purify souls.

d   Beloved sons, you have been called by me to be, today, the workers of this divine wonder.

e   I want to act through you.

f   I want to manifest myself to the world through you. By means of you I want to give my light to souls.

g   And so I have called you from all sides to consecrate yourselves to my Immaculate Heart, that I may give you the grace to live habitually in me, and thus fill your little hearts with the plenitude of my love.

h   Love all your brothers with my heart, especially those who have lost their way today, and are in great danger of being eternally lost.

i   Love above all those who are furthest away, the sinners, the atheists and those who are rejected by everyone; love even the persecutors and the executioners. Say with love, 'Father, forgive them for they do not know what they are doing.'

j   For those who hate, those who kill, those who work violence, those who do evil, those who blaspheme, those who give scandal, bear only love and say, 'Father, forgive!'

k   How many of these brothers of yours you will one day find in paradise, drawn on the way of salvation by the irresistible force of your love!

l   For this, I have called you to prayer.

m   Your priestly prayer, offered with me and joined to your suffering, has incalculable power. Indeed, it has the capacity to bring about a far-reaching chain reaction for good, in which the good effects spread and multiply everywhere in souls.

n   Through it, you will always be able to reestablish equilibrium and to equalize the balance of the scale of God's justice.

o   Precious is your life of prayer: the Liturgy of the Hours, meditation, the holy rosary, but above all the lived-out celebration of Mass which truly renews the sacrifice of the Cross.

p   Oh, what weight Holy Mass has to compensate for, and to destroy, the evil which is daily brought about by so many sins and by such a widespread rejection of God!

q   And so I have called you to trust.

r   Now that darkness covers everything and the forces of evil are being unleashed with horrible fury, you must above all grow in trust.

s   God alone ever has been, and still is, in every circumstance, the victor, God conquers especially when He appears defeated.

t   Therefore you must today imitate your heavenly Mother in exulting in God and in singing his immense mercy.

u   You must believe that the Light will always shine, even in those times when the darkness will become deeper still. And the Light is Christ, and He must shine through you, his faithful disciples, prepared and molded in my motherly heart.

v   A great wonder is about to be accomplished in your time, even though for the present it is happening in silence and mystery.

w   In the struggle between the Red Dragon and the Women Clothed in the Sun, in which heaven and earth are taking part, the heavenly powers and those of hell, your Mother and Queen is each day accomplishing an important step in the realization of her victorious plan.

x   Therefore I say to you: soon the desert will blossom and all creation will become that marvellous garden, created for man to reflect in a perfect manner the greatest glory of God."

187

Nairobi (Kenya), December 3, 1979
Feast of Saint Francis Xavier

Look at the Heart

a   "Even in this great continent, where I am bringing you for the first time, you see everywhere the wonders of my Immaculate Heart.

b   Look at the heart of these children of mine: they are so poor, so simple and they love and honor me so!

c   Like all the very poor people in general, they are the most defenseless and the most exposed to being exploited by others. And so especially here, there is increasing activity on the part of my Adversary, who never, as in this continent, has unleashed his fury in such a violent and dangerous manner.

d   Through you, I want to offer today to these children of mine the secure refuge and the maternal protection of my Immaculate Heart.

e   Here also you are aware that my Movement has spread spontaneously everywhere. This is yet another confirmation that it is solely my work and that I act in silence and hiddenness. I continue to choose as my preferred instruments those whom no one notices, and who know how to be silent, to pray, to suffer and to love.

f   In this way, I can accomplish the marvels of love of my Immaculate Heart here also, among these children of mine who are suffering so much and in such need, who are so simple and good, and therefore so dear to me.

g   Have you observed how my beloved sons live amid such poverty, solitude and lack of understanding? And how they have managed to share completely in the painful life of so many of their African brothers?

h   Love each and every one of them, these beloved sons of mine. You yourself must be the expression of my motherly tenderness for them.

265

i Look at the heart of this whole people and there you will find
stamped the seal of love of your heavenly Mother.

j Look at the heart of your heavenly Mother and you will find
gathered there, in ever increasing numbers, children of every continent. The whole world is now held in my merciful hands, for
the coming triumph of my Immaculate Heart."

188

Douala (Cameroon), December 8, 1979
Feast of the Immaculate Conception

Mother of All

a "Today I am spreading my immaculate mantle over all the earth
and gaze upon you all with a mother's tenderness.

b On this day, I find you here in this small nation of such a great
continent. What poverty, what simplicity, what goodness have you
not encountered everywhere!

c I have caused you to love all these brothers of yours with the
heartbeat of the Heart of Jesus and that of my own motherly heart.

d Here too, you have met many of my beloved sons and daughters who have spent their whole lives amidst sacrifices and renun-
ciations, in order to bring the tidings of the Gospel to this land.

e And through them how very many have entered and become
part of the Church and of the one and only flock under the care
of the one sole Shepherd. Look before you at the immense spring
which is in preparation.

f Many of them are nevertheless still living in the error of paganism or belong to religions other than the true one which has been
revealed to you by Jesus, the eternal Word of the Father, to whom
He desires to lead you all in his Spirit of Love.

g These also must the heavenly Mother, together with Jesus, lead
to the fullness of the truth, as even now I gather all into my Immaculate Heart.

h   I am the Mother of all.

i   Especially of those who are furthest away, who are still walking in darkness. And in particular, I am the Mother of those who are poorest, simplest, most abandoned and most vulnerable.

j   And today, on the feast of my Immaculate Conception, I have wanted you here in prayer, in recollection and in suffering, to hold cenacles everywhere with me, so that you might be an expression of my maternal love and of my predilection for all these children of mine.

k   Thus here too, the triumph of my Immaculate Heart takes place daily, as the reign of Jesus extends more and more in hearts and souls bearing the standard of peace, of love and of joy.

l   With the Pope, the first of my beloved sons, I today bless all my children, especially those who are living in this great continent of Africa.

189

How Great a Light

a   "This is the holy night. Beloved sons, gather about me to welcome my divine Child.

b   There is so much darkness all about us.

c   And yet, an ever increasing light shines within the cave. And now it appears entirely from heaven, while the Mother is deeply absorbed in prayer.

d   How great a light descends from the bosom of the Father into the virginal womb of the Mother, who opens herself to his gift, to Life.

e   And completely enveloped in this divine light, I behold for the first time his body: his eyes, his cheeks, his lips, his face, his arms, his hands; I feel his little heart which has scarcely begun to beat.

Each beat is a gift of love which now will never again be quenched.

f   There is so much cold about us: the severity of the cold and the frost of those who have shut all doors on us.

g   But here, within the cave, there is a pleasant and welcome warmth. It is the shelter that this poor place offers us; it is the warmth of little things; it is the help which a little straw gives us, and a manger which offers itself as a cradle . . .

h   No place is so warm, now, as this most chilly cave. And the Mother bends happily over her Baby who has been given her by the Father, over her Flower finally come to bloom, over her Heaven now for ever opened, over her God who has been awaited for so long.

i   And my tears mingle with my kisses, while I gaze enraptured on my Son and my God, who has been born of me on this holy night.

j   There is still a great night lying over the world. There is a great cold freezing hearts and souls.

k   But the light has now conquered the darkness, and love has forever defeated all hate.

l   My beloved sons, on this holy night, keep watch in prayer. In my Immaculate Heart, remain in readiness.

m   His glorious return is now near. And new light and great fire will renew this world."

190

Your Last Hour

a   "Beloved sons, keep watch with me in prayer and trust.

b   This year, which has been for each of you one of extraordinary graces and gifts on the part of your heavenly Mother, is coming to a close.

c   From my Immaculate Heart, I have poured out upon you each day torrents of light and love. And thus I have nourished and clothed you, prepared and strengthened you.

d   Under my motherly and silent action, you have grown in your life of consecration, and in imitation of your Mother. You have become littler, more humble and docile, more trusting and strong.

e   I gaze on you, one by one, with motherly tenderness, sons singled out and nurtured by me in the garden of my Immaculate Heart, to be offered to the glory of the Most Holy Trinity.

f   In the course of this year, I have gathered up many from among you to take them up here into paradise, to form a great crown of glory for Jesus and myself.

g   You, on the other hand, are still to remain on this earth and to prepare yourselves to carry out whatever has already been prepared for each one of you, according to my plan of love.

h   You are now in your last hour: the hour of the great battle, the hour of the great immolation, the hour of the great victory.

i   But everything has already been prepared for you by me. Even the time has been measured in accordance with the beating of my heart, which no longer knows time. Here, all has already been accomplished which, in time, is yet to take place.

j   Here, I see you all at the end of the journey which you have yet to complete, living and sacrificing yourselves for the glory of God. Here, I see you already in the glory which awaits you, at the end of your painful sufferings.

k   You also should think of yourselves as being in the light of my Immaculate Heart, and live serene and content.

l   Live in joy, because your names have already been written in heaven. (. . .)"

1980

YOUR VICTORIOUS MOTHER

Your Victorious Mother

a   "Priests, whom I am calling from every part of the world to enter into the refuge of my Immaculate Heart, sons so loved by me and so exposed to dangers, begin this new year with great trust in your heavenly Mother!

b   Today the Church invites you to contemplate me and to venerate me as Mother. I am truly the Mother of Jesus and I am truly your Mother. I am your Mother because I have given you my Son Jesus.

c   So it is that the feast of Christmas becomes truly the feast of your whole life.

d   Because I am the Mother of Jesus, I have been able to become your Mother also. And as I carried out well my motherly duty in regard to my divine Son, so too must I now carry it out well in regard to you, my sons.

e   It is in the joyous mystery of my motherhood that the source of your trust and your hope, at the beginning of this new year, is to be found. You are now being called to enter a time in which great sufferings await you.

f   First of all, my Church will have to suffer as it is called to a more intense and painful process of purification.

g   I am close to it at every moment to help it and comfort it. The more the Church must ascend Calvary, the more will it feel my help and my extraordinary presence. It must now enter into the precious moment of its redemptive passion, in preparation for its most beautiful rebirth.

h   It is for this moment that, in my Immaculate Heart, a sure help has been provided for you: it is the Vicar of Jesus, the Pope, whom I have given you that he might be loved, listened to, and followed by you.

i   For him also, the hours of Gethsemane and of Calvary are now drawing near; and you, my beloved sons, must be his comfort and his defense.

j   The world too is beginning to live through its most dramatic and painful hours.
k   In this new year, many things that I foretold you at Fatima will come to pass.
l   Do not fear; have confidence!
m   At the most violent hour of the storm, you will see my great light grow brighter and more apparent; the Woman clothed in the sun, with the moon at her feet and about her head a crown of twelve stars!
n   This is the sign of my victory and yours!
o   It is your victorious Mother who today, with the Pope, the first of her beloved sons, gathers you all into her Immaculate Heart and blesses you."

192

A Great Net of Love

a   "Walk in trust.
b   The times foretold by me have come, and so you must leave to me all preoccupation.
c   I am your heavenly Mother and I am at the side of each one of you.

d   I am protecting and leading you.
e   I am sheltering and defending you. Do not be worried about what is going to happen to you, because everything has already been arranged in my motherly heart.
f   Humanity is now on the brink of that destruction which it could bring upon itself by its own hand. Indeed, that which was predicted to you by me at Fatima, concerning the final closing of this age of yours, has already begun.
g   How can I any longer hold back the hand of divine justice, when the perversion which humanity has reached, as it walks

along the road of obstinate rebellion against God, becomes greater day by day? How many nations could be involved and how
many people killed, while many others would have to undergo
unspeakable sufferings! . . .

h   Famine, fire and great destruction: this is what the scourge,
which is about to strike humanity, will bring you!

i   Beloved sons, heed, all of you, my urgent request; because my
Immaculate Heart trembles: it is in anguish at the fate which
awaits you.

Cenacles of Prayer

j   *Pray more and more.*

k   Pray together with me, through the recitation of the holy
rosary.

l   Pray and do penance that the times be shortened, and that the
greatest possible number of my children may be eternally saved.

m   Pray that suffering may serve to convert all those who have
strayed far from God.

n   Pray that you may never doubt the love of the Father, who
always watches over you and provides for you, and makes use of
suffering as a means of healing you from the sickness of corruption, of infidelity, of rebellion, of impurity, of atheism.

o   I now ask you for more prayer.

p   Multiply your cenacles of prayer.

q   Multiply your rosaries, recited well and in union with me.
Offer me also your suffering and your penance.

r   I ask you for prayer and penance for the conversion of sinners,
that even my most rebellious and most distant children may
return to God, who awaits them with the merciful eagerness of a
Father.

s   And then, together we will form a great net of love that will
envelop and save the whole world.

t   Thus my motherly and supreme intervention can be extended
everywhere, for the salvation of all who have gone astray."

193

February 2, 1980
Presentation of the Child Jesus in the Temple
First Saturday of the Month

Offer Yourself to the Glory of God

a "Beloved sons, let your heavenly Mother present all of you today to the Lord, upon her Immaculate Heart.

b The more complete the offering of yourselves which you make to me through your consecration, the better can I fulfill my motherly task, which is that of offering you to the perfect glorification of the Most Blessed Trinity.

c In the Temple of Jerusalem, I first offered my child, Jesus, according to the prescriptions of the Mosaic Law. And now I must also offer each of you, my little children, according to the will of my Son Jesus who, before dying on the cross, entrusted you to me.

d Beneath the cross, and by the will of Jesus, I became the true Mother of each one of you. And in what does my duty as Mother consist if not in offering you to the perfect glory of God?

e *I offer you to the glory of the Father.*

f As in your heavenly Mother, He wishes to see shine forth in you with increasing brilliance the great design He has imprinted on the masterpiece of his creation; thus is He able to receive today from you, his little children, his perfect praise.

g *I offer you to the glory of the Son.*

h He wants to see realized in you, his brothers, his own likeness in such a manner that he can live once again through you and love, pray, suffer and work in order that the Father may be ever glorified in you.

i And thus the Son lives again perfectly, through you.

j *I offer you to the glory of the Holy Spirit.*

k He communicates himself to you to bring you into the very heart of the divine life and to transform you into burning flames of love and zeal, in order to shed his most pure light everywhere.

l   And seeing you in the motherly arms of his spouse, who is reproducing her image in you, He is drawn to come down in fullness upon you and to communicate himself to you just as He communicated himself to her. Thus the Holy Spirit is being given to you increasingly as a gift by the Father and the Son.

m   In the temple of my Immaculate Heart, I offer you all today to the glory of the Most Holy Trinity.

n   I offer you as a sign of reparation, as a sign of motherly supplication and as a sign of perfect glorification, that God may receive this poor straying humanity and, through the great power of his merciful love, come to the aid of the world, purified by your reparative offering. Thus, by the Spirit of the Lord, the whole face of the earth will be renewed."

194

Under My Immaculate Mantle

a   "I look upon you, beloved sons, with my eyes of mercy.

b   This is the gaze of your heavenly Mother, which follows each one of you in every part of the world.

c   My motherly gaze falls upon you today with special pleasure and draws you gently to enter, each and all, under the protection of my immaculate mantle.

d   I want to bring you together in love which must grow constantly greater among yourselves, to the point of making you truly one.

e   Thus, I can give you to my Son Jesus to accomplish, according to his most intimate desire, that which He left you as his testament: 'As I and You, O Father, are one, so also may they be one in Us.'

f   And where can this unity be built up each day if not in the Immaculate Heart of your Mother, who loves you all and who is leading, gathering and uniting you?

g   I want to heal you of sin and of the consequences which it leaves in you: that sense of weakness and instability which so often casts you down and discourages you.

h   You feel so frail and insecure, so uncertain and fearful of again becoming victims of the evil that surrounds you.

i   You will not fall back into sin if you live ever under the immaculate mantle of your heavenly Mother!

j   Here, I heal your injuries, I pour balm on your painful wounds. I give you food that nourishes you and I clothe you in my most beautiful garments; with maternal firmness I mold you and lead you to sanctity.

k   Through you I call all my children, this day, to take refuge under my mantle, especially those who have wandered far from Jesus and from me, who have allowed themselves to be carried away by the present storm and now find themselves in great danger. They have, for that reason, greater need of my motherly help.

l   And so, let no one despair; let no one feel abandoned by me.

m   The hour has come when the love of your Immaculate Mother will shine forth resplendently for all."

195

March 1, 1980
First Saturday of the Month of Lent

With Jesus in the Desert

a   "Beloved sons, in this period of more intense prayer and penance, you too should go with Jesus into the desert. Offer yourselves with Him for the perfect carrying out of the Father's plan. Prepare yourselves for the important mission which awaits you, because my time has come and I must count with certainty on each one of you.

b   My plan does not correspond with yours, and my ways are not yours. You will be able to understand my plan and walk in my ways, only if you have a pure heart.

c   Blessed are the pure of heart because they will be able to see.

d   In the desert, your hearts will be made ever purer by me that, in the light of wisdom, you may see the plan of the Father and, as did Jesus, you too may dispose yourselves to carry it out, drinking to the last drop the chalice which has already been prepared for you.

e   For this, your hearts will have to be still more purified by me. The desert is the place where I bring you for this, my motherly work of purification.

f   *In the desert, Jesus suffered* hunger and thirst, the cold of night and the great heat of day.

g   In the desert, where I am leading you, you will feel great hunger and thirst solely for the word of God, while you will experience something like a nausea for all other words.

h   I will have you experience both the painful cold because of sin which has descended upon the world to make it cold and barren, as well as the burning heat of the Spirit of God who will diffuse everywhere the flame of his love so that all things may be renewed and all may thus flourish once again.

i   *In the desert, Jesus lived alone* and, with Him, I will bring you to interior solitude, detaching you from your own selves, from creatures, from the world in which you live and from your occupations, so that you may listen to the voice of the great silence.

j   It is only in the cradle of this great silence that your heart can be formed in the pure and perfect love of God and neighbor.

k   *In the desert, Jesus prayed* to the Father without cease. And so, with Jesus, I am leading you to prayer which must become unceasing and continous.

l   *Pray always: with your life, with your heart, with your work, with your pain, with your weariness, with your wounds.*

m   Oh, dear sons, it is only in the desert that your heavenly Mother can train you to have a taste for prayer, that in this way you may perceive always at your side the Father who loves you, leads you and protects you.

You Will Be Tested

n   *In the desert, Jesus was tempted.*

o   In this desert, into which I am leading you, you too will be tested by the fire of innumerable temptations and afflictions, and your faithfulness and confidence will be put to a great test.

p   My Adversary has been given a period of time in which to tempt you. Thus he will set snares for you in all sorts of ways with pride, with lust, with doubts, with discouragement, with curiosity. You will be sifted like wheat and many will be allured by his dangerous deceits.

q   Follow Jesus in ever resisting his seductions; above all be on the watch because today there are many false christs and false prophets, who are seducing many souls and bringing them to perdition.

r   Do not be discouraged, my dear sons, I am at your side to point out to you the snares of my Adversary and to help you overcome his seductions. Thus I am strengthening you with the word of God, which was the light that, during her life, guided your heavenly Mother.

s   In the desert, as was Jesus, you too will be prepared for the mission which you must carry out.

t   For this, your hearts must become purer, you must feel hunger and thirst for the word of God, you must pray and suffer in order to say, with your brother Jesus, upon my Immaculate Heart: 'Father, your will alone be done. You have taken delight in neither holocausts nor sacrifices; but you have prepared a body for me. O God, I come today to do your will.' "

My Yes and Yours

a   "Beloved sons, contemplate your heavenly Mother today, at the moment when she said her yes to the will of the Lord.

b   This yes blossomed in my soul as the fruit of much silence.

c   *In interior silence*, in which I habitually lived, disposing me to seek only the Word of God. In the most profound silence, the Word communicated himself to my soul, while my mind opened to receive Him and my heart closed itself in its jealous custody of Him.

d   *In exterior silence*, which withdrew me from clamor, from distractions and from the events that were taking place about me, in order to recollect myself for the perfect acceptance of the will of God, which I sought to fulfill in my humble and ordinary manner of living.

e   Thus silence hid the great plan of the Father, and when this was made known to me, yet still in silence I had to guard it jealously within my heart.

f   My motherly assent was therefore invisible and secret, since the Father alone awaited it and received it.

g   My yes blossomed from my heart also as the fruit of *much prayer*.

h   Now my life was completely an encounter of love with the Father, who, in secret, revealed to me ever more and more the mysterious plan of the Word, who was to become flesh in my virginal womb.

i   I understood the true meaning of Sacred Scripture and everything became clearer to me, concerning that to which I was being called. It was my duty to prepare myself to give my flesh and my blood to the Word of the Father, who was to make himself incarnate in my womb in order to offer himself on the cross as a sign of salvation for all.

Withdraw from the Clamor

_j   And so my yes was also a complete *assent to suffer*, because at that moment I welcomed into my virginal womb all the suffering of the Son.

_k   With my soul I saw, even before He was born, the wounds in his hands and his little feet, and the horrible gash in the heart, even before I felt its beating. I saw Him stretched on the cross, even before contemplating Him, newborn, in a crib.

_l   Beloved sons, contemplate your heavenly Mother today, at the moment when she spoke her yes to the will of the Father. You also are called to repeat it now, that the designs of the Father for you may be fulfilled. I welcome into my Immaculate Heart your yes, which each of you pronounces today. This yes must come to blossom in you as the *fruit of much silence.*

_m   Keep in your heart the Word of the Father; guard in the secret of your soul the plan which the Mother is revealing to you.

_n   Withdraw yourselves from the noisy clamor of the world. Shield yourselves from that surge of words and images, which sweeps everything before it and contaminates it. At the present time, almost no one knows how to keep this interior silence. It is in this way that my Adversary succeeds in leading you astray and in profaning hearts and souls.

_o   Say your yes that the will of the Father may be accomplished. In this way, you are called to penetrate ever more deeply into his own secrets.

_p   You do this by your prayer, which brings you to communicate with God.

_q   And thus you are able to become, today, the very voice of God, his word lived out. At the present time, Jesus asks only this of his priests, while He is being betrayed by many of them, who misuse his very own divine words.

_r   Pronounce with me your yes *to the cross*, dearest sons of mine, because for you also the hours of the passion and of Calvary have come.

_s   As in my virginal womb I received the Word of the Father, so also I enclose each one of you today in my Immaculate Heart,

while I already contemplate you at the moment of your offering of reparation.

t Your yes, my little children, within the yes which your heavenly Mother continually repeats, with joy, to her God! . . .

u Then, in you also, the will of the Father can be fulfilled, and my Immaculate Heart will become the altar upon which you will be immolated for the salvation of the world."

197

April 4, 1980
Good Friday

In His Greatest Abandonment

a "Beloved sons, remain today with me beneath the Cross.

b I am at the side of Jesus, who is dying, to envelop all his immense suffering with my mother's love. And I become totally associated with Him in the drinking of the bitter chalice of his great abandonment.

c Not here beneath the Cross are those friends and disciples; not here are all those who were helped by Jesus in so many ways.

d His divine gaze is dimmed because of this interior and so very human bitterness. And my mother's gaze opens out and ranges about, searching among those present for someone to offer to Him, to appease his painful thirst for love: 'I sought consolers but I found none.'

e Not here beneath the Cross is that crowd who sang hosannas, or the people who received Him rejoicing, or the multitudes fed by Him with his bread.

f There is here a group of poor children, blinded by hate and driven to inhuman ferocity by their religious leaders, to make the ingratitude yet more bitter for Him, and his abandonment more complete.

g Thus, for his pain there is scorn; for his falls, contempt; for his wounds, insults; for his immolated body, outrage; for the moans of his agony, blasphemies; for the supreme offering of his life, contempt and rejection.

h   The Heart of my Son is rent by this great abandonment, even before this is done by the lance of the Roman soldier.

i   The heart of the Mother is wounded by a sorrow so great that it cannot be assuaged by the presence of a few faithful persons.

One Has Stayed

j   Not here beneath the Cross are his twelve apostles. One has betrayed Him and already taken his own life; another has denied Him and is weeping, far away; the others have scattered and are filled with great fear.

k   But one at least has stayed with me: little John.

l   I hear his innocent heart beating; I see his fear, the fear of a bewildered little child; his sorrow, the sorrow of a sincere friend; and I press him to my heart to support him in the help which he is called to give me.

m   From the Cross, the gaze of Jesus, who is about to die at the moment of his supreme abandonment, is fixed intently upon the two of us and is illuminated by an infinite love: 'Woman, behold your son!'

n   And, beneath the Cross, where my Son has just died, I press to my Immaculate Heart my new child, who has just been born in such great pain.

o   Thus, all is accomplished!

p   Here, beneath the Cross, where I begot you, I want you today, beloved sons of mine.

q   At the moment when the Church is being called to live out the hours of her passion and her great abandonment, you are the sons I give her, that she may be consoled and helped by me.

r   And so, with John, stay all of you, beneath the Cross of Jesus, close to your Sorrowful Mother, that the Father's plan may be fulfilled!"

198

Have Confidence

a   "Do not let your heart be troubled. Have confidence in Jesus, risen and ascended to the right hand of the Father, where He has already prepared a place for each one of you.

b   Beloved sons, have confidence also in your heavenly Mother. My plan is enclosed within the heart of the Blessed Trinity.

c   *I am the Virgin of Revelation.* In me, the masterpiece of the Father is realized in such a perfect manner, that He can shed on me the light of his predilection. The Word assumes his human nature in my virginal womb, and thus can come to you by means of my true function as Mother. The Holy Spirit draws me, like a magnet, into the depths of the life of love between the Father and the Son, and I become interiorly transformed and so assimilated to Him as to be his spouse.

d   Through me, the great plan hidden in the very mystery of God is made manifest.

e   My Son Jesus is the manifestation of this mystery. In Him alone dwells the fullness of the divinity.

f   Through Him, all humanity is led back to full communion with the divine nature itself. Only with Him, can the great plan of the Father be accomplished.

g   *Have confidence, beloved sons!* In these present times, so dense with darkness and threats, look to your heavenly Mother. I will reveal to your souls the secret of the Word, become flesh in my maternal womb.

h   I will bring you to the full understanding of Sacred Scripture. Above all, I will read to you the pages of its last book, which you are living. In it, everything is already predicted, even that which must still come to pass. The battle to which I am calling you is clearly described, and my great victory is foretold.

For this reason, I repeat: do not fear; have confidence! In my Immaculate Heart, you will experience the joy and the peace that, even today, my risen Son gives to all of you."

199

The Same Dimensions As the World

a "You see here also the marvels of my Immaculate Heart. What a generous response I am receiving from my beloved children, especially from so many of the faithful who listen to me, love me and allow themselves to be led docilely by me!

b Have you seen how so many have come together, from every part of this nation, to take part in cenacles of prayer and to renew their consecration to my Immaculate Heart?

c By means of them, my heart grows ever larger to receive in ever increasing numbers my more needy children, so exposed to dangers.

d From every part of the world, they are hastening to enter into this refuge, which has been prepared by your Mother. Here they become illumined by my light, strengthened by my action, comforted by my motherly love and prepared according to my plan.

e And now my Immaculate Heart has the same dimensions as the world. It embraces all poor humanity, redeemed by my Son Jesus, and now so menaced by my Adversary, who has succeeded in extending his domain in it.

f And so, I am offering you, as a sign of salvation, the love of my Immaculate Heart, which has expanded to tremendous proportions to receive all my poor children, in need of my maternal intervention.

g My heart is stretched out like a great tent of peace and salvation, to gather you in from the stormy waves which would submerge the world!"

The Time of Battle

a   "This is my great battle!

b   What you are seeing and what you are living through forms part of my plan, hidden in the secret of my Immaculate Heart.

c   The Most Holy Trinity has entrusted to me the task of leading its army in the terrible struggle against Satan who, as ever, is the most astute and ruthless enemy of God.

d   God has entrusted the carrying out of his victorious plan to me, the littlest slave of the Lord, because the spirit of pride and rebellion may still be conquered by the humility and obedience of your heavenly Mother.

e   My Adversary has dared to attack the Most Holy Trinity, obscuring its great work of love and of glory.

f   He has obscured the work of the Father, by seducing other creatures to rebellion against God, by means of the spread of atheism to a degree that mankind has never before known.

g   To render fruitless the redemptive work of the Son, he has attempted to bedim his Church with error which has entered into her interior, and with infidelity which has spread like a terrible cancer. This has reached the point of confrontation with the Pope, whom Jesus set in the Church as the center of unity and as the guardian of truth.

h   He has obscured the work of the Holy Spirit, succeeding in extinguishing the light of divine life in many souls, through sin. It is readily committed and even justified by many; and by some, it is no longer even confessed.

i   But the 'Woman Clothed in the Sun' who has begun her great battle, continues to wage it each day through you, my faithful little cohort.

j   By means of you I want to restore to its splendor the work of creation, of redemption and of sanctification, in such a way that the Most Holy Trinity will receive the greatest degree of glory.

k   Do not become disturbed by the darkness which has spread about, because this is part of the plan of my Adversary; it is on the other hand part of my own victorious plan, namely, that of dispelling the darkness so that the light may everywhere return.

l   And the light will shine resplendently throughout creation when it will once again sing the love and glory of God, following on the defeat of every form of atheism and of proud rebellion.

m   The light of truth, of fidelity and of unity will once again shine fully in the Church. My Son Jesus will manifest himself fully in such a way that the Church will become light for all the nations of the earth.

n   I will make the light of grace shine in souls. The Holy Spirit will communicate himself to them in superabundance, in order to lead them to the perfection of love. (. . .)"

201

June 14, 1980
Feast of the Immaculate Heart of Mary

A Torrent of Water

a   "Beloved sons, today is your feast because it is the feast of the Immaculate Heart of your heavenly Mother, to whom you have consecrated yourselves.

b   Spend it in recollection, in prayer, in silence, in trust.

c   I have now imprinted my sign on the forehead of each one of you. My Adversary is no longer able to do anything against those who have been signed by their heavenly Mother.

d   The Star of the Abyss will persecute my sons, and therefore they will be called to ever greater sufferings; many will have to offer even their own life. It is with their sacrifice of love and of pain that I will be able to achieve my greatest victory.

e   I am the Woman clothed in the sun, I am in the heart of the Most Holy Trinity.

f   Until I am acknowledged there where the Most Holy Trinity has willed me to be, I will not be able to exercise my power fully, in the maternal work of co-redemption and of the universal mediation of graces. For this reason, as the battle between me and my Adversary enters its decisive phase, he has tried by every means to obscure the mission of your heavenly Mother.

g   In order to succeed in dominating the earth, the Red Dragon has set out first of all to persecute the Woman clothed in the sun. And the serpent has spewed out a torrent of water from his mouth at the Woman in order to submerge her and sweep her away.

h   What is this flood of water if not the ensemble of these new theological theories, by which an attempt is being made to bring your heavenly Mother down from that place where the Most Holy Trinity has put her? Thus it has been possible to obscure me in the souls, in the life and in the piety of many of my children, even to the point of denying some of those privileges with which I have been adorned by my Lord.

i   To take flight from this great torrent of water, the 'wings of a great eagle' were given to the Woman and thus she was able to find a place for herself in the desert.

j   What is this desert if not a place which is hidden, without noise, set apart and arid?

k   This place, hidden and silent and made arid by so many struggles and so many wounds, in which the Woman now finds a place for herself, is the soul and the heart of my beloved sons and of all who have consecrated themselves to my Immaculate Heart.

l   I am accomplishing the greatest prodigies in the desert in which I find myself. I carry them out in silence and hiddenness to transform the souls and the lives of these sons of mine who have entrusted themselves completely to me.

m   Thus each day I make their desert blossom within my garden, where I can still carry out my work fully and where the Most Holy Trinity can receive perfect glory.

n   Sons, let yourselves be transformed by my powerful action as

Mother, mediatrix of graces and co-redemptrix. Do not fear, because in the desert of your heart I have taken refuge and have set up my permanent dwelling place.

o Live in joy and confidence, because you have been marked with a seal by me and have come to form part of my property.

p Today I gather your little hearts into the immense, Immaculate and Sorrowful Heart of your heavenly Mother who watches over you with delight and blesses you together with the Pope, the first of my beloved sons, who sheds such great light upon all the Church."

202 *Fatima, June 29, 1980*

The Desert Where I Withdraw

a "Today I have wanted you here in Fatima, to conclude the cenacles which, during this year, I have been able to hold throughout Europe. My sons, I have accepted the generous response which you have made to me everywhere.

b This is my hour. This is also the hour of your battle, because the victorious action of the heavenly leader, the Woman clothed in the sun, will become more and more manifest.

c But for half a time yet, I must remain withdrawn in the desert. Here I work the greatest prodigies, in silence and hiddenness.

d You are the desert where I withdraw, you sons consecrated to my Immaculate Heart: that desert is your heart made arid by so many wounds, in a world flooded with rebellion against God and his law, marked with hatred and violence which spreads menacingly.

e Your parched hearts, your thirsting souls, sons: this is the place where the heavenly Mother now sets up her refuge.

f Because of my presence, this desert is transformed into a garden, cultivated by me with special care.

g Each day I water the aridity of your hearts with the tenderness of my immaculate love, the aridity of your souls with the grace with which I am filled because, as a Mother, I must distribute it to all my children.

h   Then I bind up your wounds with heavenly balm, I clean you by helping you to set yourselves ever freer of sins, of your numerous defects and of inordinate attachments. In this way I prepare and make fertile the soil of my garden.

i   Then I sow in you the seeds of love for my Son Jesus, that it may spring up and blossom in an ever more perfect and luminous way. And in his Spirit of love I cause you to open to the sun of the Father's good pleasure, so that thus the Most Holy Trinity may shine resplendently and be reflected in the heavenly dwelling place, built in my Immaculate Heart.

j   And thus you grow, cultivated by me, as little flowers which open only to sing the glory of God and to spread everywhere the splendor of his love.

k   I give you also the colors and the fragrance of my virtues: prayer, humility, purity, silence, trust, littleness, obedience and perfect abandonment.

l   Grow and develop, while each day I transform your desert into the most beautiful garden, guarded jealously by me. (. . .)"

203

July 13, 1980
Anniversary of the third apparition of Fatima

The Work of Co-Redemption

a   "Assent to my plan, beloved sons, and allow yourselves to be formed by your Mother. Thus I am able, more and more, to associate you with my maternal work of co-redemption.

b   Jesus is the only Redeemer because He alone is the mediator between God and men. He has however willed to take into partnership in his redemptive work all those who have been redeemed by Him, so that the merciful work of his love may shine forth in a greater and more wonderful way.

c   Thus you, who have been redeemed, can co-operate with Him in his redemptive work. He in you, who are so intimately united with Him so as to form his very Mystical Body, can gather in your day the fruit of what He accomplished once for all on Calvary.

d   I am for you the perfect model of your co-operation in the redemptive work accomplished by my Son. In fact, as Mother of Jesus, I have become intimately associated with Him in his work of redemption.

e   My presence beneath the Cross tells you how my son has willed to unite his Mother completely to all his great sufferings, at the time of his passion and his death for you.

f   If the cross was his scaffold, the pain of my Immaculate Heart was like the altar on which my Son offered to the Father the Sacrifice of the new and eternal covenant.

g   As Mother of the Church, I was also intimately associated with Jesus in the accomplishment of his redemptive work, which is carried out in the course of history, by offering to all men the possibility of accepting that salvation which He obtained for you at the time of his bloody immolation. Thus the more numerous they are who attain salvation, the more fully is the masterpiece of his divine love realized.

h   My task as a Mother is that of helping my sons in every way to attain salvation; and today still, it is that of co-operating in a very special way in the redemption accomplished by my Son Jesus. My role as true Mother and Co-Redemptrix will become manifest to all.

i   I want to carry out this action today through you, my beloved sons. This is why I have wanted to withdraw myself into the desert of your life, where I have set up my safe refuge.

j   In this way I mold you as a mother so that, through you, I may carry out the great work of co-redemption. And so, I call you to prayer, to the perfect offering of yourselves, to suffering, to self-immolation.

k   I lead you along the way of the cross and gently I help you to climb Calvary in order to transform you all into sacrificial victims pleasing to the Father, for the salvation of the world.

l   This is the time of my silent action. In the desert of your life, I daily work the great prodigy of transforming you more and more, that Jesus Crucified may again live in each one of you.

m   When this work of mine is completed, the greatness of the loving plan which I am now carrying out will become apparent to the whole Church. My merciful work of co-redemption has now become more necessary and urgent than ever.

n   The task which the Most Holy Trinity has entrusted to me will be acknowleged by all; I will be able to exercise my great power fully, so that the victory of my Son Jesus may shine forth everywhere, when He will restore, through you, his glorious reign of Love."

204

Mediatrix of Graces

a   "Beloved sons, I am the Mediatrix of Graces. Grace is the very life of God which is communicated to you. It springs from the bosom of the Father and is merited for you by the Word who, in my virginal womb, became man to share with you that same divine life, and for this He offered himself as a ransom for you, becoming thus the one and only mediator between God and all humanity.

b   From the bosom of the Father, grace, in order to reach you, must therefore pass through the divine Heart of the Son, who communicates it to you in his Spirit of love. Just as a ray of light, which passes through a window, assumes its shape, color and design, so too divine grace, merited by Jesus, can come to you only through Him and it is for this reason that it reproduces in you his own image, the very same image which shapes you ever more and more to his own person.

c   Divine life can reach you only in the form of Jesus, and the more this increases in you, the more you are assimilated to Him, in such a way that you can really grow as his little brothers.

d   By means of grace, the Father communicates himself to you ever more and more, the Son assimilates you, the Holy Spirit transforms you, bringing about a relationship of life with the Most Holy Trinity, which becomes ever increasingly strong and active. Within souls who are in grace, it is the Most Holy Trinity itself which takes up its dwelling place there.

e   This life of grace has also a relationship with your heavenly Mother.

f   As I am truly the Mother of Jesus and your Mother, my mediation is exercised between you and my Son Jesus. This is the natural consequence of my divine motherhood.

g   As the Mother of Jesus, I am the means chosen by God by which my Son can reach you. In my virginal womb this first act of mediation of mine is carried out.

h   As your Mother, I was the means chosen by Jesus that through me all of you may reach Him.

i   I am truly the mediatrix of grace between you and my Son Jesus. My task is that of distributing to my little children that grace which flows out from the bosom of the Father, is merited for you by the Son and is given to you by the Holy Spirit.

j   My task is that of distributing it to all my children, according to the particular needs of each one, which the Mother is very good at knowing.

k   I am ever carrying out this duty of mine. However I can carry it out fully only in the case of those children who entrust themselves to me with perfect abandonment. I am above all able to carry it out in respect to you, my favorite sons who, by your consecration, have entrusted yourselves completely to me.

l   I am the way which leads you to Jesus. I am the safest and shortest way, the necessary way for each one of you. If you refuse to go along this way, you run the danger of being lost in the course of your journey.

m   Today many have wished to put me aside, considering me an obstacle in reaching Jesus, because they have not understand my function as mediatrix between you and my Son.

n   And so, never before as in these present times, are so many of my sons running the risk of not being able to reach Him. The Jesus whom they meet is often only the result of their human research, and corresponds to their aspirations and desires; he is a Jesus formed according to their measure: he is not Jesus, the Christ, the true Son of God and of your Immaculate Mother.

o   Entrust yourselves to me with confidence and you will remain faithful, because I will be able to carry out fully my work as mediatrix of graces. I will take you each day along the way of my Son, in such a way that He may increase in you to his fullness.

p   This is my great work, which I am still carrying out in silence and in the desert. Under my powerful action as mediatrix of graces, you are ever more transformed into Christ, that you may become fit for the task which awaits you. Forward then, with courage, along the way traced out by your heavenly Mother. (. . .)"

205

The Powerful Weapon

a   "You are here in the place which I have prepared for you, for your rest. You have spent these past days in the unity of prayer and life with X . . ., whom I have given you as your little brother, upon whom I have great designs for this work of mine.

b   My beloved sons, how great is the love and the sorrow of my Immaculate Heart!

c   I look upon you with great tenderness. My light penetrates your life, your soul, your heart, your existence.

d   How many difficulties you must overcome: how many sufferings await you each day! Pain has become for you your daily food; and thus often you are brought to discouragement and distress.

e   Live in the immaculate love of my heart. Be little, poor humble! Accept, as a gift, your fragility. Never seek either to affirm yourself, or to stand out above the others. The way along which I am leading you is that of hiddenness and of humiliation.

f   Don't be curious to know what is awaiting you, but, at each moment, live in perfect love. Then you will be able to give yourself ever more for souls, because as you begin to do each thing there will be a corresponding help of the Lord, proportioned to your work. Go forward with courage, without ever stopping, carrying your cross, as your brother Jesus did on his journey to Calvary, along a way which seemed impossible and out of proportion to the little strength that remained to Him.

g   Your mission is sublime, and you must not let it come to a stop through weakness or human discouragement.

h   My time has come and soon I will leave the desert, in which I find myself, for the decisive phase of this battle of mine. I therefore have need of you and of the powerful weapon of your love, — pure, priestly love! Open your heart to the dimensions of my Immaculate Heart and then we will trace out a great path of light, along which my poor wandering children will be able to be led back and to be saved."

206

August 15, 1980
Feast of the Assumption of the
Most Blessed Virgin Mary into Heaven

My Glorified Body

a   "I am your Mother, assumed into heaven.

b   Today I gaze on you all with these merciful eyes and I enclose you in my Immaculate Heart, which never ceases to beat with love for you.

c   I am the Woman clothed in the sun. My glorified body is a sign for you of my complete victory. The eternal Sun of grace and love now illumines, penetrates and surrounds my glorified body, intimately associated in glory with that of my Son Jesus.

d   From my heart flows the fountain of my light, with which I wish to envelop and illumine this world filled with darkness. Hasten along in the wake of my immaculate light, let yourselves be drawn by the exquisite fragrance of my glorified body!

e   Beloved sons, in order to succeed in drawing you away from me, my Adversary now rages against you with great fury. He succeeds in sweeping down from the sky a third of the stars, and you too are these stars in the firmament of the Church. But how much greater is the number of those whose splendor becomes bedimmed!

f   Thus he ensnares you in every way; he fights you often through those souls who are closest to you and most loved by you, in order to bring you to discouragement, so as to extinguish in you the zeal and the fervor of your apostolic action.

g   Step out with perfect trust in your heavenly Mother.

h   Seek the answer for your thirst for love solely in my Immaculate Heart. Here you will not experience any disappointment. Here you will be led to the heroism of love. Here all your wounds will be bound up and healed and you will receive new strength and new enthusiasm to spend yourself for souls.

i   My Immaculate heart has a great design upon you, a design which is being realized at this very time.

j   Look to paradise into which your Mother has been assumed, and live on earth letting yourself be guided and led by her. Thus you will shed my light, and you will contribute ever more and more to the triumph of my maternal love in the souls and the lives of so many of my children infected with evil and hatred.

k   The desert of your life will blossom in my garden and you will spread about you the fragrance of all those virtues which here below adorned the soul and the body, now glorified, of your immaculate Mother."

The Rock of the Great Division

a "I have wanted you here today in this great city of this continent to begin cenacles, which you will be able to hold in many other states of this immense nation.

b Beloved sons, this is your hour. I am calling you all to fight along with me the final phase of the battle. Your MOther is on the eve of her greatest victory.

c In you I have chosen the smallest and poorest child, and I am taking you to every part of the world to gather all into my Immaculate Heart. By means of you I now receive from all sides the homage of your lives consecrated to me, and I fill your hearts with pure love for Jesus, so that you may thus save a great number of souls.

d I accept your suffering and I heal your many wounds. I love you with a motherly and merciful heart. I have special love for you because of your extreme littleness and fragililty. I am leading you because it is your duty to carry out the most important task at the moment of the decisive struggle.

e Look at the great light which my Immaculate Heart has given to the Church: it is the first of my beloved sons, Pope John Paul II. From this time on this light will become much stronger, as the struggle becomes more bitter.

f This Pope is a sign of my extraordinary presence at your side; he is becoming the stumbling-stone for all my enemies and the rock against which the great division will take place.

g He has been even here, and has spoken with firmness, but how few they are who follow his trustworthy and inspired teaching! . . . Even some of my beloved sons continue to ignore him, and thus slip into a greater darkness and the Church in this country becomes so ill and wounded.

h May you, sons consecrated to my Immaculate Heart, be living examples of love for, of fidelity to, and of full unity with the Pope. Thus you will draw a great number of poor, confused children along the road of unity and of salvation in the true faith.

i Within a short time the apostasy will become manifest; only those who will be with the Pope will be saved from the threat of shipwreck in their faith. With him, I bless you all and I encourage you to walk in trust and in filial abandonment."

208   Inverness (Florida—USA), September 8, 1980
                Feast of the Nativity of the Blessed Virgin Mary

He Will Come to You As Fire

a "Today, my beloved sons, I bring you together here in great numbers; you come from the most distant states of this nation to spend two days of cenacle with me.

b This is the time to gather together with me in prayer and in love, which must increase in your midst, so as to make you completely one.

c Through your persevering with me in prayer, I will be able to prepare you to receive the gift of the Holy Spirit, who wants to communicate Himself to you in an ever fuller way. This is his hour, because through his powerful loving action the whole world will be purified and renewed.

d He will come to you as an ardent and burning fire; He will come as witness of my Son, who has never been so despised and betrayed in his person and in his words.

e He will come to lead back the world to the perfect glorification of the Father. Prepare yourselves to receive this great gift, which my Immaculate Heart has obtained for you.

f I am your infant Mother. Look upon me in order to become littler. Your littleness is my great strength.

g Gather together today about my cradle and offer yourselves to me as little flowers, having the fragrance of love and of trust. And let us second together the will of the Father, so that what He has ordained for the salvation of the world, may soon be fulfilled."

The Sufferings of the Church

a   "I am your sorrowful Mother.

b   The sword, which pierced my heart beneath the Cross, continues to wound me through the great suffering which the Church, the Mystical Body of my Son Jesus, is living through at the present time.

c   All the sufferings of the Church are in my Immaculate and Sorrowful Heart. It is in this way that I still carry out today my maternal duty, begetting in pain this daughter of mine, to a new life. For this reason the function of the Mother becomes ever more important at the present time of its painful purification.

d   All the sufferings of the Pope, the bishops, the priests, of consecrated souls, and of the faithful are enclosed in my heart of a Mother.

e   I too share with you in living out these hours of great pain. And the Passion of my Son continues in his Mystical Body.

f   Today, with Him, for the Church I relive the very hours of Gethsemane, of Calvary, of the crucifixion and of his death.

g   Have trust and patience; have courage and hope! Soon from our pain will rise a new era of light. The Church will again flourish, under the powerful influx of the love of God. (. . .)"

A Great Design on This People

a   "Look at this immense archipelago and see how my work has also spread here, in an extraordinary way.

b   You behold my marvels in every part of the world. I have also revealed to you the times and the places where the triumph of my Immaculate Heart is being realized.

c   Look at the hearts and the souls of all these children of mine: they are so faithful to Jesus, so devoted to me, and so united to the Church. Through them the light of my heart is spreading through all the countries of this continent.

d   I have a great design on this people. They please me with their simplicity, their devotion, their great poverty, their humility and patience.

e   I am the Mother of all peoples. I look at the hearts of nations, to gather the seeds of good and to make them blossom in the garden of my Immaculate Heart, that I may save them in greater numbers, at the time of the decisive trial, when some of these will disappear from the face of the earth.

f   I look with tenderness and with joy at these children of mine, and I bring you into their midst to hold cenacles of prayer and to renew together the consecration to my Immaculate Heart.

g   Your coming is a sign of my special presence at their side. Give to me all the crowns of fragrant flowers with which they encircle you. They are signs of the great crown of love, which my children from every part of the world are now offering me, to take from me the painful crown of thorns. With you are the guardian angels, who lead you into the light, so that my garden may soon be filled with flowers.

h   And then the Church and the world will see the masterpiece of love, which for the present I am jealously guarding in my Immaculate Heart."

211

Manila (Philippines), October 13, 1980
Anniversary of the last apparition of Fatima

Do Not Sin Any More

a   "Today you are gathering here, in a cenacle of prayer, and recalling my final apparition at the Cova da Iria which was confirmed by the miracle of the sun.

b   From this land, dear to me for the love and devotion with which I am loved and venerated, I make again to the world the

300

anguished appeal which I made on that same day at Fatima and which summarizes, in a few words, the message which I came from heaven to communicate to you.

c   Do not sin any more!

d   Do not offend any more my Son Jesus, who has already been too much offended. Return to God by your conversion, along the way of prayer and of penance.

e   Alas, this message of mine has remained unheeded. And thus humanity has continued to hasten along the road of rebellion against God, in the obstinate rejection of his law of love. Thus it has come even to the denial of sin, to the justification of even the gravest moral disorders, in the name of a falsely conceived liberty. Thus Satan, my adversary, has succeeded in making you fall into his seduction.

f   Many have thus lost the awareness of sin and so, it is more and more committed and justified. The sense of guilt, which is the first step to take along the road of conversion, has practically disappeared.

g   Even in those countries of the most ancient Christian tradition, the great crime of killing children still in their mother's womb has gone so far as to be legitimized. This crime cries for vengeance in the sight of God.

h   This is the hour of justice and mercy. This is the hour of chastisement and salvation. The heavenly Mother intercedes before God for you because never, as in the present time, have you been so menaced and so close to the supreme test.

i   For this reason I beg you to repent and to return to God. Through you, sons especially chosen by me and consecrated to me, my apostles in these latter times, I want this anguished appeal to reach to the very limits of the earth.

j   From this blessed nation, upon which I have a great design of love and of light, I gather you all into the refuge of my Immaculate Heart."

The Marvels of Love and of Light

a   "I have brought you even to this new continent, to have you meet so many of my children, some of whom have come expressly for this from New Zealand and the most distant islands.

b   You see how my Movement has spread everywhere. (. . .) Now this light enwraps every part of the world; there is no place to which the sweet invitation of your Mother has not yet been brought. I have made use of you, the smallest and the poorest of my children, to make of you a messenger of peace, of mercy and of salvation.

c   My time has now come. The painful hours foretold by me have arrived. The great prodigy of the Woman clothed in the sun, who has decided to hasten the time of her victorious intervention, will be made manifest.

d   And so you see that everywhere my triumph has already begun. My mother's heart triumphs in the hearts of those children, who, on every side, answer me by saying yes. They are the littlest, the humble, the poor, the unknown.

e   In the heart of my children, who have accepted the invitation and have offered themselves to the love and the perfect glory of Jesus, each day the triumph of my Immaculate Heart is being prepared. Through them the glorious reign of Christ will soon come in all the fullness of power, of light and of victory."

213   *Melbourne (Australia), October 27, 1980*

The Way of Unity

a   "You see how my Adversary has succeeded in extending his dominion here, inducing so many of my children to get along without God, seducing them with the venom of atheism and of neo-paganism.

b   Never before as in these present times and in these places must the Church, which Jesus founded as a united body, present itself in all the power of its unity, that the light of the Gospel may reach out to all who are wandering.

c   I am the way of unity.

d   It is the Mother's role to lead back to mutual love, to concord and esteem, and to full communion all those who, by means of baptism, have been incorporated into the very life of my Son Jesus.

e   Some have wanted to put your heavenly Mother aside, precisely in the deceptive prospect of making the reunification of Christians easier. This on the contrary has brought about a new and more serious obstacle. In fact, disunity has entered into the very interior of the Catholic Church.

f   A true reunification of Christians is not possible unless it be in the perfection of truth. And truth has been kept intact only in the Catholic Church, which must preserve it, defend it and proclaim it to all without fear.

g   It is the light of the truth which will draw many of my children to return to the bosom of the one and only Church founded by Jesus.

h   A true reunification of Christians is not possible except in the perfection of love.

i   And who, better than your heavenly Mother, can help you to love, understand and have compassion for each other, to know and esteem each other? For this reason a true reunion of Christians is not possible without an effort towards interior conversion and purification, in order to attain solely the fulfillment of the divine will.

j   This is the divine will for you: that all may be one. And who better than I can help her children travel along this difficult road?

k   I am for you the way of unity. When I am accepted by the whole Church, then, as a Mother, I will be able to reunite my children in the warmth of one single family.

l   For this reason, the reunion of all Christians in the Catholic

Church will coincide with the triumph of my Immaculate Heart in the world. This reunited Church, in the splendor of a new Pentecost, will have the power to renew all the people of the earth.

m   The world will believe in Him whom the Father has sent, and will be completely renewed in his Spirit of Love. (. . .)"

214   *Calcutta (India), November 3, 1980*

Mother of the Poorest

a   "I have wanted you to come also to this great country to hold cenacles, to gather together in ever greater numbers my chosen ones, all these children of mine, in the refuge of my Immaculate Heart.

b   Most of them, however, are still living in ignorance of the Gospel, which my Son Jesus has taught you with the command given to the apostles, and passed on to you, to go and proclaim the Good News to all the people of the earth.

c   How many of these are still in the darkness of paganism or belong to other religions and therefore are in need of being led to the fullness of the truth, which is present only in the Catholic Church, founded by Jesus to bring the Gospel of salvation to all nations!

d   In no other place as this have you seen, however, how many of my children live in conditions of extreme misery and immense poverty. How many of them have neither home, nor work, nor food, nor clothing and, dressed in scanty rags, spend their lives on the sidewalks along the roads, where they suffer and die in the midst of general apathy and indifference.

e   Your coming is a special sign for them of my presence at their side, and of my painful motherly anxiety. I am the Mother of those who are ignored and abandoned by all.

f   Today I take all their suffering into the immense sorrow of my heart. I pour balm upon their wounds and I greatly value all the sufferings of these poor children of mine: the suffering of those who do not yet know Jesus and walk in darkness; the suffering of those who are cast aside and experience no help from anyone: the suffering of those who possess nothing; the suffering of those who live and die on the sidewalks along the roads, without anyone stopping to bring them help.

g I am the Mother of the poorest of the poor, of the most miserable, and my Immaculate Heart wants to bring them the help that they need: help to reach Jesus and to accept his Gospel of salvation – brought by so many of my missionary sons and daughters who, for this purpose, are expending their whole lives here and I am helping them to live with the dignity of sons of God, by a more becoming and human existence.

h I am now making myself the voice of these poor children of mine, who have no voice, to repeat to all: think of these brothers of yours, of those who even today are dying of hunger and need. Give to these little ones of mine that which you have in abundance! Do not busy yourself with gathering riches, when those goods which your Creator has put at the disposition of all should be distributed among all.

i I am the Mother of all, but especially of thoese who are poorest. I gather up their suffering and I bless it and I join it to the prayer of those who plead for the coming of the reign of Jesus, through the triumph of my Immaculate Heart. It will be a reign of truth and grace, of love and justice, and my poor children will have the best place in it."

215 *Bangalore (India), November 14, 1980*

The Power of the Gospel

a "What you have lived through here, my little son, is for you a sign that this is my hour, and that the heavenly leader has now gathered together her cohort from every part of the world.

b   Each day, in different dioceses, you have met in cenacles with hundreds of my beloved sons and with tens of thousands of religious and faithful, making in the cathedrals your consecration to my Immaculate Heart.

c   Through you who have responded, my light spreads ever more in the Church. And thus the Church takes on vigor, confidence and a new impetus in the evangelization and salvation of all nations.

d   Look at this immense nation and the huge number of my children, who still do not know Jesus and who walk in darknes, in the expectation that for these also the light of truth and grace may shine forth. This is the time when the Gospel of salvation must be announced to all the peoples of the earth.

e   And the Gospel must be preached to every creature, just as Jesus preached it to you, as the Holy Spirit gave it to the Church. The Gospel must be kept today to the letter. The Gospel must be lived today to the letter. The Gospel must be preached today to the letter.

f   The attempt, undertaken by many, to explain the Gospel in a purely human manner, to ignore its historical and supernatural content, to reduce to national interpretation that which is contained in it of a divine or miraculous nature, has brought about the weakening of its message and the enfeebling of the efficacy of its proclamation.

g   The power of evangelization is in its fidelity and its authenticity. It is not in the adapting of the message of Christ to the various cultures, but in the bringing of all cultures to Christ that the duty of evangelization, entrusted to you, is carried out.

h   How many of these children of mine would already belong to Christ, if today the power and the impact of evangelization were not weakened!

i   I am for you Mother and teacher. Just as I accepted, guarded and lived the Word of God, so too today I cause it to be accepted, guarded and lived by all of you, my little ones. The divine Word must therefore be lived and proclaimed by you to the letter.

j   And so I want to communicate to all of you an enthusiasm for the Gospel. Illumined by its light, announce it to all the peoples of the earth! I am Mother and teacher of all peoples, and the triumph of my Immaculate Heart cannot come in all its fullness, until I have brought them all to my Son Jesus.

k   Live in my Immaculate Heart and give Jesus to all the peoples of the earth. Soon the deepest desire of my Son will be fulfilled and, from every part of the five continents, under my guidance, all will hasten to enter into and become part of the one flock under the one Shepherd.

l   For now, I look with the tenderness of a mother on these children of mine, still far away, and through you I now bless them all and enfold them in my Immaculate Heart."

216

Great Mercy

a   "Beloved sons, I gather you all today under my immaculate mantle. It is the shield with which I cover you, to shelter you from every attack in the great battle to which I call you. You must gird yourselves once again with this powerful shield, which I give you for your defense and your salvation.

b   How numerous today are the snares of my Adversary, who appears to be reaching the peak of his great offensive! In every way and by the most subtle means, he seeks to seduce you, if only he can succeed in striking your soul, in wounding you with sin, so as to draw you away from Jesus, who is your only Savior.

c   The whole of humanity is defiled with this invisible venom, and now needs to be healed by the merciful love of Jesus. He will manifest himself to you in an extraordinary manner, through the intervention of your immaculate Mother.

d   The weapon, which I give you to fight with, is the chain which joins you to my Heart: the holy rosary. Beloved sons, recite it often, because it is only with your priestly prayer, gathered into my Immaculate Heart that I will be able, in these times, to move — to force, so to speak — the great mercy of the Lord to manifest itself.

e   At the hour when all will seem lost, all will be saved through the merciful love of the Father, which will be made visible through the greatest manifestation of the Eucharistic Heart of Jesus.

f   The standard, under which I rally you, is that of Jesus Cruci-fied, which must be displayed by you because, even for your perverse generation, there is no other salvation but in the Cross of Jesus.

g   With the rosary in one hand and the standard of the Crucified in the other, fight as of now the decisive phase of the battle.

h   This maternal intervention of mine is also being powerfully im-plored through the confident prayer of the first of my beloved sons, the Pope, who has called upon the mercy of God on your behalf.

i   This powerful cry of his has penetrated heaven and has moved my motherly heart to hasten the time of victory. (. . .)

j   For this I now gather you into my cohort and I give you the shield, the weapon and the standard for the battle. I strengthen you all and I bless you."

217

About the Crib

a   "Beloved son, this is the holy night. Spend it with me in prayer, in silence, in recollection, in waiting.

b   The day which I have spent, with the precious help of my spouse, in covering the final stage of an exhausting journey, has now gone by.

c   This has been the longest day of my life. But in the evening, as we enter the city which should receive us, every door is closed. At every request of ours a new refusal is ready for us.

d   And so the cold, which has so benumbed my members, begins to enter my soul and, like a painful sword, wounds me in the very depths of my life.

e   I must give you the Expected of the nations, at the very moment when no one receives Him. Love is about to be born and the chill of egoism shuts the hearts of all. Only the compassion of one poor soul points out a nearby cave.

f   In the darkness and the cold, near a manger on which a little straw has been placed, the divine prodigy takes place.

g   The stars, the song of the angels, the light which pours down from heaven; but about the crib there is only the warmth of two human hearts which love, the heart of my most chaste spouse and my virginal heart of a mother.

h   But for the Child who is born, the warmth of this love is enough.

i   Beloved sons, on this holy night, I want you all with me, about the crib of my divine Child.

j   Once again the doors of the houses are closed. The nations are in rebellion against the Lord who comes, and plot to fight against his royal dominion.

k   The greatest cold envelops the hearts of men. It is so cold in the world today! This is the coldness of hatred, of violence, of unbridled egoism. It is the coldness of the lack of love which kills.

l   But on this holy night, about the crib, with my heart and that of my spouse, Joseph, I want all your little hearts also.

m   Together let us love, let us pray, let us make amends, let us warm up by our love the baby Jesus, who once again is born for you. Your hearts, which love, are for Him his only comfort, his great comfort.

n   Through you, formed in the Immaculate Heart of your Mother, this little Babe wants to open the whole world to love. (. . .)"

The Greatest Cry

a   "Beloved sons, spend the last hours which close this year with me in prayer.

b   Your time is measured by the beating of my Immaculate Heart, which is shaping its plan of love and salvation. Each day, each hour is scanned and arranged according to this motherly plan of mine.

c   The moments you are living through are moments of emergency. This is why I have called you all to a more intense prayer and to live with the greatest trust in the merciful love of your heavenly Father.

d   The golden door of his divine Heart is about to open and Jesus is about to pour forth upon the world the torrents of his mercy. These are floods of fire and of grace, which will transform and renew the whold world.

e   On the waves of sufferings, never before known to this day, and of prodigies never before accomplished, you will reach the safe haven of new heavens and a new earth. An era of grace, of love and of peace is about to be born from the painful days in which you are living.

f   And so I invite you to end this year on your knees, uniting yourselves spiritually with the Pope, the first of my beloved sons, who is now suffering and praying so much, to implore the mercy of God upon the world.

g   May your prayer be a powerful force of intercession and of reparation. Let it be the greatest cry which has ever been heard, strong enough to pierce heaven and to constrain the Heart of Jesus to pour out the fullness of his merciful love.

h   For this, watch and pray with me. My hour and yours has now come. It is the hour of justice and of mercy."

1981

THE LIGHT AND GLORY OF THE LORD

The Only Possibility of Salvation

a   "Begin this new year in the light of my divine maternity. I am the way along which peace will come to you.

b   The inability of the men of today to establish peace, is caused by their obstinate denial of God. So long as humanity continues to go along the way of rejection of God and of rebellion against his law, you will have no peace. On the contrary, egoism and violence will increase and wars will follow upon wars, ever more cruel and bloody.

c   As has been many times foreseen, a third world-wide war, which will have the terrible capacity of destroying the greater part of the human race, can take place, if men do not seriously resolve to return to God.

d   The Lord is ready to pour out upon even your straying and so very threatened generation the floods of his mercy, only on the condition that this generation return with repentance to the arms of its heavenly Father.

e   I myself have sung of his divine mercy, which extends to all generations of men who acknowledge the Lord, and the one and only possibility of salvation for you is in this return to the love and fear of God.

f   On the first day of the new year, on which you venerate the joyful mystery of my divine maternity, I direct to you, my poor sons, my merciful eyes. With an afflicted soul and an anguished voice, I implore you to return to God, who awaits you with that love with which the father, each day, awaited the return of the prodigal son. (. . .)

g   I invite you to a loving crusade of reparative prayer and to works of penance. Together with me implore of God the grace of return for so many of my estranged children.

h   Multiply everywhere cenacles of prayer to compel the mercy of God to descend, as a dew, on the immense desert of this world. And prepare yourselves to see that which human eyes have never before seen.

I am the way of peace. Through me, all humanity is called to return to God, because only in its complete return can my mother's Heart triumph. (. . .)"

220

The Light and Glory of the Lord

a   "Entrust yourselves to me, beloved sons, with complete abandonment and with the greatest confidence in your immaculate Mother. As I did my own child, Jesus, I take you too today into my arms, to present you each day in the temple of the Lord.

b   Let yourselves be offered by me to God, on the altar of my Immaculate Heart:

c   *to be his light*, which must ever shine more and more in the midst of the darkness which has recently covered the earth.

d   The light shines, even though the darkness still does not want to receive it. This light must shine through you, my beloved sons, because this forms part of your priestly mission.

e   Spread about you the light of the truth which is contained in the Gospel, which is the very light of my Son Jesus.

f   My motherly duty is that of making Jesus live in each one of you, to his very fullness. Never before as in these difficult times is it so necessary that all priests be Jesus alone, lived and living, to be once again the light of all nations.

g   His merciful eyes in your eyes; his divine heart in your heart; his soul in your soul; his love in your love, to spread everywhere in the Church the fullness of this light.

h   *to be his glory*, which through you must be reflected in every part of the world.

i   At the same moment, in fact, in which humanity is experiencing the greatest rejection of God in all history, you are being immolated on the secret altar of my Immaculate Heart, to sing today the glory of the Father, the mercy of the Son and the love of the Holy Spirit.

j   The glory of the new people of Israel, called to prepare humanity for the return of Jesus.

k   The glory of the renewed Church, which will experience its new Pentecost of fire, of grace and of light.

l   The glory of a new humanity, purified in the great tribulation, now ready to live the ineffable moment of its complete return to the Lord.

m   This is a grave hour, my dear sons. Therefore live out each day, with love and faithfulness, the consecration which you have made.

n   Allow yourselves to be always carried in my arms as my little Jesus, leaving everything to your heavenly Mother, that for each one of you also the plan of the Father may be fulfilled."

221

I Look Upon You with Pleasure

a   "Beloved sons, you are called today to carry out a great task, which has been prepared for you in all its details by your immaculate Mother.

b   For years I have traced out the road for you. I have taken you by the hand and I have led you, supporting you and teaching you to take one step after the other, just as a mother does for her children.

c   How many times I have taken you in my arms, after each fall; how many times I have bound up your painful wounds, and have given you strength in your great weakness!

d   How many times, without your even having been aware of it, have I intervened personally to rescue you from the dangerous snares which my Adversary and yours sets each day for you!

e   And now I look upon you with the pleasures of a mother, who sees a reflection of herself in the life of her children.

f   My cohort is ready; my hour has come; my battle is already in its final phase. (. . .)

g   Walk in this light of purity. You must spread about you only the fragrance of my Son Jesus and of your heavenly Mother, who never knew sin.

h   Let the fragrance of the very life of God be in you: the fragrance of the grace which clothes you, of the wisdom which enlightens you, of the love which leads you, of the prayer which sustains you, of the mortification which purifies you.

i   Do not be troubled by the assaults of my Adversary, who rages at you with fury to rob you of the precious virtue of purity, which is mine and which I give—to those sons who respond to me and consecrate themselves to my Immaculate Heart—as a sign that they belong completely to me. No one will snatch you from my heavenly garden, in which I have gathered you with such care.

j   In it grow every day more beautiful and pure, to sing to all the glory of the Father, who is pleased to be reflected in you, of the Son who wants to be perfectly relived by you, of the Holy Spirit who gives himself to you with inexhaustible abundance. And thus, many of my poor sons, who are today in such great need of grace and purity, will be able to run and wash themselves at the fount of that immaculate love which is both mine and yours!"

222

Mortify Your Senses

s   "Beloved sons, accept the invitation to conversion which the Church offers you especailly at this time of Lent.

b　　At this time your heavenly Mother asks of you works of penance and of conversion. Prayer should always be accompanied by fruitful interior mortification.

c　　Mortify your senses, that you may exercise dominion over yourselves and over your unruly passions.

d　　Let the eyes be truly mirrors of the soul. Open them to receive and to give the light of virtue and of grace and close them to every evil and sinful influence.

e　　Let the tongue free itself to form words of goodness, of love and of truth and therefore let the most profound silence always surround the formation of each word.

f　　Let the mind open itself only to thoughts of peace and mercy, of understanding and salvation and never let it be sullied by judgment and criticism, much less by malice and condemnation.

g　　Let the heart be closed firmly to every inordinate attachment to self, to creatures and to the world in which you live, that it may open itself only to the fullness of the love of God and neighbor.

h　　Never as at the present time have so many of my fallen sons need of your pure and supernatural love, in order to be saved.

i　　In my Immaculate Heart I will fashion each of you in the purity of love. This is the penance which I am asking of you, dear sons; this is the mortification which you must perform, in order to prepare yourselves for the task which awaits you and flee the dangerous snares which my Adversary sets for you.

j　　In purity, in silence and in fidelity, daily follow your heavenly Mother, who leads you along the same road as Jesus Crucified.

k　　It is the road of renunciation and complete obedience, of suffering and of immolation.

l　　It is the road of Calvary which you also must travel, carrying your cross each day and following Jesus to the consummation of the Pasch. And thus you will also put at my disposal a great power of intercession with which I will be able to break open the golden gate of the Heart of my Son and pour out the fullness of his mercy. (. . .)"

"Yes, Father"

a   "Beloved sons, entrust yourselves to me and I will bring you to perfect docility to the will of the Father.

b   Just as it was for my Jesus, so too on the plan for the life of each one of you it is written: 'Behold, I come to do your will, O Lord.'

c   Your heavenly Mother wants today to help you fulfill well — and only — the divine will. This is the will of God: your sanctification!

d   By the gift of your sanctity, you place on the altar of the Lord a powerful force of intercession and reparation. For how many evils, how many sins reparation is offered each day on the part of my beloved sons who, led by their heavenly Mother, journey along the painful way of their own sanctification!

e   Do not look at the great evils which are still perpetrated and spread about by the highly refined means of social communication.

f   Under the ashes of the immense desert, to which this poor world has today been reduced, many new buds of life and salvation are sprouting. These are the lives, hidden and unknown but how precious, of my priests and of all those children whom I lead, each day, along the road to sanctity.

g   Let your yes to the will of the Father be realized in your daily effort to shun and to free yourselves from sin, to live in grace and in the fullness of love; in the effort to recollect yourselves in the intimacy of prayer and of life with Jesus, of reflection and of the understanding of his divine word; in the interior suffering in the face of the great abandonment and the solitude in which man today finds himself.

h   *Yes*, Father, to your will, that as in heaven, so also on this earth, your will alone may be done.

i   *Yes*, Father, that as in heaven, so may it be done on earth, abandoned as it is and never before so threatened as today.

j   *Yes*, Father, to your scorned love, to your outraged presence, to your spurned Word.

k   *Yes,* Father, to the gift of your immense mercy which shines forth in your Son whom, through the yes of the Virgin Mother, you have once for all given us, Jesus-salvation, Jesus-life, Jesus-truth, Jesus-fount of divine mercy, Jesus-perfect fulfillment of the divine will.

l   May your yes, beloved sons, be placed in the yes which the heavenly Mother forever repeats to her God: for the soon-to-come triumph over my Immaculate Heart in the triumph of mercy and love, of truth and justice. (. . .)"

224

April 17, 1981
Good Friday

Today the Passion Is Repeated

a   "Beloved sons, live with me today the Passion of my Son Jesus. Each day this painful Passion is repeated.

b   Enter, with me, into the depths of his divine Heart to savour all the bitterness of his chalice: the abandonment by his own, the treason of Judas, all the sin of the world which crushes Him under an impossible and deathly weight. As He is crushed in this olive-press, the drops of blood escape, trickling down his body and falling to irrigate the earth.

c   How heavily, even today, weighs on his Heart the ease with which so many turn their backs on Him, to follow the ideas of the world, or the ways of those who still reject and deny Him!

d   How many of his disciples daily sleep the slumber of indifference, of interior mediocrity, of doubt, of lack of faith!

e   Again the blow which the servant dealt to his face is repeated, and this one is more painful, this blow which his soul receives from the High Priest, as he accuses and condemns Him: 'You have heard the blasphemy! Since He proclaimed himself the Son of God, He deserves death.'

f There is another secret Sanhedrin which, every day, judges and condemns Him, often made up of those who, among his people, are invested with power.

g The attempt to recognize Him only as man continues: the tendency on the part of many to deny his divinity, to reduce his divine words to a purely human interpretation, to explain all the miracles in natural terms and even to deny the historical fact of his resurrection.

h It is this trial which is still going on; it is the same ignoble and unjust condemnation which is being repeated.

i See Him before Pilate, who tries Him and who has the grave responsibility of passing judgment on Him, and who would like to save Him. . . . But out of cowardice he subjects Him to cruel violence: the horrible scourging, which lacerates his innocent flesh and transforms his body into a single bloody wound, the crown of thorns, the condemnation and the impossible climb to Calvary. . . . Then the scaffold of the Cross, the agony and his death, with his Mother nearby, called to die with Him in spirit!

j Beloved sons, live with me in silence, in prayer and in suffering these precious hours of the Passion being repeated in the Church, which is his Mystical Body; it is being renewed in each one of you, called to be the ministers of his love and of his sorrow.

k Together with me, suffer the judgment, the rejection, the persecution of the world, and the condemnation on the part of a society which continues to deny its God and to walk in the darkness of perversion, of hatred and of immorality.

l Together with me, carry your heavy cross each day. Pour out, with love, your blood. Allow yourselves to be placed on the altar of his very scaffold.

m Meek as lambs, allow your hands and your feet to be also transfixed with nails: love, forgive, suffer and offer yourselves to the Father, with love, for the salvation of all.

n And then let your Mother place you in the new sepulchre of her Immaculate Heart, at the moment when the whole Church is called to live mystically this passion of condemnation and of death, in expectation of the hour of the resurrection. (. . .)"

225

I Have Come Down from Heaven

a   "You are journeying along the roads of many of the countries of Africa, of this great continent so dear to my heart for its poverty, its simplicity and the goodness of so many of its children.

b   This is the time when all are bound to become aware of my special motherly presence.

c   Give to all that light which comes from my Immaculate Heart. Give it especially to my dear missionary sons, whom I love with immense tenderness.

d   I, who gather up their every tear, who wipe away every drop of their sweat, who measure with joy their fatigue and count, one by one, their painful steps, how can I not express my motherly predilection for these sons who, for Jesus, have chosen to live here, amongst so many of their poor brothers, abandoned and still far from the Gospel in the midst of great sacrifices and much renunciation?

e   The light of my immaculate Heart now embraces all areas of the world, and my plan for the salvation and the comfort of all stands out with ever increasing clarity.

f   For this I appeared at Fatima to three little children.

g   I have come down from heaven to join you in your journey. Be aware then of the presence of your heavenly Mother at your side. It is a silent and serene presence. She wants to bring strength to your weariness, she sustains you in your work, she defends you from many dangers and leads you each day to carry out well whatever the Father has disposed for you, that the Most Holy Trinity may today be better glorified.

h   I have come down from heaven to manifest myself, through you, along all the roadways of the world: along those traversed by the poor and the desperate, along those lamentable roads of the sinners and the wanderers, along those of the sick, the agonizing and the dying.

i   To all those you meet anywhere along the way, you must give the light of my heart and the tenderness of my motherly love.

j   For this I want to form you ever more and more to the gentleness of love, to attentiveness to others, to complete availability to each and every one you meet along your way.

k   I have come down from heaven to live once again in you and to love with your heart, to sustain with your labor, to save through your sufferings many of my children who have gone astray and, never before as today, have such need of firm assistance.

l   Along all the roads come to your heavenly Mother. My Immaculate Heart is the refuge which gathers you all from all sides, to bring you to the God of mercy and of salvation.

m   With you and through you, I want to manifest myself, to save my children who are in such great need. For this I come down again from heaven to this poor suffering earth."

226   *Tananarive (Madagascar), June 7, 1981*
 Feast of Pentecost

"Come, Holy Spirit!"

a   "I am the Spouse of the Holy Spirit.

b   My powerful function as mediatrix between you and my Son Jesus is exercised above all in obtaining for you in superabundance, from the Father and the Son, the Spirit of Love.

c   By this divine fire, the Church must be renewed and transformed. By this fire of love, the whole world will be made new. At his powerful life-giving breath, new heavens and a new earth will at last be opened!

d   In the cenacle of my Immaculate Heart, dispose yourselves to receive this divine Spirit.

e   The Father gives Him to you to associate you intimately in his very own life and that the image of the Son, in whom He has made to repose all his pleasure, may shine forth in you ever more perfectly.

f   Jesus gives Him to you as the most precious fruit of his redemption, as witness of his person and of his divine mission.

g   Even in this distant land in which you find yourself today, brought here by me, to hold cenacles with so many of my children, you see the Gospel already spread, through the precious work of the missionaries.

h   Today the whole world must be brought to the fullness of the truth, to the Gospel of Jesus, to the one Church willed and founded by Christ, and this is achieved by the Holy Spirit.

i   The Church must be opened to his divine fire in such a way that, completely purified, it will be ready to receive the splendor of his new Pentecost, in preparation for the second, glorious coming of my Son Jesus.

j   Today I invite you all to enter into the cenacle of my Immaculate Heart in the expectation of receiving in fullness the Spirit of love which is given to you as a gift by the Father and the Son.

k   My Immaculate Heart is the golden doorway through which this divine Spirit passes to reach you. And so I invite you to repeat often: 'Come, Holy Spirit, come by means of the powerful intercession of the Immaculate Heart of Mary, your well-beloved spouse.' "

227   *San Marino-Valdragone, July 1, 1981*

This Is the Hour of My Victory

a   "Beloved sons, you are here in my house which I have prepared for you, and you are spending these days in a continuous cenacle of prayer and of brotherly sharing, together with your heavenly Mother.

b   I am always with you. I join in your prayer and I present it to the Father through my Son Jesus; I help you to know and love each other, and I lead you to the perfection of love. I pour balm on your wounds and I give you strength in your weakness. My wounded heart is consoled and my sorrow is transformed into joy by you, my little children.

c   But why have I wanted you here again this year? Because the struggle between your heavenly Mother – the Woman clothed in the sun – and her Adversary, the Red Dragon, has now entered into its conclusive phase.

d   What has taken place in these recent months has a profound significance, following on what has already been predicted regarding this time of purification in which you are now living.

e   In the Spirit of wisdom, know then how to read the signs of the times in which you are now living. For this reason I have called you and brought you up here, and given you strength because my great plan must now be accomplished.

f   But I can accomplish it only through you.

g   And so I await from you a complete response to my will. No more doubts, no more hesitation, no more uncertainty. How many of you my Adversary has paralyzed with these subtle and dangerous weapons of his!

h   Do not look to those about you; pay no attention to the criticisms you hear, to the scepticism which often surrounds this work of mine. Not to all is it given to understand my plan.

i   To you, my little ones, this has been granted by the Father through Jesus who, in his Spirit of love, has placed you in the cradle of my Immaculate Heart.

j   *Only in my Immaculate Heart is the source of your security.*

k   Here you are prepared by me for the great struggle which awaits you.

l   Here you are trained by me in prayer, because this is the weapon with which you must fight. Pray more. Pray always. Every action of yours must truly be a prayer. Live your Mass, which immolates you each day with Jesus. Pray well the Liturgy of the Hours, which consecrates to God the rhythm of your day. Recite the holy rosary with love and joy. Meditate on my words, which I have communicated to you these past years. They will bring you to understand the Gospel, which must today be lived by you and announced to all.

m   You cannot come down from this mountain without being transformed by me into living victims, offered by the Holy Spirit to the Father, for the salvation of the world and for the imminent coming of the glorious reign of Jesus.

n   Here you are being helped by me to suffer. And now, the cradle of my Immaculate Heart becomes an altar, upon which I immolate you each day, in order to appease divine justice and that the mercy of God may descend, like a rain, to renew the world.

o   For this, you are called to great suffering, following the first of my beloved sons, the Pope, who now, bathed in his own blood, is following the path that leads to Calvary along which, together with him, your heavenly Mother is leading you.

p   Here you are, above all, being formed by me to the perfection of love. All your brothers in the Movement are spiritually close to you and, during these days, extraordinary graces are being poured into the hearts of my beloved sons scattered throughout all parts of the earth.

q   The time has come when I wish to live in you and to manifest myself to all through you.

r   I want to love with your heart, to gaze with your eyes, to console and encourage with your lips, to assist with your hands, to walk with your feet, to follow your bloodied footprints and to suffer with your crucified body.

s   This is the hour of the final battle; it is therefore also the hour of my victory. And so I have called you once again and you have responded, and have come to this cenacle, where we are praying together, loving and invoking the Holy Spirit, whom the Father will give you in superabundance through the Son, that you may soon see new heavens and a new earth."

228

Refuge of Sinners

a   "Today paradise rejoices in contemplating the glorified body of your heavenly Mother, in whom the splendor of the Most Holy Trinity is reflected.

b   You too look upon me, and I will shed my light on you. In times of temptation, struggle and discouragement, look upon me and you will be encouraged and aided.

c   When you happen to fall or to feel the weight of defeat, when you are overwhelmed by evil and sin, come to me and I will give you support.

d   Today, looking with eyes of mercy on my sinful children, I say: —I am your heavenly Mother who invites you all to gather together under my immaculate mantle, to be protected and led to Jesus, your Savior.—

e   I AM THE REFUGE OF SINNERS!

f   At the moment when the fury of my Adversary is unleashed, and succeeds in sweeping away so many with the power of evil which is triumphing, I invite you, my beloved sons, to offer yourselves and to pray for the conversion and the salvation of all sinners.

g   You yourselves be, with me, the refuge of sinners, of the poor, the sick, the desperate, the little, the abandoned. From my glorified body I reflect my light upon your mortal body; from my Immaculate Heart I communicate my love to your ailing hearts; from my blissful soul I cause the fullness of my grace to descend upon your wounded souls. And so I now transform you, because I want to be, through you, a refuge for all my poor sinful children.

h   Come then to me and I will console you and lead you along the safe road which takes you up to paradise, where, in the light and the joy of God, you will attain the goal of all your earthly existence."

Mother of Mercy

a   "You have come once again to the largest country of this vast continent, to hold cenacles with my beloved sons and with all who have heeded my invitation and consecrated themselves to my heart.

b   The Church will become more and more aware of the powerful assistance which the merciful love of my Immaculate Heart gives it.

c   **I am the Mother of Mercy**. And my presence today will become stronger there where the Adversary has done greater damage and brought about greater devastation.

d   I am entering into the enclosure of the Church, which is so desolate, and there I am gathering the broken flowers in order to repair them, and those that are withering to give them back new life, and those that are bent over to straighten them up. I am trying to make beautiful once again this garden, which should blossom and give forth fragrance solely for the love and glory of Jesus. Here also, where the Adversary has so violated the Church, I want to exercise mercy in an extraordinary way.

e   And I am making use of you, my poor child, whom I have set up as the sign of my merciful love, because you have been called to bring to everyone confidence in my motherly heart.

f   Encourage, console, strengthen your brother priests. See how they are suffering! They are, as it were, abandoned and so discouraged, as a flock without shepherds, they who are called to be shepherds of the flock.

g   I want to be, with Jesus, their loving and understanding shepherdess. Let them follow me into the safe refuge which I have prepared for them: my Immaculate Heart. Bring light and strength to my poor children, bewildered as they are in the midst of the confusion in which they are living. Strengthen them in the faith and in their complete obedience to the Pope and to the hierarchy united to him, and confirm them in the truth; entrust them all to me, by the sincere and generous consecration of themselves to my Immaculate Heart.

h   I am pressed for time. Never as at the present time have you had such need of your heavenly Mother! For this reason, I desire to manifest myself through you. The time left to you is short. That you may be protected and defended, hurry—all of you—under the mantle of the Mother of Mercy."

230
Brasilia (Brazil), September 8, 1981
Feast of the Nativity of the Blessed Virgin Mary

By the Power of the Little Ones

a   "Gaze today upon your infant Mother. Learn to be little. If you do not change and become as little children, you cannot understand my plan. Its power lies in weakness, and its realization takes place each day in silence and hiddenness.

b   With the power of the Holy Spirit, which sets afire and renews everything, the kingdom of God will come to you through the way of littleness and humility.

c   If your heart is pure, it can open itself to the Holy Spirit, who comes to give witness in glory to the triumph of my Son Jesus. If your mind is docile, then you can understand and accept this invitation of mine.

d   By the power of the little ones my proud Adversary will be defeated; and the whole world will be renewed. Therefore, all of you, gather today about the cradle of your infant Mother, and repeat with me to the Lord: 'In my littleness I was pleasing to the Most High.' God has looked upon his servant in her lowliness, and thus He who is mighty has done great things in me; holy is his name."

Mother of All Sorrows

a   "I am your sorrowful Mother. Mine are all your sorrows.

b   At the present time, for you also sufferings and afflictions are increasing, because you are living at a period of time when the hearts of men have become cold, closed up by a great egoism.

c   Humanity is continuing to hasten along the road of its obstinate rejection of God, despite all my motherly admonitions and the signs which the mercy of the Lord continues to send it.

d   Thus the chill of sin, of hatred and of violence spreads increasingly, and the easiest victims are the most defenseless of my children and those most in need of protection.

e   How numerous today are the poor, the disinherited, and those who live in conditions of inhuman misery, without steady work, without means of livelihood; and how numerous are those who daily drift away from God and his law of love, swept away by the powerful cohort of those who teach atheism!

f   Humanity is living in a desert, barren and cold; and never before as now is it so threatened.

g   The pain of humanity is enclosed within my Immaculate Heart.

h   Today more than ever, I am the **Mother of All Sorrows** and tears are falling from my merciful eyes. Listen to me and do not withdraw yourselves from the love of your sorrowful Mother who wants to lead you all to salvation.

i   Beloved sons, at this time you must become the sign of my immense sorrow. In your hearts carry, with me, the suffering of the world and the Church, in this its new hour of agony and of redemptive passion. It will be only from this suffering of ours that a new era of peace for all can be born."

Montevideo (Uruguay), September 29, 1981
Feast of Saints Michael, Gabriel and Raphael

Queen of the Angels

a   "In the struggle to which I am calling you, beloved sons, you are being especially helped and defended by the angels of light.

b   **I am the Queen of the Angels.** At my orders, they are bringing together, from every part of the world, those whom I am calling into my great victorious cohort. In the struggle between the Woman clothed in the sun and the Red Dragon, the angels have a most important part to play. For this reason, you must let yourselves be guided docilely by them.

c   The angels, the archangels and all the heavenly cohorts are united with you in the terrible battle against the Dragon and his followers. They are defending you against the snares of Satan and the many demons who have now been unleashed with furious and destructive frenzy upon every part of the world.

d   This is the hour of Satan and of the power of the Spirit of Darkness. It is their hour, which coincides with the moment of their apparent victorious action. It is their hour, but the time which they have at their disposal is brief, and the days of their triumph are counted.

e   Therefore they are setting dangerous and fearful snares for you and you would not be able to escape them without the special help of your guardian angels. How many times each day they intervene to rescue you from all the treacherous maneuvers which, with astuteness, my Adversary undertakes against you!

f   This is why I call upon you to entrust yourselves more and more to the angels of the Lord. Have an affectionate intimacy with them, because they are closer to you than your friends and dear ones.

g   Walk in the light of their invisible, but certain and precious, presence. They pray for you, walk at your side, sustain you in your weariness, console you in your sorrow, keep guard over your repose, take you by the hand and lead you gently along the road I have pointed out for you.

h   Pray to your guardian angels and live out with trust and serenity the painful hours of purification.

i   Indeed, in these moments, heaven and earth are united in an extraordinary communion of prayer, of love and of action, at the orders of your heavenly Leader."

233   *Buenos Aires (Argentina), October 13, 1981*
Anniversary of the last apparition of Fatima

An Interior Wound

a   "Today you are at Lujan, in the most celebrated shrine of this great country, where I am so loved and venerated. With a cenacle, you are commemorating my last apparition at Fatima, which took place on this very day in 1917.

b   The entire plan which I am now carrying out was revealed to you at that time. You are entering into the most difficult and decisive period of time. You are living through the last years of this century in which a great part of the battle between your heavenly Leader and her Adversary has already taken place.

c   You are now living out its conclusive phase. For this reason I am preparing you each day, through confidence and prayer, to live through the most painful hours of all.

d   With the anxiety and concern of a mother, who sees how great the danger is through which you are passing, I beg you again to return to God who is awaiting you all to give you his forgiveness and his fatherly love.

e   **See with what great signs** I accompany this anguished appeal of mine!. . .With messages I have given and apparitions I have granted in many parts of the world, with my numerous weepings, even with blood, I want to make you understand that this is a grave hour, that the cup of divine justice is now full.

f   An interior wound has been inflicted on my motherly heart as I see that these extraordinary signs are neither believed in nor accepted.

330

g   What more can I do for you, my poor children, so menaced and exposed to danger?

h   In a final attempt to save you, I am giving you the secure refuge of my Immaculate Heart. I am calling you from every part of the world, through this work of mine, to enter into this refuge by way of your consecration.

i   And you, my little one who are led and guided by me, go into every part of the world to bring to all my motherly call. My hour has come. (. . .)

j   Raise up to the Father a powerful cry of supplication and reparation. From the divine Heart of the Son may rivers of mercy descend upon this world which, through the powerful action of the Holy Spirit, will be entirely renewed that in this the glory of God the Father may shine forth."

234

Peace Will Come to You

a   "In this country too, which I love so much, you have gone everywhere to hold cenacles with my priests and with many other children of mine. How much love and how much devotion to me you find along all the roads of the world!

b   The most generous response to my motherly invitation comes from the poor, the little, the humble, the suffering, the sinners. The thorns of my sorrow are thus transformed into flowers, and the tears into a smile.

c   Each day I see you increasing in numbers and in generosity, and from all sides the sound of your prayer, ever more pleasing, reaches me. How very dear I hold the rosary, which you recite so often in answer to the urgent appeal of your heavenly Mother!

d   How I welcome with joy your response to my sorrowful plea to consecrate yourselves to my Immaculate Heart, in the midst of the great indifference of the majority of my poor children.

e   Together let us keep on fighting and, each day, you will add new forces to my cohort, for the victory which has already been announced.

f   **From my Immaculate Heart, peace will come to you!**

g   At the moment when everything will seem lost, it is then that you will see the extraordinary prodigy of the Woman clothed in the sun, who will manifest herself in all her power.

h   The darkness will be conquered by a light which will cover the whole world; the cold of hatred, by the fire of love; the great rebellion against God, by a universal return to his merciful fatherly love.

i   Yes, my beloved sons, you too will have to suffer and some of you, in my Immaculate Heart, will be immolated, but through your generous response the time of the great trial will be shortened.

j   More quickly than you yourselves could think, there will come to you the reign of love and of peace of my Son Jesus, to whom alone is due honor and power and glory for ever and ever."

235

Quito (Ecuador), November 1, 1981
Feast of All Saints

The Communion of Saints

a   "I am the Queen of all the Saints. Today you are bid to lift up your eyes to paradise, where so many of your brothers have preceded you. They are praying for you and helping you, that that reign of Jesus, which in heaven is the cause of our joy and glory, may soon come also upon earth.

b   May this living communion with all your brothers who are already in paradise become ever more intense. The communion of the saints must be lived out still more fully at these times, because there is only one Church in which my Son Jesus lives and reigns and is glorified by his brethren, who are still struggling, or suffering, or rejoicing in eternal beatitude.

c   As you go about, bringing my invitation everywhere and gathering my children into my cohort, how greatly you are assisted, protected and defended by your brothers who have already attained these heavenly heights!

d   They form a crown of light about my Immaculate Heart. Each one of these lights is reflected on each of you, and illumines and guides you on your journey.

e   Your heavenly Mother wants to strengthen the bonds of love which unite you to heaven, so that you may daily benefit from the communion of the saints, and go forward united with them."

236

Puebla, November 12, 1981
Six-day cenacle for the Directors of the MMP in Mexico

The Great Trial

a   "You are gathered here for a continuous cenacle of one week, and my beloved sons have come from the most distant parts of Mexico, this land which loves me so much and which I am protecting with special solicitude and which I am defending from the many evils which are today menacing it.

b   I am your sweet and merciful Mother. Many years ago, I imprinted my image on the cloak of my little Juan Diego, to whom I appeared; today I want to imprint my image in the heart and the life of each one of you.

c   You are thus signed with the seal of my love, which distinguishes you from those who have allowed themselves to be seduced by the Beast and bear his imprinted blasphemous number. The Dragon and the Beast can do nothing against those who have been signed with my seal.

d   The Star of the Abyss will persecute all those who are signed with my seal, but nothing will be able to harm the souls upon whom I myself have impressed my image. By the blood which many of them will have to shed, divine justice will be appeased and the time of my victory will be hastened. (. . .)

e   By your prayer, your suffering and your personal immolation, I will bring my plan to completion. I will hasten the time of the triumph of my Immaculate Heart in the reign of Jesus, who will come to you in glory. Thus a new era of peace will begin and you will at last see new heavens and a new earth. (. . .)

f   I have great designs on you. Respond, each and all, with generosity! In this extraordinary cenacle, I have obtained for you from the Father, through Jesus, the gift of the Holy Spirit. He will transform you into 'apostles of these last times.' (. . .)

g   Give me your prayer, your suffering and your trust. Do not be afraid if my Adversary attacks you with terrible snares, to lead you to discouragement.

h   You are my very little children, my beloved sons, my apostles. Your light will increase day by day, and you will be a source of guidance and safety at the time of the great tribulation.

i   Pray, most dearly beloved sons, because for your homeland, as for all the world, the great trial has come."

237   *New York (U.S.A.), December 8, 1981*
Feast of the Immaculate Conception

On the Road of Perfect Love

a   "You are here today, on the feast of my Immaculate Conception, to conclude by a great cenacle this long and extraordinary journey, which has been strewn with true miracles of grace from my Immaculate Heart.

b   I am the Immaculate Conception.

c   I am your all-beautiful Mother.

d   I am the Woman clothed in the sun.

e   Being without the least shadow of sin, even of original sin, from which I was preserved by a singular privilege, I could reflect completely the plan which the Father had in the creation of the universe. Thus, in a perfect way, I could give the greatest glory to the Lord.

f   Because I was all-beautiful and full of grace, the Word of the Father chose me as his dwelling place and, stooping to my extreme littleness, through a divine prodigy of love, He descended into my virginal womb; He assumed his human nature and became my Son. Thus I became truly the Mother of Jesus and your true Mother.

g   Because I am truly your Mother, Jesus has entrusted to me the mission of begetting you constantly into his likeness, by leading you along the road of love, of divine grace, of prayer, of penance, of your interior conversion.

h   In this daily struggle against Satan and against sin, my place is that of victorious Leader.

i   I am today the Woman clothed in the sun, who is doing combat against the Red Dragon and his powerful army. The Holy Spirit gives strength and vigor to the great cohort of my little sons.

j   Jesus is awaiting the moment to establish, through you, his reign of love, to carry out the will of the Father in a perfect way. He will thus lead back all creation to its pristine glorification of God. (. . .)

k   Go forward with the very greatest confidence. Follow the light of your immaculate Mother.

l   I am covering you with my very own splendor, I am clothing you with my virtues, I am signing you with my seal, I am revealing to you the secrets of divine wisdom, **I am leading you each day along the road of perfect love.** From your mouths, little ones, may the Most Holy Trinity receive today praise and glory. You are the greatest joy of my Immaculate Heart: you are already part of my victory. Today I am casting my light upon you all, I am protecting you, I am consoling and blessing you."

In the Cradle of Suffering

a "Beloved sons, watch with me in prayer and in expectation. This is the holy night.

b At the moment when the greatest silence envelops everything, there unfolds upon earth the great prayer of the Mother, which penetrates heaven and opens it to send down upon you my divine offspring.

c I look into his eyes, I feel the beating of his little heart, I stroke, with my motherly hands, his little hands. I place Him in the cradle, made of a poor manger, in the penetrating chill of the night and the cold which closes the hearts of all.

d The cradle in which I place my heavenly child, on this holy night, is formed from the suffering and the pain of all. For this Christmas also, the prayer of your heavenly Mother becomes more intense. It embraces the suffering of all and the desperation of many of my children.

e I look at the sufferings of the Polish people, who have all been consecrated to me and who, in recent days, have been repeatedly entrusted to me by my Pope. They are living through the dramatic hours of their Calvary and carry the cross of a mortal suffering.

f I look, with motherly apprehension, upon their children, who are suffering from cold and hunger; upon their young people who have been imprisoned and deported; upon their families which have become broken up; upon their men who are carrying on an unequal struggle to defend their human rights; upon their women who again are shedding so many bitter tears.

g On this Christmas day, may the people of Poland, so loved by me, be a warning sign for all and a symbol of that which now awaits poor humanity.

h   In the cradle of this immense suffering I am today placing my heavenly child.

i   Pray that the hearts of all may open to Him. Throw open wide the doors to Jesus Christ who is coming. At the moment of your greatest tribulation, from his birth will stream forth abundant light for a new birth of all humanity."

239

A Gentle and Sad Voice

a   "Spend with me, in prayer and in profound silence, the last hours of this year which is about to end. You will then hear in your heart the gentle and sad voice of my motherly lament.

b   And you will see many tears fall from my merciful eyes. And you will notice that the beating of my Immaculate Heart becomes more anxious and anguished.

c   Because, in my mother's heart, you will feel beating the heart of the whole Church, never before so violated by its Adversary and betrayed by its own children; the heart of your homeland, never so threatened in its life and liberty; the heart of all poor humanity, now on the point of living the painful moments of its terrible trial. You are on the threshold of grave and painful events. In my heart, your own preoccupation, anxiety and bewilderment is now reflected.

d   Turn your gaze, this night, to your immaculate Mother. In my motherly Heart, your prayers and sufferings are offered by me at each moment to the justice of God, as a sign of reparation and supplication for all. Thus, by the mercy of the Father, each new day and each new year is made ready for you.

e   May the new year, which is now about to be born, open up upon this straying world the road of your return to the God of salvation. The great hour of justice and of mercy is about to open upon the world. For this reason I bid you, beloved sons, to spend on your knees, in prayer and reparation, these very precious hours of this last night of the year."

1982

I AM THE MOTHER OF CONSOLATION

I Am the Mother of Consolation

a   "Today you are beginning a new year in the light of my divine maternity. On this first day, the Church invokes me as mother and asks that I extend my motherly protection to all.

b   Today you also unite in asking God for the gift of peace. And you beg for it through the intercession of her whom you call the Queen of Peace.

c   Peace is the greatest gift of the Lord, which was lavished upon you appropriately on Christmas day.

d   The infant Jesus, whom you see, so frail, at the moment of his birth in Bethlehem, is the eternal Prince of Peace. His name is 'Peace'; his gift is peace; his mission is that of bringing peace to all.

e   Glory to God in the heights of heaven and peace on earth to men of good will – this is what the joyous angels sang, about the crib on the night of his birth.

f   **Peace between God and men** – and it was for this that the Word of the Father became incarnate in my virginal womb, was born in Bethlehem and sacrificed himself on Calvary.

g   **Peace amongst all men** – because you are all children of God, true brothers of Jesus and of each other. In living out your brotherhood lies the source of peace among men. Because the gift of peace is found only on the road of love, which one journeys by observing the laws of God and his commandments. In these, we are taught to love God, ourselves and our neighbor; with these is built that harmony which is founded upon justice, upon truth and upon love. As long as the God of peace is not accepted, but on the contrary men continue obstinately to deny and reject Him, they will not even be able to safeguard the demands of respect for human and civil rights.

h   If the laws of the Lord are not observed, but on the contrary are more and more openly violated, humanity will run along the road of confusion, of injustice, of egoism and of violence. This is the reason why humanity is menaced with war. How much suffering I see scattered over all the roadways of the world, as this new year begins!

i   The sufferings of little ones who have no food or help; of youth abandoned and deluded; of men whose dignity is trampled upon and who are made into tools of domination and tyranny; of women who mourn over the destruction of their homes . . . !

j   Humanity is close to the danger of a new world war. How great is my anguish over that which awaits you, my poor children, so threatened by hunger, by war, by hatred and by violence.

k   Take shelter today under the mantle of your Immaculate Mother! Never, as in these times, have I felt the motherly need of bringing you comfort in your sorrow, confidence in your discouragement, hope in your disillusionment and safety in your tribulations.

l   You will now be constantly aware of the consoling presence of your heavenly Mother! It will become stronger as the sufferings you must undergo become greater, now that you are entering into the most painful period of the great purification.

m   **I am the Mother of Consolation**. You are becoming aware of my great comfort, which will give you courage and protection, especially as you live through the bloody hours of the trial, which has been foretold by me for so long. And so, I am covering you all today with my mantle, I am gathering you into the refuge of my Immaculate Heart, I am stirring up your confidence and spirit of filial abandonment and I am giving you my blessing."

241

February 2, 1982
Feast of the Presentation of the
Child Jesus in the Temple

The Light of Love and of Hope

a   "Today I am gathering you all on the altar of my Immaculate

Heart, dear sons scattered throughout every part of the world, and I am presenting you, with love and joy, in the temple of the Lord.

b   Here, you are offered to his glory. Here, you are immolated for the salvation of all. For how long now have I been calling you to respond to my loving plan!

c   From the time when the hearts of men became closed because of the coldness of unbridled egoism, hatred, violence and inability to love, I have wanted the light of my motherly love to shine through you.

d   You, my children, are being offered by me to the Lord, in order to spread this light everywhere. Love all my children ever more and more, with my own motherly tenderness. From among them, be especially kind and merciful to those who have lost their way, who are far from God, who are often the unconscious victims of sin and of evil, of corruption and of violence. Never so much as at the present time have I wanted to assist and save, through you, all my poor sinful children, who are running the danger of being lost.

e   Here, you are also being immolated for the perfect glorification of God. This world is experiencing such a rebellion against God as has never before been experienced in the whole course of its history. It is running the danger of self-destruction, and menaced with ruin and death.

f   Beloved sons, let yourselves be offered on the altar of the Lord, as docile and meek lambs, for the salvation of the world. For this reason, I am bringing you all today into the temple of the Lord to present you, as a hymn of perfect glorification, to the Most Holy Trinity. Your little voices will become strong, like the roar of a hurricane and, joined to the powerful victory-cry of the co-horts of angels and saints, they will go out through all the world to proclaim everywhere, 'Who is like God? Who is like God?'

g   You have been called to live through pains and sufferings without number. Today, through you, I want to encourage and console my children. At the time of the great tempest, the Mother wants to gather her children in her arms, that they may be consoled. Together, we will live through the agonizing hours of the purification; together we will pray, suffer and trust in the mercy of the Father.

h   Together we will be tested; together we will also be consoled. For the present, through you, my beloved sons, I want to spread throughout the world the light of hope, of trust in God and of my motherly consolation."

242

Jerusalem, March 5, 1982
First Friday of the Month

The New Jerusalem

a   " 'How often have I yearned to gather your children, as a mother bird gathers her young under her wings, but you refused me. If only you had known the days of your peace!'

b   I hear again the sorrowful lament of my Son Jesus. How often have I, too, as your Mother, called you to gather you under the wings of my motherly love. And now, the days of the tribulation have come.

c   My requests have not been accepted. My extraordinary interventions have been given no credence. An attempt has been made to nullify everything that I have done these years in order to meet your needs and free you from the dangers that hang over you.

d   Just as in Jerusalem all the prophets were put to death, just as in this city the very Son of God, the Messiah promised and awaited for so many centuries, was rejected, outraged and condemned, so also today in the Church, the new Israel of God, the salvific action of your Mother, the heavenly prophetess of these last times, is too often obstructed by silence and rejection.

e   In so many ways have I spoken, but my words have not been harkened to. In many ways I have manifested myself, but my signs have been given no credence. My interventions, even the most extraordinary, have been contested. O New Jerusalem, Church of Jesus, true Israel of God! How often have I yearned to gather all your children, as a mother bird gathers her young. . . . If you had known the days of your peace!

f But now, great tribulations will come upon you. You will be buffeted by the wind of a tempest and a hurricane; of the great works built in you by human pride, not a stone will remain upon a stone.

g O New Jerusalem, accept today my invitation to conversion and interior purification. And thus the new era of justice and holiness can shine forth upon you; your light will spread to all the nations of the earth. And my Son Jesus will establish in your midst the glorious reign of love and peace."

243

Yes to the Gospel of Jesus

a "Beloved sons, I want you at my side at that ineffable moment of my life, when the Archangel Gabriel had announced to me that I had been chosen to become the Mother of the Word, the Son of God, the long-awaited Messiah.

b That which is known to you is nothing compared to that which your heavenly Mother experienced at that moment. That which is narrated in the Gospel of Luke is part of an event which truly took place; it is a true account, not a legend or a literary form.

c The Archangel truly came to me and his light, more resplendent than the sun, completely filled my poor little house in Nazareth: my eyes saw it; my ears heard his gentle voice; there was a real conversation between us. To my questions, there were his replies; to my interior apprehension, his serene and comforting explanations.

d   It was also through his precious assistance that my mind was opened to understand the plan of the Father, that my heart was opened to receive the Word of God and my life was united in a perfect manner to the Holy Spirit whose most beloved spouse I became.

e   And it was the Archangel who received my yes and placed it upon the heavenly altar, for the perfect glorification of the Most Holy Trinity and for the greater joy of all the angelic hosts, whose mistress and queen I became at that moment.

f   Beloved sons, say your yes today to the will of the Father; your yes to the Gospel of the Son; your yes to the love of the Holy Spirit. In these times, the will of the Father is not being accomplished and the action of the Holy Spirit is being impeded, because the Gospel of Jesus is not being accepted.

g   Often, a purely human interpretation is given to it, an interpretation which tends to exclude any supernatural intervention whatsoever. Many of its events are thus explained as legends or literary forms; never before has the great mystery of God been given such a banal and paltry interpretation. As a result of this, the faith of many has become extinguished and grave errors are spreading more and more throughout the Church.

h   You will remain in the true faith only if you will give your full assent to all that is said in the Gospel of Jesus. Announce it to the letter, live it to the letter.

i   Be living gospels and then the plan of the Father will be accomplished and the fire of the love of the Holy Spirit will purify this world. Let your yes as obedient children be placed within the yes which your heavenly Mother repeats continually to her God.

j   Then you will understand the mysteries of the kingdom of God, which are hidden from the proud and the mighty, but revealed to the little ones."

This Is How I Found My Son

a   "Draw near, beloved sons, to the fount of grace and mercy, which gushes forth from the pierced Heart of Jesus Crucified. Today, let yourselves be led with me up Calvary that we may live, together, through the painful and precious hours of his agony.

b   He is nailed to the Cross, about midday, after having reached, with great difficulty, the summit of Golgotha.

c   His body is crushed with suffering: the scourging has covered Him with bleeding wounds; the crown of thorns has surrounded his head with rivulets of blood which trickle down and disfigure his face; his body is overwhelmed by the immense weight of ingratitude; his eyes, so lively and penetrating, are now obscured by the veil of treason and abandonment...

d   This is how I found my Son, on the road to Calvary, on the Friday of his Passion. John is there with me and, beneath the Cross, we live out together the tremendous hours of his agony.

e   We see the nails transfix his hands and feet, his tormented body; we hear the impact of the Cross in the earth, which causes Him to start with pain, his moans of distress, his silent prayer, the loud cry to Heaven, the throbbing of his heart as it gives its final beats.

f   O my beloved ones, with me and with your brother, John, live beneath the Cross on which my Son has been hung and on which He is agonizing and dying, out of love, and for the salvation of all.

g   This is how I find the Church today, the Mystical Body of Jesus Crucified. She too is climbing Calvary, carrying a heavy cross; she too is experiencing the hour of such abandonment and of betrayal; her body, also, is being tormented by the scourges of sin which strike at it and by sacrileges which open up deep wounds in it...

h　And still, the Church looks upon this lost humanity with motherly and merciful eyes, and trustingly makes her way to the summit of Golgotha, for its crucifixion and agony.

i　This is how I find my daughter today. She is close to the painful hour of her Good Friday. With John, who is living again in each of you, my beloved sons consecrated to my Immaculate Heart, together let us be willing to help her in this, her agony.

j　Let us kiss her hands, likewise transfixed; let us cover with love her body, likewise stripped bare; let us pour balm upon her numerous wounds; let us surround with prayer and hope the bloody moments of her crucifixion.

k　In the sure expectation of her resurrection! By the work of the Holy Spirit she will again be completely renewed and know a wondrous splendor. For her too, the Good Friday of her passion will certainly be followed by a joyous Easter and a new Pentecost of grace and of life."

245

Look to the Pope!

a　"With the first of my beloved sons, Pope John Paul II, who has come today on a pilgrimage of love and prayer before my image in the very place where I appeared, I want you all to be spiritually united, gathered around your heavenly leader, the Woman clothed in the sun.

b　**Look to the Pope: He Gives an Example of Prayer.**

c　His life, which belongs entirely to me, has been molded by me in the spirit of incessant and trusting prayer. His voice penetrates heaven and, united with my maternal intercession, brings down, still today, a shower of graces upon this lost humanity.

d　You too, together with the Pope, must form a strong barrier of prayer to obtain the conversion of sinners, a return to God on the part of many straying children, peace for this humanity which is so threatened and a true and interior renewal for all the Church.

e Pray often, using the holy rosary, which I came here also to ask of you. If the most grave problems for the Church and for the world have not yet been successfully resolved, despite all the human means which have been taken, this is a sign for you that you must now put all your trust in the power of prayer.

f **He Gives an Example of Fidelity.**

g He is faithful to the mandate received through his succession to the Chair of Peter; he is faithful to Jesus Christ whom he announces by word and the witness of his life. Thus the light which he spreads everywhere is one and the same with the light of the Gospel.

h You must all be united with him in giving witness to the life of my Son Jesus and in announcing faithfully the truth of his Gospel. The Pope is often surrounded by a great void and by loneliness. His words are those of a prophet, but often they fall upon an immense desert.

i You must be a powerful echo of his word which must be more and more propagated, listened too and acted upon. Until this light is once again enkindled, walk behind him in the secure wake of this great brilliance, because soon the darkness may become even greater upon the world and the Church.

j **He Gives an Example of Fortitude.**

k He is going forward everywhere without fear, with the power that comes from his great love as universal Pastor and as Vicar of my Son Jesus. he fears neither criticism nor obstacles; he does not halt before threats and attempts upon his life. Led and defended by me, he proceeds along the way that I have pointed out to him, like a trusting child that always allows itself to be led by the hand. And thus each day he climbs his painful Calvary, carrying a great cross for the good and the salvation of all.

l What he is now living there has already been foretold him by me. Remain ever with him, beloved sons whom I am gathering from every part of the world into the refuge of my Immaculate

Heart, and carry with him today the great cross of the whole Church. Today you are now being called to be immolated, that the plan of the Father may be fulfilled.

m   Have confidence and hope. Have courage and patience. The hour of justice and of mercy has begun and soon you will see the wonders of the merciful love of the divine Heart of Jesus and the triumph of my Immaculate Heart. And so, from the Cova da Iria where, on the 13th of May, 1917, I came from heaven to reveal myself to you and to walk with you, together with the Pope, the first of my beloved sons, I bless you all in the name of the Father, and of the Son and of the Holy Spirit."

246   *Blumenfeld (Germany) May 30, 1982*
Feast of Pentecost

The Hour of the Holy Spirit

a   "In the cenacle of my Immaculate Heart, prepare yourselves to receive the fire of the love of the Holy Spirit, which will lead my Church to live the joyous moment of its Pentecost and which will renew the whole face of the earth.

b   This is its hour. It is the hour of the Holy Spirt who, from the Father and by means of the Son, is given to you ever more and more as a gift, as a sign of the merciful love of God who wants to save mankind.

c   By the fire of the Spirit of Love, the work of the great purification will be quickly accomplished. The Church groans as it awaits his merciful work of purification.

d   Through interior sufferings and by means of trials which will bring it to relive the bloody hours of the Passion through which my Son Jesus lived, the Church will be led to its divine splendor.

e   It will be healed of the wounds of error, which have spread like a hidden cancer and which threaten the deposit of faith. It will be cured of the leprosy of sin, which obscures its sanctity. It will be purified of all those human elements, which separate it from the spirit of the Gospel.

f   It will be deprived of its earthly goods and purified of many of its means of power, that once again it may become poor, humble, simple and chaste. In its pastors and its flock, it will again be crucified, that it may give perfect witness to the Gospel of Jesus.

g   Through the power of fire and of blood, the whole world will also be renewed. Humanity will return once again to the glorification of the Father, through Jesus, who will at last have established his reign in your midst.

h   This is, then, the hour of the Holy Spirit. He will come to you in all his fullness, by means of the triumph of the Immaculate Heart of Mary, his most beloved spouse."

247

Split (Jugoslavia), June 19, 1982
Feast of the Immaculate Heart of Mary

In You the Mother Is Glorified

a   "Enter into the refuge of my Immaculate Heart. This year, I have called you from every part of the world and you, my little ones, have responded with generosity and have entered into the garden which your Mother has prepared for you. You have listened to my voice and you have accepted my call.

b   And now, through you, I have formed my victorious cohort. With how many snares has my Adversary sought to impede your response to my anguished appeal. He has not succeeded because I have always intervened to defend my plan of love.

c   Thus, despite all the snares of Satan and the difficulties that have been encountered, my call has gone out to the very limits of the earth. And from the five continents, my children have hastened in very great numbers to enter into the secure refuge of my Immaculate Heart. Today I gaze upon you with delight and love.

d **In you, the Mother is glorified**, because I am able to offer
you all to the perfect glorification of the Most Holy Trinity.
Thus, in these times of rebellion against God, through you, the
Mother can offer her hymn of glory to the Lord.

e Not to the great, or the powerful, or the rich, or the proud is
it given to understand my voice and to penetrate the mystery of my
Heart. It is granted to the little, to the poor, to the humble servants of the Lord. With them, I have formed my cohort. And now,
the time of preparation is complete. Now we must enter into the
moments of the conclusive battle.

f Humanity has reached that time when it is to live through the
bloody hours of the great scourge, which will purify it through
fire, hunger and devastation.

g The Church will be purified by the blood of Jesus and by your
blood and by the fire of the Holy Spirit, and it will be totally
healed of the wounds of infidelity, of hypocrisy, of impiety and of
apostasy.

h The time has come when the task which the Most Holy Trinity
has entrusted to my Immaculate Heart in this age must be
acknowledged by the world and the Church. I embrace you all
and bless you."

248

Valdragone di San Marino, June 30, 1982
Cenacle of the Directors of the M.M.P.

The Secret of My Immaculate Heart

a "Beloved sons, I have brought you again up this mountain, for
a week of continuous cenacle with me, your heavenly leader. I
want to reveal to you the secret of my Immaculate Heart, in order
to have you share in the mystery of my maternal love and
sorrow.

b Never as in these present times has my heart trembled with a
most pure love for those whom Jesus entrusted to me when I
stood beneath the Cross on which He was about to die.

c The Church today has need to feel itself loved by me.

Humanity today has need to feel itself loved by me. My poor sinful and wandering children have need today of feeling themselves loved by me.

d I Want to Love Through You.

e I want to help humanity, the Church and all my children through you who are called to enter into the mystery of my Immaculate Heart. For this, I am bringing about an ever deeper union between my mother's heart and your hearts, my beloved priests.

f The luminous ray which shines forth from my heart will spread to all parts of the world. It will be like a strong anchor to which all will be able to cling, with confidence, in order to be saved at the moment of the decisive test.

g I Want to Suffer Through You.

h I will expand your heart that you may also be able to understand the mystery of my motherly suffering. See if there is today any suffering greater than mine: my Son Jesus is outraged, despised; He is again abandoned and betrayed by his own . . . the sacrileges, which are constantly increasing, make up a new crown of thorns, which surround the tabernacles scattered throughout all parts of the earth.

i The Church, his Mystical Body, is again scourged by division and threatened by error. Those children who are faithful are called to bear great sufferings, and to endure insult and outrage on the part of those who do not listen to me.

j Humanity, in rebellion against the Lord, is rushing inexorably along the road of rejection of God and this brings it to fall into the abyss of death and desolation. How many there are who are lost each day, swept along by this widespread and dangerous confusion!

k Share in my motherly sorrow! Judge no one; condemn no one. Pray, love, carry the cross of this great suffering with me for the salvation of all.

l I Am Your Heavenly Leader.

m I am the Woman clothed in the sun. I have gathered you together again in this cenacle, extraordinary for its graces, to obtain for you from the Father, through Jesus, the fullness of the Holy Spirit.

n   He will complete in you the work begun by me. He will mold your hearts to the perfection of love. He will bring you to understand everything. He will strengthen you and give you courage for the supreme witness for which I, as a Mother, have formed you.

o   The times of the great trial have come. Go down from this mountain and spread throughout every part of the earth the light from the merciful love of Jesus, which today is being poured out upon all humanity, by means of the love and the sorrow of my Immaculate Heart, in which I have enfolded you all forever. I bless you in the name of the Father, and of the Son and of the Holy Spirit.

249

August 13, 1982

Instruments of My Mercy

a   "Beloved sons, I am turning my merciful eyes upon you. I am the Mother of Mercy, of fair love and of holy hope, and my Immaculate Heart trembles with preoccupation for you. How many dangers are menacing you; how many snares my Adversary is setting for you!

b   In this hour of his rule and his triumph, numerous indeed are my children who are exposed to the danger of being eternally lost.

c   You see in what a grave situation you find yourselves today: humanity has rebelled against the God of love and is walking along the road of hatred and of sin, which is put forward as something good through the means of social communication.

d   You are living in a corrupted and unhealthy atmosphere and you succeed only with great difficulty in remaining faithful to the commandments of God, which lead you to walk along the road of love, flee sin and live in grace and holiness.

e   Thus each day the number of my poor children who allow themselves to be seduced by unbridled egoism, envy and impurity grows greater and greater. The easiest victims, and those who are less guilty, are the young people whose unhappy lot it is to be living at this time when the world has become worse than at the time of the flood.

f   That is why I feel that I am a gentle and merciful Mother especially to my young children, and I am sowing in their lives words of confidence and salvation. I am opening up their souls to a great thirst for good, I am opening up their hearts to the joyous experience of true love and self-giving, I am healing their numerous wounds, while I encourage all those who are good to come to their help through prayer, good example and penance.

g   If you, my beloved children, suffer and pray with me, you will succeed in leading many souls each day along the road which leads to paradise. You then, O children consecrated to my Immaculate Heart, must be today the instruments of my maternal mercy.

h   'How many souls go to hell because there is no one to pray and sacrifice for them!,' I said to Jacinta, Francisco and Lucia when I appeared to them at Fatima.

i   Today I say: how many souls you can save from the fire of hell and lead to paradise if, together with me, you pray and sacrifice each day for them! . . . It is above all in this, my merciful Work of salvation and yours, that the triumph of my heart is being brought about."

250

It Will Be Saved

a   "My chosen ones, remain about the crib of your infant

Mother. I will lead you to understand the secret of littleness and of spiritual childhood.

b   I will teach you to walk along the way of humility and of trust. I will obtain for you the gift of wisdom of heart and of purity. Great joy fills heaven and earth today in the recalling of the birth of your heavenly Mother.

c   You too must share in this interior and profound joy. Today I bless each one of you who, about my crib, form a crown of fragrant flowers of love, of purity and of trust. You are living through tempestuous and difficult days: men are withdrawing further and further from God and their hearts are being closed, in the chill of egoism and hatred.

d   The world in which you are living has become a cold and arid desert, but over this world of yours there throbs my motherly and Immaculate Heart, which beats with love for all and is ever causing the dew of grace and of mercy to descend upon the earth. Thus am I able to cause the parched hearts of so many of my children to open up to love. (. . .)

e   It is through you that I will be able to bring to fulfillment the loving plan of salvation which has been entrusted to me by the Most Holy Trinity. You will see a new birth of this poor humanity in its complete return to the God of salvation.

f   (. . .) You are here, today, holding a cenacle with my chosen ones in this land where the great contestation on the part of my Adversary had its beginning. Here, you see the Church deeply humiliated and wounded, while an immense number of my poor children are confused and wandering. Satan may seem to be singing his song of victory, especially in this country. But from this place, I have also begun my irresistible action.

g   For this, I am making use of all my little children who have said 'yes' to me: through littleness I will conquer the power of the great; with humility I will defeat pride; with docility all rebellion will be overpowered. You will be increasingly aware of my presence. (. . .)"

A Great Force of Reparation

a   "Today, I bend with love over the sores and wounds of all my children. I am your sorrowful Mother. My duty as Mother binds me to you in a strong and personal way. As your joys increase my happiness, so too each of your sufferings brings new sorrow to my motherly heart. Today I see you all under the weight of an unspeakable suffering. See if there is any sorrow as great as my motherly sorrow.

b   In a world where egoism and pride have taken the field, the most numerous victims are the innocent. Today they are killed by the millions while still in their mother's womb, through the crime of abortion which is now legalized everywhere.

c   Why such cruelty? Why is such inhuman impiety so widespread in the world today? The blood of these innocent ones cries out daily for vengeance in the sight of God and causes wounds of deep sorrow in my motherly heart.

d   Little children who are just opening out to life are being presented absolute transgressions of God's law as values to be sought after; young people are disoriented and deceived; families bewail the destruction of their home-life; the immense multitude of my poor children who are hastening along the road of sin and perdition: see if there is any sorrow as great as mine!

e   Above all, I look today with sorrowful apprehension at the Church, especially entrusted by Jesus to my motherly action. I see how it is violated by sin, its unity shattered, profaned by sacrileges, its truth obscured.

f   How many pastors there are today who no longer defend the flock which has been entrusted to them by Jesus! Some remain silent when they should speak courageously to defend the truth and to condemn error and sin. They tolerate to avoid risk, they descend to compromise simply to maintain their privileges. Thus error is spread under the form of ambiguous formulae and reparation is no longer made for sin, in a progressive apostasy from Jesus and from his Gospel.

g   Today there is need for a great force of prayer. There is need for a great chain of suffering, raised up to God in reparation! I call upon you, my chosen ones, and upon all the children who are consecrated to my Immaculate Heart to unite yourselves to the sorrow of your heavenly Mother, that what is lacking in the Passion of Jesus be completed in each one of you. (. . .)"

252

I Am the Dawn

a   "In the stormy sea in which you are sailing, hasten all to my Immaculate Heart. I came down from heaven to give you this anchor of salvation. Cling to the anchor which has been prepared for you by my merciful love.

b   Come to me, children, never before so menaced by the cold of sin, by the torment of hatred, by the tempest of rebellion against God and his law, by the earthquake of moral disorder, by the danger of war, destruction and famine.

c   In this world, which has become worse than at the time of the flood, you are truly running the danger of being lost, along the wicked roads of sin and infidelity, in this life, and the threat of perdition for all eternity, in the next.

d   How many souls there are, in fact, who go each day to hell, because the request I made of you in this very place, to return to God along the road of prayer, of penance and of interior conversion, has not yet been acted on.

e   These then are times of chastisement and of salvation, of justice and of mercy. In view of these times, I have prepared a secure refuge for you where you must gather together to be comforted and saved.

f **This Refuge Is My Immaculate Heart!**

g From my heart there issue in ever increasing reflected strength, the rays which come forth from the Heart of Jesus, so that you may walk along the way of grace and of holiness, of love and of mercy, of truth and of fidelity.

h If the world is filled with the darkness of sin, these rays descend like a dew and they urge it to open itself to the radiant noonday of its renewal. All creation will know the new and long-awaited time of its perfect glorification of God.

i If the Church is, in its human reality, darkened and wounded, these rays will open it to the light of the Gospel of Jesus, to the custody of the deposit of faith which has been entrusted to it alone, and to the full witness of its unity and holiness.

j **I Am the Dawn Which Precedes the Day.**

k My light, which shines out in the night which still enwraps the world, is you who are consecrated to my Immaculate Heart, you who are totally entrusted to me that you may listen to me and follow me. Increase in prayer, in humility, in suffering and in confidence.

i Soon you will see the great day of the Lord, prepared for by so much sorrow and so many tears, by so much love and so much hope, by many prayers and by unceasing suffering. From the Cova da Iria, on the sixty-fifth anniversary of my final apparition which was confirmed by the miracle of the sun, I bless you all in the name of the Father and of the Son and of the Holy Spirit."

253

Rome, November 20, 1982

Obedient, Chaste and Poor

a "Live in my maternal predilection, responding to my call for prayer and trust. Allow yourselves, beloved sons, to be formed by me each day.

b   **I want you docile** and obedient to the will of the Father, in perfect imitation of my Son Jesus: for this, you must always be obedient to the Church.

c   The virtue which I love most in my priest-sons is that of obedience. Today, you must be an example to everyone, by obeying with joy your superiors, especially the Pope.

d   How is it possible that when he speaks today he is no longer listened to by many, and when he gives directives, he is no longer obeyed? And it is sometimes some of my bishop-sons and priest-sons who are the first to disobey him! In this way the Church becomes truly threatened in its interior unity. (. . .)

e   **I want you chaste** in mind, heart and body.

f   Through purity of mind, you will see the truth with greater clarity and you will be always faithful to it; the Gospel of Jesus will appear to you in all its divine splendor.

g   Through purity of heart, you will attain perfect communion of love with Jesus and you will be led by Him to understand the mystery of his burning love. You will become truly able to love everyone and the flame of his love will set you afire and transform you.

h   Through purity of body you will experience the joy of living in greater intimacy with me and of being increasingly in communion with the heavenly spirits and with the souls of your deceased brothers; the power of the spirit will transform you, freeing you of the many limitations of the flesh. And thus, you will spread about you the light of divine grace and of holiness.

i   Let celibacy, willed by Jesus and ardently sought by the Church, be loved, esteemed and lived by you: you will become the source of life for an immense number of souls, even of your own brother-priests.

j   Take courage, O dearly beloved sons of mine! Follow me along the way of hiddenness and humility.

k   **I want you poor** in material goods and in spirit.

l   Only thus will you be able to understand the anxieties and the sorrows of many people and share in the concerns and the sufferings of your poorer brothers; of those who have no work or means of livelihood; of those who are pushed aside and persecuted; of those who are considered as nothings, while they are, for me, most precious treasures.

m Whoever meets you must be aware of the presence of their heavenly Mother who, through you, again caresses and consoles, who again helps, even materially, who encourages and saves and who embraces and defends everyone."

254

My Plan

a "I am your Immaculate Mother: allow yourselves to be led by me, beloved sons, for the perfect fulfillment of my motherly plan.

b **It Is a Plan of Enmity.**

c 'I will put enmity between you and the Woman, between your offspring and hers.' Thus did the Lord speak of me, addressing Himself to the serpent when, by means of him, sin entered in at the beginning of the history of the human race. Enmity between me and Satan; between the Woman and the serpent; between my cohort and his; between good and evil; between grace and sin.

d To walk along my way, there can be no descending to compromise with evil, because this road winds its way only over [the terrain] of enmity between these two opposed realities. My Son Jesus became the sign of this contradiction and has been given to you by the Father for the salvation and the ruin of many.

e You are now living in obscure times, because in all kinds of ways an attempt is being made to reach a compromise between God and Satan; between good and evil; between the spirit of Jesus and the spirit of the world. Many are running the danger of becoming victims of this general confusion; and even in my Church a false spirit, which is not that of Jesus the Son of God, is seeking to spread itself about. Like a cloud of invisible poison gas, a spirit which jumbles the things of God with those of the world is expanding and succeeding in depriving the Word of God of its vigor and in despoiling the announcement of the Gospel of its force!

f   It Is a Plan of Struggle.

g   Assisted by me and following along the road which Jesus has traced out for you, you must fight against the Evil One, against sin, against error and infidelity.

h   If, by divine privilege, I have been exempt from all sin, even original sin, it is because I have been appointed by the Most Holy Trinity as Leader of this terrible battle, which involves heaven and earth, heavenly and earthly spirits. It is a great and continuous struggle, often invisible, and at this time it has become general.

i   In the Apocalypse, it has been foretold how the Woman clothed in the sun will conduct the battle against the Red Dragon and all his followers. If you want to second my plan, you must do battle, my little ones, as children of a Mother who is a leader in battle. Fight against sin and against compromise with the weapon of prayer and of suffering. In hiddenness and confidence, in the humble fulfillment of your daily duties, in the perfect imitation of Jesus and in poverty and contempt for the world and for your own selves, join me in waging this battle each day.

j   It Is a Plan of Victory.

k   After the presnt triumph of evil, which has succeeded in subduing the world, in the end the victory will be solely that of my Son Jesus. He alone is the victor. The outcome of the great struggle, through which we are living, will be his glorious reign of peace and of goodness, of justice and of holiness, which will be established in the world and will shine forth resplendently in the hearts of all. Thus will be brought to completion the plan of enmity, of struggle and of victory in the triumph of my Immaculate Heart."

God Is with You

a "A great silence enwraps the world. Darkness covers everything. Hearts keep vigil in prayer and expectation. A sense of confident hope opens the doors which have been closed by hatred and egoism.

b The powers of hell feel themselves unexpectedly overpowered by a new force of love and of life.

d In the darkness an increasing brightness is enkindled. In the silence the harmonies of celestial hymns are heard. And in the heavens a great light suddenly appears.

d **This Is the Holy Night.**

e The light now enwraps the poor shelter, where the greatest event in history is about to take place. The Virgin Mother gives you her Child, who is born poor and defenseless, trembling and in need of everything, weeping and tender as a lamb, who is to make visible, already in his little body, the great mystery of meekness and of mercy.

f The life of every man takes on a new meaning from this night, because the little Child who is born is also his God. He is man like you and He is God with you. He is Emmanuel, prophesied for centuries.

g He is your brother. He is the heart of the world. He is the heart-beat of an immortal life. He is the caress laid upon every human suffering. He is the victory which covers over every defeat.

h He is the balm for the wound of egoism, of hatred, of sin. He is the light which shines resplendently forever for all who walk in the darkness. He is the only hope of this bewildered world.

i With the concerned voice of a Mother, who hears a thousand voices which still reject Him and who listens with dismay to the sound of a thousand doors which are closed upon Him, I say to you: Do not be afraid; God is with you. Today there is born to you a Savior for all!

j   With a heart wounded by the great coldness which still permeates the roads of the world, and with a soul made desolate because of this great rejection of God which has turned the earth into a great desert, in the face of such vast hopelessness, I say to you again: *Do not be afraid; God is with you!*

k   This is especially so today, when you are being called to live through the painful moments when it appears that my Adversary reigns in the world, as he spreads his deadly poison in the hearts of men.

l   In the face of such suffering which cannot be assuaged, of such great slavery which cannot be shaken off, of situations of injustice which cannot be successfully healed, of dangers of war which cannot be checked, of fierce threats which grow more and more ominous, on this holy night, here is the message which springs from my Immaculate heart as a source of hope and comfort for all: *Do not be afraid; God is with you!*

m   Just as the Word of the Father made use of my humble assent for his first coming into your midst, in the frailness of human nature, so now does my Son Jesus make use of my prophetic announcement to prepare his second coming into your midst in glory.

n   Do not be afraid, O children so exposed to dangers. With the triumph of my Immaculate Heart, Jesus will manifest himself to you in his glorious reign of love and of peace!"

256

December 31, 1982
Last night of the year

Watch in Prayer

a   "On this night, while the greater part of my children spend the last hours of the year in amusement and dissipation, watch with me, my beloved ones, in silence and more intense prayer.

_b_   **Prayer of thanksgiving**: for all the graces which, in this period of time, have been granted you by the Father, in the Holy Spirit, by means of my Son Jesus and through the unceasing intercession of my Immaculate Heart.

_c_   This world is at the mercy of my Adversary, who is ruling it with his spirit of pride and rebellion, and who is leading an immense number of children of God along the road of pleasure, of sin, of disobedience to the laws of God, and of contempt for his will.

_d_   It is immersed in the deepest of nights and no beginning of a year can dissipate the great darkness in which it is walking. Indeed, it has been created for the glory of the Father; it has been redeemed and saved by the Son and it continues to be transformed by the action of the Holy Spirit.

_e_   Nothing can resist the power of the merciful love of God, which wants to transform this poor world into a new creation. And so, the interventions of my Immaculate Heart will become steadily more numerous, extraordinary and miraculous.

_f_   For this, give thanks with me to the Most Holy Trinity which is making use of me — its little handmaid — to lead all creatures to the perfect glorification of God.

_g_   **Prayer of supplication**: to obtain from the merciful Heart of Jesus days of peace and not of affliction, days of serenity and not misfortune. There is a real danger of another war. Under the appearance of fragile promises of agreements, the most refined means of dealing death are being prepared, and humanity is being led along the road of hatred and of self-destruction. May your prayer obtain for all the grace which leads to the defeat of sin and that concord which causes violence and terror to cease so that universal peace, in truth and justice, may finally be yours. There is need of a great miracle; there is need to wrest through the power of prayer, this miracle from the mercy of God. Only thus can salvation come to you.

_h_   **Prayer of reparation**: because the cup of divine justice is full, very full; it is overflowing! See how hatred and sin burst all bounds. Today the majority of mankind no longer observes the

Ten Commandments of the Lord. Your God is publicly ignored, denied, offended and blasphemed. The day of the Lord is more and more profaned.

i   Daily an attack is being made upon life. Each year, throughout the world, by the tens of millions, innocent children are being slaughtered in their mother's womb and the number of murders, robberies and acts of violence and kidnappings are increasing.

j   Immorality is spreading like a flood of filth and is being propagated by the means of social communication, especially the cinema, the press and television. By means of this last-mentioned, a subtle and diabolical tactic of seduction and corruption has found its way into every family. The most defenseless victims are children and youth, whom I look upon with the tender preoccupation of a mother.

k   Only the powerful force of prayer and reparative penance will be able to save the world from what the justice of God has prepared because of its obstinate refusal to accept every demand for repentance.

l   Listen at least to the voice of your heavenly Mother! I need much prayer of reparation and suffering, offered with faith. Pray your rosary always. Live, together with me, in trust and trepidation, because there are in preparation decisive hours which can determine the destiny of all humanity.

m   I bless you in the name of the Father, and of the Son and of the Holy Spirit."

1983

(Extraordinary Holy Year of the Redemption)
OPEN WIDE THE GATES TO CHRIST

Mother of Hope

a   "At the beginning of this year, the Church looks to me with confidence and venerates me in the mystery of my divine and universal motherhood.

b   And in the midst of the innumerable sufferings of the present moment, of the great uneasiness, of the threats which hang over your future, raise your eyes to your heavenly Mother, as to the fount of divine mercy and as a great sign of hope for you.

c   *I am the Mother of Hope.*

d   This is the theological virtue which must be especially lived in the bloody hours of the purification.

e   In how many ways my Adversary seeks to bring you to discouragement, in order to make you harmless and to weaken the power of my victorious cohort! Do not be afraid, because Satan has already been defeated by Jesus, and every apparent victory of his prepares a great new and real defeat for him.

f   If hatred still causes blood to flow in your streets, if sin chills the souls and hearts of many, if humanity is not returning along the way of love, if rebellion against God becomes greater every day, your trust in the mercy of your heavenly Father must be all the greater, and you must look to me as the sign of your hope.

g   I am the Mother of love and of grace, of pardon and of mercy, and therefore, at the beginning of this year, marked by important events in the plan of Providence, I am going along the deserted roads of the world to scatter in the hearts of my children seeds of repentance, of goodness and of hope. There is such need today of light and of comfort, there is such need at this time for consolation and motherly encouragement for all my children! I look, with sorrowful compassion, at the innumerable crowds of my sinful children; at the young people who have been seduced and betrayed by the society in which they live; at the adults who remain slaves of unbridled egoism and hatred; at the sons of the

Church who have become slothful through indifference and lack of faith. To all, I repeat today: *I am the Mother of your hope.*

h   The great coldness which covers the world must not discourage you, because each day I am spreading everywhere seeds of life and of resurrection.

i   I am the daybreak which precedes the Sun; I am the dawn which begins the new day. I am the Mother of holy joy.

j   Live in the joy of knowing you are loved by God, who is a Father to you, you who are carried by the Spirit as children, and sustained by Jesus as his little brothers.

k   In the joy of living in the heart of the Most Holy Trinity and of being safe in the garden of my Immaculate Heart, begin this new year in order to live it wholly with me."

258

February 2, 1983
Presentation of the Child Jesus in the Temple

I Am Asking You for a Spiritual Childhood

a   "If you consider with love the mystery the Church commemorates today, beloved sons, you will learn how the consecration you have made to me should be lived.

b   The child Jesus whom, in company with Joseph, my most chaste spouse, after forty days I presented in the Temple of the Lord, is truly God, our Savior, the Messiah so long awaited.

c   As a mother I brought Him into this earthly life, yet He is the author of life, for He is the Creator.

d   With my yes I permitted Him to enter into time, yet He is outside of time, for He is eternal.

e   I hold Him in my arms and support Him, yet it is He who upholds all things, for He is omnipotent.

f   In fulfillment of the divine Scripture I carry Him into the Temple of Jerusalem, yet He is the fountain of Revelation, for He is the eternal Word.

g   The Word of the Father, Creator, omnipotent and omniscient God, willed to clothe himself in weakness, and subjected himself to the limitations of time, took upon himself the frailty of human nature and was born of me; like every infant, He experienced all sorts of needs.

h   How often, while kissing Him with the tenderness of a mother, I said to Him: and yet You are the eternal kiss of the Father; and while I caressed Him; I thought: You are the divine caress conferring beatitude upon souls; while I clothed Him in his little garments, I whispered: it is You who clothe the earth with flowers and the immense universe with stars; and while nourishing Him, I sang to Him: it is You who provide food for all living creatures. When with maternal love I called him 'My Son!', adoring Him in my soul, I prayed to Him: You are the Son of the Father, his eternal Only-Begotten, his living Word. . .

i   Oh! Penetrate today into the ineffable mystery of the infancy of my Son Jesus, whom I carried in my arms to the Temple of the Lord, if you wish to journey along the road of spiritual childhood I have traced out for you.

j   All must travel along this road, even those who are further advanced in age, and who occupy important posts; even those who are learned, formed by years of study and experience; even those who are rich in culture and who have been called to perform tasks of great responsibility.

k   Allied with your human growth, which unfolds itself over the years, I am asking you for a spiritual childhood, an interior littleness leading you to robe yourselves in the humility and in the very fragility itself of my child Jesus.

i   I want to see in you the candid hearts of children, knowing nothing of egoism and sin, open to love and to giving, expecting everything from the Heavenly Father so as to be able to give everything.

m   I want to see in you the virginal hearts of children, still firmly shut to the snares of deceit and duplicity, opening like flowers to receive the rays of knowledge, truth and wisdom.

n   I want to see in you the docile wills of little ones, like fragile clay vessels ready to let themselves be formed with trust and abandonment; wills which must be molded by the good and the true, strengthening themselves by pursuing what is good and what is beautiful.

o   Oh! This way of spiritual childhood must of necessity be traversed by you, beloved sons, if you wish to live in a perfect manner the consecration to my Immaculate Heart.

p   It is only in this way that I can carry you, like my Infant Jesus, and offer you in the temple of the Lord for the realization of the designs of love and mercy He has upon you, for the salvation of all my children."

259

February 11, 1983
Apparitions of Our Lady at Lourdes

Love One Another

a   "Come in procession!—I told the simple child Bernadette, when I appeared to her in the humble grotto at Massabielle.

b   Why did I make this request?

c   Because I want all my children to walk together, united in prayer and in love.

d   Today my Adversary is trying in every way to divide you, to isolate you, to set you against one another. He who from the beginning was the father of lies and the sower of hatred, seeks more and more to break up your fraternal unity.

e   Thus it is that often—even under the specious appearance of good—one rises against another, this group struggles with that group in an endless quest for self assertion that leaves so many good efforts fruitless.

f   I want you to walk together toward me, because I am the Mother of all, and because I want to form all of you together in prayer, in penance, and in your reciprocal love.

g   In these times it is more than ever necessary to live the new commandment given you by Jesus on Holy Thursday evening during the Last Supper: 'Love one another, as I have loved you.' I want to form you in a mutual and reciprocal love. It is necessary to give this testimony of ecclesial charity that unites you all in the perfection of love, in order to combat the tactics of division and isolation used by my Adversary.

h   Come to me, all of you, making your way along the difficult paths of your times, praying together, giving praise together, and loving one another.

i   Come to me, therefore, not in isolation or in division, but in procession, strengthening those who are weak, leading on those who have come to a standstill.

j   Come to me because I wish to lead all of you in unity to my Son, present in the Eucharist.

k   Jesus is present in the sacrament of the Eucharist to help you build this unity of yours, to give you an example of how one must love, in total giving to all one's brothers.

l   Come to me together, therefore, that I may bring you to Jesus in the sacrament of the Eucharist, awaiting you in his silent immolation, really present among you in all the tabernacles of the world.

m   Then you will be able to accomplish what I am asking of you, for the realization of my maternal designs of salvation."

260

The Path of Penance

a   "Beloved sons, follow me along the path of penance.

b   The weapons with which you are to fight my battle are those of prayer and penance. Today I want to show you the path of penance which is to be traversed by each of you.

c   The first stage is that of renunciation and self-denial.

d   It is necessary to renounce oneself, as well as all disordered attachments, passions, immoderate desires, ambitions. Even in your apostolic labors, you are never to seek success and human approval. Rather have a love for being hidden, for an apostolate carried out in silence, in humility, and the daily and faithful fulfillment of your duties.

e   In this way you will mortify egoism which constitutes your greatest peril, the easiest and most customary of the snares by which my Adversary attempts to impede your journey.

f   Then you will become free interiorly, and it will be easy for you to discern in the light the will of God, and you will find yourselves more suitably disposed to carry it to perfection.

g   The second stage is that of carrying one's cross properly.

h   This cross is made up of the difficulties one encounters when one desires to fulfill solely the will of God, because this involves the task of daily fidelity to the duties of one's state in life. It is a fidelity in which even the very smallest tasks are performed with perfection. Everything is done in the fulness of love; every moment of the day is lived in fulfilling the divine will.

i   How precious, above all for you, my beloved sons, is this second stage of suffering!

j   In this you are shaped into the likeness of Jesus Crucified, and this interior crucifixion will take place each day, and in every mo-

k ment of your priestly day: in moments of prayer, which is so greatly necessary and which must be the center of your life; in that most precious moment of the celebration of holy Mass, when with Jesus you too are interiorly immolated for the life of the world; in your fidelity to the priestly duties proper to the ministry of each one; in evangelization, in catechizing, in teaching, in the apostolate of charity; with each person you meet, especially the very poor, the lonely and forsaken—those who feel themselves despised and rejected by all.

l   In your priestly apostolate never seek to please yourselves, or to procure some personal advantage; give yourselves always with all the inexhaustible force of love, and do not let ingratitude stop you, or misunderstandings stand in your way; indifference should not make you hesitate nor should lack of cooperation cause you to become weary. It is above all in your priestly suffering that souls can be begotten by you to the life of grace and to salvation.

m The third stage is that of following my Son Jesus toward Calvary.

n During his life, how often I found Him turning his glance with desire toward Jerusalem, where He would one day go to be betrayed, arrested, judged by his own, condemned, scourged, crowned with thorns and crucified. How greatly Jesus longed for this moment. He was always journeying toward the consummation of his Pasch of love and immolation for you.

o Therefore, you, my beloved, who are his priests, you too are called to follow him each day toward the consummation of your paschal immolation for the salvation of all.

p Never lose courage. Today the voices of condemnation are for you the shouts of those who reject and challenge you. Sins, committed but then justified and no longer atoned for, are for you the painful strokes of the scourge. The errors which threaten to estrange great numbers of souls from the faith, are for you the crown of thorns. Today, to remain faithful to your calling is to follow the stern path that leads to Calvary.

q The obstacles found today in staying united and obedient in all things to the Pope, and to the hierarchy united with him, the lack of understanding on the part even of your brothers, the sense of being pushed aside with which you are often overwhelmed, are for you the painful falls.

r But, the entrusting of yourselves to my Immaculate Heart by means of your consecration, is today for you the meeting with your Mother, so full of sorrows.

s Together, from now on, let us go forward in the perfect imitation of Jesus, who invites us to follow Him on the way of the cross.

t Some of you will even have to shed your own blood in the decisive moment of this bloody purification.

u Beloved sons, you see now described for you the road you must travel to reach a genuine experience of conversion.

v It is the simple and evangelical road, pointed out to you by my son Jesus when He told you: 'He who wishes to come after Me, let him renounce himself, take up his cross each day, and follow Me.'

_w Along this path, evangelical and sacerdotal, your heavenly Mother wishes to lead you."

261

March 25, 1983
Annunciation of the Lord and
Opening of the Holy Year of the Redemption

Open Wide the Gates to Christ

_a "Beloved sons, today live this moment of grace which the Heart of Jesus has prepared for you.

_b It is his feastday!

_c Today adore the mystery of his coming among you. In my virginal womb, the eternal Word of the Father assumed his human nature, permitting him to become a man like you, your true Brother.

_d At that same moment, humanity was redeemed, weakness found its support, poverty was ennobled, and for every human being the gate of true, supernatural and divine greatness was thrown open.

_e But it is also my feastday!

_f The feast of the Son, conceived in me by the work of the Holy Spirit, is also that of the Mother who gave Him life, preserving forever the ineffable charm of perpetual virginity.

_g His yes of the Son to the Father; my yes of the Mother to the Son, united us wholly and forever after, in the perfect realization of the divine will.

_h Since neither holocausts nor sacrifices were acceptable, then I said: I come, O God, to do your will.

_i But today, O sons, is also your feastday.

_j At that same instant in which the Word became incarnate in my virginal womb, there sprang into being the real and practical possibility that each of you might become true sons of God, brothers of Jesus, recipients of the great gift of the Redemption.

_k Also at that very moment of the Incarnation, I became for all of

you a true Mother in the supernatural order, Mother of your divine life.

l For these reasons, today, following an inspiration of the Holy Spirit experienced in a moment of intense prayer, my Pope is opening the holy door and beginning the Jubilee Year of the Redemption.

m The Redemption had its beginning at the moment of the Incarnation of Jesus. It continued throughout his life and culminated in the sacrifice of his body, offered for you, and that of his blood, shed for you, a sacrifice consummated on the summit of Calvary and still renewed mystically upon the altar.

n Let all correspond to this extraordinary period of grace which the merciful love of Jesus has prepared for this generation, so remote and perverse, so rebellious and endangered, so dominated by Satan and the spirits of evil, and consequently in immense need of being saving.

o This holy year becomes the final effort of the divine Heart of Jesus and of my Immaculate Heart to make all of you walk the road of a return to God, in sincere repentance for your sins and with a serious commitment to conversion, such as will lead you to active works of justice and charity, of goodness and giving, for the good of all.

p Today my maternal summons becomes urgent. Through you, my beloved sons, I wish to address it to all my children.

q To those of my poor children who are straying, because they have been seduced by the atheism that is prevailing everywhere, and who live in a continual and obstinate rejection of God, I appeal beseechingly: 'Return to the God of your salvation and of your peace!'

r To those of my poor children who are sinners, seduced by evil, by hatred and violence, I repeat with the heartfelt lament of a Mother: 'Return to God, who awaits you with the love of a Father; let yourselves be washed in the Precious Blood and purified by the infinite mercy of my Son, Jesus'

s To the children of the Church, today living the hour of its agony and its redemptive passion, I repeat my maternal invitation to walk the road of love and unity, of fidelity and holiness, of prayer and penance.

t To all of humanity, with the strength of an anguished Mother, who sees the mortal dangers threatening it, I want to cry out: 'Open wide the gates to Christ who is coming! He alone is God with you! He alone is your Redeemer! He alone is your Savior!'

u If you welcome my invitation, there will soon come upon you the new era of justice and peace, and my Immaculate Heart will experience its triumph, beholding all of you advancing along the road of the glorification of the Father, the imitation of the Son, and full communion with the Holy Spirit."

262

All Is Accomplished

a "All is accomplished!

b These were the last words before the loud cry with which my Son Jesus gave up his spirit.

c Linger today with me beneath the Cross, beloved sons, to understand the meaning of these words.

d It is Good Friday. It is the day of his Passion and of his death upon the Cross. It is the precious moment of your redemption.

e Let us enter into the recesses of the Heart of Jesus to taste the bitterness of his soul, and to penetrate the profound mystery of his immolation.

f Everything was accomplished at the moment his body was immolated and his blood was shed for you.

g In his life, everything has been ordered toward this supreme moment: on each day of his earthly life, how greatly he had desired to consummate this, his Pasch, his Passion and death on your behalf!

h Today I am to be found beneath the Cross on which my Son Jesus lived his tremendous agony, with John, who represents all of you, close by. In union of soul with Jesus, with whom I am intimately associated in his redemptive work, let us together retrace the moments that led Him to its perfect accomplishment:

i   –the joyous moment of the Annunciation when the Word of the Father became incarnate in my virginal womb, assumed the body prepared for Him enabling Him to begin immediately the precious work of the Redemption;

j   –the radiant day of his birth in the poor little shed in Bethlehem, when I could already see the signs, in his infant's tender frame, of the true Lamb of God, called to offer himself in a perfect sacrifice for the salvation of the world;

k   –after returning from the exile endured in Egypt, the serene years of his childhood, when each day I watched Him open Himself up, like a flower, to the sun of beauty, of grace and of divine wisdom;

l   –the long years of his adolescence, during which I saw his body grow, that body in which was reflected the synthesis of every human perfection, intent on daily labor, marked by perspiration and fatigue;–Oh! Frequently in spirit I could already see his hands and feet pierced by wounds and his body covered with blood . . .and then I would bend over Him with the renewed tenderness of a mother . . . ;

m

n   –the short years of his public life, when He announced to all the Gospel of salvation, curing and pardoning, healing wounds and dispelling illnesses, pardoning sins and performing innumerable miracles; how many times, near to me, his Mother, to whom He confided everything, He went in spirit to the summit of Calvary, and together with me lived the moment of his sorrowful departure!

o   All is accomplished.

p   And Jesus seeks to prepare his disciples for the scandal of this moment. 'The Son of Man must go up to Jerusalem, where He will be handed over to the pagans, and will be spat upon, scourged, condemned and crucified, but on the third day He will rise again.'

q   Now I see Him hanging on the Cross, and I behold his hands and feet torn by horrible wounds, the crown of thorns opening fissures of blood that stream down and disfigure his countenance. And while his body is shaken with tremendous spasms of fever and agony, his lips open once again for his last words: 'All is accomplished'.

r   The will of the Father has now been done. Every circumstance of his life has been oriented towards this perfect fulfillment. . .His work is here summed up in the deed toward which it was ever directed: in the divine gift, the ineffable and precious gift of the redemption.

s   Like Him, you too, beloved sons, have been prepared by me for this supreme moment, so that the Father's design may be accomplished in this new hour of redemptive passion for the Church. Everything in your life has had this profound meaning. Read with me, the Mother of Sorrows, in the sealed book of your existence.

t   In it everything has been prepared by God and arranged by me with love, as I did with my Son, Jesus.

u   In a like manner, I can help you too, to accomplish today the Father's will.

v   Love all with a heart that is open and generous; bring health to the sick; close the gaping wounds; bestow grace and peace; forgive sins.

w   And prepare yourselves to ascend, with me, your own Calvary. (. . .)."

263

April 3, 1983
Easter Sunday

Let Nothing Disturb Your Peace!

a   "Jesus has risen, alleluia!

b   Today I communicate to you and to all your brother-priests, and to all my beloved children, the joy experienced by my heart when Jesus came into the little room in which I was staying, and, in the divine splendor of his glorified body, leaned down to implant a kiss upon the face of his Mother, while in profound adoration I bathed the marks of his luminous wounds with tears of joy. Peace to you, peace to all! With my risen Son, I repeat it again to you. Let nothing disturb your peace!

c —Not the world in which you are living, rebelling against God, perverted and in the hands of the Evil One. Jesus has already overcome the world.

d —Not the darkened and divided Church, into which have come idolatry and apostasy. Jesus loves his Spouse with a divine love, and in these moments of its purification He is closer to it than ever.

e —Not the disconcerting succession of events; not the persecutions and fratricidal struggles; not the fire and the red scourge that has already spilled out over the world.

f Jesus, risen and alive, is among you!

g He is guiding the vicissitudes of the world and of history, according to the designs of his merciful love, for the salvation of all of his redeemed brothers.

h Therefore, in Jesus, Life and Resurrection, peace to you in a joy that is pure and supernatural. Peace to all in the paschal joy of Christ. To the Pope and to all, my blessing in the name of the glorified Father, the risen Son, and the Holy Spirit, bestowed upon you as a gift."

264

This Month of May

a "During this month of May try to live more intensely the consecration you have made to my Immaculate Heart, beloved sons, for it is only in this way that I can be venerated by each of you.

b Bring me little flowers of mortification, to console my great sorrow in seeing all the appeals addressed to humanity, for a return to God, going unheeded.

c How greatly saddened is Jesus by the great numbers who are traveling the road of sin, of impurity, of corruption and of unbridled egoism! For these poor diseased children of mine, offer the assistance of your penance and your mortification.

d   On each day of the month consecrated to me, give me little flowers of silence and docility, of complete availability, of humility and patience, of meekness, of your renunciation of comforts and the gratification of the senses.

e   In this way you will walk the road of self-contempt, effecting in yourselves that renunciation of the world and its seductions that constitutes the most important daily obligation assumed by you in your baptismal and sacerdotal consecration.

f   Give me the garlands of your rosaries, recited more frequently and with a greater intensity.

g   Gather the religious and the faithful around you in cenacles of unceasing prayer, offered with me.

h   Above all, I am asking you to pray with fervor and joy by means of the holy rosary. It is the weapon which is to be used by you today in fighting and winning this bloody battle; it is the golden chain that binds you to my heart; it is the lightning rod that will keep far from you, and from those who are dear to you, the fire of the chastisement; it is the sure means of having me always close to you.

i   Finally I ask you to renew often and to live the consecration to my Immaculate Heart.

j   Enter at once into this refuge to be protected by me.

k   My protection should become ever more manifest to all, because the days in which you are living are marked by great sufferings, and for so many of my poor, menaced children the danger of being lost is increasing.

l   Let this month of May, especially consecrated to me, be a precious occasion for you to entrust yourselves to me with the offering of your little flowers of mortification, the frequent recitation of the holy rosary, and a more intense living of the consecration to my heart."

New Heavens and a New Earth

a   "Everything is about to be fulfilled, beloved sons, whom for so long I have called to enter into my refuge, in order to assist in my plan of salvation and mercy.

b   For this reason I gather you into the cenacle of my Immaculate Heart, to form you to a life of prayer with me, to a life of mutual love, of giving, and of holiness.

c   In this new cenacle, let us together invoke the gift of the Holy Spirit who, coming from the Father and the Son, through my maternal intercession again today wishes to pour out his fulness on the suffering Church, on all humanity shrouded in such deep darkness.

d   Under the influence of his mighty work of love, the desert of this world can be entirely renewed by an immense profusion of the dew of grace, and thus transformed into a garden of life and beauty, wherein it may please God once again to display his reflection.

e   Give us, O Spirit of Love, new heavens and a new earth, where the Most Holy Trinity will be loved and glorified; where men can live together as in a single large family; where the wounds of egoism and of hatred, of impurity and injustice, may be entirely healed.

f   Give us, O Spirit of Love, a Church renewed by the irresistible force of your divine action, straightening what is contorted, bending what is inflexible, healing what is wounded, bringing water to what is parched, throwing open what is closed.

g   Give us, O Spirit of Love, a Church faithful to the Gospel, a herald of truth, resplendent in sanctity.

h   Give us, O Spirit of Love, a humble Church, evangelical, poor, chaste and merciful.

i   By your divine fire, burn away whatever in it is imperfect; despoil it of so many human means of power; free it from compromise with the world in which it lives and which it should save; cause it to come forth from its purification completely renewed, ever more beautiful, without stain or wrinkle, in imitation of Mary, its immaculate Mother and your most loving Spouse.

j   It is only in the triumph of my Immaculate Heart that the task I have entrusted to my Movement of priests will be fully accomplished."

266

The Gate of Heaven

a   "My Immaculate Heart is the Gate of Heaven through which passes the Spirit of Love of the Father and of the Son, to come to you and to renew the whole world.

b   For this reason I am inviting you today to enter even further into the depths of this, my heavenly garden; you will then be covered with the light of the Most Holy Trinity.

c   In my Immaculate Heart, the Father gazes upon you with complacency, seeing that you have been formed by me to glorify Him in a most perfect manner.

d   My maternal task is to help each of you realize in all its fulness the design of the Father, who created you to participate in his being, his love and his glory.

e   Accordingly I help you to open yourselves to the sunshine of God's love which makes you grow in what is beautiful and good and true. The glory of God, in all its divine harmony, manifests itself through the ordered cadences of your existence.

f   How many mysterious modulations vibrate through the melody of your prayer, your suffering, your silence, of all the virtues that should comprise the epic poem of your existence.

g   In your life you are opening your hearts to the chant of the glory of the Father, who would have his complacency reflected in you while, by the mystery of his paternity, you are being generated to a new fulness of life and joy.

_h_ In my Immaculate Heart the Son assimilates you to make you more completely resemble himself, and to associate you with his own life. It is in my heavenly garden that the wonder of your transformation takes place.

_i_ It is above all through me that this happens; through me because Jesus, finding me to be as it were the purest and most supple clay, molded me so perfectly in his image that no other creature will ever be able to produce that image as did your heavenly Mother.

_j_ And so it is that I, though Mother, became the daughter of my Son; and so it is that I became the first and most perfect of his disciples; and so too it is that while I am leading you to Jesus I am able to manifest myself to you as a model for imitation, if you want to succeed in reliving his life in your own.

_k_ I form you in his likeness in your minds, and I obtain the Spirit of wisdom for you, to lead you to seek and receive, to meditate upon and to preserve, his divine word.

_l_ In this way it is possible for you to live the Gospel with the simplicity of little children, with the fidelity of the martyrs, and with the heroism of the saints.

_m_ I form you in your hearts, and bring you to the plenitude of love for God, so that you may love all your brothers with the same divine charity. For this I make you always more sensitive, purer, more understanding and merciful, more compassionate and meek, more courageous and humble.

_n_ And every day Jesus enters through the gate of this, my heavenly garden, to experience the great joy of seeing himself imitated and relived by all of you, my sons and his little brothers.

_o_ In my Immaculate Heart the Holy Spirit communicates himself to you in an ever more munificent manner, to produce in your souls that union of life and of love which He achieved in your heavenly Mother.

_p_ And seeing you in my maternal arms, He breathes upon you with the vehemence of love, transforming you into sparks of fire, flames of grace, stars of sanctity and zeal for renewing the firmament of the Church.

_q_ He communicates himself to you with his seven holy gifts, and makes you suitable instruments for converting the world to the God of Mercy and Salvation, preparing the kingdom in which Jesus will rule with his divine power and the Father will be everlastingly glorified by all creation.

r   Enter, therefore, through the heavenly gate of my Immaculate Heart, if you wish to participate in the divine prodigy, the new Pentecost for the Church and the complete renewal of the world."

267

Valdragone di San Marino, June 29, 1983
Spiritual Exercises — Cenacle of the Directors of the M.M.P.

Why I Wanted You Here

a   "This year I have again summoned you here, and from all over Europe you have come to spend these days in a continuing cenacle with me.

b   Here my heart is being consoled by you in these times of so much tribulation. How greatly glorified in you is your heavenly Mother! I reflect my light in your hearts and pour out the fullness of grace upon your souls.

c   I am always close to you; I associate myself with your prayer; I increase your love; I strengthen the bonds that unite you; I rejoice to see you so little and so docile, so prompt to understand and help one another, to walk together along the difficult road of the consecration you have made to me.

d   Why have I wanted you here this year?

e   To make you understand that now you must walk together, united in love, so that you form but a single entity. During these days in the cenacle of my Immaculate Heart I want to form all of you into a single heart and a single soul.

f   The tactic of my Adversary is one of hatred and division. Where he penetrates, by his deceitful and malignant action he succeeds in bringing rupture, misunderstandings and antagonism. Even within the Church he is making ever greater efforts to wound its interior unity. Therefore I am assembling you from every part of the world, to help you to love one another, to unite with one another, to grow in the perfection of love.

g   I have also summoned you here to make you understand that your public mission is now about to be consummated by your personal and precious immolation.

h   This is the Holy Year of the Redemption accomplished by my son Jesus upon the Cross.

i   And now for you too, my Immaculate Heart, once a cradle, has become an altar upon which I must fix each of you on the cross the Father has prepared for you for the salvation of the world.

j   For this reason, my beloved sons, ready yourselves to live with trust and abandonment the bloody hours now awaiting you, while each day I make you more conformed to Jesus Crucified.

k   The errors spreading through the Church and obscuring her faith are the crown of thorns. Sins committed and not atoned for are the painful lashes. The deluge of impurity is reducing your sacerdotal body to a single wound. The hatred of the world, the lack of understanding, and even the ostracism that surround you, these are the nails that transfix you. You have been called to ascend Calvary with me, and there you are to be immolated for the salvation of the world.

l   I have also called you here to obtain for you the Holy Spirit, given to you in superabundance by the Father and the Son, through your unceasing prayer united to my maternal intercession. He will transform you into ardent flames of zeal for the glory of God, and into courageous witnesses of Jesus, in these times which have become so evil.

m   The struggle between your heavenly Mother and her Adversary has now entered its decisive phase.

n   The Woman clothed with the sun is, with her cohorts, openly waging war against the cohorts submissive to the Red Dragon, at whose service is placed the Black Beast come up from the sea.

o   The Red Dragon is Marxist atheism, which has now conquered the whole world, and which has induced humanity to build a new civilization of its own, without God. In consequence, the

386

world has become a cold and barren desert, immersed in the ice of hatred and in the darkness of sin and impurity.

p   The Black Beast is also Masonry which has infiltrated the Church and attacks it, wounds it, and seeks by its subtle tactics to demolish it. Like a poisonous cloud, its spirit seeps in everywhere, to paralyze faith, extinguish apostolic ardor and produce an ever greater alienation from Jesus and his Gospel.

q   Apostles of these last times, the time has come to fight with courage under the command of your heavenly Leader.

r   To discord and division I wish to respond through you, strengthening your communion and the love that unites you, so that you will become a single entity. To the flood of sin and iniquity, I respond with your priestly immolation, and to achieve this I help you to ascend Calvary and I place you upon the cross upon which each must be immolated. To the attack of the Red Dragon and the Black Beast I respond by summoning all to the battle, so that God may be ever more glorified and the Church, in its children, healed from the wounds of infidelity and apostasy.

s   Pray, love, do penance! Walk the road of humility and littleness, have contempt for the world and for yourselves, following Jesus who loves you and is leading you.

t   Soon victory will be resplendent everywhere. Through the triumph of my Immaculate Heart there will come upon you the glorious reign of Jesus who, in his Spirit of Love, will bring all of creation to the glorification of the Father, and at last the face of the earth will be renewed.

u   Wherefore, before you go down from this mountain, I look upon you one by one with maternal tenderness, and fill your hearts with graces that you will understand only later on. I bless you in the name of the Father and of the Son and of the Holy Spirit."

The Holy Mountain

a   "Ascend with me, beloved sons, the holy mountain of your perfect conformity to Jesus Crucified.

b   How many times my Son Jesus lovingly ascended the mountains, impelled by an ardent desire for solitude and silence, to live with greater intensity his union with the Father!

c   From the time of his adolescence He often sought refuge in the hills surrounding Nazareth; it was on a mountain that He promulgated the evangelical law of the Beatitudes; it was on Mount Tabor that He experienced the ecstasy of his transfiguration; in Jerusalem, a city on a mountain, He gathered his own together for the Last Supper, and endured the sorrowful hours of his interior agony; on Mount Calvary He consummated his sacrifice, on the Mount of Olives his final separation from his disciples took place, in the glorious Ascension into heaven.

d   Today ascend with me the holy mountain which is Jesus Christ, so that you can enter into a life of intimacy with Him. In these times of my decisive battle, each of you has been called to combat, armed with the very light of Christ, because you must be his own presence in the world.

e   For this reason, ascend the holy mountain of his wisdom, which is revealed to you if you remain little, humble and poor. Your minds will be drawn towards his divine mind, and you will penetrate into the secret of truth revealed in Holy Scripture; you will be captivated by the beauty of his Gospel, and with courage you will pronounce the word of Jesus to the men of today, that word which alone illumines and can lead to the fullness of the truth.

f   Ascend the holy mountain of his Heart, so that you may be transformed by the burning ardor of his divine charity.

g   Then your hearts will be dilated and molded after his, and in the world you will be the very pulsations themselves of the Heart of Jesus, which seeks above all those who are furthest away, and wishes to envelop all in the flames of his infinite mercy.

h   You will become meek and humble of heart; you will be truly able to love; you will pour balm on the grievous wounds of the suffering and of those most in need; you will give your priestly help especially to those who have lost themselves along the road of iniquity and sin. In this way with your love you will bring an immense number of my children to the path of salvation.

i   Ascend the holy mountain of his divine humanity, in order to become reflections of his perennial immolation for you: his eyes in your eyes, his hands in your hands; his Heart in your hearts; his sufferings in your sufferings; his wounds in your wounds; his Cross in your crosses.

j   In this way you will become the potent presence of Jesus who, by means of you, can still today work mightily to bring all to salvation. In this salvation is the triumph of my Immaculate Heart; in it is to be found the conclusion of the battle to which I have summoned you, and the realization of my heralded victory.

k   Therefore, beloved sons, it now becomes more urgent than ever to follow me, your heavenly Leader. Ascend with me, then, the holy mountain that is Christ, to become perfectly assimilated to Him, so that He may live again in each of you, in order to bring all men to salvation."

269

In The Light of Paradise

a   "Today, beloved sons, I want you to be spiritually here above in paradise that I may fill you with trust and hope in the spectacle of your heavenly Mother assumed, body and soul, into the glory of heaven.

b   With heart and soul behold the paradise that awaits you. Paradise is your goal. You have not been made for this earthly life that now so greatly absorbs, wearies and consumes you.

c   Life on earth is a long and sorrowful antechamber through which one must pass before entering the kingdom prepared for you by the heavenly Father.

d   In this kingdom my Son Jesus is already arranging a place for each of you. The angels joyfully await your arrival and all the saints pray and burn with love in expectation that all of these places will one day be forever occupied, and occupied by you.

e   Today you should look more intently at the paradise awaiting you, if you wish to walk in serenity, in hope and in trust.

f   In the light of paradise you will better understand the times in which you are living. It is a time of suffering. It is the time described in the Apocalypse in which Satan has established in the world his reign of hatred and death.

g   Those who are the very poorest, the weakest, the most defenseless, my little ones, are so often overwhelmed by sufferings, sufferings which become greater day by day.

h   Oh, the Lord will shorten the time of trial, mindful too of the sorrow and fidelity He sees in you.

i   But that you may be consoled, today you should look up at the paradise prepared for you.

j   In the light of the paradise awaiting you, you will be better able to read the signs of your times.

k   The days in which you live are evil, for the hearts of men have become cold and barren, closed tight by so much egoism, no longer capable of love.

l   Humanity is travelling the road of rebellion against God and of obstinate perversity. And so it is that the fruits you are harvesting today are themselves evil: hatred and violence, corruption, impiety, impurity and idolatry. The body is lifted aloft as an idol, and pleasure is sought after as if it were the supreme good.

m   How many signs the Lord sends you, to call you to repentance and change of heart: sickness, misfortune, a virtual flood of incurable ills, ever widening wars, threats of imminent harm! Lest you despair in these times, and to keep you ever astride the path of secure and unshakeable faith, it has become urgent for you to live with your gaze upon paradise where, with Jesus, your heavenly Mother loves you, and in her glorious body she even follows you.

n In the light of the paradise awaiting you, above all you will know how to fulfill to perfection the design I have for each of you, in these times of the great struggle between the Woman clothed with the sun and her Adversary, the Red Dragon.

o In profound detachment from the world and from creatures, you will become truly little, trustful, humble and good; you will walk along the road of contempt for the world and for yourselves; you will be capable of mortifying your senses, and once again you will offer me the gift of your penitence.

p It is my desire that you also return to the practice of fasting, recommended so much by Jesus in the Gospel. Thus you will become true disciples of Jesus, and in this time of pervasive darkness, you will shed his light around about you.

q For these reasons I invite you today to look up to paradise, which exults in the mystery of the bodily assumption of your heavenly Mother who encourages all and blesses all."

270

Toronto, Canada August 26, 1983
Our Lady of Czestochowa

Mother of the Purification

a "Beloved children, look with my most merciful eyes at the evils afflicting humanity and the Church today, and you too will shed tears of sorrow and deep compassion.

b With my heart love all your brothers and you will feel the immense sufferings of my poor children as if they were your own. I am the Queen of all nations and my regency is one of love. I wish to convey the hearts of all to the greatest possible life of union with Jesus, in a way that will glorify the Father in the triumph of his Spirit of Love.

c   In your lives carry the sufferings of the peoples reduced to slavery by those who reject God and use every means to spread atheism.

d   Poland, of whom I have been officially proclaimed Queen, is a symbol of this unending and bloody persecution.

e   In these nations how many are prevented from professing their faith; how many are pushed aside by reason of their fidelity to Jesus and to the Church!

f   For so many years the Red Dragon has extended his dominion over these peoples and persecuted my children by the most subtle and refined means.

g   Feel in your hearts the deep wounds caused me by the millions of infants slaughtered in the wombs of their mothers; by sin which overabounds and seduces souls; by immorality which, like a terrible cancer, corrupts consciences; by the disorientation of the youthful victims of vice, drugs and violence; by the breakdown, in so many instances, of domestic harmony.

h   Participate too in the sufferings of the Church as it lives through the hour of its greatest abandonment. How ailing she is, this my most beloved daughter!

i   In your hearts carry the sufferings of Jesus, and my sufferings as well as for the agonizing condition in which the Church now finds itself in every part of the world. Error is being taught and propagated beneath the ambiguous formulas of a new cultural interpretation of truth; the spirit of the world finds welcome; it spreads its malignant influence and leads so many souls to accept sin, to justify it and to live in it; loss of faith is becoming a deluge, and in many places of worship the images of the saints have been removed, even those of your heavenly Mother.

j   The apostasy has now been spread into every part of a Church betrayed by some of its bishops, abandoned by many of its priests, deserted by so very many of its children, and violated by my Adversary.

k   You, my little child, are to go again into every part of the world, and to announce with power my message to all.

l These are the terrible and painful times of your purification. Never so much as now has it been so necessary to look to me, in order to be consoled, to be defended, and to be saved.

m I am the Mother for these, your times. I am a Mother for you in the present hour of purification."

271

Vancouver (Canada), September 3, 1983
First Saturday of the month

Ministers of the Redemption

a "Beloved sons, respond to my maternal invitation to become the faithful ministers of the Redemption accomplished by my Son, Jesus.

b To you has been entrusted the precious task of baptizing and of pardoning, of announcing the Gospel, of renewing, in the celebration of holy Mass, the sacrifice consummated upon Calvary, of communicating grace by means of the sacraments instituted by Jesus.

c Cause his blood to flow down once again and wash away all the sins of the world. Each day with love and with sorrow, with the intimate participation of your own lives, celebrate the holy Sacrifice of the Mass. It has the power to make reparation, and to destroy so much evil in the world.

d With the Heart of Jesus, have love for your brothers and my children. How many of them are walking the roads of this world like sheep without a shepherd, exposed to every kind of danger! How many have been wounded by sin, made into slaves of evil, victims of hate! How many there are who are poor, who are exploited, weak, suffering. . . .All the sufferings of my children are like a desperate cry for help reaching up to me, and deeply wounding my mother's heart.

e   I am with you on all the by-ways of the world.

f   With maternal mercy I help those of my little ones who find themselves in greater need; I save the perishing, restore health to the sick, console the afflicted, encourage the down-hearted, raise up those who have fallen, find those who have lost the way.

g   This is the hour of the triumph of the Immaculate Heart of your heavenly Mother; it is the hour of the great miracle of divine mercy.

h   But I wish to act through you, my beloved sons. For this I invite all of you to consecrate yourselves to my Immaculate Heart. I can then make you perfect ministers of the Redemption accomplished by Jesus.

i   From this city on the Pacific Ocean, the dividing line, as it were, between East and West, I call all of you to respond to my design, a design that from day to day will make itself more apparent. The Church and the world are to see wrought before them the greatest of the miracles of the divine mercy."

272
Montreal, Canada, Sept. 8, 1983
Feast of the Nativity of Mary

The Smallest of My Children

a   "From every part of the world I am gathering the smallest of my children, to assemble them in my cohort, and to place them in the depths of my Immaculate Heart.

b   Beloved sons, listen to their voices as they cry for help. Go forward to meet them, take them into your arms, and carry them all to your heavenly Mother.

c   To me, little ones are all those infants who, already conceived, are to be put to death purposely while still in the wombs of their mothers. The love and the anxiety of your heavenly Mother, and of the Church, for their salvation, with the innocent blood being spilled by those who despise and disobey the law of God, are a baptism of blood and desire saving all of them.

d   To me, little and defenseless ones are also the children who live and grow up, yet are educated in errors and taught values which are really transgressions of God's law.

e   To me, little ones are those who are young and just beginning to venture out into life, but in a world reduced to a desert because of its want of love. These are being initiated into lives of most bitter experience with every sort of evil.

f   To me, little ones are the poor, those who lack means for getting along in life, who have neither shelter nor work, who are often exploited.

g   To me, little ones are all of my persecuted children, those who are rejected, oppressed.

h   They are those who suffer, who weep, who are alone, who have neither help nor comfort.

i   Little ones are all those of my children who are victims of sin and hatred, who travel along the roads of life without hope or trust. Who can help to save these poor sinful children of mine?

j   Today, around my crib, beloved sons, bring me a wreath of all these my infant children, that I may gather them together as a bouquet of flowers which you are pleased to offer me on the glorious feast of the birth of your heavenly Mother."

273   *St. Francis, Maine (U.S.A.), September 15, 1983*

I Am Beneath the Cross

a   "Look upon your sorrowful Mother, beloved sons, beneath the Cross upon which Jesus is hanging, upon which He is in agony and upon which He dies. From that moment, this has been my place: to remain beneath the cross of each of my sons.

b   I am beneath the cross of the first of my beloved sons, Pope John Paul II, who loves and prays and suffers because of the agony now being lived by the Church, and because of the fate that awaits poor humanity. Do you not recognize that the scourge of war has already come upon you? How many innocent victims will be called upon to endure unspeakable sufferings!

c   I am beneath the cross being carried today by the bishops who remain faithful, while the number of those who prefer to go their own way grows ever greater, heedless of and refusing to follow the Holy Father, whom Jesus has placed at the very foundation of his Church. They are preparing another Church, one separated from the Pope, and this will cause a further scandal, that of a sorrowful division.

d   I am beneath the cross carried today by my beloved sons, the priests, who have been called to live in absolute fidelity to Jesus, to his Gospel and to his Church. Often they must endure the interior martyrdom of feeling themselves misunderstood, ridiculed and even rejected by their own confreres.

e   I am beneath the cross of consecrated souls who wish to live their consecration in fidelity, in opposition to the spirit of the world which has now entered into so many religious houses, bringing into them tepidity, impurity, laxity and the pursuit of every kind of worldly satisfaction.

f   I am beneath the cross of so many of the faithful who have received my invitation courageously and with generosity. Amid enormous difficulties, they hope and have trust in me; in the thick of great trials, they pray with faith and perseverance; amid countless sufferings, in the spirit of reparation they offer whatever the Lord is disposed to place in their lives.

g   I am beneath the cross of my poor sinful children, to lead them back to the road of repentance and reconciliation; beneath the cross of the sick to bring them comfort and resignation; of those who have wandered away, to bring them back to the way of salvation; of those who are soon to die, to help them do so in the grace and love of God.

h   Oh! In these times in which sufferings and tribulations are multiplying, more than ever before I am your sorrowful Mother,
your Consolatrix. I am here beneath your cross, and that of all
my children, to suffer with you, to pray for you.

i   I offer the Father, together with you, the precious contribution
of your personal collaboration in the Redemption accomplished
by my Son Jesus."

274   Curacao (Archipelago of the Antilles), September 29, 1983
         Feast of the Archangels Michael, Gabriel and Raphael

The Role of the Angels

a   "Today the Church is celebrating the feast of the Archangels
Michael, Gabriel and Raphael.

b   It is also your feast, beloved sons, because the angels of the
Lord have a very important part to play in my victorious plan.

c   See, now, what a role is theirs: under my command, they are
fighting a terrible battle against Satan and all the wicked spirits.
It is a struggle proceeding more particularly on the level of spirits,
fought with intelligence and a perfect adhesion to the plans of the
two great opposing leaders, the Woman clothed with the sun and
the Red Dragon.

d   To St. Gabriel has been given the task of clothing you with the
strength of God himself.

e   He fights against the most dangerous of the snares of Satan,
which is that of weakening you, bringing you to discouragement
and to weariness. How many of you have stopped along the way
of the consecration you have made to me, because of your
human weakness!

f   It is weakness that leads you to doubt, to uncertainty, to fear,
to uneasiness. This is the temptation of my Adversary, to render
you spiritless, locked up inside yourselves, hampered by your own
problems, incapable of any real apostolic offensive.

g   The Archangel Gabriel has the task of helping you to grow in
trust, by clothing you in the strength of God. And so it is that

every day he leads you along the path of courage, of firmness, of a faith that is heroic and pure.

h   To St. Raphael is given the task of pouring balm upon your wounds.

i   How often Satan succeeds in wounding you with sin, harming you by his deceitful allurements! He makes you feel the weight of your misery, of your incapacity and frailty, and stops your advance along the path of perfect giving.

j   Finally, to St. Raphael is given the task of accompanying you along the road I have traced out for you, supplying you with the medicine that will heal all your spiritual ailments.

k   Each day he makes your footsteps more secure, your resolutions less uncertain, your acts of love and of the apostolate more courageous; he makes your response to my wishes more decisive, and your minds more attentive to my maternal plan, and you fight your battle, strengthened by his heavenly balm.

l   To St. Michael is given the task of defending you from the frightful attacks Satan unleashes against you.

m   In these times, you my beloved ones, and those who have accepted my invitation and are consecrated to my Immaculate Heart, and all my children who have come to be part of my victorious cohort, are targets assailed with particular fury and ferocity on the part of my Adversary and yours.

n   Satan attacks you on the spiritual field with evey kind of temptation and suggestion, to bring you to evil, to disorientation, to doubt and to distrust. Often he uses his favorite weapon, which is that of diabolical suggestion and impure temptation.

o   He attacks you with terrible snares, frequently forcing you into a position of danger. Even physically he makes attempts upon your life and personal safety.

p   It is the Archangel Michael, Patron of the Universal Church, who, with his great power intervenes and joins combat to liberate you from the Evil One and his dangerous snares.

_q   For this reason I invite you to invoke his protection with the daily recital of that brief but so very efficacious prayer of exorcism composed by Pope Leo XIII.

_r   You see now that the angels of the Lord have an important role in the battle plan for the present conflict: you should always live in their company.

_s   Theirs is a function which is invaluable and irreplaceable: they are close to you, engaged in the same struggle; they give you force and courage, heal your many wounds, defend you from evil; and with you they form the mightiest part of the victorious cohort commanded by the heavenly Leader."

275

Fort Lauderdale, Florida, U.S.A. October 7, 1983
Our Lady of the Holy Rosary

The Dragon Will Be Shackled

_a   "Beloved sons, in the battle in which you are daily engaged against Satan and his crafty and dangerous seductions, and against the mighty armies of evil, apart from the special help given you by the angels of the Lord, it is necessary for you to employ a weapon which is both secure and invincible. This weapon is your prayer.

_b   With prayer you are always able to snatch back from the enemy whatever territory he has conquered; to make blossoms of goodness spring up on the desert of sin and evil; and especially you can free an immense number of souls whom Satan has succeeded in imprisoning. Prayer possesses a potent force and starts a chain reaction in good that is far more powerful than any atomic reaction.

_c   The prayer of my predilection is the holy rosary.

_d   For this reason, in my many apparitions I always ask that it be recited. I unite myself with those who say it; I request it from all with solicitude and maternal preoccupation.

_e   Why is the holy rosary so efficacious?

f   Because it is a simple prayer, a humble one, and it forms you spiritually in littleness, in meekness, in simplicity of heart.

g   Today Satan is successfully conquering everything with the spirit of pride and of rebellion against God, and he is terrified by those who follow your heavenly Mother along the road of littleness and humility. While this prayer is despised by the great and the proud, it is recited with so much love and so much joy by my little ones, by the poor, by children, by the humble, the suffering, by the many, many faithful souls who have welcomed my invitation.

h   Satan's pride will again be conquered by the humility of little ones, and the Red Dragon will find himself decisively humiliated and defeated when I bind him not by a great chain but by a very frail cord: the holy rosary.

i   It is a prayer that you say together with me.

j   When you invite me to pray for you, I accede to your request and mingle my voice with yours, and I unite my prayer to yours.

k   Consequently it always becomes efficacious, because your heavenly Mother is suppliant omnipotence.

l   What I ask for I always obtain, because Jesus can never say 'no' to what his Mother requests of Him.

m   It is a prayer that unites the voices of the Church and of humanity, because it is said in the name of all, and never exclusively on behalf of a single person.

n   By contemplating its mysteries, you are led to understand the plan of Jesus, as spelled out in all of his life, from the Incarnation to the consummation of his glorious Pasch, and thus you penetrate ever more profoundly into the mystery of the redemption.

o   And you begin to understand this mystery of love through your heavenly Mother; moving through the passage-way of her heart, you gain possession of the immense treasure of the divine and burning charity of the Heart of Christ.

p   In the rosary you become formed for the perfect glory of the Father with the frequent repetition of the prayer Jesus taught you: 'Our Father who art in heaven; hallowed be thy name, thy kingdom come.'

q   You are also formed for the everlasting adoration of the Most Holy Trinity with the recital of the 'Glory be to the Father, and to the Son, and to the Holy Spirit.'

r   Today your heavenly Mother asks you to make use of the holy rosary as the most efficacious weapon for fighting in the great battle, under the command of the 'Woman clothed with the sun.'

s   Give your support to my invitation; multiply your cenacles of prayer and fraternity; consecrate yourselves to my Immaculate Heart; frequently recite the holy rosary! Then the powerful Red Dragon will be shackled by this chain, and his margin of action will become ever more restricted. In the end he will be left impotent and harmless.

t   The miracle of the triumph of my Immaculate Heart will be made manifest to all."

276

November 1, 1983
Feast of All Saints

Leader of a Single Cohort

a   "Beloved sons, an invaluable help for fulfilling the task I have entrusted to you is bestowed upon you by those of your brothers who have already arrived here above in paradise, and now participate in its beatitude without end.

b   Today is the feast of All Saints, and you should look up at them with joy, with trust and with great hope.

c   How many of these brothers of yours have lived through difficulties identical to your own, endured the same sufferings, shared in the same sorrows. They responded to my maternal invitation and consecrated themselves to my Immaculate Heart.

d   Here above they form a great crown of light, which together with your Mother, opens in an everlasting chant of praise to the Most Holy Trinity.

e   Those who while on earth lived as my children, listened to me with docility, and followed me along the road I myself pointed out, now are components of a most luminous crown around my Immaculate Heart, a crown of love, of joy and of glory. How many of these my children have you known during these years! Now they are closer than ever to you, fighting the same battle under the command of the heavenly Leader.

f   My mother's heart today unites you in an extraordinary communion of life with all your brothers who are in paradise, and with those who now possess certitude as to their salvation but are still suffering the moment of their personal purification in purgatory.

g   This is an immense part, invisible but most valuable, of my cohort, because my holy children are now clothed with the very power of God and with the strength that is my own, while the souls in purgatory can give me the contribution of their suffering and their unceasing prayer.

h   For this reason you need never feel alone. Strenghten your bonds with the saints in heaven, and with those still being purified in purgatory. They are very near to you. They see all your difficulties. They are aware of the terrible snares being laid for you by my Adversary, and they help you always in a very efficacious way. Look up today at all who have gone before you, leading lives on earth marked by the sign of faith, and now awaiting you with love and with joy.

i   I am the Mother and the Queen of all the saints.

j   I am the Leader of a single cohort!

k   I am the Mother of the entire Church: the militant, the suffering, and the triumphant Church, and my Immaculate Heart vibrates with joy to see you so united in the fraternal bonds of a single communion of life and of love.

l   From paradise, together with your brothers, these my beloved sons who are already here above, and with all the souls still praying and suffering in purgatory, I bless you today in the name of the Father, and of the Son, and of the Holy Spirit."

Along the Roads of Africa

a "Enter into the temple of my Immaculate Heart, beloved sons, if you wish to contemplate the wonders of my merciful love.

b In these times your Mother is exerting her action of solicitous admonition in all parts of the world, to bring you to walk along the good road, that of love, of a return to God, your Redeemer. Everywhere I am revealing myself to little ones, to the simple, to the poor, to the pure of heart.

c Even in this part of the African continent, you see how my invitation is being received by them with gratitude and great appreciation.

d How much love for me you are finding along the roads of Africa! Here, amid such great poverty, where houses still made of mud and my children often have neither food nor clothing, what I obtain from them is more than what is given me in other more advanced parts of the world.

e I receive a love that is open and sincere, a generous response, a correspondence that is enthusiastic and contented, prayer that is ardent and persevering.

f You have seen with what great fervor they recite the holy rosary, and with what deep veneration they surround my images, how they place me in every room of their poor homes.

g To these I will continue to manifest myself, by apparitions and by means of my maternal presence, aiding them and soliciting Providence so that they may not lack food and clothing.

h In these days, my little son, you have been able to see with your own eyes how the heavenly Mother is working along the roads of this immense continent.

i The hour of my greatest wonders has come. These are the times of the triumph of my maternal love.

j For this reason I invite all, from all five continents, to enter the temple of my Immaculate Heart, that you may thus further my design."

278   *Grand Bassam (Ivory Coast, Africa), December 8, 1983*
Feast of the Immaculate Conception

The Medicine You Need

a   "I am the Immaculate Conception.

b   Participate, beloved sons, in the great joy of the whole Church as she contemplates today this singular privilege with which the Most Holy Trinity adorned me, in view of my divine maternity.

c   I am your Mother all beautiful, and as such I am invoked by you. I wish to clothe you with my own beauty, and I exhort you to follow after me on the road of grace and of holiness, of purity and virginity.

d   It is sin alone that offends your interior beauty. For this reason I invite all of you to fight every day against so great an evil.

e   Sin is a consequence of that original disorder by which you unfortunately have been prevented from being conceived and born as I was, wholly immaculate.

f   All of you were born burdened by the weight of this evil inheritance. You were released from it at the moment of your baptism, but its consequences have remained with you, leaving you so very fragile and still so easily attracted by sin, to which you fall victim often during the course of your lives.

g   The first thing you must do is to recognize sin as an evil, and to repent immediately with an act of pure and supernatural love.

h   How many of my children today no longer recognize it as an evil. Often they welcome it as something good, and as such they let it penetrate into their souls, into their hearts and into their lives. They are then no longer capable of repentance, and live habitually infected by this grave disease.

i   You should resort to the medicine which the mercy of Jesus has prepared for you: the sacrament of reconciliation.

j Never as in these times has the usage of frequent confession been so necessary. Today confession is disappearing from the lives and practices of so many of my children, and this is a sign of the crisis the Church is undergoing.

k By means of you, beloved ones, I wish to have the sacrament of reconciliation in the Church brought back to its splendor. I wish all of my children to hasten in great numbers to this fountain of grace and of divine mercy. And I invite you, my beloved ones, to confess frequently, and, if possible, every week.

l I ask you to go to the confessional and be at the disposal of all those who need this sacrament.

m Thoroughly educate the faithful on the necessity of using this sacrament, above all when they find themselves in a state of mortal sin.

n This is the medicine you need if you wish to walk along the road of divine grace and of holiness. In this way you will follow your heavenly Mother who, in the train of her heavenly perfume, would draw you after her.

o Then you yourselves will be clothed in the splendor that is mine, and the life of Jesus can cast deep roots within your being.

p From the African continent, today I am addressing to all, with maternal solicitude, my invitation to walk on the road of love and holiness, fighting against Satan and all his seductions. Soon, by means of you, I will be able to obtain the victory, when I will crush the head of the infernal Dragon who today with his wonted treachery is seeking to ensnare you."

279

His New Birth

a "In the garden of my Immaculate Heart, beloved sons, live the beautiful and precious hours of this holy night. Spend it in prayer, in silence, in the sweet company of myself and my spouse, Joseph.

b   Participate in the moments of ecstasy and of ineffable joy lived by your heavenly Mother as she prepared to give you her divine Child. Prayer enveloped me like a mantle; silence took ever greater possession of my life, for the moment had come, so long awaited, of his birth in time. Hence I did not remember the fatigue from the long journey we had completed, nor did I feel discouragement at the refusals to open doors; I was drawn by the secluded quiet of the grotto, and not troubled by its dreariness and want of everything.

c   Then, suddenly, Paradise bent down on my nothingness, and I entered into a rapture of love and of life with the heavenly Father; when I realized that I was still on earth, I now had in my arms my God, miraculously become my Son.

d   Relive the industrious silence of my most chaste spouse, Joseph; his fatigue from conducting us down the long road, his persistence in looking for a house; his repeated patience with each refusal to open a door; his confidence as he led the way to a safe and protected place; his loving efforts to make the miserable grotto more hospitable; his prayerful awaiting for what was about to take place; and finally, his incomparable bliss as he leaned down to kiss and to adore his God, now born from me on this holy night.

e   Let the light that appeared to the shepherds in the darkness of the night be upon you, and also the chants of the angels, and the joy of hearing the glad tidings: 'I announce good news to you, of great joy for all; today a Savior is born for you, who is Christ the Lord!'

f   In the thickness of the night that today has fallen over the world; in the suffering now reaching the point of bloodshed that the Church has been called to experience, while the doors of men and of peoples are again shut to Jesus, who is returning in glory, imitate your heavenly Mother, her most loving spouse, Joseph, and the shepherds who immediately rose up at the invitation

406

addressed them by heaven.

g   Pray and be silent, so that you can hear the voice of God, and recognize the great signs He is sending you today, and by your personal collaboration further his merciful design.

h   Like Joseph, devote yourselves to the task of attentively preparing all for his near return. Enkindle in hearts the lights that have gone out; open souls to grace and to love; throw wide all the gates for Christ, who is coming!

i   And following the example of the shepherds, those simple little ones, so also you must not shut your ears to the voices still more than ever before being given you by heaven.

j   Among them know how to recognize and follow that of your heavenly Mother, who in so many ways and with such great signs repeats to you her prophetic admonition: prepare yourselves for the return of Jesus in glory.

k   His second birth is close at hand. Live with me the decisive hours of this second coming: in trust, in prayer, in suffering that is accepted and enlightened, in the expectation that the great day of the Lord is near.

l   The desert of the world will open to receive the heavenly dew of his glorious reign of love and of peace."

280

December 31, 1983
Last night of the year

Return to Your Redeemer

a   "Spend the last hours of the year in silence, in recollection, and in prayer.

b   Beloved sons, I am your heavenly Mother, and I am presently arranging a great plan of love, to hasten the advent of the triumph of my Immaculate Heart. For never as in these moments has the world been in such need of my maternal presence.

c   The world is walking along the roads of hatred and obstinate rejection of God, of violence and immorality. Despite all the continuing invitations sent by the Divine Mercy, humanity persists in remaining deaf to every summons.

d   The signs the Lord sends are neither understood nor accepted; the dangers pointed out by 'my Pope' who courageously and anxiously is predicting the storm awaiting you, are not believed.

e   The messages which I give, through simple and little souls chosen by me in every part of the world, are not taken into consideration.

f   The appearances which I am still making, often in faraway and dangerous places, are ignored. And yet you are only inches from your ruin. When all are shouting for peace, a new world war could suddenly fall upon you, spreading death and destruction everywhere.

g   When they say: tranquillity and security! then could begin the very greatest overthrow of peoples and individuals. How much blood I see flowing in all the streets of the world!

h   How many of my poor children I see weeping because of the scourge of fire, famine and terrible destruction.

i   The Lord is at the doors of this generation, and during the Holy Year of his Redemption, He still knocks on the hearts of all, with insistence and love.

j   Return to your God, who wishes to save you and to lead you to peace! Return to your Redeemer! Open your hearts to Christ who is coming!

k   The moments you are living are fraught with emergency. For this reason I would ask you to spend the last hours of the year on your knees, in confident and unceasing prayer. Unite your voices with the powerful supplication of your heavenly Mother, who is imploring for all the great miracle of the Divine Mercy."

1984
I ASK THE CONSECRATION OF ALL

Have Courage

a   "Begin this year in the light of my divine maternity. Beloved sons, this feast should be a sign of confidence and of hope for all of you.

b   Have courage; I am the Mother of grace and of mercy. If the new year is opening amid clouds that menacingly thicken on the horizon; if humanity is incapable of finding its way back to God; if the disintegrating forces of evil and death in the world are increasing; if insecurity and fear mark the passage of your days, look to me as to the Mother of Divine Mercy.

c   Today I bend down over this generation, so ailing and so threatened, with the love a mother has for the neediest of her children, and for those exposed to danger. With my immaculate hands I gather up all the sufferings and immense miseries of humanity, and present them to the Heart of my son, Jesus, that He may cause the river of his merciful love to flow down upon the world.

d   Have courage, because Jesus loves you with his divine tenderness, and your heavenly Mother is always among you to share your difficulties and dangers.

e   Have courage; I am the Mother of the Savior and of your Redeemer.

f   On the Cross Jesus redeemed you forever, suffering and dying for you. His sacrifice has an infinite value, transcending time. His blood, his wounds, his painful agony, his atrocious death upon the Cross, possess the value of salvation even for this generation of yours, which without Him would have gone to perdition.

g   His sacrifice is mystically consummated in every holy Mass which is celebrated.

h   To the general and renewed rejection of God, the answer is still that of his renewed prayer, with its infinite capacity for reparation: 'Father, forgive them, for they know not what they say or what they do'.

i   If sin and evil are overflowing, today there is offered anew to the Divine Justice the innocent blood of the true Lamb of God, who takes away all the sins of the world.

j   To the threat of war and of destruction, the answer is the certainty of having the real presence among you of Jesus in the Eucharist, he who is Life and who has conquered sin and death forever.

k   At the beginning of this new year, look to Jesus your Redeemer and to your heavenly Mother, who console you and lead you to penetrate into the wonderful plan of your salvation.

l   Have courage: I am the Mother and the Queen of peace. Through me peace will come to you. Listen to my voice and let yourselves be led by me with docility.

m   On the eve of the great trials awaiting you; in the threat, now feared by all, of a new and frightful war, know that my presence among you, confirmed today in so many ways and with such great prodigies, is a sign which tells you how, at the end of the great suffering, my Immaculate Heart alone will triumph.

n   The victory of love and of peace will be throughout the whole world!"

282   *Sanctuary of Castelmonte (Udine), January 21, 1984*
(During the concelebration, just after the Gospel)

My Book

a   "I accept the homage from you, who have come up to my Sanctuary here, to give thanks to your heavenly Mother for the book. How many difficulties 'my book' has encountered, but how much good has it already done in every part of the world, translated now into so many languages!

b   It has been the instrument for carrying to the hearts and souls of so many beloved children the voice of the heavenly Mother, the manifestation of my maternal plan, my invitation to receive you all within the refuge of my Immaculate Heart.

411

c   How should this book be read?

d   With the simplicity of a child who is listening to his mother. He doesn't ask why she speaks, or how she speaks, or where her words are going to lead him. He loves her and he listens to her. He does what she says. And then the child is happy, because he feels that in this way he is guided and illumined by his mother. Led by her and formed by her words, each day he continues to grow in life.

e   So should it be for you. Read it with simplicity, without minding about such problems as how I speak, why I speak, where I am speaking. My only concern is that you live everything I have told you. Then your hearts will be inflamed with love, your souls will be illumined by my light, and I will transform you interiorly to lead you to do each day what pleases the Heart of Jesus.

f   If you are consecrated to me, I take you just as you are, with your limitations, your defects and sins, your frailty, but then each day I transform you to bring you to be in accordance with the plan which God has entrusted to my Immaculate Heart.

g   What do I say in this book of mine?

h   I trace out a simple and beautiful road, but a difficult one, oh how difficult! How necessary it is to travel it, if you wish to live the consecration.

i   I teach you how to live; I form you in a practical way to live with me.

j   I tell you the things which I have most on my heart, because they are the very things which Jesus has told you in the Gospel, which today should be lived with the simplicity of little ones, with the ardor of martyrs, and with the fidelity of courageous witnesses: it should be lived to the letter!

k   Accordingly I am calling you to prayer, to penitence, to mortification, to the practice of virtue, to trust, to hope, to the exercise of an ever more perfect charity.

l   This is what I want to tell you. Don't be delayed, therefore, by the predictions I give you in the effort to make you comprehend the times in which you are living.

m   Like a mother, I am telling you the dangers through which you

412

are góing, the imminent threats, the extent of the evils that could happen to you, only because these evils can yet be avoided by you, the dangers can be evaded, the plan of God's justice always can be changed by the force of his merciful love. Also when I predict chastisements to you, remember that everything, at any moment, may be changed by the force of your prayer and your reparative penance.

n Do not say therefore: how much of what you predicted to us has not come true! Instead, give thanks with me to the heavenly Father because at the response of your prayer and consecration, your suffering, and on account of the immense suffering of so many of my poor children, again He alters the period of justice, to permit that of the great mercy to come to flower. (. . .)"

283 *Zompitta (Udine) January 24, 1984*

My Signs

a "Beloved sons, I welcome this rosary you are reciting together with such great love and fervor.

b As a mother I wish to speak to you, I who am here with you, represented by the statue you have here. Every statue of mine is a sign of my presence, and reminds you of your heavenly Mother. Therefore each of them should be honored and put in a place of greater veneration.

c Just as you look with love at a photograph of a cherished person because it transmits to you a reminder and a likeness, so too you should look with love at every image of your heavenly Mother, because it transmits to you a reminder of her, or rather it becomes a particular sign of her presence among you.

d How deeply saddened I am by the circumstance, today so frequent, of being ousted from the churches. Sometimes I am placed outside, in a corridor, like some trinket; sometimes I am put in the back of the church, so that none of my children can see or venerate me.

e   A sign also of how much I like the fitting veneration given to my images is what I am effecting through this little statue. It is a triple sign I give you: that of my eyes, which suddenly come alive; that of the color of my countenance, which changes its hue; and that of my heart, which exudes a fragrance, now a delicate one, now one of greater strength.

f   By the sign I give you in the eyes, I want to show you that your heavenly Mother, never so much as in these times, is watching you with merciful eyes. She is never far from you; she takes cognizance of you in all the difficulties in which you find yourselves, in the difficult moments you are living, with all the sufferings besetting you, with the great cross you must carry.

g   And with these eyes I look at all, at those far away, at the atheists, at the drug addicts, at my poor sinful children, to know them just as they are, to guide them along the path of goodness, of a return to God, of conversion, prayer, fasting and penance.

h   In a particular way I look at you, my beloved, objects of my maternal complacency. Especially you, beloved of my sacerdotal Movement, who form for me an object of great gratification.

i   I look at you and I illumine you with my own beauty. In you I reflect the candor of heaven that is mine. You should be lilies in your purity, roses in your fragrance, cyclamens in your littleness. In this way you compose this beautiful crown of love that makes the thorny crown of my sorrow break into blossom.

j   By the sign I give you in the color of my visage, I want to show you that I am a Mother for all, and today I share in all your needs, and I rejoice in all your joys. But I also suffer in all your numerous sufferings.

k   When a mother is happy and jumps for joy, you see the color of her face become rosy; when she is worried about the fate of her children, you see her face turn completely pale. If this happens to an earthly mother, it also happens to me, and the sign I give you, so human and maternal, is to tell you that as a Mother I truly share in all the moments of your mortal life.

l   When you suffer, I suffer. When you rejoice, I rejoice. When you are good, I jump for joy. When you love me, my face is all aflame because of the joy you give me.

m   By the sign I give you with the fragrance I exude, sometimes of lesser, sometimes of greater strength, I wish to show you that I am always among you, but especially when you are more in need of me.

n   If you do not recognize the perfume, or you notice it in a very faint way, it is not because I do not love you, or because you are wicked. A mother loves even with merciful predilection those who have the greater need for her!

o   Understand then why my maternal compassion goes out to sinners, all, but especially those who are furthest away, those most in need of divine mercy. Appearing at Fatima, I taught you to pray to Jesus in this way. 'Bring all souls to heaven, especially those most in need of thy mercy.'

p   I love all, beginning with the furthest away, those of my children who are sinners, for whom I am a secure and maternal refuge.

q   Look at my merciful eyes which shed tears of sorrow and compassion. In so many parts of the world I give this sign, causing copious tears to stream from my eyes, even tears of blood.

r   To give a sign of my maternal presence, and to accord to your lives a secure support, and amid the tribulations you are living, to call you to joy and to trust, in so many parts of the world I am still giving my maternal messages. They announce to you the certitude that I am following you and am with you. I live with you, I prepare everything for you, I lead you by the hand along the difficult road of this time of purification.

s   A fragrant sign of my maternal presence is to be found in the apparitions I am still making in many regions of the world. Yes, in these times I am appearing in Europe, in Asia, in Africa, in America, and in distant Oceania. The whole world is wrapped in my maternal mantle.

t   In the struggle, now conclusive, between me and my Adversary, my extraordinary presence tells you that my victory has already begun. My beloved sons, how much I love you!

u From you, to whom I have given so much, this I ask; that you increase your love for me! (. . .)"

284

My Gift To You

a "(. . .) Everything in life has been arranged for you; in every particular, by the providence of God the Father and of your heavenly Mother: the moments of suffering, those of spiritual trial and interior difficulties, the moments of joy and of consolation, the moments of special fervor and of union with me.

b Everything is the gift of God to you, which Jesus gives you through the Immaculate Heart of your heavenly Mother. For this reason it is also a gift from me.

c When my heart which is replete with grace and with love opens and pours out upon you my maternal predilection, encouraging and consoling you, what is this unfolding of my maternal tenderness, of the fullness of my immaculate love, if not a gift I am giving you?

d The task of the Mother is to prepare this gift each day for her children, for all; for the furthest away, it is a gift of mercy and pardon; for sinners it is a sorrowful gift, one recalling them to the road of goodness; for the many who suffer, it is a gift of compassion and comfort; for those soon to die, it is a gift of support, helping them to close their lives here below in a good way, and opening the golden gate of the life awaiting them after death.

e And for you, my beloved ones, the gift is one of most particular predilection, expressing itself by the ordering of all things, the arranging of every circumstance of your day like an embroidery of perfect beauty woven by the fingers of your heavenly Mother.

f My being present among you; the gathering of you together in prayer; the frequent reciting of my prayer, the holy rosary; the caring for you, and this even with your weaknesses and human miseries, all is a gift of my Immaculate Heart!

g   Walk forward always united, hand in hand like so many little brothers, praying together, loving together, rejoicing and suffering together, because I have now revealed to you my plan, which should be realized in a most perfect unity.

h   Also a gift of my Immaculate Heart, oh! a most particular gift, is the book containing my messages.

i   In my book what you should know has already been revealed. If you know how to read it, it is my total plan, in its preparation, in its sorrowful actualization, and in its luminous and victorious completion.

j   Read it, my beloved sons, meditate on it, live it! Have no doubt but that in it I am speaking to you; through its words I am present in it and manifest myself. Only tomorrow will you understand the importance of this maternal message of mine.

k   A gift of my Immaculate Heart is the plan I have revealed to you. When I speak to you I use your human words, but whereas you speak in virtue of the experience you have from your earthly life, I speak to you in virtue of the light of paradise. In the Heart of my Son Jesus, and in the profound mystery of the Most Holy Trinity, a single reality is comprised, binding together in a true communion of life the present, the past and the future, the Church that is triumphant and rejoicing in heaven, that which is suffering and being purified in purgatory, and that which, as a pilgrim on your poor earth, is still struggling.

l   In the vision of this divine communion that now unites you, I speak to you always in the vision of eternity, so that for me there is no difference between my children living here in paradise, between those still in purgatory, and those yet walking upon earth, pursuing day after day their human pilgrimage.

m   (. . .) For this reason I see close to you, still members as valuable as ever of my Movement, your brothers and my beloved ones who have arrived here above and compose so beautiful a harmony (. . .). You should feel that your brother priests who have arrived here above are near to you, because they are forever a part of my Movement. Perceive them as members who are living, working, fighting and of great value to my victorious cohort, which battles at my command!

417

n　A gift of my Immaculate Heart to the Church is this, my Movement. It is my work alone.

o　For eleven years I have been diffusing it in every part of the world; I call my sons and they respond. For eleven years I have been achieving a masterpiece of love and mercy for the triumph of my Immaculate Heart. Everything that I have told you will be fulfilled to the letter. The Church will come to an ever greater realization of how the Marian Movement of Priests is a gift of my Immaculate Heart; and with it too I wish to give the Church the certainty of my perennial presence and my maternal protection (. . .).

p　But above all the new Pentecost will be a gift of my Immaculate Heart. Just as in the Cenacle of Jerusalem the apostles, reunited with me in prayer, prepared for the moment of the first Pentecost, so now in the cenacle of my Immaculate Heart, and consequently in the cenacles where you, apostles of these last times, reunite yourselves in prayer with your heavenly Mother, you can obtain a new effusion of the Holy Spirit.

q　It will be the Spirit of Love, with his powerful action of fire and of grace renewing the very foundations of the whole world.

r　It will be He, the Spirit of Love, with his great force of holiness and of light, bringing my Church to new splendor, making it therefore humble and poor, evangelical and chaste, merciful and holy.

s　It will be the Spirit of Love, through the fire of innumerable sufferings renewing all creation, that it may become that garden of God, that terrestrial paradise in which Jesus will always be with you, like a sun of light reflecting its rays everywhere."

285

February 2, 1984
Presentation of the Child Jesus in the Temple

The Soul Transpierced

a　"At the moment I presented my Son Jesus in the Temple and my heart was overwhelmed by maternal bliss in seeing how the

Spirit had revealed the secret plan of the Father to two simple and elderly creatures, my soul was transpierced by the prophetic words addressed to me: 'He is to be as a sign of contradiction, for the salvation and the downfall of many. . .and a sword will transpierce your soul!'

b   See now how the profound mystery of my divine and universal maternity was also revealed.

c   It is a mystery of love.

d   My mother's heart opens itself to love in a perfect manner. No other creature can ever possess as profound a capacity for love as does mine.

e   If the compass of maternal love can be measured by the number of the children, consider how great must be the love of your heavenly Mother, to whom Jesus has confided all mankind as her children.

f   How great is my mother's love! It embraces all and each one in particular; it follows each one along his road; it participates in difficulties, shares in your sufferings, helps you in all your necessities; it assists you in dangers, keeps vigil in decisive moments. No one is ever abandoned or forgotten.

g   Penetrate into the secret of my maternal love and you will always be consoled.

h   It is also a mystery of sorrow.

i   At the moment my infant Jesus was put back into my arms by the priest, and I comtemplated Him, then forty days old, in all his beauty with the freshness of a flower that has just begun to bloom, the prophetic voice of the aged Simeon caused me to behold Him mentally already stretched out on the Cross, and then my soul was truly transpierced by a sword.

j   I am the Mother of the transpierced soul! Therefore all your wounds are now mine, O sons, just as those of my Son Jesus were mine!

k   You are living days of great sufferings that are ever increasing, especially for you, my beloved ones. The time in which you are living is marked by wounds of every kind, caused by a persistent and general rejection of God, by a great neglect of your duties, by the widespread habit of ignoring and no longer obeying the commandments of God's law.

l   Within the Church the confusion grows; too few are those who accept my invitation to let themselves be formed by me, and led with the humble docility of my infant Jesus; and consequently the darkness deepens in minds, in hearts and in souls.

m   I am your Mother of the transpierced soul. I am close by you to close your wounds.

n   Do not lose heart! Pray, do penance, be little and docile, let yourselves be formed by me, let yourselves be carried in my heart over the stormy waters. Courage!

o   Above all, my transpierced soul today wishes to pour down upon you the fullness of its light and grace.

p   I hold you in my heart; each day I carry you to the temple of the Lord and from my maternal arms I place you upon his altar, victims prepared by me and pleasing to Him, for the salvation of the world."

286

Look at My Spouse Joseph

a   "My beloved sons, today look at my most chaste spouse Joseph, who is an example for all of you in furthering God's plan with love, with purity, with faith, and with perseverance.

b   During his life he was a chaste and faithful spouse for me, a valuable collaborator in the loving care of the child Jesus; a silent and provident worker, careful to see that none of the things necessary for our human existence were lacking, just and firm in daily fulfilling the tasks entrusted to him by the heavenly Father.

c   How much he loved and followed each day the wonderful growth of our divine Son Jesus! And Jesus repaid him with an affection that was filial and profound; how He listened to him and obeyed him; how He comforted him and helped him!

d   So also in you, beloved sons, I wish those virtues to flourish which made him so perfect in the fulfillment of the providential design for him.

e   May his silence and effacement be in you, necessary in these times to enable you to carry out the plan I have entrusted to you.

f   Live far from noise and commotion, from shouting and the din that to an ever greater degree surrounds you. Maintain your interior quiet in silent colloquy with Jesus and with your heavenly Mother.

g   Take no part in worldly shows, and shut your eyes to the loose seductions of the world. Know how to avoid the subtle tactics of moral perversion, today disseminated in so insidious and dangerous a way by the press and the television.

h   Do not waste time in front of the television, stealing precious moments from prayer and from listening to my word.

i   May his virginal purity also be in you, in a detachment—which I wish to be as great as possible—from yourselves, from creatures, from human affairs, so that you will be interiorly free, able to love and to fulfill with faithful perseverance whatever the Lord asks of you.

j   Imitate my most loving spouse, Joseph, in his humble and trusting prayer, his heavy labors, his patience and great goodness.

k   Entrust yourselves and my Movement to his powerful protection. Just as once he knew how to protect the menaced life of the infant Jesus, so now he will protect this, my work of love, during those moments in which it will be attacked and furiously combatted by my Adversary.

l   With him, and together with our divine infant Jesus, we encourage you today, and we bless you."

I Ask for the Consecration of All

a "Consider the ineffable moment of the Annunciation made by the Archangel Gabriel, sent by God to receive my yes for the realization of his eternal plan of Redemption, and for the great mystery of the Incarnation of the Word in my virginal womb, and then you will understand why I ask to consecrate yourselves to my Immaculate Heart.

b Yes, I myself manifested my wish at Fatima, when I appeared in 1917; I have asked it many times of my daughter, Sister Lucy, who is still on earth for the accomplishment of the mission I have entrusted to her; during these years I have insistently requested it through the message entrusted to my sacerdotal Movement; today I renew my request that all be consecrated to my Immaculate Heart.

c Before all I ask it of Pope John Paul II, the first of my beloved sons, who on the occasion of this feast, performed the consecration in a solemn manner, after writing to the bishops of the world and inviting them to do so in union with him.

d Unfortunately the invitation was not welcomed by all the bishops; particular circumstances have not permitted the explicit consecration of Russia which I have requested many times. As I have already told you, this consecration will be made to me when the bloody events are well on the way to actuality.

e I bless this courageous act of my Pope in his wish to entrust the world and all the nations to my Immaculate Heart; I receive it with love and gratitude, and because of it I promise to intervene greatly to shorten the hours of the purification, and to lessen the gravity of the trial.

f But I ask this consecration also from all the bishops, from all the priests, from all religious, and from all the faithful. This is the hour in which the Church must assemble itself in the secure refuge of my Immaculate Heart!

g   Why do I ask you for the consecration?

h   When a thing is consecrated, it is removed from all uses other than the sacred one to which it has been assigned, and so it is with an object designated for the divine worship.

i   But this can also be the case with a person, when such a one is called by God to render Him perfect worship. Understand then how your true act of consecration is that of baptism.

j   By this sacrament, instituted by Jesus, grace is communicated to you placing you in an order of life higher than your own, namely the supernatural life. Through this you participate in the divine nature, you enter into a communion of love with God, and your actions, accordingly, have a new value exceeding that of your nature, because they have a value which is truly divine.

k   After baptism you are then destined for the perfect glorification of the Most Holy Trinity, and consecrated to live in the love of the Father, in the imitation of the Son, and in full communion with the Holy Spirit.

l   The fact that characterizes the act of consecration is its totality: when you are consecrated you are then wholly so, and forever!

m   When I ask you for the consecration to my Immaculate Heart, it is to make you understand that you must completely entrust yourselves to me, in a total and everlasting way, that I may dispose of you according to the will of God.

n   You must entrust yourselves in a manner that is complete, asking me for everything; you should not give me one thing and hold on to another, for yourselves; you should truly be wholly mine.

o   And then you should entrust yourselves to me not on one day yes and on another day no, or for a period of time as you would have it, but forever.

p   It is to emphasize this important aspect of a complete and lasting dedication to me, your heavenly Mother, that I ask for the consecration to my Immaculate Heart.

q   How should the consecration be lived by you?

r   If you consider the ineffable mystery the Church commemorates today, you will understand how the consecration I have asked of you should be lived.

s The Word of the Father was entrusted completely to me, in love. After my yes, He came down into my virginal womb.

t He was entrusted to me in his divinity.

u The Eternal Word, Second Person of the Most Holy Trinity, after the Incarnation, was received and hidden in the tiny dwelling, miraculously prepared by the Holy Spirit, of my virginal womb.

v He was entrusted to me in his humanity, in a manner as profound as the way any son is entrusted to the mother, from whom everything is expected: blood, flesh, breath, food, love, to enable him to grow in the womb each day, and then—after birth—each year, always close to the mother.

w For this reason, just as I am the Mother of the Incarnation, so also I am the Mother of the Redemption, which had on this occasion its wonderful beginning.

x And so you see me intimately associated with my Son Jesus; I collaborate with Him in his work of salvation, during his infancy, his adolescence, his thirty years of hidden life at Nazareth, his public ministry, during his sorrowful Passion until the end under the Cross where I offer and suffer with Him, receiving his last words of love and sorrow, in which I am given to all humanity as a true Mother.

y Beloved sons, called to imitate Jesus in everything because you are his ministers, imitate Him also in this, his complete reliance on the heavenly Mother. For this reason I ask you to offer yourselves to me with your consecration.

z I will be able to be an attentive Mother for you, concerned to make you grow in God's plan, to realize in your lives the great gift of the priesthood to which you have been called; I will bring you each day to an ever better imitation of Jesus, who must be your only model and your greatest love. You will be true instruments, faithful collaborators in his Redemption.

A Today this is necessary for the salvation of all humanity, so diseased and so far from God.

B By an extraordinary intervention of his merciful love, the Lord can save this humanity, and you priests of Christ and my beloved sons, are called to be the instruments of the triumph of the merciful love of Jesus.

c   Today this is indispensable for my Church, which must be healed from its wounds of infidelity and apostasy in order to return to its splendor and to renewed holiness.

D   Your heavenly Mother wishes to heal the Church through you, my priests. I will do this soon, if you will allow me to work in you, if you entrust yourselves with docility and simplicity to my merciful maternal action.

E   Again today, with sorrowful supplication, I ask you all to consecrate yourselves to my Immaculate Heart."

288

Close to Every Altar

a   "I am your Mother, so very sorrowful. I am close to my Son Jesus at the moment. He ascends Calvary, exhausted by immense suffering and by the weight of the Cross which He carries with meekness and with love.

b   His feet leave their bloody imprint on the ground; his hands grip the Cross, which weighs upon his wounded shoulders; his body is bruised and lacerated by the terrible scourging it has undergone; from his head fall streams of blood, flowing from the wounds opened by the crown of thorns. . .

c   What weariness the ascent costs Jesus; what suffering is imposed upon Him by each step He makes towards the summit of Calvary!

d   He staggers; He stops, He is shaken by spasms of fever and sorrow; He bends down as if to recoup new energies; this no longer avails Him and He falls to the earth.

e   Behold the Man. Behold, O sons, your King.

f   With an outburst of my mother's love, I would help Him to his feet, to succor Him with the force of my sorrow, to comfort Him with the strength of my presence, I caress Him with the moan of my prayer; I accompany Him with the anguish of a wounded mother; and upon my Immaculate Heart, now united with his in a single offering to the will of the Father, I lead Him towards the summit of Golgotha.

g   I am close to Him when they strip Him of his garments, and with a mother's impulse, understood and accepted by the executioners, I give my white veil so that his modesty will be protected. I watch Him as they stretch Him out on the gibbet; I hear the hammer on the nails which pierce his hands and feet; the terrible thud of the Cross upon the ground penetrates my soul, and makes Him quiver with pain.

h   I am beneath the Cross on this Good Friday, to live together with my Son the long and terrible hours of his Passion.

i   Like a mantle, the peace that comes from his immolated body envelops me; like a river of grace, it flows into me and I feel myself opening to an immense capacity for love; a new and greater maternal vocation discloses itself to my soul, while my Immaculate Heart receives every precious drop of his sorrow during the hours of agony.

j   This Good Friday has truly illumined every day granted you by the Lord for your earthly pilgrimage, O my sons, because it was on this day that you were redeemed.

k   Let all behold Him whom today they have pierced!

l   Let yourselves be washed in his blood; penetrated by his love; be generated by his sorrow, hidden in his wounds, restored by his ransom, redeemed by his new and eternal Sacrifice.

m   This Good Friday is repeated when Jesus is again immolated by you, although in an unbloody manner, in the sacrifice of holy Mass. The supreme gift of this day is mystically renewed by you.

n   But, close to Jesus who is immolated, the sorrowful oblation of your heavenly Mother is also repeated. She is always present close to every altar upon which holy Mass is celebrated, just as she was during the long and sorrowful Good Friday.

o   Let your confidence be great and irresistible!

p   Evil, every evil, and the Spirit of evil, Satan your Adversary from the beginning, has been vanquished and reduced henceforth to perpetual bondage.

q   His great commotion of today should not frighten you, should not disturb you. Live in the joy and in the peace of Jesus, the gentle and meek Victim, offered on the Cross to the Father as the price of your everlasting ransom.

r   Now that darkness has again fallen over the world, and the night envelops a straying humanity, on this, his Good Friday, behold Him whom they have pierced, so that you will understand how the victory over evil, over hatred, and over death, has now been forever obtained for you by the force of the merciful love of Jesus, your Redeemer."

289

May 13, 1984
Anniversary of the First Apparition at Fatima

Be Converted!

a   "These are my times. Today while you recall my first apparition which took place at Fatima in 1917, you are living the events I then predicted to you.

b   You are in the period in which the struggle between me, the Woman Clothed with the Sun, and my Adversary, the Red Dragon, is moving now toward its conclusion, and for this reason I am appearing in a new and more extraordinary way to assure you that my presence in your midst is habitual.

c   I am communicating to all my maternal will with a message which today has become anguished and urgent:

d   Be converted and repent of your sins!

e   Be converted and return to the God who saves you!

f   Be converted and walk along the road of goodness, of love, and of holiness!

g   This is still for you the precious time of conversion. Receive my invitation, which in so many ways, I still wish to address to my children who are so endangered.

h   Pray more; pray with the holy rosary; pray among yourselves in the cenacles; above all, pray in the family.

i   I want Christian families to return to the practice of praying with me and by means of me, so that they will be saved from the great evils threatening them.

j   Mortify yourselves with penance and fasting.

k   It is fasting from evil and from sin that I prefer, of renunciation of smoking, alcohol, motion pictures and television. Do not watch television shows which corrupt your interior chastity and bring so much dissipation into your souls, sowing the germs of evil in your hearts.

l   I am also asking for bodily fasting, at least every now and then, just as it has been requested of you by my Son Jesus, in the Gospel, when He said: 'Certain kinds of demons can be ejected only by prayer and fasting.'

m   Consecrate yourselves continually to my Immaculate Heart, and live in daily communion of life with me.

n   I am the Mother of the faith; I am the faithful virgin, and today you should ask me for help to remain in the faith. For this reason I summon you to listen to and follow the Pope, who has from Jesus the promise of infallibility, and to recite The Creed often as a renewed profession of your faith.

o   If you do everything I ask you, you are walking each day with me towards your conversion. Live well this space of time which the merciful love of Jesus still gives you.

p   You will live with trust and with joy the impending moment of the triumph of my Immaculate Heart."

The Mystery of My Immaculate Heart

a   "Venerate my Immaculate Heart, beloved children. Today the Church is inviting you to look at the mystery of love and of mercy enclosed in my Immaculate Heart.

b   *If you venerate* my heart, you give praise to the Most Holy Trinity, which receives its greatest glory in it, because it has made of this, my heavenly garden, the place of its divine delight.

c   In it the Father is reflected with joy, the Word is placed therein as in a precious cradle, and the Holy Spirit burns with the purest light of his divine love.

d   If you venerate my Immaculate Heart, you also give praise to your heavenly Mother, because within it is enfolded the mystery of my predilection and of the privileges of grace with which I have been adorned by God. And thus you also venerate my singular privileges of the immaculate conception, of the divine motherhood, of the bodily assumption into heaven, of the fullness of grace and of perpetual virginity. Through the way of my heart, enter in so that you may understand and delight in the divine masterpiece which is your heavenly Mother.

e   *If you love* this heart, you yourselves become clothed with my motherly love and my immaculate mercy. In the depths of my Immaculate Heart, there takes place the wonder which I accomplish everyday with you in order to make you ever more like myself and to transform your soul into the image of my own soul.

f   I also communicate my spirit to you in order that you may truly grow in my life and become, today, the expression of the presence of your heavenly Mother. I form you in purity of mind, of heart and of body; and thus you will spread about you the brightness of my immaculate light. I communicate to you my capacity to love, and your hearts will open up as a refuge of salvation to all who have strayed along the path of error and of sin. I give gentleness to your way of acting so that you may be good and merciful to all. I give comfort and balm to your actions, that you may heal the painful wounds of the sick and of all my poor sinful children.

g   And thus you yourselves become, today, the concrete expression of my motherly love.

h   *If you offer reparation* to the sorrow of my Immaculate Heart, you become a source of great joy and consolation for me, because through you I am able to take action, in these years, in order to carry out my plan of salvation.

i   It is a plan which I am still keeping secret; I reveal it only to my little ones, who accept my invitation to venerate, to love, and to offer reparation, as they are led by me to understand more and more the great mystery of love and of mercy of my Immaculate Heart."

291

San Marino, July 5, 1984
Spiritual Exercises in the Form of a Cenacle with the Priests of the M.M.P. of the Italian Language

Mother of Jesus, the Priest

a   "Beloved children, how pleasing to my heart is this continuous cenacle of fraternity and prayer which you are making together with me, your heavenly Mother!

b   *I am the Mother of Jesus, the Priest.*

c   My Immaculate Heart has always been the altar upon which Jesus has wished to present his priestly offering to the Father. From the ineffable moment of the Incarnation, when the Word of the Father was placed in my virginal womb and divinity annihilated itself, assuming therein the beginnings of human nature, my Immaculate Heart became the altar upon which the first priestly action of my son, Jesus, took place.

d   I always accompanied Him in every most perfect accomplishment of his continuous offering as priest and victim. From his birth in poverty to his infancy spent in exile; from his youth passed in humble labor and obedient service to his public life quickly expended amidst so many sufferings and misunderstandings until its painful completion in his bloody agony and death on the cross; the whole life of Jesus was a continuous priestly action, offered with love to the Father for our salvation.

e   At every moment of this offering, Jesus willed to have his Mother with Him that she, too, might suffer and offer. In this, I became co-operator with Him in his work of redemption, truly co-redemptrix, and I am, above all, the Mother of Jesus as priest.

f   And so you understand why I feel a particular predilection for you, my sons, to whom has been entrusted the great gift of the priesthood.

g   I am at your side in every moment of your day, so that it may be completely sacrificed and given to the Father in a continuous priestly offering. I am at your side at the time of prayer and of work, in the hours of joy and of suffering, of solitude and of abandonment.

h   I am always at your side when you celebrate the Holy Sacrifice of the Mass, which renews that accomplished by Jesus on the cross. With Jesus who, by means of you, today carries out his sacrifice, I am always at the side of each altar to offer with you to the heavenly Father, on my Immaculate Heart, the precious Victim of our redemption.

i   Today it is necessary to shed greater light upon the value of Holy Mass as the sacrifice which renews, in an unbloody but true manner, that accomplished by Jesus on Calvary.

j   These are my times and I am at your side, sons, to receive your continuous priestly action. For this reason, allow yourselves to be formed by me with docility.

k   In these spiritual exercises in the form of continuous cenacles, which I wish to be multiplied more and more, I am gently preparing you for your offering.

l   As little lambs I have gathered you into my sheepfold to prepare you for the immolation which awaits you. And now I look upon you with pleasure because you are co-operating with my action which disposes you to be offered to the Lord, on the altar of my Immaculate Heart, for the salvation of the world."

August 15, 1984
Feast of the Assumption
of the Blessed Virgin Mary into Heaven

Walk in the Light

a   "From paradise, into which I have entered with my body as well, I look upon you today with my motherly and merciful eyes. I am shedding upon you the rays of my immaculate light and, in the deep darkness in which you are more and more enveloped, I invite you to walk along the light-filled path which comes from my heart. Little children, walk in the light of your heavenly Mother; allow yourselves to be carried upon the wave of her heavenly perfume.

b   *Walk in the Light of Faith.*

c   These are the times in which my children run the grave risk of straying from the true faith. Errors are being spread; they are listened to and followed; they are publicized and disseminated especially through the press, even that which professes to be religious. How great a need there is today for a press which spreads the truth of the faith in all its clarity and integrity!

d   And so it is necessary to be vigilant, to pray and to remain strongly faithful to the authentic *Magisterium* of the Church. For this reason I invite you to listen to the teaching of the Pope and to recite often The Creed as a profession of your Catholic faith and also to meditate upon the complete profession of faith composed by my beloved son, Pope Paul VI, who is already up here. You will then remain in the true faith, beloved children of your Mother, who is for all the model of how you must believe, guard, love and live the one and only Word of God.

e   *Walk in the Light of Grace.*

f   As a terrible cancer, sin is today infecting souls more and more and leading them to death. If you looked with my eyes, you would see how this real spiritual epidemic has spread, causing slaughter among so many of my children and making them victims of evil.

g   You must become instruments which I will make use of for the healing of all poor sinners. For this I invite you to walk along the way of love and of divine grace, of mortification and penance, of prayer and of holiness.

h   *Walk in the Light of Love.*

i   In these times, in an ever more dangerous way, hatred and unbridled egoism are spreading everywhere. My Adversary is bringing about division on all sides: in families, in religious communities, in the Church, in all human society. How difficult it is becoming to understand one another today, how hard it is to live together with understanding and in mutual agreement!

j   And so I ask of you to remain always in my peace, to become instruments of peace for all. For this reason I invite you, with gentle severity, to silence, to concrete gestures of charity and communion, to help whoever is in need, always to speak words of peace and reconciliation with everyone.

k   Thus you will diffuse my immaculate light in the darkness which has spread about and you will contribute to the transformation of your earthly life according to the model which is lived here above in paradise, where your heavenly Mother has been assumed, even with her glorious body."

293

Altötting (Germany), August 30, 1984
Spiritual Exercises in the Form of a Cenacle
with the Priests of the M.M.P. of the German Language

Mother of Faith

a   "I am the Mother of Faith. I am the faithful virgin. Beloved sons of Germany, Switzerland, Austria, Holland and Hungary, how happy I am with these days of spiritual exercises which you are making with me, in the form of a continuous cenacle! How your fervent and persevering prayer consoles my Immaculate Heart, now more than ever surrounded by a great crown of thorns!

b   In these countries of yours, you are facing a great danger which causes concern to my motherly heart, because errors are being spread much more, efforts are being made to weaken the bond which unites you to the Pope and moreover many souls are being led away from devotion to your heavenly Mother.

c   And so, during these days of cenacle I am causing extraordinary graces to shower down from my Immaculate Heart upon you and upon all my consecrated children. I want to obtain for you from the Holy Spirit the gift of your spiritual transformation to lead you to be courageous witnesses today.

d   *Be Witnesses of Faith.*

e   Preserve in the true faith all those who have been entrusted to you. So therefore defend yourselves from the danger, so widespread today, of falling into error. Do not give acceptance to any error: unmask it when it presents itself hidden under the appearance of truth, because it is then even more dangerous. Do not be afraid if, because of this, you are judged as being backward and not up-to-date, because just as for Jesus, so also his Gospel is the same: yesterday, today and always.

f   Renew often with the faithful your profession of faith and ask of me, the Mother of Faith, the grace to remain always in the truth which my divine son, Jesus, has revealed to you.

g   *Be Witnesses of Unity.*

h   Above all you must be united with the Pope, whom Christ has placed as the foundation of his Church. Today only those who remain united to the Pope can be saved in the faith. Listen to him, follow him, spread his teaching with courage.

i   Be also united to your bishops with prayer, with good example and with effective collaboration. By the witness of your life may they be assisted in rooting out error from the holy Church of God, and by your obedience and your filial love may they receive encouragement in their difficult ministry.

j   Bring all the faithful to this unity of life with the biships and the Pope. And thus you will console my heart, so sorrowful and wounded today because of the profound disunity which has entered into the interior of my Church.

434

k   *Be Witnesses of True Devotion to Me.*

l   In your countries there is under way a strong attempt to remove me from the life and piety of many of my children. It is your duty to have me shine once again upon your path. For this reason, I invite you to multiply the cenacles of prayer and of life with me. Hold them everywhere. Gather the faithful about you to recite the holy rosary, to meditate on my word, to renew and to live the consecration to my Immaculate Heart.

m   The more I will begin again to shine within the life of the Church the more the darkness of error and infidelity will recede from it.

n   Courage! Take leave of this cenacle with my motherly blessing. And in times of greater danger, I will be your defense and your protection. Many evils will be spared you because of your response, so generous and fervent, in consecrating yourselves to my Immaculate Heart and in walking with me.

o   With you, I bless all my priest-sons and faithful of the surrounding countries, who are especially suffering and who are praying in the hope of an early liberation."

294   *Strasbourg (France), September 13, 1984*
Spiritual Exercises in the Form of a Cenacle
with the Priests of the M.M.P. of the French Language

In Cenacle with Me

a   "Beloved sons, how happy I am with your homage of prayer and brotherhood, which you are offering to my Immaculate Heart during these days of continuous cenacle. These are the times in which I wish my beloved priests and all the children consecrated to me to gather together in cenacles of prayer and life with me.

b   *In cenacle with me,* I form you to prayer, which it now becomes necessary to employ increasingly as the weapon with which you must fight and conquer in the battle against Satan and all the spirits of evil who, in these times, have been unleashed with great violence.

It is above all a battle which is waged at the level of spirits, and so you must fight with the spiritual weapon of prayer.

c   How much power you bring to my motherly work of intercession and reparation when, together, you pray the Liturgy of the Hours, the holy rosary and above all when you offer the Sacrifice of the new and eternal Covenant, through your daily celebration of the Eucharist.

d   *In cenacle with me,* I encourage you to continue along the difficult road of your times, in order to respond with joy and immense hope to the gift of your vocation.

e   In these times, how many of my priest-sons there are who find themselves more and more isolated, surrounded by so much indifference and lack of response, with such a great burden of work to carry out, and thus they are often overcome with weariness and discouragement.

f   Courage, my beloved sons! Jesus is always at your side and gives vigor and strength to your weariness, makes your work efficacious and causes everything you do in the exercise of your priestly ministry to be fruitful in graces. These abundant and wonderful fruits you will see only in paradise and they will be an important part of the reward which awaits you.

g   *In cenacle with me,* I teach you to look on the evils of today with my motherly and merciful eyes and I form you, because I wish you yourselves to become the remedy for these evils.

h   Above all in your countries, you see how the Church is violated by my Adversary, who is seeking to obscure it with error which is being accepted and taught, to wound it with moral permissiveness which leads many to justify everything and to live in sin, to paralyze it with the spirit of the world which has entered its interior and has also rendered fruitless many consecrated and priestly lives.

i   There are especially three wounds which, in your countries, cause my Immaculate Heart to suffer:

j   —*Catechesis,* which is frequently no longer in conformity with the truth which Jesus taught you and which the authentic *Magisterium* of the Church still sets forth for all to believe.

k — *Secularism* which has entered into the lives of so many of the baptized and especially so many of the priests who, in their souls, and in their way of living, of acting and even of dressing, behave, not as disciples of Christ, but according to the spirit of the world in which they live. If you only saw with my eyes how great this desolation is which has struck the Church!

l — *The emptiness, the abandonment and the neglect* with which Jesus present in the Eucharist is surrounded. Too many sacrileges are committed by those who no longer believe in the real presence of Jesus in the Eucharist, and by those who go to Holy Communion in the state of mortal sin without any longer going to confession.

m Beloved sons, you must be the medicine for these ills by your greater adhesion to the *Magisterium* of the Church and thus may your unity of thought and of life with the Pope become ever greater.

n Give to everyone an example of a holy, austere, recollected and mortified life. Bear in your body the marks of the passion of Jesus and, outwardly also, the sign of your consecration to Him, by always wearing your ecclesiastical garb. In all things, be opposed to the secularism which surrounds you and have no fear if, like Jesus, you also for this reason become a cause for contradiction.

o Be burning flames of adoration and of reparation to Jesus present in the Eucharist. Celebrate Holy Mass with love and with intimate participation of life. Go to confession often and help the faithful to make frequent confessions. Make frequent hours of Eucharistic adoration and bring all souls to the Heart of Jesus, who is the fount of grace and of divine mercy.

p And so, *in cenacle with me*, you are preparing the second Pentecost which is about to come so that, through the irresistible power of the Spirit of Love, the Church may be healed and the whole world renewed."

Fatima (Portugal), September 20, 1984
Spiritual Exercises in the Form of a Cenacle
with the Priests of the M.M.P.
of the Portuguese and Spanish Language

Be My Apostles

a   "How my so sorrowful heart is consoled by this continuous cenacle, which you, beloved sons of Portugal and Spain, are holding with me during these days!

b   Be united in prayer. In this way, you give power to my motherly work of intercession and reparation; implore from the Father and the Son the gift of the Holy Spirit who will gently transform your entire life; you are of great assitance to many of your brothers, my beloved sons, whom Satan, particularly at this time, is ensnaring, wounding, and deceiving.

c   Be united in brotherhood. Grow increasingly in your love for one another. Overcome the snares of my Adversary who, especially in your countries, is seeking to lead you into division, putting obstacles in the way of your brotherly understanding and mutual love, which I want you to live in a perfect way.

d   For this reason, I invite you to littleness, to humility, to docility, to simplicity. Be little children who allow themselves to be carried in my motherly arms, so that my plan may be caried out through you.

e   Be also courageous witness of your heavenly Mother. I want to be glorified in you. Through you I want to be increasingly honored. You are called to be my apostles in these very difficult times of yours.

f   *Be my apostles*, in living and spreading what I have told you, during these years. I myself am leading forward my work of the Marian Movement of Priests, by means of all that I have told you through the book of my messages and the little son whom I have chosen as my instrument to spread it in every part of the world. May you all be more and more united to this son of mine; only in this way are you sure of walking in the light which I give you. You must be vigilant because, in your countries, my Adversary is seeking to do all he can to break up this unity of yours.

g   *Be my apostles*, in spreading everywhere the one and only light of Christ. Proclaim with courage and without fear the truth of the Gospel, which the Pope and the *Magisterium* of the Church continue to set forth for all to believe. And then give the example of a life which is in all things in conformity with the Gospel. I want to bring you to a great summit of holiness, to repel the attack of my Advesary who—especially in your countries—is seeking to obscure the Church with the secularism which has entered deeply into the life of so many of my consecrated sons and into many religious houses.

h   *Be my apostles*, in spreading my light and in leading everyone into the refuge of my Immaculate Heart.

i   How great is the work of Masonry and Communism which, in a hidden way, is being carried out for the destruction of my Church, which has always shone forth and flourished in your countries. Respond to these dark attacks by spreading my light everywhere. Give to all the security which I have prepared for you in view of the bloody days which are awaiting you: the refuge of my Immaculate Heart. Fight with prayer and penance; let the rosary be your victorious weapon.

j   I am the Queen of the Holy Rosary.

k   I am the Mother of Faith.

l   I am the Queen of Peace.

m   From this place, where I appeared as the Woman Clothed with the Sun, I bless all of you in the name of the Father, and of the Son, and of the Holy Spirit."

London (England), October 24, 1984
Spiritual Exercises in the Form of a Cenacle
with the Priests of the M.M.P. of the English Language

Do Battle, Beloved Sons!

a   "I welcome with joy the prayer and fraternal sharing which, during these days, brings you together in a cenacle of life with me, dear sons of my Movement from England and Ireland, this land which is so threatened today by my Adversary, but so loved and protected by me.

b   I unite myself to your unceasing prayer, to obtain for you from the Father and the Son the gift of the Holy Spirit, that He may confirm you in your vocation, give courage to your apostolic action, efficacy to your work and consolation to your souls.

c   Take courage, beloved sons of mine, because these are my times, and I am calling you, who form my cohort, to do battle for the triumph of my Son Jesus, in the triumph of love and of good.

d   You are being formed by me to spread the light of Christ, of his truth and of his Gospel in these days of obscurity and darkness. You are being called to be my apostles in the difficult times in which you are living.

e   *Do battle, my beloved ones, by means of love*, which must become ever greater within you, until it reaches the very dimensions of the divine charity of the Heart of my Son Jesus.

f   You see how, in your countries, my Adversary is fighting above all with hatred, which brings division and discord, unbridled egoism and violence everywhere. And thus many of my children often fall victims to terrorism, and blood flows in your streets.

g   You must make love and goodness triumph. Quench the fire of hatred with the dew of your priestly love. Become my instruments for building up unity and brotherhood around you. For this, approach all, but especially those who are most in need and most alienated, with the tenderness of my motherly love.

h   *Do battle, my beloved ones, by means by prayer*, which must be made in union with me and must be offered to God as your most precious contribution for the salvation of the world.

i In these countries of yours, the Church is seen as still divided, although the problem of its unity is keenly felt by many. I bless the efforts which are being made on the part of so many to bring about the restoration of the unity of the Church. But I confide to you, my children, that this can only take place through a special miracle on the part of the Holy Spirit and through a special intervention of my Immaculate Heart.

j For this I need much prayer. More is obtained through one day of intense prayer than through years of continuous discussions. Pray with faith and trust, with recollection and perseverance. Recite well the Liturgy of the Hours and the holy rosary, and let Holy Mass be the center of your apostolic day. Multiply everywhere the cenacles of prayer and fraternal sharing. I promise you that, after the triumph of my Immaculate Heart, these countries of yours will have the joy of seeing once again a renewed and united Church, which will reflect everywhere the splendor of Christ.

k *Do battle, my beloved ones, by means of your personal immolation.* Give me all your sufferings. They are precious to me because I can offer them to Jesus, that they may be united to his perennial and priestly intercession for you.

l Above all in these countries of yours, my Adversary is seducing you with the venom of neopaganism and with an immorality which is spreading more and more and claiming victims among many of my children. How many young people are seduced by vice in their quest for all kinds of pleasure and, allured by the great spread of impurity and of drugs, live like sick people in need of healing!

m Your priestly sufferings are the effective remedy for so many wounds which today, in ever-increasing numbers, are afflicting my poor children. Because of this, I am calling you each day to a greater immolation.

n May the peace of Jesus and my peace be in you. Live in peace of heart. Spread peace around you. I am the Queen of Peace. I am the Mother of Consolation.

o Through you I bless today all my beloved ones and all those children who are consecrated to me, both in these countries of yours and throughout the whole world."

The Shrine of Castelmonte (Udine), November 9, 1984
(During concelebration, immediately after the Gospel)

My Messages

a   "Beloved sons, today you have once again come up here to my shrine before my image which is so venerated because it is a sign of my very special presence among you. You have come here to invoke my protection on the Church, on the world and on the whole Marian Movement of Priests scattered throughout the world.

b   How pleased I am with the Holy Mass which you are celebrating in my honor! I desire that all the beloved sons of my Movement from all the five continents be spiritually present with you because my times have at last come.

c   In these years, as a Mother, I have formed you *through my messages.* They are so many words of wisdom, which I have caused to come down from my Immaculate Heart to form you according to my plan. *My messages* trace out, above all, a simple and luminous way which I have pointed out to you and upon which you should travel, each day, in order to live the consecration which you have made to me, to grow in my love and in life with me and to be ever more mature and prepared to carry out the task which I have shown you.

d   If any, after having consecrated themselves to me, have come to a halt, it is because they have no longer listened to, meditated upon, or lived my messages. Oh, after my triumph, they will be a light for the whole Church; then will be understood just what I have done for you during these years!

e   Meditate on my messages and live them. If you live what I have shown you and travel the road which I have traced out for you, you will walk securely along the way of the consecration which you have made to me and you will bring to fulfillment the great plan of the triumph of my Immaculate Heart.

f   Otherwise you will be halted by doubts, discouragement, difficulties, and the opposition which you will encounter. You will come to a halt and will not be ready to accomplish what I have arranged for you and which today is so necessary for the salvation of the world and the renewal of the Church, whose Mother I am.

g   *In these messages*, I also reveal to you my plan in its silent preparation, in its painful realization, and in its victorious fulfillment. You are already about to reach the most painful and bloody conclusion of the purification which will take place in these years, before the great triumph of my Immaculate Heart in the coming to you of the glorious reign of Jesus.

h   This is a plan which embraces this century. In 1917 at Fatima, I anticipated it, as in a prophetic announcement, at the moment when the great struggle between the Woman clothed with the sun and the Red Dragon became evident, a struggle which was to last throughout the whole century, as a proud challenge to God on the part of my Adversary, who was certain that he would succeed in destroying the Church and in bringing all humanity to a universal rejection of God. The Lord has granted him this space of time, because in the end the pride of the Red Dragon will be broken and conquered by the humility, the littleness, and the power of your heavenly Mother, the Woman clothed with the sun, who is now gathering all her little children into her army, drawn up for battle.

i   Now that you are coming to the most painful and bloody years of this great struggle, I have intervened personally in order to form for myself my cohort through the Marian Movement of Priests, which is my work. For this I have chosen as my instrument a son from among the weakest and humanly speaking least gifted, and I have brought him to every part of the world to show to all that what is to take place is due solely to my personal and extraordinary intervention.

j   However do not be afraid, son, of the difficulties which you encounter when it seems to you that some instrument chosen by me, deceived by Satan, no longer wishes to respond to my plan. Have confidence in me; I alone am the leader of my cohort, I alone am the mother and queen of my Movement. I make use of the instruments who respond to me; I choose others when those who have been chosen by me no longer respond.

k   I myself am leading this work forward each day for the great battle which we are fighting. . . ."

Zagreb (Yugoslavia), November 14, 1984
Spiritual Exercises in the Form of a Cenacle
with the Priests of the M.M.P.
of the Slovenian and Croatian Languages

My Urgent Invitation

a   "Beloved sons, I joyfully welcome this continuous cenacle of priestly fraternity and of prayer, which you are making together with me, your heavenly Mother.

b   You are in this land where my children are in pain and carrying the burden of innumerable sufferings, in this land which is so threatened by my Adversary and yours but which is so loved and protected by me. I spread over all of you my luminous mantle and I enclose you in the sure refuge of my Immaculate Heart.

c   Through you, beloved sons, I want to spread everywhere in these countries of the East, my urgent and heartfelt message, so that it may reach all my children.

d   *I am the Queen of Peace.*

e   Never before as today has the human race been so threatened by the danger of war and of an immense destruction. Look to me as to her who has the task from God of bringing peace to the world.

f   For this, I invite you to beg for it through a prayer which is continuous, trusting and always made with me. Above all, recite the holy rosary. In this way you can obtain from the Lord the great grace of a change of heart, that all may open themselves to sentiments of love and of goodness. Thus peace can enter into the hearts of men and then be spread into families, nations and the whole world.

g   *I am the Mother of Consolation.*

h   In these so troubled times, I am taking my place at the side of each one of you, to share in the difficult moments of your life. I am at your side when you pray and work, when you walk and rest, when you rejoice and suffer.

i   It is to give you a sure sign of my motherly presence, and to give you joy and comfort in the midst of your many sorrows, that I myself have chosen this land in which to appear in a new way, more prolonged and more extraordinary. The pure of heart know how to see me; the poor, the little, the simple know how to listen to me; the humble, the sick and the sinners know how to find me.

j   If there are difficulties or obstacles which make it impossible for you to come to the place of my apparitions, do not be saddened. When you pray and do penance and listen to my motherly invitation to walk along the way of conversion and of love, you come to meet spiritually with your heavenly Mother, who thus manifest herself, present in your midst.

k   *I am the Mother of Trust.*

l   In these times, how many of my poor children there are who have distanced themselves from God, because they become victims of the error of atheism, so widespread today, sustained and propagated through all the means of social communication! Innumerable is the company of those who walk in the darkness of the rejection of God, of the lack of faith, of immorality, of injustice, and of impiety. Evil is covering the whole earth like a thick coat of ice and the cup of divine justice is already full and flowing over.

m   And now I am revealing myself to you to show you the road of salvation: it is the road of return to God. If humanity does not accept my motherly invitation to return to the Lord, it will be inevitably lost. And so I repeat again to you this, my heartfelt message: walk along the road of your return to the Lord. Be converted because, for yet a little while, this is the favorable time of conversion. Be converted and return to your God.

n   From here, through you, I bless all my children who live in these countries, so loved and protected by me because they must bear great trials and sufferings: those of Yugoslavia, Albania, Bulgaria, Rumania, Hungary, Czechoslovakia, East Germany, Poland, Russia and the whole world, whom I want to enclose as soon as possible in the sure refuge of my Immaculate Heart."

The Will of God

a   "Today you are sharing, beloved sons, in the joy of paradise, which exults in the contemplation of your heavenly Mother, so filled with privileges, with graces and with the fullness of holiness by her Lord, whose least servant she feels herself to be.

b   The exemption from every stain of sin, even from the original one, has made my life a pure reflection of the life of God. Thus my soul was filled with grace, and its powers were always directed to carrying out the divine plan in a perfect way. My mind was opened to seek and love the will of God, and my heart was impelled, with joy and complete abandonment, to fulfill only the divine will.

c   This is the road which today I want to point out to you also, for you to journey along, if you wish to follow your heavenly Mother in her plan of immaculate purity and of sanctity.

d   *The Will of God*: this is where, even for you, sanctification is achieved! It is the will of God that, in your lives, you walk along the road of an ever more perfect knowledge of Him. Let the word of God be the daily food with which you nourish your spirit. Seek this word in the sacred book of Divine Scripture; savor all its beauty in the Gospel of my Son Jesus. Through the wisdom which I am giving you, I am leading you to understand more profoundly the secret of Holy Scripture, so that you may fathom it, delight in it, guard it and live it.

e   The word of God became Flesh and Life in Jesus Christ, who is the revelation of the Father, the image of his substance, and the reflection of his glory. The will of God is carried out through you only by your following, with love and complete trust, my Son Jesus. Jesus must be much more loved, listened to and followed by you, his brothers, his ministers, and my beloved sons.

f   The more you penetrate into the deep mystery of his divine love, as into a blazing furnace, the more you will be purified from sin, from frailty, from miseries, and from all your impurities. If you love and follow Jesus, you too will always walk along the road of an immaculate purity and of a great sanctity. When you happen to fall again into sin, his mercy will set you free and, in the sacrament of reconciliation, will restore you to the life of grace and of intimate union with Him.

g　　When discouragement takes hold of you, the bond with Him which is established in prayer and especially in the Eucharist will give you strength and infuse you with new energy for good. When aridity threatens you, communion with Him will open you up to new and profound experiences of love and joy. Then you too will carry out the divine will, which is that of living to know, love and serve the Father, in a profound intimacy of life with the Son, whose mystery will become ever increasingly revealed to you in its fullness by the Holy Spirit.

h　　Thus you will respond to the plan which I have for you for the triumph of my Immaculate Heart, which is carried out only in the reign of love, justice and peace of my Son Jesus. By his divine mercy all evil, sin and impurity will be washed away in such a way that the renewed world will be able to sing again the glory of the Lord."

300

December 24, 1984
The Holy Night

Everything Has Already Been Revealed

a　　"Beloved sons, be recollected with me in prayer during these hours which precede the birth of my baby Jesus. Live in my Immaculate Heart the moments of the holy night. Follow me along the way of incessant prayer so that it may become a colloquy of love, of trust, and of filial abandonment to the plan of salvation of the Lord our God.

b　　This abandonment carried me on the wave of a joyous experience of the presence of my Son, of which I was aware in a most powerful way, because the moment of his birth in time had come. My journey toward Bethlehem became nothing but a sweet and motherly bowing down to his divine wish to come and live among you as a brother. And I spoke with Him in a conversation made up of silence and listening, contemplation and love, adoration and expectation.

c   Thus unceasing prayer enwrapped the long journey, undertaken in order to reach the hospitable grotto, and there it became even more intense and more recollected, to the point of lifting the veil which separated me from entering into a profound ecstasy with heaven, from which I emerged with my divine baby already born.

d   Follow me along the road of a suffering understood, welcomed, and lived by me, as a humble response to what, at this time, the Lord was asking of me. An interior suffering, brought about by unfolding circumstances, which presented themselves to me as a claim on my motherly collaboration with his plan of love.

e   The necessity of abandoning the house in Nazareth, which had been made ready with such care; the exhausting journey to Bethlehem in my condition of motherhood already brought to term; the uncertainty of that which we were to find there; the refusal to put us up in any house; the squalid shelter in a freezing cave: all these things were like so many thorns which pierced my motherly heart. But I understood that this suffering was asked of me by the Father, in order to prepare a more precious cradle for my child who was about to be born.

f   Now I ask of you also, my beloved children, prayer and suffering, as your personal collaboraton in preparing a fitting dwelling place for Jesus who is about to return in glory.

g   Understand the meaning of my motherly interventions, which today have become more frequent, extraordinary, and urgent. On this holy night, my message, which I give you as heavenly prophetess of the last times, appears clearer to you.

h   Prepare yourselves for the second birth of Jesus in glory: He is about to come to reign in your midst. The ways by which He will come are those of prayer and suffering. Already these are the times in which you must all recollect yourselves in a continuous and trusting prayer, as was mine during the long journey made to Bethlehem.

i   The time for projects and discussions is over.

j   *For those who wish to listen and understand, everything has now already been revealed.*

448

k The hearts of men have been dried up by hatred and sin; nations and people are rebelling against their God and a great darkness is surrounding them; humanity no longer wishes to throw open the doors for Christ, who is coming. So then let the poor caves of your hearts be opened which, in the deep night, must blaze in the light of an unshakable faith, of a sure hope and of a burning love.

l And suffer with patience and with trust. As for Me, so also for you, the sufferings which the Lord asks of you form part of a loving plan of his. The pangs must increase for everyone the closer his new birth approaches. Accept them just as your heavenly Mother did.

m Walk in the light of the star, which tells you that the time has already come in which the prophetic announcements that have already been given you during these years are coming to pass. And live each hour of your life in the greatest trust and in the joyous expectation of the glorious return of my Son Jesus."

301

December 31, 1984
Last night of the year

The Signs of Your Time

a "Beloved sons, pass the final hours of the year, which is about to close, in sweet intimacy with me.

b How many of my children spend these moments in amusements and clamor and are inebriated with emptiness amidst so many frivolities and diversions which are often licentious and against the law of the Lord! . . .

c I invite you on the contrary to spend these hours in prayer, in recollection, and in interior silence, so that you may enter into a conversaton with me, your heavenly Mother. Then, with the same familiarity that a mother has for her children, I will reveal to you the cares, the anxieties and the deep wounds of my Immaculate Heart and, at the same time, *I will help you to understand and to interpret the signs of your times.*

d   Thus you can cooperate in the plan of salvation, which the Lord has for you and which He wishes to carry out in the course of the new days which await you.

e   — You are living under an urgent request made by your heavenly Mother, who is inviting you to walk along the road of conversion and of return to God. Beloved children, share in my anxious motherly concern as I see that this call of mine is neither welcomed nor followed. And yet I see that the only possibility of your salvation is bound up uniquely with the return of humanity to the Lord, with a strong commitment to follow his law.

f   Be converted and walk along the road of the grace of God and of love. Be converted and build up days of serenity and peace. Be converted and take part in the plan of divine mercy.

g   With how many signs has the Lord manifested to you his will to at last put a fitting halt to the flood of impiety: incurable diseases which are spreading; violence and hatred which are exploding; misfortunes which are occurring; wars and threats which are spreading. Know how to read the signs which God is sending you through the events which are taking place and accept his strong admonitions to change your life and to return along the road which leads you to Him.

h   — You are living under your heavenly Mother's concerned and constant request to remain in the true faith. And yet I see, with anguish, that errors continue to be spread, taught, and propagated. The danger of losing the precious gift of faith in Jesus and in the truth which He revealed to you is thus becoming ever greater among my children. Even among my chosen ones, how great is the number of those who doubt or who no longer believe.

i   If you only saw with my eyes how vast this spiritual epidemic is which has struck the entire Church: it brings its apostolic action to a halt, wounds it and paralyzes its vitality, often even making its effort at evangelization empty and ineffective.

j   — You are living under my very painful anxiety as I see that you are still the victims of widespread sin. I observe how, by the means of social communications, experiences of life contrary to those indicated by God's holy law are being proposed to my poor children everywhere. Everyday you are being fed with the poisoned bread of evil and given to drink at the polluted spring of impurity. Evil is being proposed to you as something good, sin as a value, and transgression of the law of God as a way of exercising your autonomy and your personal freedom.

k   And so you arrive at losing even the consciousness of sin as an evil, and injustice, hatred and impiety cover the earth and make of it an immense desert, deprived of life and love. The obstinate rejection of God and of return to Him, the loss of the true faith and the iniquity which is spreading and leading to the diffusion of evil and sin: *these are the signs of the evil time through which you are living.*

l   But at the same time see in how many ways I an intervening to lead you along the road of conversion, of goodness and of faith. With extraordinary signs which I am giving in every part of the world, through my messages and through my so frequent apparitions, I am pointing out to everyone the approaching of the great day of the Lord.

m   But how much sorrow my Immaculate Heart feels in seeing that these admonitions of mine are not heeded and are frequently and openly rejected and opposed, even by those who have the duty of being the first to accept them. For this reason, I am revealing myself today only to the little ones, to the poor, to the simple, to all my children who still know how to listen to me and follow me.

n   Now, as never before, I have need of a great force of supplication and reparation. For this reason, I am turning to you, beloved children, and inviting you to spend the hours of this last night of the year on your knees in a continuous prayer with me."

1985

I AM THE BEGINNING OF THE NEW TIMES

I Am the Beginning of the New Times

a "Beloved children, you are united today with the whole Church in venerating me as true Mother of God and your Mother, in the order of the supernatural life of faith and of divine grace.

b   On this day, which for you marks the beginning of a new year, while all of you in the Church – bishops, priests, religious and faithful – look to me as to your mother, I say to you if that is what I am and if you honor me as such, I must be loved, listened to, and followed by each one of you.

c   And so it is today, on the solemnity of my divine maternity, that I wish to give a message to the Church to be heard and welcome by her.

d   *It is a message of trust and of hope.*

e   Notwithstanding the difficulties and the sufferings which the Church is called upon to bear, and the painful hours of agony and of passion which mark the time of her bloody purification, the moment of a renewed splendor and of a second pentecost is in preparation for her.

f   My dearly beloved children, never lose confidence and hope. Beneath the great and vast clamor which evil is managing to spread everywhere, many sprouts of goodness and holiness are budding forth in silence and hiddenness. These precious sprouts of new life are being daily cultivated in the secret garden of my Immaculate Heart.

g   However be on your guard against three serious dangers which are threatening your growth in goodness and which have been pointed out to you by me many times: that of departing from the true faith by following the many errors which are being taught today; that of separating yourselves from the interior unity of the Church through contestation directed against the Pope and the hierarchy, which is still spreading within ecclesial life; and that of falling victims to secularism and moral permissiveness, which leads you to yield in the daily struggle against evil and sin.

h   If you allow yourselves to be led by me, you walk along the sure road of love and of holiness.

i   *It is a message of comfort and of consolation.*

j   Entrust yourselves, all of you, to your heavenly Mother that you may be consoled. In the great battle which you are fighting, find strength and comfort there and never lose your courage in the face of the difficulties which you meet.

k   During the new year, the trials and sufferings which await you will become even greater, because you have already entered into the final phase of what I have foretold to you. A great and bloody trial is about to shake the whole earth, to prepare it for its complete renewal in the triumph of my Immaculate Heart.

l   But the more severe the trial will become, the greater will be my presence at the side of each one of you, that you may be comforted and encouraged by me. If you live in my Immaculate Heart, nothing that can happen will be able to disturb you; within this motherly refuge of mine you are always safe, wrapped in the light and the presence of the Most Holy Trinity, who loves you and surrounds you with its divine protection.

m   *It is a message of salvation and of mercy.*

n   You must be my powerful help, which I wish to offer today to all humanity in order to lead it to return along the road of goodness and of love.

o   I am the way of this, its return. I am the doorway of divine mercy. I desire that, through you, all my lost children may be able to come back to the Lord, who awaits them with the anxiety and the joy of a father who loves them and wants to save them. Thus you also become instruments of divine mercy, in these times in which the greatest triumph of the merciful love of my Son Jesus is in preparation.

p   It is in order to be your trust, your consolation, and your salvation in the last times through which you are living, that I am manifesting myself today in such a powerful way, through the messages which I am giving, by means of this little son of mine and the apparitions which I am carrying out, in a continuous and extraordinary way, in many parts of the world.

q   Believe in my invitations, accept my messages, and look at my signs! I am the Queen of Peace; I am the beginning of the new times; I am the dawn of the new day.

r   With the Pope, the first of my beloved sons, I bless you all today in the name of the Father and of the Son and of the Holy Spirit."

303

I See Your Littleness

a   "Beloved children, contemplate me in the mystery of the presentation of my child Jesus in the Temple. I want to reveal to you today what the sentiments were which filled my heart as I passed my child, forty days after his birth, from my arms into those of the priest.

b   *My heart burned with gratitude* towards the Lord, who had at last fulfilled the plan of salvation for his people. For how many centuries had this moment been awaited! With my soul I saw the face of the Father, bending down with pleasure, while the Holy Spirit came down upon some of those present and revealed to their minds the hidden plan of the Lord.

c   *My heart beat violently with ineffable motherly love,* in the contemplation of the whole of divinity enclosed in the members, so tiny, of my baby, who was only forty days old.

d   *My heart exulted with joy* at the moment when the Lord entered the Temple and I felt that the vast cohorts of angels and all the heavenly spirits were accompanying Him, as He was led to take possession of his dwelling place.

e   *My heart was also wounded with sorrow* at the prophetic voice of old Simeon, who announced to me how my motherly mission was also a call to a profound suffering, to an intimate and personal participation in the sorrowful mission of my Son Jesus.

f   With these same sentiments I am leading you, dear children, each day to the altar of the Lord, to help you fulfill well his divine will.

'Sacrifice and offering you did not desire, but a body you have prepared for me; I have come to do your will, O God.'

g   I am filled with gratitude to my son Jesus because, through you who have responded to me, I am able today to carry out my motherly plan of preparing the greatest triumph of his merciful love. I feel my heart filled with love for you who, through your consecration, have offered yourselves to me as little children.

h   I see your littleness, I look upon your weakness and fragility and at the innumerable snares set for you by my Adversary. I see you as so small that you are not even able to take a single step without my motherly help. For this reason I stoop over you with the renewed tenderness of a mother.

i   I am happy too with the great degree of generosity with which you have responded to me. You have said 'yes' to my request for consecration; you have offered me your entire life, that I might freely intervene to order it according to my plan, which is the will of the Lord.

j   Finally, I am also sorrowful because, as for Jesus so also for you, the mission which awaits you is that of suffering and of immolation. It is above all by means of this that I am able to offer to the Father, to the Son and to the Holy Spirit a great force of intercession and of reparation, so that the golden door of divine mercy may be soon opened, and the greatest miracle of complete transformation of the world be accomplished.

k   For this reason, beloved children, each day, on my grateful heart, happy and at the same time sorrowful, I carry you to the temple of the Lord and place you upon his altar, so that you may be offered to the perfect fulfillment of his divine will."

304   Shrine of Castelmonte (Udine), February 9, 1985
(After the recitation of the holy rosary)

My Word

a   "Beloved children, you have come to my Shrine in a spirit of prayer and of reparation. On pilgrimage, you have come up here, where I await you to fill you with graces, with comfort, and with motherly consolation.

b   Each time you come to the feet of my image, so venerated, to bring me your filial homage of love, I cause many graces to come down from my Immaculate Heart upon you, upon all my beloved children throughout the world, upon the Church, upon my poor sinful children, and upon humanity which is so threatened by evil, by hatred, by violence, and by war and which is dried up by sin and by an ever more widespread immorality.

c   In this House, your heavenly Mother consoles and encourages you, molds and leads you, strengthens and confirms you by the word which she gives you to show you the way. Oh! How necessary is my motherly word for you today! For this reason I cause it to gush forth from my heart in an ever more abundant manner. Feel its deep desire; receive it with humility and docility; meditate it in your heart; put it into practice in your life.

d   *My Word is above all a flower of wisdom*, which I cause to come down from heaven. It sets out from the eternal Wisdom, from the Word. It is He who is the uncreated Wisdom, who reveals the plan of the Father whose perfect image He is. This Wisdom, made flesh in my virginal womb, from Word became man, and has the task of always giving men the gift of eternal Truth. This divine Word, contained in Holy Scripture and above all in the Gospel, is the only Light which must guide you.

e   But today it is being surrounded by many doubts, because there is a desire to interpret it according to the human way of reasoning and of seeing things, and is often no longer presented in its integrity. Errors are spreading and, when you come to the plan of God, you are impeded from understanding it in its fullness, because you are making use of an attitude which is too human and which seeks to understand only by means of reason. This is an attitude of pride and it is the very least to be recommended for approaching the great mystery of God.

f   To understand his truth it is necessary to be little; to see it in its proper light it is necessary to be poor; to keep it in its integrity one must be simple; to give it to others in the splendor of its authenticity, one must be humble. For this reason, with my word, I am forming you to humility, to simplicity and to littleness. I want to lead you to be like so many little children, because only then can I speak to you.

g *My word is a flower of wisdom,* which forms you through the Holy Spirit, given to you by the Father and the Son and who leads you to an ever more complete and deep understanding of the Gospel. In the obscurity which today has fallen everywhere, my word of wisdom becomes a ray of purest light which points out to you the way you must follow and the road along which you must go in order to remain always in the truth.

h Darkness, with a thick, cold fog, has entered the Church, obscuring it in the splendor of its truth. For this reason, everyday, my word is forming you to the spirit of wisdom, that you may always see, in the light, the truth which my Son has taught you and proclaim it with courage to all in its integrity.

i The time has now come when only the little children, consecrated to my Immaculate Heart and entrusted completely to their heavenly Mother, will have the gift of keeping themselves intact in the faith and of bringing to the true faith the souls entrusted to them.

j *My word is also a drop of dew,* which I cause to fall upon the earth, which has become an immense desert, and upon human life, so dried up by sin and suffering. How many of my children are like dried up trees without life; and in the Church, how many among my beloved ones have allowed themselves to be seized by aridity and discouragement! They continue to exercise their ministry but without enthusiasm and without joy, because they have become hindered by difficulties and become crushed by the enormous weight of the purification which you are living through.

k You have need for my word to cause a rain of motherly tenderness to fall into your dried-up hearts, a rain of freshness, of filial abandonment and of hope for the beautiful days which await you, in the new era, which is even now about to blossom upon the desert of the last times. My word is therefore like a drop of dew which I cause to fall from my Immaculate Heart into your hearts, that they may be able to open up to the warmth of the new life which I am cultivating within you, to offer you as fragrant

459

flowers, now finally opened, to the perfect homage of the Most Holy Trinity.

l   My *Word is lastly a spring of graces*, which I cause to flow over you, to open up your souls to a new splendor of beauty and holiness and to cleanse you also, once again, of every least stain of sin, because I want you to be beautiful, pure and luminous, opened to the divine gift of grace, so that the fullness of love and of the most perfect charity may blossom in your life. My graces come to you through the gift of my word, which becomes light to the mind, life to the heart, and support for your journey.

m   In the fearful and bloody final period of the purification which awaits you and which, in these very years, will make itself felt in a particularly painful way, I am preparing you to receive, with greater docility, the motherly gift of my word. Thus, in the midst of great darkness, you are able to walk in the light of wisdom; in aridity you can always be consoled by my tenderness, a balm which is placed on so many open and bleeding wounds. In every circumstance of your life you can obtain the grace of responding to the love of Jesus and of singing today the glory of the divine Trinity, walking along the road of a holiness which I want to be ever greater.

n   In these very years of the great purification, I want to offer you to the Church as an ever more visible sign of my motherly triumph."

305
Shrine of Castelmonte (Udine), February 14, 1985
(After the recitation of the holy rosary)

My Purity and Yours

a   "My beloved children, I have wanted you here today, on a brilliant day, with a blue sky, a warm sun and the snow which gives a tone of purity to the high mountains which form a crown for this place, from which rises the blessed house of your heavenly Mother. I enfold you with my motherly rays; I enlighten you with the light which comes from my Immaculate Heart; I cover you with my heavenly mantle to make you also ever purer.

b   *I am the Mother of purity.* I am the ever Virgin Mother. I am immaculate whiteness the splendor of heaven which reflects the light of the Most Holy Trinity upon the world, the dawn which puts an end to night, the Mother of Grace who drives away every sin from you, the Medicine of Paradise which, like soothing balm, closes up all your wounds.

c   *I am the all-beautiful Mother: tota pulchra, tota pulchra!*

d   *Mine is above all a purity of mind.* Oh, my reason was always directed to seeking, to meditating upon, to keeping and to living the will of the Lord! His Word was received by me with docility and with virginity; I was always diligent in understanding it and keeping it in its entirety. Throughout my whole life, not even the slightest shadow of a doubt or of an error ever grazed the virginal integrity of my mind, which was open only to receive the gift of divine wisdom.

e   This purity of mind was the road that led me to a *deeper purity of heart.* My heart was completely formed to receive the love of God and to give it back to Him, with the virginal and motherly impulse of a creature cultivated in the garden of the Trinity, in the divine sun of a love received and exchanged in a perfect manner.

f   No human heart has ever loved nor will it ever be able to love, as has that of your heavenly Mother. It opened up like a flower which unfolds its petals to shed all about it the brightness, beauty, and fragrance of heaven. For this reason I was able to form the flesh and the blood for Him who is the Lily of the Valley and who loves, in a special way, the pure of heart.

g   I was also the purest in love of neighbor. After Jesus, no creature has been able to love humanity as has the heart of your Mother; in this perfect love toward all is to be found the intimate source from which there springs the working of my divine and universal motherhood.

h   From purity of heart, enter yet further with me into the innermost depths of my life to discover *how I was pure in soul.*

i   The soul becomes impure when it is darkened or beclouded by even the least shadow of sin. The slightest stain of venial sin defiles its whiteness and causes the enchantment of its light to fade and be spoiled.

j   I, through a singular privilege, was preserved from original sin and was filled with grace. Throughout my whole life, my soul was never, not even for an instant, touched by sin, even venial sin; it has ever been all light, all beautiful, all pure.

k   If every soul created by God, being spiritual and raised to the state of sharing in his divine nature, reflects the light of the Trinity, you can understand how no soul will ever be able to reflect, as in a perfectly clear mirror, the splendor of the Father, of the Son and of the Holy Spirit, as has the soul of your heavenly Mother.

l   The wrapping which was to enclose the precious treasure of a perfect purity of mind, of heart, and of soul was *to be this body of mine*. And so then my body too was completely wrapped by a light of inviolate purity.

m   *I have been pure in body*, not only through having always kept it intact from the slightest sin of impurity, but also because the Lord has willed to make his divine masterpiece shine forth in it in a marvellous way. My body which, through its function of motherhood, had to be opened at the moment of the gift of the Son and to break the enchantment of its integrity, through a singular privilege remained intact. Thus I was able to give you my Son, while the virginal wrapping, by means of which even at the moment of my gift of motherhood I remained *ever a virgin*, remained intact:

n   Virgin before birth, because that which took place in me was solely the work of the Holy Spirit;

o   Virgin during birth, because that which was accomplished at that moment was the working of the Most Holy Trinity;—enwrapped by the light of God and by his secret, before Him alone took place the miraculous birth of my divine Son—

p   Virgin after birth, because nothing ever disturbed the inviolate charm of my most pure body, called to guard my immaculate soul, so that in the person of your heavenly Mother there should be able to shine out, in a perfect way, the most holy splendor of the divine Trinity.

q   Defend this privilege of mine, which is denied by many today in a facile and banal manner; defend it always.

r   And I ask all of you as well to be pure.

s   How great is my suffering when I see that, today, this virtue is no longer taught and cultivated in the hearts of the young and of adolescents, and even of those who are consecrated to God. In the name of a false freedom they are led into experiences which take this delight of paradise from their souls.

t   How sorrowful is your heavenly Mother today as she sees so many priestly and consecrated lives dried up through impurity, which has spread everywhere like a terrible cancer! This is why you are no longer able to understand the plan of God, and to be so simple and small as to listen with docility also to the voice of your heavenly Mother.

u   Only to the pure are the mysteries of the reign of God revealed:

v   —the pure of mind, because they know how to recognize his plan and to accept it with humility,

w   —the pure of heart, because they are detached from goods, from creatures and from their own way of seeing things, which impedes one from receiving my light because one wants to filter and judge it through one's own human and limited intelligence,

x   —the pure of soul, who flee the least shadow of sin, because it obscures the light of God within you and makes you unable to accept his divine mystery,

y   —the pure of body, because, consecrating it to God in celibacy and in the vow of chastity, it becomes more conformed to that of Jesus Crucified and enlightened by the immaculate light which clothes my glorious body.

z   Beloved children, I want you all to be pure of mind, of heart, of soul, and of body in imitation of your all-beautiful heavenly Mother. Then, upon the world of today, so permeated with coldness and hatred, you will be the light of the sun, coming down to warm souls and open them up to the life of God. Amidst the threatening clouds which have appeared upon humanity's present moment, you open up a clear blue patch in the sky. Over the rotting and putrid swamp to which the world has been reduced, you will be a mirror of purity; in it the world will be reflected and will be helped to be slowly transformed into a new garden.

A   Only in this way, beloved children of mine, will you be able to become the rays which shine down from my Immaculate Heart to light up the terrible time of purification through which you are living, and to give to everyone the sure sign of my presence and of my victory.

B   I bless you in the name of the Father and of the Son and of the Holy Spirit."

306

Dongo, March 16, 1985
A Saturday of Lent

The Fast Which I Ask of You

a   "Walk along the road of penance and of mortification.

b   *I am asking of you a bodily fast* as a means of mortifying your senses, in order to ward off the widespread deceit by which so many of my children are being seduced today, driven as they are to seek happiness only in the complete satisfaction of bodily and material pleasures.

c   How many there are who are nourished with the poison food of impurity and drugs! How the putrid sore of immoral literature and pornography is spreading! The means of social communication are often becoming instruments for the moral corruption of consciences, for the diffusion of vice and obscenity, and for sin which is now proposed as a good and as something of value.

d   For this reason I am asking you, my beloved ones and children consecrated to me, to provide me with a great force of reparation, with which I will form a dam against the flooding of so contagious and dangerous an evil. I am asking of you a bodily fast in order to mortify your senses, so as to witness today to the necessity of putting a limit to the mad quest for pleasure. By your good example you must teach that man does not live by bread alone, but by every word which comes from the mouth of God.

e   *I am asking of you a spiritual fast* from every form of evil, so that you may be nourished only by what is good, by grace and by love. The food which is the word of God nourishes you spiritually and gives strength to your existence in the life of grace. I am requesting of you a fast of the mind, preserving it from every error as you welcome the truth which Jesus has revealed to you.

f   Nourish yourselves—I tell you again—with the precious food of divine Scripture, above all with the Gospel of Jesus. Receive, meditate upon and live the messages which today, in so many ways, your heavenly Mother as well is giving you.

g   For this, you must be careful to reject all ideologies which are contrary to your faith and which contain subtle and dangerous errors and so much damage your growth in fidelity to the commitments assumed at the time of baptism.

h   *I am asking of you a fast of the heart,* closing it to disordinate attachment to yourselves, to goods, and to creatures.

i   How many there are who can only think of themselves and who allow themselves to be devoured by an unbridled egoism, which closes them up to any possibility of true communion with others! How many are slaves to a mad attachment to goods, and to money, which they seek as the only object of their lives, and they become consumed with avarice, which is the source of many other vices and sins! And thus they close their hearts to the tremendous needs of the little people, of the poor and the marginalized; they are unable to see those who are in difficulties and are in need of being helped.

j   *I am asking of you a fast of the soul,* by keeping it far from any sin even the least, so that it may be nourished only by the life of grace and by the light of God. Flee mortal sin as the greatest of all evils; make your examination of conscience every day; allow yourselves to be led with docility by the Spirit. Let the custom, which is so very useful, of frequent confession, return.

465

k   Flee also from the easy occasions of sin. For this, I ask you to close your eyes and ears to television and to the cinema, in order to preserve your soul in the light of purity and of grace.

l   If you carry out this fast which I am asking of you, you will build about yourselves a strong barrier against the flood of evil and of sin, and you will offer to the Lord a holocaust of immolation and of reparation, to obtain the return to Him of many of my poor sinful children.

m   In this way you will become instruments of my peace, you will spread about you peace of heart, walking along the road which your heavenly Mother has traced out for you."

307

The Hour of a New Agony

a   "Beloved sons, live these hours in the depths of my Immaculate Heart, that you may be able to penetrate with me into the blazing furnace of the infinite and merciful love of my Son Jesus. During his life, how much He awaited this moment! 'I have greatly desired to eat this Passover with you before I suffer.' It is Holy Thursday.

b   *It is the day of the institution of the Eucharist.* This great sacrament allows Him to be really present in your midst, to renew mystically his Sacrifice of the new and eternal covenant and to give Himself in a personal communion of life with you.

c   *It is also the day of the institution of the priesthood.* It is perpetuated through his commandment given to the apostles and to those who succeed them in the exercise of the sacred ministry: 'Do this in memory of me.'

d   *It is your day, beloved sons.* The heavenly Mother looks upon you with particular and sorrowful concern at the moment when, reunited in concelebration about your bishops, you renew the commitments assumed on the day of your priestly ordination.

e How many are the dangers which surround you, the obstacles which my Adversary places in your way, the seductions of the world in which you live, the difficulties which weigh upon the faithful exercise of your priestly ministry.

f The institution of the Eucharist was immediately followed by the terrible and bloody agony of Gethsemane during which Jesus was left alone, at the moment when He had the greatest need of assistance and comfort, felt the bitter abandonment by his own, and was betrayed by Judas and denied by Peter.

g Today, among my beloved ones, how many there are who flee from and abandon Jesus and the Church, seduced by the easy attractions of the world in which they live . . . How many of them betray Him, driven on by the desire to be more accepted and followed, in greater harmony with the tastes and ideologies of your time. How many repeat the gesture of Peter, who denied the Master out of cowardice and fear. This is for many the fear of not appearing up-to-date and in line with the cultural demands which are fashionable today.

h On this Holy Thursday, allow your heavenly Mother to gather you into the sheepfold of her Immaculate Heart to form you to be ever more faithful to Jesus and to his Gospel. Be humble, strong, courageous. Do not allow yourselves to be seized either by fear or by discouragement. The night of error, of apostasy, and of infidelity has already descended upon the world and into the Church.

i The Mystical Body of Jesus is living through the hour of a new painful agony. For this reason, there are repeated again today, in a much greater way, the same things that were done at that time: the abandonment, the denial, the betrayal.

j You, O little sons formed in the Immaculate Heart of your heavenly Mother, must, like the apostle John, keep watch in prayer and in trust during the painful hours of this new Holy Thursday."

Your Sorrowful Passion

a   "The cross for you, O son, is the will of the Father, which you carry out well only if, at each moment, you second the plan of my Immaculate Heart.

b   Carry your cross each day and never depart from the divine will. Your wounds are the misunderstandings, the doubts, the perplexities and the numerous abandonments. These are the real wounds of the soul, which no one sees, more precious than gold, the blood from which I am always gathering up to water the garden of the dried up and thirsty souls of your brother-priests.

c   Your climb to Calvary is the journey you must undertake for me, advancing alone and full of trust, in the midst of your many fears and the proud scepticism of those who surround you and who do not believe. The immense weariness which you feel, that sense of exhaustion which so prostrates you, is your thirst. The scourges and the blows are the snares and the painful temptations of my Adversary.

d   The cries of condemnation are the venomous serpents which obstruct your way and the briars which pierce your frail body of a child, which has been struck so many times.

e   The abandonment to which I am calling you is the bitter taste of feeling yourself to be ever more alone, far from friends and disciples, rejected sometimes even by your most fervent followers.

f   But at your side is the sorrowful Mother; together with her, live out, with love and trust, *your sorrowful passion*, which no one is able to see, but which consumes you each day, as a victim immolated by me for all your brother-priests.

g   Your death is the very great silence, the hiddenness, the humiliation and rejection which I am always asking of you. The virginal bosom of your Mother is the new sepulchre for this, your pasch, which has now been perpetuated in the depths of my Immaculate Heart, my littlest and most loved from among the sons of predilection."

Your Reparation

a   "Walk along the road which I have traced out for you, without allowing yourselves to be seized by lack of confidence or discouragement. This is the most dangerous snare with which my Adversary seeks today to check the force of my victorious cohort. And in this way he tries to bring misunderstanding and division into your midst; he makes you feel the burden of the difficulties which weigh upon the exercise of your priestly ministry; he emphasizes the sense of misunderstanding and rejection with which you are sometimes surrounded.

b   Do not stop before these snares which Satan places in your way, because he feels fear of my cohort, which I have formed for myself in every part of the world, with the little ones who have accepted my invitation to consecrate themselves to my Immaculate Heart.

c   Respond with the greatest confidence and with your filial abandonment to me. Offer me, with the simplicity of little children, everything that happens to you: joys and sorrows, interior trials and physical sufferings, the numerous wounds of your soul and everything which, in whatever manner, becomes a source of suffering to you.

d   Answer with that prayer which must become intensified and continual. Then you will have the strength from Jesus to resist all the subtle seductions of the Evil One; you will receive from the Holy Spirit the light of the wisdom which enlightens you and leads you to see every dangerous snare which is set along your path. From the Father there is given to you the joy of a tender and filial abandonment to his divine action which predisposes with love for each one of you every circumstance in your life.

e   In this month of May, consecrated to me, intensify as well your *filial reparation* for the sacrilegious and diabolical way in which the life of your heavenly Mother is being publicly presented. All heaven trembles with indignation before the public and grave outrage tendered to the honor of your heavenly Mother, and Jesus is now personally taking up the defense of the Creature who is most loved and glorified by Him.

f   Not much time will go by before a great chastisement will strike the whole of your poor country, so loved and protected by me and which has publicly willed to permit this sacrilegious outrage tendered to your heavenly Mother.

g   My heart bleeds to see how only the first of my beloved sons, my Pope, has willed to protest publicly and to make reparation and has raised his voice in a courageous act of condemnation. But no other member of the hierarchy has had the courage to do this; indeed some bishops and some priests have had the audacity to publicly justify this horrible sacrilege.

h   For this, there has now come for the Church the time of its greatest division, of the apostasy which has entered its interior, which will lead it to live through the moment of its gravest crisis, of its bloody and terrible persecution.

i   For this reason, I invite you to make reparation in a continual act of prayer and of penance, of trust and of filial abandonment. Then you, my beloved children, will pour the balm of love on the open and bleeding wounds of my Immaculate and so Sorrowful Heart."

310   Cagliari (Sardinia), May 26, 1985
Pentecost

Come, Spirit of Love

a   "Beloved children, who have entered into the cenacle of my Immaculate Heart to let yourselves be formed by me for the great task which the Lord has entrusted to you, pass this day in an unceasing prayer, addressed to the Father and to the Son, so that they may grant you the gift of the Holy Spirit.

b   For this reason alone have I invited you to enter into the cenacle of my motherly Heart. For this reason alone I invite today the whole Church to gather together in the cenacle of my Immaculate Heart in a continuous prayer made with me and through me. For this reason alone I recommend to you to gather together often in your cenacles, in order to give me a great force of prayer, with which I may be able to intervene before my Son Jesus, that He may quickly obtain for you from the Father the gift of a new and second Pentecost for the Church and for all humanity.

c   *Come, O Spirit of Love and renew the face of the earth*; grant that it may entirely become once again a new garden of grace and of sanctity, of justice and of love, of communion and of peace, so that the Most Holy Trinity may once again be reflected, pleased and glorified.

d   *Come, O Spirit of Love and renew the whole Church*; bring it to the perfection of love, of unity and of holiness, that it may become today the greatest of all lights which shines upon all in the great darkness which has spread everywhere.

e   *Come, O Spirit of Wisdom and Understanding* and open the way for hearts to the understanding of the truth, whole and entire. With the burning force of your divine fire root out every error, sweep away every heresy, so that the light of the truth which Jesus has revealed may shine forth for all in its integrity.

f   *Come, O Spirit of Counsel and Fortitude* and make us courageous witnesses of the Gospel we have received. Sustain the persecuted; encourage the spurned; give strength to the imprisoned; grant perseverance to the downtrodden and tortured; obtain the palm of victory for those who, again today, are being led to martyrdom.

g   *Come, O Spirit of Knowledge, of Piety, and of Fear of God* and renew, with the lymph of your divine love, the life of all those who have been consecrated in baptism, and signed with your seal in confirmation, of those who have offered themselves in service to God, of the bishops, the priests and the deacons, that they may all be enabled to correspond to your plan which you are bringing about in these times of the second Pentecost, so long implored and awaited.

h   Only then will the task which I myself have entrusted to my Marian Movement of Priests be completed. Only then will there have taken place the triumph of my Immaculate Heart, at the beginning of a time in which the new heavens and the new earth will at last be able to be seen by all."

311

San Marino—Spiritual Exercises, July 5, 1985
First Friday of the Month
At the end of the evening procession;
message given orally

Instruments of My Peace

a   "My beloved sons, how I have welcomed this evening the homage which you have offered to me, at the conclusion of a week in which you have all been gathered together here in the precious refuge of my Immaculate Heart. Never as in these present times has my Immaculate Heart been for each one of you the refuge and the sure way which leads you to God.

b   That which I predicted at Fatima to my daughter, Sister Lucy, is today becoming a reality. For humanity and for the Church there is great need of my motherly and immaculate refuge, because you are all living within my times. These are the painful times foretold by me, in which everything is moving towards its most painful and bloody fulfilment.

c   For this reason, I have again wanted you here on this mountain, on a week of Spiritual Exercises, so extraordinary in graces. These Exercises have a great and particular importance, which you will understand only later on.

d   During these days, I have formed you for prayer. I have taught you to pray, to pray well, with me. In your prayer, which must come from the heart, you must see and feel with mind, heart, and will the reality you address in prayer. Your heavenly Mother wants to form you ever more and more in the prayer of the heart, so that this prayer may be the way which leads you to peace of heart.

e   I want to obtain for each one of you the gift of peace and heart. You came with your hearts burdened with difficulties, with sorrows, with hopes, with cares and with expectations; I have taken everything into my Immaculate Heart and I give you peace of heart.

Go in the peace of your hearts and to all about you become *instruments of my peace.*

f   To this end, gather souls together ever more and more in cenacles of intense prayer, of deep prayer, so that I may be able to give them peace of heart. At a time when peace is departing ever further and further from men, from families, from nations, and from humanity, the sign of my motherly triumph is peace, which even now I want to bring into the hearts of all my children: of those who listen to me, follow me, and consecrate themselves to my Immaculate Heart. For this, I am again asking you to continue in your cenacles of prayer because, through the grace which springs from my heart and which brings you to a fullness of love for my Son Jesus, I wish to give my children, today, the precious gift of peace of heart.

g   Here also I have taught you to love one another. How happy the Mother is when she sees you as so many little brothers who love one another and who want to grow in love, notwithstanding the difficulties which come from your limitations, from your numerous defects, and from the subtle snares which are laid for you by my Adversary. He seeks only to rob your hearts of peace and to spread discord, misunderstandings, and divisions among you!

h   As with prayer I lead you to peace, so also with my motherly presence I bring you to brotherhood. You must increase more in your mutual love; you must know how to love one another more. The Mother rejoices when you love one another and when, after every least breach in this love, you know how to be reconciled with one another, to extend the hand to each other and to walk together, because I love each one of you individually and all of you together.

i   You cannot come to me alone. If you come alone, I ask you: 'And your brothers, where are they?' You must come to my heart all together, joined by the divine bond of your ever increasingly perfect and reciprocal love.

j   Because my Adversary is laying many snares for you along this road, before you go down from this mountain, I want you to make me a promise: that of loving each other ever more and more, that of walking all together, taking each other by the hand because, in a world where my Adversary is succeeding in dominating through egoism, hatred, and division, the sign of my triumph is this mutual love of yours.

k   I want it to become even greater, as an anticipation of the new world which you are preparing and which awaits you, and which will be a world thrown open only to the perfect, immense, and true capacity of your loving one another.

l   But before you go down from this mountain, I am also accepting the gift of your personal suffering. As I foretold to you in the country where I am still appearing, as it were by way of anticipation and motherly preparation for that which was awaiting you, I have in the course of this year, profoundly purified my Movement. I have burdened it with a cross the weight of which you still feel, deep to be sure, very deep, so that my work might be purified and might increasingly respond to my plan.

m   Do not be discouraged. Have strong faith in me. Something great and new is also about to open up for my work, because you have entered into the full phase of its fulfilment.

n   How much pain you will find along the roads of the world! As you go down from this cenacle in which I have gathered you, bring everywhere the motherly reflection of my merciful assistance. Pour balm on the many open and bleeding wounds; speak my sweet word to those who walk in aridity, in darkness, in discomfort, and in desperation.

o   You are the sign of my motherly presence, the rays of light which come forth from my Immaculate Heart to descend upon a devastated humanity and upon a darkened and divided Church.

p   Soon this division will become open, powerful and widespread and then you will have to be the bonds which unite those who want to remain in the unity of faith and of obedience to the hierarchy and, through innumerable trials, want to prepare the new times which are awaiting you. I have not let you go without speaking to you my motherly word and without giving you the comfort which comes down from my Immaculate Heart. I am always with you. You will always feel me close to you. I am your tender Mother who leads you to Jesus and brings you to peace.

q   With joy and gratitude for whatever good you have done and for whatever comfort you have given to the deep sorrow of my

Immaculate Heart, I, this evening, as your Mother, thank you all and bless you in the name of the Father and of the Son and of the Holy Spirit."

312

Do Not Be Afraid

a   "Today look at the Paradise which await you, beloved children, if you want to walk in the light of joy and of hope. On this day the whole heavenly cohort of angels and saints, especially of your brothers who have preceded you here and who await you, forms a great crown of glory about the glorious body of your heavenly Mother, assumed into heaven.

b   From my motherly and Immaculate Heart, I cause an extraordinary rain of graces to come down upon each one of you, to encourage you, to console you and to help you walk along the road which I have traced out for you.

c   Never before as today has the world in which you live become such a desert which produces poisonous and rotten fruit. Never before as today has my Adversary attempted in every way to obstruct you, to seduce you, and to strike you. Never before as today has Satan, exercising the great power which has been conceded to him, done everything to ruin my project and to destroy my work of love, which I myself am carrying out in these last times of yours.

d   For this, the Adversary is tormenting you in every way, is placing snares upon your path, is sowing misunderstandings and divisions to bring you to discouragement and is seducing you with temptations of all kinds, in order to intimidate you and cause you to halt. This is the time when his attacks against my Movement are becoming strong and continuous and when above all he is seeking to sow confusion and division among those whom I have chosen as directors in this work of mine.

e *Do not be afraid!* I am covering you with my immaculate mantle and protecting you. I am always at your side and I am leading you along the way which I have traced out for you. I allow his snares in order to purify you, but then I personally intervene in order to help you conquer them and to overcome them.

f With my glorious body I often make myself present to give you signs of my motherly assistance. For this reason I am still appearing in a continuous, daily, and extraordinary manner. Even now the light of my motherly presence is uniting the heavenly world to the earthly one, in a perennial communion of love and of prayer, in the terrible moments which are awaiting you in this concluding period of the great purification."

313

Fulda (Germany), September 8, 1985
The Birthday of the Blessed Virgin Mary

The Hour of Public Witness

a "Beloved sons, accept my invitation today to enter into my Immaculate Heart and to let yourselves be led by me. All those who accept this invitation of mine and consecrate themselves to my Immaculate Heart form part of my victorious cohort.

b On this day, the feast of my birth, I want to have you all about my cradle as a fragrant crown of love and of prayer.

c Today I am calling you all to a public and courageous witness. Look at your heavenly Mother who is born 'like the rising of the dawn, beautiful as the moon.' What is it that is darkening the life of men today? It is the darkness of rebellion against God, of their obstinate and so very widespread denial. You must spread everywhere the powerful cry: 'God is! Who is like God?'

d Only in return to God is the possibility of salvation opened up for humanity. And so you must spread with courage my motherly invitation to *conversion* and to return to the Lord, along the way of prayer and of penance, of charity and of fasting. For a little while yet, this is still the favorable time granted to humanity for its conversion.

e   Look at your heavenly Mother who is born 'bright as the sun.' What is it that is obscuring the beauty and the brightness of the Church? It is the smoke of the errors which Satan has caused to enter into it. These are becoming constantly more and more disseminated and are bringing very many souls to the loss of the faith.

f   The cause of such a vast diffusion of errors and of this great apostasy rests with unfaithful pastors. They remain silent when they should speak with courage to comdemn error and to defend the truth. They do not intervene when they should be unmasking the rapacious wolves who, hidden beneath the clothing of lambs, have insinuated themselves into the flock of Christ. They are dumb dogs who allow their flocks to be torn to pieces. You, on the other hand, must speak out with force and with courage to condemn error and to spread only the truth. The time of your public and courageous witness has come.

g   The splendor of the Church is also darkened by the profound division which has entered into its interior and which is growing greater every day. And so you must bear witness to this unity, with a strong commitment of union with the Pope and with the bishops united to him. Do not follow those bishops who oppose the Pope. Make of yourselves courageous defenders of the Pope and denounce openly those who are opposed to his *Magisterium* and who teach in a manner contrary to it. Look to your heavenly Mother who comes forth 'terrible as an army in battle array.'

h   What is it that makes your strength ineffectual and halts you with fear in the face of the great attack of my Adversary? It is the tolerance of sin which draws you away from the life of my Son Jesus. It is the great neglect of prayer, which gives you his very own strength.

i   So then be today courageous witnesses in fighting against sin. Through you, let the great gift which Jesus has made to you in the sacrament of reconciliation shine forth once again in the Church. Return to the practice of going often to confession and pray more. Pray with me; pray the holy rosary.

j   Everything that my Pope has said in this place corresponds with the truth.

k   You are close to the greatest chastisement; and so I say to you:

entrust yourselves to me and remember that the weapon to use in these terrible moments is that of the holy rosary. Then you will form my cohort which I am leading, in these times, to its greatest victory."

314

The Two Cohorts

a   "From here, where I appeared as the Woman clothed with the sun, I am calling all of you to gather together about your heavenly Leader.

b   These are the times of the great battle between me and the powerful cohort which is under the orders of the Red Dragon and the Black Beast. Marxist atheism and Masonry are guiding this army, which has been mustered to lead all humanity to the denial of God and to rebellion against Him.

c   At its head is Lucifer himself, who is repeating today his act of defiance in placing himself against God to make himself adored as God. With him are fighting all the demons who are, in these times, being poured out from hell upon the earth, in order to lead the greatest possible number of souls to perdition.

d   United with them are all the souls of the damned and those who, in this life, are walking in rejection of God, whom they offend and blaspheme, as they walk along the road of egoism and hatred, of evil and impurity. They have made their one and only aim the quest for pleasures; they satisfy all their passions, they fight for the triumph of hatred, of evil, and of impiety.

e   The cohort which I myself am leading is made up of all the angels and saints of paradise, guided by Saint Michael the Archangel, who is the head of all the heavenly militia.

f   This is a great battle which is being waged above all at the level of spirits.

g   On this earth, my cohort is made up of all those who live by loving and glorifying God, according to the grace received in holy baptism, and who are walking along the sure road of perfect observance of the commandments of the Lord. They are humble, docile, little and charitable; they flee from the snares of the demon and from the easy seductions of pleasure; they journey along the way of love, of purity, and of holiness. This cohort of mine is made up of all my little children who, in every part of the world, are answering me today with a 'yes' and are following me along the road which, in these years, I have traced out for you.

h   It is with my cohort that I am bringing on my victory in these times. It is with my cohort that I am building up, each day, the triumph of my Immaculate Heart. It is with my cohort that I am preparing the way along which the glorious reign of Jesus will come to you, and it will be a reign of love and of grace, of holiness, of justice, and of peace.

i   From this place where I appeared, I repeat to you again today my motherly appeal: join together, all of you, as quickly as possible in this my cohort! The hour of the great battle has already arrived. Fight with the weapon of the holy rosary and walk along the way of love for Jesus, of comtempt for the world and for yourselves, of humility, of charity, of simplicity, of purity. Then you will be ready to bear the great trials which will soon begin for the Church and for humanity.

j   From this blessed place, with my Pope and with my beloved ones and the children consecrated to me, I bless you all in the name of the Father, and of the Son and of the Holy Spirit."

315
My Path

Auckland (New Zealand), November 12, 1985

a   "From this land of the Far East, where I have brought you to spread my motherly message and to gather together my children in the refuge of my Immaculate Heart, I am again calling the whole Church and all of humanity to follow the path traced out by your heavenly Mother. It is the sure path which brings you to the God of salvation and of peace.

b   Upon it you experience the love of the Father, who loves you very much and leads you, who prepares everything for you through his divine providence, and who calls you to an ever greater happiness. Allow yourselves to be carried at every moment by this fatherly love, like little children who entrust themselves completely to his divine will.

c   Upon it you meet the divine person of my Son Jesus, who, with his glorified body and his divinity, is ever close to each one of you. He wants to be your joy and your peace. He wants to be loved, followed and imitated by each one of you. The path upon which I am leading you is that of perfect imitation of my Son Jesus. In this way you live out the consecration of your baptism, and you renounce the world and its seductions, in order to walk along the way of divine grace, of love and of holiness.

d   Upon it you become transformed each day by the powerful action of the Holy Spirit, my most beloved Spouse, who is leading you to the perfection of your witness.

e   I have ordained that it is to be, for you, a painful witness. The times of the purification and of the bloody trial are drawing close. It is necessary for the salvation of my children and to purify the Church from the wound of apostasy and infidelity.

f   My motherly love constrains me to shorten the times. Within a short time, you will begin to understand all that I have been telling you for years.

g   Then all my little children who, from every part of the world, have answered me with a 'yes' and who have consecrated themselves to me and whom I am now cultivating in silence and in hiddenness, will open up like fragrant flowers to announce the new season of the triumph of my Immaculate Heart. I bless you all with love and with joy."

316

Melbourne (Australia), December 1, 1985
First Sunday of Advent

Blessed in Expectation

a   "My message has now reached every part of the world. Beloved children, sustain and support with generosity and trust the plan of your heavenly Mother.

b   Live in peace of heart. Love, pray, make reparation. With the simplicity of little children, live the present moment, which the Father is preparing for you as a gift of his divine providence.

c   Do not allow yourselves to be seduced by those who point to years and days, as though they wanted to impose a time-table on the infinite mercy of the divine Heart of my Son Jesus.

d   *Today, many are the false prophets* who are spreading lying messages in order to cast many of my children into anguish and fear.

e   I am the Mother of hope and of trust. Live with me through these times of your second advent. As I was the virginal Mother of the first coming of Jesus, so also today I am the glorious Mother of his second coming.

f   Live in this expectation and you will be blessed.

g   Blessed in the midst of trials and sufferings of every kind, because you have the certitude that the time of the present tribulation is preparing the time of the glorious return of my Son Jesus.

h   Blessed in the midst of misunderstandings and persecutions, because your names are written in my Immaculate Heart and because you are being guarded in my secure and motherly refuge.

i   Blessed also if you are living in a Church which is darkened, wounded, and divided because this, her hour of agony, is preparing for her the radiant dawn of a second Pentecost.

j   Live in my Immaculate Heart, blessed in the expectation of the blessed hope and the glorious coming of my Son Jesus."

317

Perth (Australia), December 8, 1985
Immaculate Conception

Your Motherly Shepherdess

a   "I am the Immaculate Conception. I am your all-beautiful Mother.

b   Beloved children, walk along the road of love, of purity and of holiness.

c   Today I am happy to see how my motherly message has now spread to every part of the world.

d   Many priests, but especially the faithful in great numbers and with great enthusiasm, have responded to my invitation to consecrate themselves to my Immaculate Heart, to be united with the Pope, to walk along the way of divine grace, to flee sin, to pray the holy rosary and to gather together in cenacles of unceasing prayer, made with me and through me.

e   And you, my little son, find yourself this day in a city, so very far away, set at the extreme south of this great continent to be the gentle shephard's staff of your motherly Shepherdess, who wants to gather you all together as quickly as possible in the safe sheepfold of her Immaculate Heart.

f   My times have now come. What I have foretold to you is now about to be accomplished. You are on the threshold of grave and painful events for the Church and for humanity.

g   And so today, when heaven and earth are united with joy in venerating the singular privilege of my Immaculate Conception, I am inviting you all to gather together in the cohort, and at the orders of your heavenly Leader, who is leading you in the battle against the Evil One and sin, so that the most pure light of divine grace and of holiness may shine forth resplendently in you."

318

Dongo (Como), December 24, 1985
The Holy Night

A Great Silence

a   "This is the Holy Night. Beloved children, spend it with me, in the joyous remembrance of the moments which I lived through, while the birth in time of the Word of the Father, of the true Son of God, was in preparation.

b   A *mysterious silence* marked the unfolding of this great mystery of love. A sweet harmony of peace enwrapped my virginal person, called to open itself to the motherly gift of the Son.

c   A *great silence* surrounded the accomplishment of this divine mystery. While silence enfolded everything, in the middle of the night, the eternal Word of the Father came down as a dew upon the world, called to receive its divine bud. And upon this great silence, behold, the heavenly voices of the angels are opened up and also hearts of the shepherds, who are able to understand that which is hidden to the great ones.

d   And thus it must be for every encounter with the Word, who becomes flesh in the life of each one of you. Thus it must be in your daily encounter with my Son Jesus. Thus it must be for the Christmas which you are called to live out each day, as you welcome with love into your hearts and your souls the Lord who saves you and leads you to peace.

e   Thus too it must be for his second coming, when He will return in the splendor of his divinity and will come upon the clouds of heaven to establish his reign in glory.

f   There is need again today of a *great silence*, in order to understand the mysterious plan of God and to know how to read the signs of the times through which you are living, and which announce to you his imminent return.

g   Open up your hearts to the humility, the simplicity, and the candor of little ones. Persevere in prayer and trust. Each day, in company with your heavenly Mother, live your perennial Christmas, which is already perpetuated in time, for the joy and salvation of all."

319

Dongo (Como), December 31, 1985
Last night of the year

Your Prayer with Me

a   "Beloved children, spend the hours of this last night of the year with me in prayer. So many of my children are spending these hours in amusements and in dissipation, in order to greet the new year with noise and diversion.

b   *You on the other hand, are to lift up to the Lord, with me, a powerful prayer of thanksgiving.*

c   His merciful love is continuing today to carry out a great plan of salvation and of mercy for the people of these times of yours who are so lost and ill. Sin is your real illness, sin which is infecting my children more and more and leading them to live in egoism, in hatred, in impurity and in the obstinate rejection of the Lord your God, who has created you and is leading you along the road of true happiness.

d   The Lord is asking you to come back along the way of return to Him, and in many ways, even during this year, He has given you signs of his invitation to conversion.

e   *Lift up to the Lord, with me, a powerful prayer of reparation.*

f   Iniquity is covering the whole earth like a deep layer of ice and has dried up the hearts and the souls of many of my children. The cup of divine justice is full, it is flowing over, and it demands to be appeased.

g   While the greatest mystery of iniquity is about to be completed in the world, I am turning to you, my children, to invite you to form with me a great chain of reparation. Offer all your prayers and your sufferings of whatever kind, uniting them each day to the sacrifice of my Son Jesus, which is everywhere being renewed in reparation and in remission for all the sins of the world.

h   Then you will be helping me to keep in suspension the chastisement, which this human race has even now drawn upon itself, because of its own impious way of life.

i   The new times are already at the gates. I am the Mother who is leading you along the way of salvation and of peace.

j   In prayer, in fasting, in mortification and in penance, dispose yourselves to live with me the new days which are awaiting you and which the mercy of the Father is preparing for you."

1986

QUEEN OF PEACE

320

Queen of Peace

a   "Look today at your heavenly Mother. This is the feast of my divine motherhood. It is also the first day of the new year, and the Church invites you today to pray in order to obtain the great gift of peace.

b   *I am the Queen of Peace.* On Christmas day, I gave you Him who is your peace, my Son Jesus. Jesus has brought you to peace with God and thus He has opened up for you the way of your salvation and of true happiness. Jesus has brought you to peace with yourselves and thus He has opened up for you the way to peace of heart.

c   This can be born only through living in divine grace, which He has merited for you by his birth in your midst, by his life and by his bloody immolation on the Cross. If you live in the grace of God, you live in peace of heart.

d   Egoism, hatred, impurity and any sin whatsoever take away your peace of heart.

e   Jesus has brought you to peace with all people and has traced out for you the way towards true brotherhood. Every human person must truly be looked upon by you as your brother.

f   I am asking you all to live in one true communion of brotherhood and of mutual love, without distinction of race, language or religion. You are all children of God, redeemed by Jesus, entrusted to my spiritual motherhood and therefore you must all live with each other as true brothers. Only along the way of a brotherhood which is truly lived out will peace be able to come to you.

g   *But peace is, today, being ever increasingly threatened.* Men are walking in a vast and obstinate rejection of God; they are victims of sin and of impurity; they are incapable of understanding and loving each other and thus human rights are trampled under foot, the poor and the hungry are abandoned, oppression and injustices are increasing, acts of violence are exploding menacingly and wars are constantly spreading more and more.

h   In this year, grave threats to peace and dangers of great evils are pressing in upon you. And so, today, on the feast of my divine motherhood, I invite you to entrust yourselves to me, who am the Queen of Peace.

i   Be converted and return to the Lord along the way of prayer and of penance, of mortification of the senses, and of fasting. The space of time which God has yet granted to humanity for its conversion is almost over. For this reason, I address this message of mine to you, with heartfelt and motherly anxiety.

j   Listen to it and you will be saved. Follow it and you will find peace of heart. Spread it everywhere and you will help to prepare, for all, days, not of misfortune and affliction, but of hope and peace."

321

The Way to the Divine Will

a   "Follow me, beloved sons, along the way which I am tracing out for you, in order to lead you all into the temple of the Lord, that you may sing today of his love and his glory.

b   While, with my most chaste spouse, Joseph, I walked along the road to the Temple of Jerusalem, carrying in my arms my divine Infant and was absorbed with Him in a profound ecstasy of love and prayer, I was carrying out a prescription of the Law and fulfilling the will of the Lord.

c   I am doing the same today with each one of you. I am leading you along the way of perfect fulfillment of the will of the Lord.

d   *I am the way to the divine will.*

e   *It is the will of God* that you fulfill to perfection the obligations of your priestly state.

f   *It is the will of God* that you give an important place to the life of prayer and of deep union with Him. For this reason, I am leading you to a scrupulous observance of your practices of piety: the Divine Office must never be neglected by you; your daily meditation must be made with calm and love; the rosary must be recited every day by you, with me; holy Mass, celebrated and lived by you, must be the point of reference of your entire day.

g   It is the will of God that also in your apostolic activity you should follow the norms set down for you by the Church. Never take part in profane shows: do not go to those places which are not suitable to your dignity as Ministers of God; know how to protect and defend the sacred character of your person.

h   You are in the world, but not of the world. Do not be ashamed of giving to all this public testimony. For this, I am asking you to always wear your ecclesiastical garb, so that it may be seen everywhere that you are priests of God and my sons of predilection. How it grieves my Immaculate Heart to see that many priests, and even some bishops, dress entirely in lay attire, openly disobeying the laws which the Church has set down for you.

i   It is the will of God that you burn with great zeal for the salvation of souls, and that you be always ready therefore for the serious task which has been entrusted to you as ministers of reconciliation. In much of the Church, this sacrament, which is so necessary, is already in the process of disappearing, precisely because many priests no longer enter the confessional to be at the disposal of those souls who have extreme need of this sacrament of divine mercy.

j   It is the will of God that you be always available for all the spiritual and material needs of your neighbor. Your priestly heart must be open, generous, sensitive and merciful. Only in this way do you fulfill the will which the Lord has for each one of you and walk along the road which leads toward holiness.

k   For this I am leading you each day along the way of the perfect fulfillment of the divine will so that, in the holy temple of your priestly life, the Most Holy Trinity may receive from you today its greatest glory."

A Divine Mystery

a   "This is your feastday, beloved sons, because it is your pasch. Remember the institution of the Eucharist and the priesthood. Jesus so much desired to eat this Pasch with his disciples before He suffered! You should also desire to consummate with great love the mystery of your priestly pasch.

b   *It is a divine mystery of love.* You are called to the purity of love. For this I am working powerfully in you each day, to transform your hearts and make them conformable to that of my Son Jesus. I am leading you into the burning furnace of his divine and most pure love, because a priestly heart must be molded and transformed by the Heart of Jesus, the eternal High Priest.

c   A priestly heart must be meek and humble, merciful and sensitive, pure and compassionate, open like a chalice to loving God in an exclusive and total manner and then, filled with the fullness of divine love, to set all his brothers aflame with inextinguishable charity.

d   Today is also the day of the new commandment: 'Love one another as I have loved you.' It is the day of his binding command: 'If I, as Teacher, have done this, you must do it also if you wish to be my true disciples.' Beloved sons, put yourselves ever at the service of all: you also must wash the feet of your brothers, by pouring balm on their wounds, by sharing with them in every way in their needs and in their poverty, and by taking upon yourselves the weight of the sin and evil in the world.

e   *It is a divine mystery of prayer.* Your priesthood is expressed in a perennial work of mediation between God and men. And this is exercised by your priestly prayer, above all with the offering to God of the daily sacrifice of holy Mass which, by means of you, makes the paschal gift of this Last Supper perennial and universal. The exercise of the priesthood in the gift, to the faithful, of the sacraments instituted by Jesus for your salvation is the perfection of prayer, that is to say, of deep union of life with God.

f   Above all, the perfection of prayer is to be found in your docile and obliging availability to the needs of souls, which often leads you to enter the confessional, as ministers of the sacrament of penance, through which you can heal the deep wounds caused by many sins. Through your good example, may the practice of frequent confession return throughout the whole Church, thereby putting into effect that which, on this day, the first of my beloved sons, Pope John Paul II, has asked in his letter written to all priests.

g   *It is a divine mystery of suffering.* The institution of the priesthood is above all ordered to a perpetual, even though unbloody, immolation of Jesus, which perpetuates that which was done by Him on Calvary. And so you too are called by me to suffer with Jesus, to immolate yourselves with Him for the salvation of souls. Climb the Calvary of this indifferent and cruel century, ready to die with Jesus, that the brothers may have life. To this purpose, I am asking of you, in these times, greater and more continuous sufferings.

h   Do not be discouraged; on the contrary, be happy. If you enter into the garden of my Immaculate Heart, you will experience ever more and more that which Jesus experienced in a perfect manner: the joy of being immolated for the sake of love and the salvation of all.

i   And so, each day, to the souls who have been entrusted to you, you can say with truth: 'How much I have desired to eat this pasch of mine with you!' "

323

Dongo, March 28, 1986
Good Friday

Why Have You Abandoned Me?

a   "I am today beneath the Cross upon which Jesus is living out the hours of his painful agony. In my motherly Immaculate Heart, weighed down by his suffering, I hear the cry of his final lament: 'My God, why have you abandoned Me?'

b Listen with me today, beloved sons, to this cry of his. It is, as it were, the summit of all his suffering, the supreme culmination of every pain. Oh, relive with me, the wounded and sorrowful Mother, these unspeakable moments of his sorrowful Passion:

c the agony of Gethsemane, the betrayal by Judas, the abandonment by the disciples, Peter's denial, the outrage and the condemnation on the part of the religious tribunal, the judgment before Pilate; the horrible flagellation and the crowning with thorns, his painful climb to Calvary, the spasm of the hands and the feet pierced by the nails, and those three interminable hours of atrocious agony, as He hung on the Cross.

d Behold the Lamb who, silent, allows Himself to be led to the slaughter. Behold the true Lamb of God, who takes away the sins of the world. Upon the Heart of this meek body of an immolated and crucified victim there weighs every sin of the world and all the iniquity redeemed by his sacrifice.

e 'My God, why have You abandoned Me?'

f Upon this divine Heart, so crushed and oppressed that He even feels abandonment by the Father, there weighs also all the lack of response and all the ingratitude of his Church, born, like a pure bride, from the womb of his great suffering.

g Again today, in his Church, Jesus continues to be abandoned, denied, and betrayed.

h He is denied by those who put Him in second place after their own comfort, their own self-seeking and their relish for being accepted and applauded. Pride leads many to deny Him in their words and in their life: 'I do not know this man!'

i He is also betrayed on the part of those pastors who do not look after the flock entrusted to them, who remain silent out of fear or for the sake of convenience and do not defend the truth from the snares of errors, nor do they protect the sheep from the terrible scourge of rapacious wolves, who present themselves dressed as lambs.

j He is abandoned by many priests and religious who leave the state of their lofty vocation or who do not live in faithfulness to their commitments and who allow themselves to be led completely by the spirit of the world in which they live.

k   He is rejected and spurned by many of the faithful who follow ideologies which are in style today but which propose values opposed to those of the Gospel, and they descend to compromises simply in order to always have everyone's approval.

l   Good Friday is truly being repeated today in a form immensely greater and more universal than that which took place at the time of the Passion and death on the Cross. For one thing that was done at that time, a thousand such are being carried out at present. For this reason, in his Mystical Body which is the Church, Jesus continues to repeat his painful cry: 'My God, why have you abandoned Me?'

m   This is the affliction of your heavenly Mother, which is being repeated today, as she sees the same sufferings which Jesus experienced being repeated in the Church on this day of its Good Friday.

n   See if there is any sorrow like mine! Share in my agony over the flood of sin, over the apostasy which is becoming ever greater because of the loss of faith on the part of many and over the unfaithfulness which is growing like a tide and submerging souls.

o   Never before as today, O Church, have you been so likened to your Crucified Spouse. For you too, this is the hour of your agony, of your abandonment, of your painful death on the cross.

p   But during your Good Friday, there stands at your side your sorrowful Mother, who is comforting you and watching in prayer and in the firm hope of your imminent and glorious resurrection."

324

Dongo, March 30, 1986
The Pasch of the Resurrection

Jesus Is Your Peace

a   "The peace of the divine Heart of your risen Brother, Jesus, and of the Immaculate Heart of your heavenly Mother which is filled with gladness at the sight of his glorious body, be always with you, my beloved children.

b   Peace be in your hearts and in your lives. May peace be the everlasting gift of your apostolate. Jesus who was humiliated, despised, spat upon, scourged, condemned, crucified, slain on the Cross and buried, *is risen today!*

c   This is the Pasch of his Resurrection! The risen Jesus is ever living and present among you.

d   *Jesus is your peace.* He alone is your life; He alone is your victory.

e   Share with me in this joy, which no one can ever disturb. Carry it in your soul so that hope may bloom therein.

f   I am the sorrowful Mother of the Passion. I am the joyous Mother of the Resurrection. I am the Mother of the risen Christ; I am the announcement of his victory.

g   To me has been entrusted the task of preparing his glorious return. In these painful times of purification, I say to you: 'Do not doubt; have great hope!' Jesus has conquered the world forever. Jesus alone is still today the true victor.

h   I am the Mother who am calling you from all sides to bring you all to Jesus and thus to prepare for you a new era of peace. I am the Queen of Peace who look upon you with the tenderness of a mother and bless you in the name of the glorified Father, of the risen Son and of the Holy Spirit who is given to you as a gift."

325

Merine (Lecce), May 8, 1986

Mother of Grace and of Mercy

a   "I am the Mother of Divine Grace. I am the Mother of Divine Love. I am the Fount of Mercy.

b   Beloved sons, walk along the road which I have traced out for you during these years, if you wish to second my motherly plan for the salvation of all my children, especially my poor sinful children.

c   *You must be my hands*, who distribute copious graces to all who find themselves in any necessity. In these times, I want to manifest myself through you. I desire to distribute my graces through your priestly hands, which must always be opened as a help and comfort for all.

d   Pour balm upon the many painful wounds; bring help to those who are in poverty and neglect; assist the suffering, the marginalized, the little people, the oppressed and the persecuted to walk along the road of confidence and hope. You must be the hands of your heavenly Mother, which are always opened to pour the fullness of graces upon all her children!

e   *You must be my heart*, which opens itself to give its motherly love. Love with the very beating of my Immaculate Heart. You are consecrated to me that I may be able to form you in the perfection of love. Be gentle and sensitive, pure and humble of heart. You must be the help which I want to give today to all who have need of love in order to be saved.

f   Love those who are far away and who are atheists; love even those who persecute you and reject you; love *all*, without any distinction of language, race or religion. In this way, each one of you becomes a beat of my Immaculate Heart, which comes down upon all, to give the comfort of my unwavering love of a mother.

g   *You must be the instruments of my mercy*. Today humanity has great need of divine mercy. Only through mercy can it be entirely renewed and saved. It is sick because of its obstinate rejection of God, which hinders it from walking along the road that has been pointed out by Him in order to lead it to salvation. It is gravely ill because it has become incapable of loving. The world has been reduced to an immense desert, devoid of love. In it there flourish the bad weeds of hatred, of division, of sin, of unbridled egoism, of impurity, of violence and of war. Only a great miracle of divine mercy will be able to save this straying and dying humanity, which has even now touched the depths of its extreme misery.

h   This is the reason why, in these times, the entire world has been entrusted to the Immaculate Heart of your heavenly Mother. You, O priests consecrated to me, must be the instruments of my motherly mercy. In this way, you will cause new buds of life and holiness, of purity and love to sprout forth everywhere. And thus you will have a part in building, with me each day, new heavens and a new earth, as the most beautiful fruit of the fullness of grace and of mercy, which the Immaculate Heart of your heavenly Mother forever gives you."

326

Anchor of Salvation

a "Today I want to express my motherly gratitude to you for your having accepted my invitation to consecrate yourselves to my Immaculate Heart. You have responded in great numbers, from all parts of the world. Continue to respond to me with generosity and allow yourselves to be led by me into the secure refuge which my motherly love has built for you.

b *In these times, you all need to hasten to take shelter in the refuge of my Immaculate Heart*, because grave threats of evil are hanging over you.

c *These are first of all evils of a spiritual order*, which can harm the supernatural life of your souls. Sin is spreading as the worst and most pernicious of epidemics, which is bringing sickness and death everywhere to many souls. If you live habitually in mortal sin you are spiritually dead and, if you come to the end of life in this state, eternal death in hell awaits you. Hell exists; it is eternal, and today many are running the danger of going there, because they are being contaminated by this mortal disease.

d *There are evils of a physical order*, such as infirmity, disasters, accidents, droughts, earthquakes, and incurable diseases which are spreading about. Even in that which happens to you in the natural order, see a warning sign for yourselves. You should see a sign of divine justice, which cannot allow the innumerable crimes which are committed every day to go unpunished.

e   *There are evils of a social order*, such as divisions and hatred, famine and poverty, exploitation and slavery, violence, terrorism and war.

f   *To be protected from all these evils, I invite you to place yourselves under shelter in the safe refuge of my Immaculate Heart.*

g   But, in these times, *you have need above all of being defended* from the terrible snares of my Adversary, who has succeeded in establishing his reign in the world. It is the reign which is opposed to Christ; it is the reign of the Antichrist. In this last part of your century, this reign of his will reach the peak of its strength, of its power, of its great seduction. The hour is in preparation when the man of iniquity, who wants to put himself in the place of God to have himself adored as God, is about to manifest himself in all his power.

h   Under the bloody scourge of this terrible trial, how are you to avoid being scattered and discouraged and to remain strong in the faith and faithful only to Jesus and to his Gospel? My Immaculate Heart will become your strongest defense, the shield of protection which will safeguard you from every attack of my Adversary.

i   *But today you have special need of being consoled.* To whom will you be able to turn in the painful moments which are awaiting you, when the great apostasy will reach its peak and humanity will arrive at the summit of denial of God and of rebellion, of iniquity and discord, of hatred and destruction, of wickedness and impiety.

j   In my Immaculate Heart you will be consoled! For this reason, I say again to each one of you today that which I said at Fatima to my daughter, Sister Lucy: 'My Immaculate Heart will be your refuge and the sure way which will lead you to God.' On this day, dedicated by the Church to its particular veneration, I desire that my Immaculate Heart appear as the anchor of salvation for all."

San Marino—Spiritual Exercises
in the form of a cenacle, July 4, 1986
After the evening procession; message given orally

A Spirit of Joy and of Consolation

a "Beloved sons, I do not want to let you go down from this mountain where, for an entire week, you have remained united with me in an unceasing prayer and in a lived-out experience of brotherhood, willed and guided by me, without telling you of all the joy experienced, during these days, by the Immaculate Heart of your very sorrowful heavenly Mother.

b Your love has been a gentle balm on all my wounds. Your prayer, made with me, has been a powerful force which you have given me to offer to the justice of the Father and in order to obtain for you, very soon, the rain of fire and of grace of the Holy Spirit, who will renew and transform the whole world, thus bringing to completion the greatest miracle of the merciful love of my Son Jesus.

c I do not want to let you go down from this mountain, without telling each and every one of you of my motherly gratitude. During these days you have entered into the heavenly garden of my Immaculate Heart. Look at my heart; enter into my heart; live always in my heart and *a spirit of joy and of consolation will come upon you.*

d You have come up here with many preoccupations, marked by many sufferings and also enveloped by an all-too-human discouragement. You have climbed up here, asking yourselves, in your heart, what new thing your Mother from heaven has to say to you this year.

e *Beloved sons, look at my Immaculate Heart and there will come down upon you a spirit of joy and of consolation.*

i I am your Mother: I see the difficulties in which you are living; the heavy sorrow of these days of yours; the bloody hours which await you in the purification through which you are living. I see with what sadness your life is sometimes marked. I see also the moments in which you are oppressed by distress and discouragement, because today my Adversary is ensnaring you, above all with doubt and mistrust.

g   Look to my Immaculate Heart and within you, like a gushing fount, *will flow forth a spirit of joy and consolation.*

h   Why do you doubt? Why are you sad? I am at your side at all times; I never leave you. I am a mother and I am drawn close to you by the weight of the great difficulties in which you are living today.

i   From my heart there comes a ray of light: it is the light of your Mother, faithful Virgin, which enlightens your mind and draws it gently to understand the mystery of the Word of God and to penetrate deeply the secret of the Gospel.

j   In the darkness which has come down upon the world and is spreading throughout the Church, how many minds are becoming obscured by errors and dried up by the ever widening spread of doubts; how many intellects are being contaminated with error which leads many to become lost and to stray from the way of the true faith.

k   These are the times in which many in the Church are losing the faith, even from among my beloved sons.

l   If you look to my Immaculate Heart and allow yourselves to be penetrated by the ray of my light, your minds will obtain the gift of divine wisdom and will be drawn by the beauty of the truth which Jesus has revealed to you. The daily food of your mind will be only the Word of God. Love it, seek it, guard it, defend it, live it. Thus, as the great apostasy spreads, you will walk in the joy and in the consolation of remaining ever in the truth of the Gospel.

m   *When you came up here, I looked at your souls,* the garden of my celestial and motherly domain, and I saw them to be still darkened by sins, which you often commit, because of your very human fragility. In you there are no grave sins, since you are seeking not to commit them any more. But even the little ones, which you call venial, displease my heart. These can be egoism, attachment to yourselves, the inability to believe and to entrust yourselves to me with the docility of little children, the daily compromises with the world and attachment to creatures and to your way of thinking. These are little shadows which obscure the beauty of your

498

soul. During these days, my motherly hand has passed along to wipe out all these shadows.

n   Walk in the joy and in the consolation of feeling that you are loved and led by me to become purer, better, more loving, holier, more beautiful. Your souls must return from this mountain more luminous and renewed by the grace of Jesus, while the Father bends down over them with a love of predilection and my divine Spouse, the Holy Spirit, transforms them into perfect copies of my Son.

o   *You came up here and I saw your hearts, one by one*: they are consumed with great aridity, closed in upon themselves and hardened by the trials in which you are living. And so, as a mother, I have drawn close to each one of you; I have taken your heart in my hands; I have placed it into the burning furnace of my motherly heart and I have brought it into the depths of the divine Heart of my Son Jesus. Look at this Heart: it has been pierced for you! Enter into the wound of the Heart of Jesus and allow yourselves to be transformed each day by the burning fire of his divine love. This Heart is a sea of infinite love and it gathers in every human weakness, burns up every sin and calls to an ever greater charity, because Love must be loved and every gift demands its own response. In here, as gold in the crucible, your hearts become continually transformed by the flame of an ardent charity, and thus you become ever more docile, humble, meek, merciful, good, little, pure.

p   *Behold, formed in the infinite sea of divine Love, your new hearts and new spirits are born, that you may be witnesses of love, bringing love everywhere and thus become, you yourselves, spirits of joy and of consolation for everyone.*

q   Do you still not understand that these are the years of the painful purification which is about to come to its most bloody finish? Why do you still ask questions? These are my years. This is the reason why I have wanted you here again and, during these Spiritual Exercises which have been a continuous cenacle, I have given extraordinary graces to each one of you. For the present you do not understand, because they are like a seed placed in your soul, but later on you will understand and then you will look up

499

here, to this mountain, and you will comprehend that which I have done for you during these days.

r Here, this has been a true cenacle, like that of Jerusalem! Here, you my apostles have been united in prayer with me, because the new Pentecost is at the doors. Here, I have introduced you to an understanding of the secret of my Immaculate Heart so that, as you go down from this mountain, you yourselves may become my sign of joy and of consolation for all.

s You cannot go back the way you came up. Go down with me. Look at this withered humanity. How many of my children are dead, because they have been slain by sin and hatred, by violence and impurity, victims of vice and of drugs. They are my children: desperate, afflicted, in need of help. With your love, speak my motherly word to them and be, for them, my sign of joy and of consolation.

t And then enter into the heart of my Church. Be signs of joy and of consolation for the Pope, the first of my beloved sons, who is suffering so much today, abandoned, criticized, and contradicted. You must be the support of love, which my motherly heart wishes to give him. Because even he has need today of a spirit of joy and of consolation and I want to give it to him through you, my priests and my beloved sons. Love the Pope; follow him; defend him.

u Enter into an understanding of the mystery of the Church as the Mystical Body of Christ, which is divided and torn today and which you must restore in its unity. This Body is being mocked today; it is being scourged once again by sins which are spreading ever more and more. Make reparation for all sins, by helping many of my children to free themselves from them, through the use of the sacrament of reconciliation which, by means of you, must once again shine throughout all the Church.

v Bend down with me to kiss the wounds of this most beloved daughter of mine, whose sons you also are, because the Church can only be renewed through the power of your priestly love.

w Thus you become signs of the new era which is beginning even now in the bitter winter of its most painful purification. In the agony through which she is still living, you are the chalice of comfort which the Immaculate Heart of your heavenly Mother is giving her to drink, that she may regain strength and walk with joy.

And so you become today a spirit of joy and of consolation for the whole Church.

x   Do not allow yourselves to become discouraged. My triumph has already begun. In your hearts and in the silence of your priestly lives, consecrated to me and immolated by me, *the triumph of my Immaculate Heart has already begun.*

y   Thank you for the comfort which you have given me. I welcome the desires and the questions which you bring to me. I bless your apostolate, the souls entrusted to you and your difficult ministry. I bless your lives. They are precious to me.

z   You will go down from this mountain tomorrow, to return to your homes. I am accompanying you with my motherly blessing. Do not be afraid any more. I am always with you. In you and by means of you, I am the beginning of the new times. I am the Mother of hope and of consolation. I am the Queen of Peace.

A   I bless you in the name of the Father, and of the Son, and of the Holy Spirit."

328

Rubbio (Vicenza), July 30, 1986

Ark of the New Covenant

a   "Beloved children, I am leading you each day along the road of your perfect imitation of my Son Jesus. Only in this way can you become today a sign of joy and of consolation for all. These are the painful years of the trial. This has already been foretold to you by me, in many ways and with many signs.

b   But who believes me? Who listens to me? Who truly pledges himself to change his life? I am caught between two swords, which pierce my motherly heart. On the one hand I see the great danger into which you are running, because of the chastisement which is already at the doors; and on the other I see your inability to believe and to accept the invitations to conversion, which I am giving you, so that you may flee from it.

c   And so I turn again to you, my beloved ones and children consecrated to me, and I invite you to climb above the world, above
your daily preoccupations, above your disordinate attachments to
creatures and to yourselves, above mediocrity and tepidity, above
an ever widening aridity.

d   Enter into the refuge which your heavenly Mother has prepared
for you, for your salvation and that you may be able to pass in
safety, in my Immaculate Heart, the terrible days of the great
tempest which is on the point of coming.

e   *This is the moment for all to take refuge in me, because I am the
Ark of the New Covenant.*

f   At the time of Noah, immediately before the flood, those whom
the Lord had destined to survive his terrible chastisement entered
into the ark. In these your times, I am inviting all my beloved
children to enter into the ark of the new covenant which I have
built in my Immaculate Heart for you, that they may be assisted
by me to carry the bloody burden of the great trial, which precedes
the coming of the day of the Lord.

g   Do not look anywhere else. There is happening today what happened in the days of the flood, and no one is giving a thought
to what is awaiting them. Everyone is much occupied in thinking
only of themselves, of their own earthly interests, of pleasures and
of satisfying in every sort of way, their own disordinate passions.

h   Even in the Church, how few there are who concern themselves
with my motherly and most sorrowful admonitions!

i   You at least, my beloved ones, must listen to me and follow me.
And then, through you, I will be able to call everyone to enter
as quickly as possible into the ark of the new covenant and of salvation, which my Immaculate Heart has prepared for you, in view
of these times of chastisement.

j   Here you will be in peace and you will be able to become signs
of my peace and of my motherly consolation for all my poor
children."

329

Climb the Mountain

a   "Climb today with me up the mountain of my peace, beloved children. Climb up the mountain of salvation and of prayer, of purity and of holiness, of docility and of meekness, of humility, of littleness and of your ever more perfect charity.

b   Climb up the holy mountain of your personal transfiguration, through an ever increasing conformation of yourselves to the divine humanity of my Son Jesus, through a filial abandonment to the love of the heavenly Father and through a daily docility to the purifying action of the Holy Spirit. Thus you yourselves will be able to benefit from the gift of a complete transformation, in the glorious light of Christ who, in you and through you, wishes to manifest Himself in a greater way, in these times, in order to renew the whole world with the power of his merciful love.

c   On this holy mountain, you will also feel the extraordinary presence and the special action of your heavenly Mother, who wants every day to transform you into the very person of Jesus, so that you may become today a powerful witness of his love for you.

d   Here I am gently preparing you for the painful moments of the cross and of martyrdom. For you also, the days of abandonment, of agony and of immolation have already come. The great events which I have foretold to you during these years have arrived. Soon you will all be called to your most painful witnessing. And then you will be able to become, for all, the rays of light which come forth from my Immaculate Heart to reach every part of the world, in order to cast light upon the dark moments through which you are already about to live.

e   Thus you will assist my motherly plan, which is that of cooperating in the fulfillment of the greatest miracle of the merciful love of Jesus, who is even now about to pour out rivers of fire and of grace upon the world."

330   Rubbio (Vicenza) August 8, 1986
                                    (After the recitation of the holy rosary;
                                                message given verbally)

Mother of the Eucharist

a   "Beloved sons, how my heart is filled with joy in seeing you here,
on a priestly pilgrimage of adoration, of love, of reparation and
of thanksgiving to Jesus, my Son and my God, present in the
Eucharist, to console Him for the great emptiness, the great ingratitude and the great indifference, with which He is surrounded
in his real and loving presence in all the tabernacles of the earth,
on the part of so many of my children, and especially on the part
of so many of my beloved sons, the priests.

b   Thank you for the joy which you are giving to the Heart of Jesus,
who is smiling upon you with pleasure, as He is transported with
tenderness for you. Thank you for the joy which you give to the
deep sorrow of the Immaculate Heart of your heavenly Mother.

c   I am the Mother of the Most Blessed Sacrament. I became such
by my 'yes' because, at the moment of the Incarnation, I made
it possible for the Word of the Father to place Himself in my virginal
womb and, though I am also truly the Mother of God because
Jesus is true God, my collaboration nevertheless took concrete form
in giving the Word his human nature. This made it possible for
Him, who is the Second Person of the Most Holy Trinity and
coeternal Son with the Father, to become also man in time, truly
your Brother.

d   By his assuming human nature, it was possible for him to carry
out the work of redemption. Just as I am Mother of the Incarnation, so also am I Mother the Redemption. The redemption was
carried out from the moment of the Incarnation up to the moment of his death on the Cross, where, because of the humanity
which He had assumed, Jesus was able to fulfill that which, as God,
it was not possible for Him to do: to suffer, to undergo his Passion
and to die, offering Himself as a perfect ransom to the Father and
making a worthy and just reparation to his justice.

e   Truly, He has suffered for you all, redeeming you from sin and
opening you up to the possibility of receiving that divine life which

504

was lost for all, at the moment when the first sin was committed by your first parents.

f   Look at Jesus as He loves, works, prays, suffers and immolates Himself, from his descent into my virginal womb to his ascent upon the Cross, in this his unceasing priestly action, so that you may understand how I am above all Mother of Jesus, the Priest.

g   *I am therefore also true Mother of the Most Blessed Eucharist.* I do not beget Him again to this mysterious reality upon the altar. *That task is reserved only to you, my beloved sons!* But your task assimilates you very closely to my maternal function because you also, during holy Mass and by means of the words of consecration, truly beget my Son. For me, the cold manger of a poor and bare cave received Him; for you, it is now the cold stone of an altar which welcomes Him. But you also, as I, give birth to my Son. This is why you cannot but be sons of a special, indeed a most special, predilection on the part of her who is Mother, true Mother of her Son Jesus.

h   But I am also true Mother of the Eucharist, because Jesus becomes truly present, at the moment of the consecration, through your priestly action. By your human 'yes' to the powerful action of the Spirit, which transforms the matter of the bread and the wine into the body and the blood of Christ, you make possible for Him this new and real presence of his among you.

i   And He becomes present in order to continue the work of the Incarnation and Redemption and in order to accomplish, in mystery, the Sacrifice of Calvary, which He was able to offer to the Father because of his human nature, assumed with the body which I had given Him. Thus, in the Eucharist, Jesus becomes present with his divinity and with his glorious body, that body given to Him by your heavenly Mother, a true body, born of the Virgin Mary.

j   Sons, his is a glorious body, but it is not a different one, that is to say, there is no question of a new birth of his. In effect, it is the same body which I gave Him: born at Bethlehem, dead on Calvary, placed in the sepulchre and risen from there, taking on however a new form, his divine form, that of glory. In heaven, Jesus, with his glorious body, remains the Son of Mary. Thus, He whom, with his divinity, you beget at the moment of the Eucharistic consecration, is ever the Son of Mary.

k   *I am therefore the Mother of the Eucharist.*
l   And, as a mother, I am always at the side of my Son. I was there on this earth; I am there now in paradise, in virtue of the privilege of my bodily assumption into heaven; and I am still to be found wherever Jesus is present, in every tabernacle on earth.
m   Just as his glorious body, being beyond the limits of time and space, allows Him to be here before you, in the tabernacle of this little mountain church but at the same time allows Him to be present in all the tabernacles spread throughout every part of the world, so also your heavenly Mother, with her glorious body, which permits her to be both here and in every other place, is truly near every tabernacle in which Jesus is kept.
n   My Immaculate Heart becomes, for Him, a living, beating, motherly tabernacle of love, of adoration, of thanksgiving and of unceasing reparation.

o   *I am the joyful Mother of the Eucharist.*
p   You know, beloved sons, that wherever the Son is, there too the Father and the Holy Spirit are always present. Just as, in the glory of heaven, Jesus is seated at the right hand of the Father, in intimate union with the Holy Spirit, so also when, at your bidding, He becomes present in the Eucharist and is placed in the safekeeping of the tabernacle, surrounded by my motherly heart, close to the Son there is always the real presence of the Father and the real presence of the Holy Spirit; there is always present the divine and Most Holy Trinity.
q   But, as in heaven, so also at the side of every tabernacle, there is the enraptured and joyful presence of your heavenly Mother. Then, there are all the angels, arranged in their nine choirs of light, to sing, in diverse modulations of harmony and glory the omnipotence of the Most Holy Trinity, as if to make its great and divine power appear in different degrees. About the choirs of angels are all the saints and the blessed who, from the very light, the love, the unending joy, and the immense glory which issues forth from

the Most Holy Trinity, receive a continuous increase of their eternal and ever greater beatitude.

r   To this summit of paradise, there also ascend the profound inspirations, the purifying sufferings and the unceasing prayer of all the souls in purgatory. Toward it they strain forward with a desire and a charity which becomes ever greater, the perfection of which is proportionate to their progressive release from every debt, owed because of their fragility and their sins, until the moment when, perfectly renewed by love, they can join in the heavenly song that arises about the most holy and divine Trinity, that is found in heaven and in every tabernacle where Jesus is present, even in the most remote and isolated parts of the earth.

s   This is why, there at the side of Jesus, I am the joyful Mother of the Eucharist.

t   *I am the sorrowful Mother of the Eucharist.*

u   With the Church, Triumphant and Suffering, which palpitates around the center of love, which is the Eucharistic Jesus, the Church Militant should also be gathered together; you should all gather together, my beloved sons, religious and faithful, in order to form, with heaven and purgatory, an unceasing hymn of adoration and praise.

v   Instead, today, Jesus in the tabernacle is surrounded by much emptiness, much neglect and much ingratitude. These times were foretold by me at Fatima, through the voice of the Angel who appeared to the children to whom he taught this prayer: 'Most Holy Trinity, Father, Son and Holy Spirit, I adore You profoundly and I offer You the most precious body, blood, soul and divinity of Our Lord Jesus Christ, present in all the tabernacles of the world, in reparation for the outrages, sacrileges and indifference with which He Himself is surrounded. . . '

w   This prayer was taught for these times of yours.

x   Jesus is surrounded today *by an emptiness*, which has been brought about especially by you priests who, in your apostolic activity, often go about uselessly and very much on the periphery, going after things which are less important and more secondary and forgetting that the center of your priestly day should be *here*, before the tabernacle, where Jesus is present and is kept especially for you.

507

y   He is also surrounded by the *indifference* of many of my children, who live as if He were not there and, when they enter church for liturgical functions, they are not aware of his divine and real presence in your midst. Often Jesus in the Eucharist is placed in some isolated corner whereas He should be placed in the center of the church and be placed at the center of your ecclesial gatherings, because the church is his temple which has been built first for Him and then for you.

z   What causes deep bitterness to my motherly heart is the way in which Jesus, present in the tabernacle, is treated in many churches, where He is placed in a little corner, as though He were some object or other to be made use of, for your ecclesial gatherings.

A   But above all, it is the *sacrileges* which today form, around my Immaculate Heart, a painful crown of thorns. In these times, how many communions are made and how many sacrileges perpetrated! It can be said that there is no longer any Eucharistic celebration where sacrilegious communions are not made. If you only saw with my eyes how great this wound is which has contaminated the whole Church and paralyzes it, halts its, and makes it impure and so very sick! If you only saw with my eyes, you too would shed copious tears with me.

B   And so, my beloved ones and children consecrated to my heart, it is you who must be today *a clarion call* for the full return of the whole Church Militant to Jesus present in the Eucharist. Because there alone is to be found the spring of living water which will purify its aridity and renew the desert to which it has been reduced; there alone is to be found the secret of life which will open up for her a second Pentecost of grace and of light; there alone is to be found the fount of her renewed holiness: **Jesus in the Eucharist**!

C   It is not your pastoral plans and your discussions, it is not the human means on which you put reliance and so much assurance, but it is only Jesus in the Eucharist which will give to the whole Church the strength of a complete renewal, which will lead her to be poor, evangelical, chaste, stripped of all those supports on which she relies, holy, beautiful and without spot or wrinkle, in imitation of your heavenly Mother.

D   I desire that this message of mine be made public and be numbered among those contained in my book. I desire that it be spread throughout the whole world because I am calling you today from every part of the earth to be a crown of love, of adoration, of thanksgiving and of reparation, upon the Immaculate Heart of her who is true Mother – joyful Mother but also most sorrowful Mother – of the Most Holy Eucharist.

E   I bless you in the name of the Father, and of the Son, and of the Holy Spirit."

331   *Bagni di Tivoli (Roma), August 15, 1986*
The Assumption of Mary into Heaven

You Will Give Peace of Heart

a   "Look at your heavenly Mother, assumed into the glory of paradise, even with her body. Today I am causing a shower of graces to fall upon you all, my children.

b   The light from my glorious body is shining on you and pointing out to you the road you must follow. It is that of purity, of love, of prayer, of suffering, of holiness. It is that of a life united intimately to Jesus. Thus you also, even while living on this earth, can be illumined and surrounded by the light which is shining up here in paradise.

c   The light from my glorious body is shining for you with increasing strength, especially in these very difficult and painful times, in order to console you and encourage you in all your daily difficulties. Today you are being called to live through the bloody hours of the purification, because the great events which I have foretold to you during these years are already upon you.

d   And so you have need of my motherly consolation in order not to become discouraged. Look to paradise where your heavenly Mother has been assumed in body and soul, and you will be consoled by me. Live, with heart and soul, in paradise, where Jesus has already prepared a place for each one of you, and nothing will disturb your peace.

e   The light from my glorious body will draw you in the wake of my most exquisite fragrance. It is the fragrance of all the virtues which have adorned the garden of my earthly existence. It is the celestial aroma of all my immaculate beauty.

f   Today I want to sprinkle you all with the exquisite fragrance of purity, of humility, of simplicity, of silence, of prayer, of docility, of obedience, of contemplation.

g   Then you too will spread the heavenly fragrance of your immaculate Mother. And thus *you will give peace of heart* to all and you will become today instruments of my peace. Because you are the beloved children of your Mother, assumed into the glory of heaven and who, in these times, desires to be invoked by all as Queen of Peace."

332

Dongo (Como), September 6, 1986
Anniversary of the miracle of the tears
and First Saturday of the Month

My Heart Is Bleeding

a   "I am your most sorrowful Mother. Again today, I am causing copious tears to fall from my merciful eyes. They want to make you understand how great the sorrow of the Immaculate Heart of your heavenly Mother is.

b   My *heart is bleeding.*

c   My heart is transfixed with deep wounds.

d   My heart is immersed in a sea of sorrow.

e   You live unconscious of the fate which is awaiting you. You are spending your days in a state of unawareness, of indifference and of complete incredulity. How is this possible when I, in so many ways and with extraordinary signs, have warned you of the danger into which you are running and have foretold you of the bloody ordeal which is just about to take place?

f   —Because this humanity has not accepted my repeated call to conversion, to repentance, and to a return to God, there is about to fall upon it the greatest chastisement which the history of mankind has ever known. It is a chastisement much greater than that of the flood. Fire will fall from heaven and a great part of humanity will be destroyed.

g — The Church of Jesus is wounded with the pernicious plague of infidelity and apostasy. In appearance, everything remains calm and it seems that all is going well. In reality, she is being pervaded with an ever widening lack of faith which is spreading the great apostasy everywhere. Many bishops, priests, religious and faithful no longer believe and have already lost the true faith in Jesus and in the Gospel. For this reason, the Church must be purified, with persecution and with blood.

h — There has also entered into the Church disunity, division, strife and antagonism. The forces of atheism and Masonry, having infiltrated within it, are on the point of breaking up its interior unity and of darkening the splendor of its sanctity. These are the times, foretold by me, when cardinals will be set against cardinals, bishops against bishops and priests against priests and the flock of Christ will be torn to pieces by rapacious wolves, who have found their way in under the clothing of defenseless and meek lambs. Among them there are even some who occupy posts of great responsibility and, by means of them, Satan has succeeded in entering and in operating at the very summit of the Church. Bishops and priests of the holy Church of God, how great today is your responsibility! The Lord is about to demand of you an account of how you have administered his vineyard. Repent, seek pardon, make amends and, above all, be once again faithful to the task which has been entrusted to you.

i — Sin is being committed more and more, it is no longer acknowledged as an evil, it is sought out, it is consciously willed and it is no longer confessed. Impurity and lewdness cover the homes built by your rebellion.

j *This is the reason why my heart is bleeding*: because of the obstinate disbelief and the hardness of your hearts.

511

k   *My heart is bleeding* to see you so closed and insensitive to my sorrowful motherly admonition.

l   *My heart is bleeding* because I see your roads even now smeared with blood, while you live in an obstinate unconsciousness of that which awaits you."

333

Milan, September 8, 1986
Nativity of the Blessed Virgin Mary

My Birth

a   "On the feast of my nativity, paradise exults and the Church Suffering and Militant look upon me as a sign of joy, of hope and of motherly consolation.

b   *My birth* is cause for your joy. At the moment your heavenly Mother is born, like the rising dawn, the radiant day of your salvation is already near at hand and certain for you. Close to my crib, heaven leaps for joy, with the countless cohorts of angels, who have been forever awaiting this ineffable moment. Round about my crib, there gather festively the spirits of the prophets and the just who have lived, prepared and hoped, in the expectation of this joyous event. Over my crib, with immense love of predilection, the Father bends down as He contemplates his masterpiece of creation; the Word, in the expectation of placing Himself in my virginal and motherly womb; and also the Holy Spirit who is already communicating Himself to my soul with the fullness of love. For this reason, my birth is above all a cause of great joy for you all, who love to call upon me as the cause of your joy.

c   *My birth* is also cause for your hope. Even now the Redemption, awaited, longed for and predicted for hundreds of centuries, is about to become a real event of your history. I am born to give birth to Jesus, your Redeemer and Savior. There breaks a new dawn for all humanity. Sin is about to be conquered and, for the Spirit of Evil, the moment of his complete defeat draws near, while all creation prepares itself to receive the gift of its total renewal. For this reason, my birth becomes also a cause of hope for all of you, who love to call upon me as Mother of Hope.

d   My *birth* is above all cause for your consolation. The little creature, scarcely born, whom you contemplate again today in her crib, is wondrously intended to become the Mother of Jesus and Mother of all humanity. And this gives you great comfort in the painful times in which you are living. Because you all have an immaculate Mother who knows you, understands you, helps you and defends you. Above all in the bloody hours of the great suffering to which you are being called, how much comfort you find in the sure knowledge that your heavenly Mother is always at your side, to share in your suffering, to strengthen your trust and to be a consolation to your many sorrows.

e   Do not be afraid. Have no fear. Feel at your side your heavenly Mother, whom you venerate today at the moment of her earthly birth, in order to become, especially in these your times, a cause of joy, of hope and of consolation for all."

334

September 15, 1986
Feast of Our Lady of Sorrows

I Am Forming You to Suffering

a   "Beloved children, learn from me always to say 'yes' to the heavenly Father, even when He asks of you the precious contribution of your suffering.

b   I am the sorrowful Virgin.

c   I am the Mother of suffering.

d   My Son Jesus was born of me in order to immolate Himself, as a victim of love, for your ransom. Jesus is the docile and meek Lamb, who mutely allowed Himself to be led to the slaughter. Jesus is the true Lamb of God who takes away all the sins of the world. From the moment of his descent into my virginal womb, to the moment of his ascent upon the Cross, Jesus always gave Himself up to the will of the Father, offering Him, with love and joy, the precious gift of all his suffering.

e   I am the sorrowful one because, as a mother, I formed, raised, followed, loved and offered my Son Jesus, as a gentle and meek victim, to the divine justice of the Father. And thus I became the greatest help and comfort in his immense suffering. In these most painful times, I am again, as a mother, at the side of each one of you, to form you, to help you and to give comfort in all your suffering.

f   *I am forming you to suffering,* by saying 'yes' with you to the heavenly Father, who is asking this of you, as your personal collaboration in the redemption carried out by my Son Jesus. In this I, your heavenly Mother, am an example and model for you, by my perfect co-operation in all the suffering of the Son, so that I became the first to collaborate in his work, through my motherly suffering.

g   I have become true co-redemptrix and now I am able to offer myself as an example to each one of you in the giving of your own personal sufferings to the Lord, to assist everyone in walking along the way of good and of salvation. It is for this reason that, in these bloody times of purification, my motherly task is that of forming you, above all, to suffering.

h   I am also helping you to suffer, by my motherly presence, which is urging you to transform all your suffering into a perfect gift of love. For this, I am training you in docility, in gentleness, in humility of heart. I am helping you to suffer, with the joy of giving yourselves to your brothers, as Jesus gave Himself. Then you will carry your cross with joy, your suffering will become sweet and it will be the sure road which will lead you to true peace of heart.

i   I comfort you in all sufferings, with the assurance that I am at your side, just as I was beneath the Cross of Jesus. Today, when sufferings are increasing from all sides, everyone will become aware, in an ever stronger way, of the presence of your heavenly Mother. Because this is my mission, as mother and co-redemptrix: to gather every drop of your suffering, to transform it into a precious gift of love and of reparation and to offer it, each day, to the justice of God.

514

j   Only in this way can we break open together the golden door of the divine Heart of my Son Jesus, so that He may be able to cause to descend soon, upon the Church and upon humanity, the river of grace and of fire of his merciful love, which will make all things new."

335

Naples, September 29, 1986
Feast of the Archangels,
Gabriel, Raphael and Michael

With You in the Combat

a   "Fight, dearest children, my apostles in these last times of yours. This is the hour of my battle. This is the hour of my great victory.

b   *With you in the combat* are also the angels of the Lord who, at my orders, are carrying out the task which I have entrusted to them. All the heavenly spirits are luminous and powerful beings and they are very close to God whom they love, serve, defend and glorify. In the light of the Most Holy Trinity, they see all the dangerous and subtle snares, set for you by the wicked spirits who struggle against God and against his royal dominion.

c   This is a terrible battle, which is being waged above all at the level of spirits: those who are good, against the wicked; the angels against the demons.

d   You are involved in this great struggle and it is for this reason that you must always entrust yourselves to their sure protection and, through prayer, often invoke their powerful assistance.

e   All the heavenly spirits know my plan, they know the hour of my triumph, and they see how the attack of hell, in these times of yours, is becoming powerful, continuous and universal. Satan has succeeded in establishing his reign in the world and he already feels that he is the sure victor. But the moment of his great and definitive defeat is close. For this reason, the battle is becoming more fierce and terrible and you too, with the angels of the Lord, are being called to battle. The weapons used by the demons are those of evil, of sin, of hatred, of impurity, of pride and of rebellion against God. The weapons used by the heavenly spirits, who are at your side to do battle, are those of good, of divine grace, of love, of purity, of humility and of docile submission to the will of the Lord.

f   The heavenly spirits have also the task of strengthening you, of healing you from your wounds, of defending you from the snares of my Adversary, of protecting you from evil and of leading you along the luminous way of my will.

g   The Archangel Gabriel was sent by God to accept the 'yes' of your heavenly Mother; now, he has the duty of accepting your 'yes' to the will of the Father. He strengthens you and sustains you; he leads you along the way of courage and of a heroic witness to Jesus and to his Gospel.

h   The Archangel Raphael gives refreshment to your weakness, pours balm on every painful wound and lifts you up from the weight of your weariness and discouragement, in order to continue the struggle, with the shield of faith and with the armor of love and of holiness.

i   The Archangel Michael defends you from all the terrible attacks of Satan, who is particularly raging against you who form part of my cohort and are allowing yourselves to be led with docility by your heavenly Leader. How many times would you have become victims of the attacks of Satan, had not the Archangel Michael intervened in your defense and for your protection! Invoke him often with that so very efficacious prayer of exorcism against Satan and the rebellious angels, because he is guiding you in this battle in such a way that each one of you may be able to fulfill the task which has been entrusted to him by the heavenly Mother.

j   And so, be united in an affectionate and fraternal communion of life, of prayer and of action with all the heavenly spirits, who are engaged, together with you, in fighting the same battle and preparing God's great victory in the glorious reign of Christ, which will come to you with the triumph of my Immaculate Heart in the world."

336

The Rosary Brings You to Peace

a   "I am the Queen of the Holy Rosary. I am your leader who is guiding you in the terrible battle against Satan and all the spirits of evil. If you allow yourselves to be led with docility by me, you will always feel at your side the precious help which is given to you by the angels of the Lord, the blessed and the saints of paradise, and all the souls who are still being purified in purgatory.

b   I am, in fact, the leader of one single cohort.

c   Today, as you recall the date of one of my great victories, I want to call upon you to fight, with courage and confidence, without allowing yourselves to become alarmed at the subtle and dangerous tactics made use of by my Adversary to bring you to discouragement.

d   For this reason, I want to uncover for you three traps which form part of a particular strategy employed by my Adversary, in this great battle.

e   —*The first* is that of spreading about the certainty that he has already succeeded in conquering the whole world; that he has established his reign in it and that he fully exercises his power there. His great conquest is this human race, which has rebelled against God and which is repeating his proud act of defiance: 'I will not serve the Lord!' A most dangerous means, made use of by Satan in these times, is that of giving the impression that there is no longer anything more to be done, that one will no longer succeed in changing anything, and that it has already become useless to make any kind of an effort to lead humanity along the road of return to God and to good.

f   And so your heavenly Mother is assuring you that even this humanity forms a precious part of the people of God, won by Jesus at the price of his blood, shed to the last drop for its salvation. God, especially today, is alone the victor and He loves all the poor sick humanity which has been snatched from Him, and He is preparing the moment when, by the greatest miracle of his merciful love, He will lead it along the road of return to Himself, that at last it may be able to know a new era of peace, of love, of holiness and of joy. For this reason, I am inviting you always to make use of the the powerful weapon of trust, of filial abandonment, of a great and boundless charity, of a complete availability for all the spiritual and material needs of your neighbor and of a motherly and unlimited mercy.

g — *The second* is that of having succeeded in putting the Church in a state of grave difficulty, shaking it to its foundation, by the wind of contestation, of division, of infidelity and of apostasy. Many are losing courage, as they see how numerous today are those pastors who are allowing themselves to be deceived by his subtle and dangerous action.

h The means by which you must use to fight back against this ambush of his is that of your consecration to my Immaculate Heart, because the Church, even though it appears wounded, darkened and routed today, has been entrusted by Jesus to the loving protection of your heavenly Mother. I want to help it, console it and heal it through you, beloved children consecrated to my heart and docile instruments of my motherly will. Through you, I am pouring balm upon its painful wounds, comforting the hours of its desolate passion and preparing the moment of its greatest renewal.

i I am doing this, in these times, in a very special way, through my Pope, John Paul II, who is bringing the sign of my motherly presence everywhere. He is giving you the battle sign; he is guiding you in the struggle; he is teaching you courage and confidence; he is already announcing to you my sure victory. Follow him along the road which he points out, if you wish to prepare, with me, a new and radiant Pentecost for the whole Church.

j — *The third* is that of succeeding in spreading everywhere, through all the means of social communication, his wicked works of destruction and death. Thus, divisions are multiplying; impurity is being exalted; corruption is extensive; violence is becoming more and more widespread; hatred is flooding the land and wars are expanding menacingly.

518

_k To fight and conquer all this evil, which is attempting to submerge the entire human race, you must have recourse to the powerful weapon of prayer. In fact, the new era will be able to come to you only as a gift of the Spirit of the Lord, not as the fruit of the work of man. And so it is necessary to ask for this gift through a continual, incessant, and trusting prayer.

_l Pray with me. All the Church must enter into the cenacle of my Immaculate Heart, to invoke, with the heavenly Mother, a very special outpouring of the Holy Spirit, which will lead it to live the experience of a second and radiant Pentecost.

_m Pray above all with the prayer of the holy rosary. Let the rosary be, for everyone, the powerful weapon to be made use of in these times.

_n *The rosary brings you to peace.* With this prayer, you are able to obtain from the Lord the great grace of a change of hearts, of the conversion of souls, and of the return of all humanity to God, along the road of repentance, of love, of divine grace and of holiness.

_o Then you will no longer say: 'But, always and everywhere, everything remains just as it was. Nothing ever changes!'—This is not true, my beloved children. Each day, in silence and in hiddenness, the heavenly Mother is waging her battle against the Adversary and is working, by means of most extraordinary signs and manifestations, to change the heart of the world."

337 Sant' Omero (Teramo), October 27, 1986
World Day of Prayer for Peace

The Task Entrusted to the Church

_a "Today you are imploring peace, through a day which is bringing together representatives of all religions in a communion of prayer and of fasting. This is the road that I have pointed out to you. Peace can come to you only as a gift of God. The more you want to build peace through human discussions and reciprocal agreements, the more it will remove itself from you. For this reason,

it is necesary for humanity to return to God along the road of conversion and of a change of heart.

b   Jesus Christ alone has shown you the way to reach the Father in his Spirit of Love. It is necessary that all men come to a knowledge of the truth and to accept and to follow the Gospel of Jesus.

c   *This is the task entrusted to the Church.*

d   This is what her ministers, her consecrated ones, and all her faithful must do today: with the courage of martyrs and the strength of confessors of the faith, there is need to announce to the whole world the good news that Jesus Christ alone is your Savior and your Redeemer! Only Jesus Christ can bring you to peace. It is necessary to preach Him to all, without fear and without compromise, carrying out his divine mandate: 'Go into the whole world and proclaim my Gospel to all creation; whoever believes and is baptized will be saved.'

e   The attempt to bring together all religions, even those who adore false and lying gods, with the prospect of forming a world-wide religious union for the defense of human values, is vain, dangerous and not in conformity with the desire of my Immaculate Heart. It can on the contrary lead to an increase of confusion, to religious indifference and even make the attainment of true peace more difficult.

f   For this reason, I say to you today: announce Christ to everyone; be faithful only to Christ and to his Gospel and you will become true builders of peace."

338

Dongo (Como), November 1, 1986
Feast of All Saints

Your Place in Paradise

a   "Today, look at those who have already gone before you into glory. Round about my Immaculate Heart, they form a luminous crown of love, of joy and of glory.

b   *This is also your place in paradise.* It is being prepared for all of you who listen to my voice, who consecrate yourselves to my Immaculate Heart, live in filial dependence upon me and offer yourselves completely for the perfect fulfillment of my plan. Be, here below, my dearly beloved children. Be my apostles, called to spread everywhere the light of my motherly presence and to point out to all the road that they have need to follow in order to reach Christ, from whom alone can come the new era of holiness, of justice and of peace.

c   For this reason, feel at your side, each day, the saints and the blessed of heaven; call upon them for help and protection. Feel also at your side the souls of the just, who are still suffering and praying in purgatory, awaiting the moment of their full beatitude in the perfect contemplation of the Lord. With you they form one single cohort, under my orders. For all, I am the Mother and the Queen. Each one has an irreplaceable part to play in my victorious plan.

d   In these times, I want to make deeper, stronger and more extraordinary your communion with those who have preceded you in the earthly life and now enjoy eternal salvation. As a motherly gift of my Immaculate Heart, I offer you, as a precious help, the souls of the saints in paradise and of the just in purgatory. You are being exposed to grave dangers and they can assist you in overcoming them. You are victims of the subtle snares of my Adversary and they can give you light that you may be able to see them, and strength that you may flee from them. You are fragile and weak and often happen to fall again into sins; they can always lend you a hand to walk along the road of good and of holiness.

e   Travel therefore, together with them, along the road which I have traced out for you. Together, I am leading you to peace.

f   Peace will come to you from my Immaculate Heart when this, your communion of life, of love and of joy will have then been perfectly accomplished."

The Way Which Leads You to His Kingdom

a   "Today, in the glory of paradise and in the purifying light of purgatory, I am accepting the homage of the whole pilgrim Church on earth, in order to offer, together with you all, the crown of his royalty to Jesus Christ, our God, our Saviour and our King.

b   *Jesus must reign above all in the hearts and in the souls of all*, because his is a royalty of grace, of holiness and of love. When Jesus reigns in the soul of a creature, it becomes transformed by a divine light, which renders it increasingly beautiful, luminous, holy and beloved of God.

c   For this, my motherly task is that of driving away from the souls of my children every shadow of sin, any snare whatsoever of egoism, any predominance of the passions, in order to lead everyone along the road of great sanctity. Then Jesus will truly be able to establish his reign in your hearts and in your souls and you will become the precious domain of his divine royalty.

d   *Jesus must reign in families*, which must open themselves like buds to the sun of his royalty. For this reason, I am working in these times, in order that there may increase, in families, harmony and peace, understanding and concord, unity and faithfulness.

e   *Jesus must reign in all humanity*, that it may become again a new garden where the Most Holy Trinity may receive charm and beauty, love and fragrance from every creature and thus be glorified and establish its habitual dwelling place in your midst. For this, I am working powerfully today to lead all humanity along the road of return to God, by way of conversion, of prayer and of penance. And I myself am leading the cohort, called to fight against the army of evil so that the power of those who deny and blaspheme God and who work tirelessly to build a civilization without Him may be defeated as quickly as possible.

f   *Jesus must reign in the Church*, the privileged portion of his divine and loving domain. The Church is all his because she is born of his rent Heart, brought up in his love, washed with his blood, espoused to Him by an inviolable pact of eternal fidelity. For this reason, I am working as a mother, in these painful moments of her purification, to cleanse the Church once again from every stain, to set her free from every human compromise, to defend her from the subtle attacks of her Adversary and to lead her along the road of perfection, that she may reflect everywhere the very splendor of her divine Spouse, Jesus.

g   My motherly action is preparing, in this time of yours, the coming of the glorious reign of my Son, Jesus.

h   *My Immaculate Heart is the way which leads you to his reign.* In fact, the triumph of my Immaculate Heart will coincide with the triumph of my Son, Jesus, in his glorious reign of holiness and of grace, of love and of justice, of mercy and of peace, which will be established in the whole world.

i   For this reason I am inviting you today to prayer and to trust, I am calling you to peace of heart and to joy because the glorious reign of the Lord Jesus is already at the gates."

340

Dallas (Texas, U.S.A.), December 3, 1986
Spiritual Exercises in the form of a cenacle
with the priests of the M.M.P.
of the United States and Canada

My Remedy for Your Illnesses

a   "How happy I am with these days of continuous cenacle which you, the priests of my Movement, are making, coming as you do from even the most distant states of this great country, in order to live together in brotherhood and in prayer with me, your heavenly Mother. Your love, your docility and your generosity give much joy to my Sorrowful and Immaculate Heart.

b   Today I want to give you my motherly word, that it may be a source of comfort in your sufferings and of confidence in the midst of the many difficulties you encounter.

c   Be the smallest of my little children; be my courageous apostles; be the rays of light that come forth from my heart and spread about everywhere, to bear witness to my motherly presence.

d   There are three wounds, in this country of yours, which are causing pain to my motherly heart and making it bleed.

e   *The first wound is caused by the apostasy,* which is spreading, because of the errors that are being taught and promoted more and more even in Catholic schools, and which are leading an immense number of my poor children to separate themselves from the true faith.

f   The responsibility for this grave situation rests above all with those who have consecrated themselves to God because, having been seduced by the spirit of pride, they continue on their way, despite my motherly admonitions and the directives given by the *Magisterium* of the Church.

g   You, my beloved sons, are to be my remedy for this illness, by preaching more and more the truth which Jesus has taught you and which the Pope and the bishops united with him are still presenting today to everyone with clarity and courage.

h   You must oppose anyone who teaches doctrines which are different and, above all, you must speak openly to all the faithful of the grave danger, which they are encountering today, of swerving from the true faith in Jesus and in his Gospel. Recite often the profession of faith, composed by the first of my beloved sons, Pope Paul VI, now up here with me, as he foresaw these difficult moments.

i   *The second wound is caused by the disunity* that has entered into the Church which exists in your countries. How it makes the Heart of Jesus and my motherly heart suffer to see that many bishops, priests, religious and faithful are no longer united with—and are even openly opposing—the Pope, whom Jesus has set up as the foundation of his Church.

524

j This division is becoming daily more extensive and deeper and soon it will become even open and proclaimed. How much pain I feel in seeing that often the greatest supporters of this rebellion are those who have consecrated themselves to God and have vowed to follow Jesus along the road of humility, of poverty, of chastity and of obedience.

k You, my beloved sons, are to be my remedy for this deep wound by being ever more united with the Pope, by helping your bishops to be united with him, through prayer, love and your good example, and by leading all the faithful to this unity.

l *The third wound is caused by the infidelity* that has entered into the life of many children of the Church, who no longer follow the commandments of God and the teachings given by Jesus in his Gospel. Thus they walk along the wrong road of evil and of sin. Sin is no longer recognized as an evil. Often justification is made for even the gravest sins against nature, such as abortion and homosexuality. Sins are no longer confessed. To what a grave state of sickness have you now come!

m You, my beloved sons, are to be my remedy for such a grave and so extensive an evil, by helping my children to walk along the road of purity and of holiness. Return again to teaching everyone true Catholic morality. Give a helping hand to my poor sinful children, to lead them to the observance of the law of God. Make them understand the necessity of frequent confession, which becomes indispensable before one who is in the state of mortal sin may receive Holy Communion. The Church here is all wounded because of communions received sacrilegiously.

n If you accept this motherly invitation of mine, you will then be the gift of love which my Immaculate Heart is offering today to the Church and to all of humanity which is living in this great country of yours.

o *You will thus become my remedy for your illnesses.*

p You are the instruments of my peace.

q Together with all the members of my Movement, I bless you in the name of the Father and of the Son and of the Holy Spirit."

My Candor of Heaven

a   "My candor of grace and of light, of holiness and of purity seeks to cover the whole earth like a mantle.

b   For this reason, my little child, I have brought you here today, to this island from which the evangelization of all the great continents of America began, in order to lead as quickly as possible my beloved ones and all my children into the safe refuge of my Immaculate Heart.

c   I am the dawn which precedes the great day of the Lord. I am the longed-for luminous cloud which will cause the heavenly dew of grace and of holiness to descend upon the desert of the world, wasted by evil and by sin.

d   Join my victorious cohort, all you who wish to fight the great battle for the triumph of good and of love. There where the ray of my light reaches, the darkness of evil, of egoism, of hatred, of sin and of impurity vanishes. Bring my motherly announcement everywhere.

e   *Spread my candor of heaven throughout every part of the world.*

f   These are the times when I must gather all of you again under my immaculate mantle, at the orders of your heavenly leader.

g   Through you, who have responded to me, my light will grow stronger from day to day, because the moment of the glorious triumph of my Son, Jesus, is already at hand.

h   From this land, I bless you today, together with all those who have accepted my invitation, listened to me and followed me."

The Crib at His Glorious Return

a   "Accept my motherly invitation to pray, to meditate upon my word, to guard it in your heart, to keep vigil, remaining on the watch expectantly.

b   This is the holy night.

c   Spend it with me, beloved children; live it in the depths of my Immaculate Heart. You will then be able to penetrate the mystery of your salvation, which reveals itself to the poor, to the little, to the simple, to the pure of heart.

d   My soul is flooded by a divine light and my person becomes surrounded with a profound sense of peace and of blessedness, while my virginal womb opens itself to the divine gift of the Son.

e   All about us, it is deep night: the doors, closed upon our plea for hospitality, the hearts of men, made hard through egoism and hatred, minds blinded by error and a great coldness upon the world which has become incapable of love!

f   But in the poor cave, a little light is enkindled, in the sign of expectation and of hope; two human hearts are beating with love, to prepare the crib in which to place the newborn child; my most chaste spouse, Joseph, is readying himself to make the squalor of the place more hospitable, while the heavenly Mother is absorbed in a profound and intense prayer with the Father.

g   It is at this moment that heaven espouses itself to earth, that the shoot awaited for centuries comes to flower, that God is born among us, that the Savior enters his regal domain, that the Redeemer begins to pay the price of our ransom.

h   And peace descends from heaven with the song of the angels, the earth opens to receive the dew of divine mercy, while the simple hearts of the shepherds open themselves to the voices which announce the wondrous event: 'Today there is born for you a Savior who is Christ the Lord.'

i   Everything is again repeated for his second nativity. His return in glory is just as it was then. The night of the denial of God has descended upon the world; the coldness of rebellion against his law of love has reduced humanity to an immense desert; error has closed minds to the understanding of the greatest mystery of love; hearts have become hardened by egoism and hatred which is spreading everywhere. Doors are still obstinately shut to the Lord as He comes.

j   You, O beloved ones, throw open your hearts to blessedness and hope and, in imitation of your heavenly Mother and of her most chaste spouse, Joseph, undertake to make yourselves attentive in preparing the roadways for Christ who is returning in glory.

k   His second nativity is already at the doors. And so open your minds to the heavenly voices which, in many ways and through many signs, are telling you that his return is near. As the love of my motherly heart was the most precious crib for his first nativity, so also *the triumph of my Immaculate Heart will be the crib at his glorious return.*

l   On this holy night, I am gathering you all together to keep watch, with me, close to the little Child, who has such need of love. On this holy night, I am inviting you to open your hearts and your minds to receive the joyful announcement that his second nativity is near."

343

Dongo (Como), December 31, 1986
Last night of the year

And Peace Will Come to You

a   "During these last hours of the year, beloved children, I want all to gather close to me in an unceasing prayer.

b   *Pray* in order to give thanks to the heavenly Father, who is guiding human events toward the fulfillment of his great plan of love and of glory.

c   *Pray* in order to console the divine Heart of the Son, wounded by so many sins and surrounded by an immense sea of human ingratitude. Jesus loves you. His Heart is a furnace of most ardent love for you. But this Heart is being continually pierced by offenses and sins. It is you who must be the consolers of the Heart of Jesus. My beloved ones, I am asking you to fill up, with your priestly love, all the emptiness, the negligence and the indifference with which He is surrounded.

d *Pray* in order to invoke the Holy Spirit, that He may be able to accomplish as quickly as possible the prodigy of a second Pentecost of holiness and of grace, which may truly change the face of the earth. Pray and do penance. Recite the holy rosary with love and with confidence. With this prayer, made by you together with me, you are able to influence all human events, and even the future events which are awaiting you. With this prayer, you can possess the grace of a change of hearts and you can obtain the much-desired gift of peace.

e *Peace will come*, after the great suffering to which the Church and all humanity are already being called, through their interior and bloody purification.

f *Peace will come*, after the event of the terrible chastisement, which I have already announced to you beforehand, at the dawn of this century of yours.

g *Peace will come*, as a gift of the merciful love of Jesus, who is about to pour forth upon the world torrents of fire and of grace, which will make all things new.

h *Peace will come*, as the fruit of a special outpouring of the Holy Spirit, who will be given by the Father and by the Son, in order to transform the world into the heavenly Jerusalem and to lead the Church to the summit of its sanctity and of its divine splendor.

i *And peace will come to you* from the triumph of my Immaculate Heart, as that space of time, which has been granted by the Lord to humanity for repentance and for its conversion, is about to come to an end.

j Even now the great events are coming about and all will be accomplished at a faster pace, so that there may appear over the world, as quickly as possible, the new rainbow of peace which, at Fatima and for so many years, I have already been announcing to you in advance."

ACTS OF CONSECRATION TO
THE IMMACULATE HEART
OF MARY

ACT OF CONSECRATION
TO THE
IMMACULATE HEART OF MARY
(for Priests)

Virgin of Fatima, Mother of Mercy, Queen of Heaven and Earth, Refuge of Sinners, we who belong to the Marian Movement of Priests, called to form the cohort of your priests, today consecrate ourselves in a very special way to your Immaculate Heart.

By this act of consecration we intend to live, with you and through you, all the obligations assumed by our baptismal and priestly consecration.

We further pledge to bring about in ourselves that interior conversion that will free us of all human attachment to ourselves, our career, our comforts, or to easy compromises with the world so that, like you, we may be available only to do always the will of the Lord.

And as we resolve to entrust to you, O Mother most sweet and merciful, our priesthood, so that you may dispose of it for all your designs of salvation in this hour of decision that weighs upon the world, we pledge to live it according to your desires, especially as it pertains to a renewed spirit of prayer and penance, the fervent celebration of the Holy Eucharist and of the Liturgy of the Hours, the daily recitation of the holy rosary, the offering of holy Mass in your honor on the first Saturday of every month, and a religious and austere manner of life, that shall be a good example to all.

We further promise you the greatest loyalty to the Gospel, of which we shall always be genuine and courageous heralds, even, if necessary, to the shedding of our blood. We promise loyalty to the Church, for whose service we have been consecrated.

Above all, we wish to be united with the Holy Father and the hierarchy, firmly adhering to all their directives, so as thus to set up a barrier to the growing confrontation directed against the *Magisterium*, that threatens the very foundation of the Church.

Under your maternal protection, we want to be apostles of this sorely needed unity of prayer and love for the Pope, on whom we invoke your special protection.

And lastly, we promise to lead the faithful entrusted to our care to a renewed devotion to you.

Mindful that atheism is causing shipwreck in the faith to a great number of the faithful, that desecration has entered into the holy temple of God, not sparing even many of our brother priests, and that evil and sin are spreading more and more throughout the world, we make so bold as to lift our eyes trustingly to you, O Mother of Jesus and our merciful and powerful Mother, and we invoke again today and await from you the salvation of all your children, O clement, O loving, O sweet Virgin Mary.

(with ecclesiastical approval)

ACT OF CONSECRATION
TO THE
IMMACULATE HEART OF MARY
(for Religious and Laity)

Virgin of Fatima, Mother of Mercy, Queen of Heaven and Earth, Refuge of Sinners, we who belong to the Marian Movement consecrate ourselves in a very special way to your Immaculate Heart.

By this act of consecration we intend to live, with you and through you, all the obligations assumed by our baptismal consecration. We further pledge to bring about in ourselves that interior conversion so urgently demanded by the Gospel, a conversion that will free us of every attachment to ourselves and to easy compromises with the world so that, like you, we may be available only to do always the will of the Father.

And as we resolve to entrust to you, O Mother most sweet and merciful, our life and vocation as Christians, that you may dispose of it according to your designs of salvation in this hour of decision that weighs upon the world, we pledge to live it according to your desires, especially as it pertains to a renewed spirit of prayer and penance, the fervent participation in the celebration of the Eucharist and in the works of the apostolate, the daily recitation of the holy rosary, and an austere manner of life in keeping with the Gospel, that shall be to all a good example of the observance of the law of God and the practice of the Christian virtues, especially that of purity.

We further promise you to be untied with the Holy Father, with the hierarchy and with our priests, in order thus to set up a barrier to the growing confrontation directed against the *Magisterium*, that threatens the very foundation of the Church.

Under your protection, we want to be apostles of this sorely needed unity of prayer and love for the Pope, on whom we invoke your special protection.

And lastly, insofar as is possible, we promise to lead those souls with whom we come in contact to a renewed devotion to you.

A4

Mindful that atheism has caused shipwreck in the faith to a great number of the faithful, that desecration has entered into the holy temple of God, and that evil and sin are spreading more and more throughout the world, we make so bold as to lift our eyes trustingly to you, O Mother of Jesus and our merciful and powerful Mother, and we invoke again today and await from you the salvation of all your children, O clement, O loving, O sweet Virgin Mary.

(with ecclesiastical approval)

DIARY INDEX

1973

THE MOVEMENT IS NOW BORN

[Chapter]		[Date]	[Page]
1	I will always be near you	July 7	4
2	The Movement is now born	8	4
3	Your mission is taking shape	9	4
4	The reason for my tears	13	5
5	I will be your Leader – In Humility	16	6
6	Let it be I who act	21	7
7	Only and always a Mother	24	8
8	Watch and pray	28	9
9	The heart of my Priests	29	9
10	It will be a new Church	Aug. 1	11
11	The purpose of your life	9	12
12	Close to my Heart in prayer	21	13
13	The great goal of sanctity	24	13
14	Night has fallen upon the world	28	15
15	For all my Priest-Sons	29	16
16	The Mother must be loved and lived	Sep. 19	17
17	These are my Priests	23	17
18	I will do everything for you	24	19
19	Foolishness is confound wisdom	27	20
20	A way of acting different from yours	Oct. 13	20
21	I want to save them – I will given them a new purity	16	20
22	The light of the Gospel	20	23
23	The hours of agony – Always with the Pope	30	24
24	From the hands of my Adversary	31	27
25	My faithful cohort	Nov. 1	27
26	The Demon fears and hates them	14	29
27	Only for my Son Jesus	27	30
28	The spirit of rebellion against God	Dec. 1	31
29	The triumph of my Immaculate Heart – Wisdom of Heart	19	33
30	The caress of a Mother	26	35
31	My Church will be renewed – They will love Him alone	28	36
32	They become intoxicated with emptiness	31	37

B2

1974

CENACLES OF LIFE WITH ME

[Chapter]		[Date]	[Page]
33	My Heart will be your refuge	Jan. 5	40
34	Cenacles of life with Me—The purpose of the Cenacles	17	41
35	The sign that I will give to each one	23	43
36	What a Mother can do	28	44
37	Rely on Me alone	Feb. 10	44
38	Let them live out the trust of the present moment	11	45
39	It is time that I myself gather them together	18	46
40	It will begin with my Priests	23	48
41	Great in Love	Mar. 11	49
42	I give you the joy of the Cross	23	50
43	Place them in my maternal Heart	27	51
44	Let them offer Me their sufferings	Apr. 1	52
45	I will give them this water	18	53
46	My beloved Priests	30	54
47	The prayer of my Priests	May 20	55
48	The Work I am accomplishing	27	56
49	I want to make Jesus live again—All your nothingness	June 8	57
50	In the furnace of the Heart of Jesus	21	58
51	I have no need of human means	24	59
52	I accept your crown of love	July 10	60
53	My triumph and that of my children	24	61
54	I will lead you by the hand	30	62
55	In heaven to be more a Mother	Aug. 15	63
56	My Reign	22	64
57	Pray for the Holy Father	28	64
58	No one passes beyond this point	Sep. 16	65
59	Prayer and docility to my voice	Oct. 23	66
60	How much you have need of a Mother!	29	66
61	The altar on which they will be immolated	Nov. 19	67
62	The sign which God gives	30	68
63	Revealed to the little ones	Dec. 7	69
64	Moments of anxiety—All poor in this way	24	70
65	The power of the Spirit	26	72
66	Your only light	31	73

1975

LIVE IN JOY

[Chapter]		[Date]	[Page]
67	Faithful to my voice and that of the Pope—The voice of the Church	Jan. 4	76
68	The time left to you	28	78
69	The joy of making you grow	Feb. 15	80
70	Without thinking of tomorrow	Mar. 15	81
71	The way of the Cross Good Friday	28	82
72	Do not grieve Me by your doubts—Prayer and trust	Apr. 25	83
73	Respond to my supreme call—Each thing in its place	June 7	85
74	Your heaviest cross—For the salvation of all	July 9	86
75	Serene in this time of your repose—A sign of reparation	24	88
76	Behold the handmaid of the Lord	29	90
77	The Priests are responding to Me—Your prayer	Aug. 5	91
78	Satan breaks loose	13	93
79	You will have them walk toward Me	23	94
80	Little to others, great to Me	Sep. 12	95
81	Offer and suffer with Me—Live in the present moment	15	96
82	What it means to be a Mother	Oct. 7	98
83	Be joyous—It is not the end!	18	99
84	Your silence	24	101
85	I am calling them all—Present in person	30	103
86	Live your consecration—Totally at my disposal	Nov. 9	105
87	This time will be shortened	25	107
88	I will be victorious—My Heart will triumph	Dec. 8	108
89	Do not fear—Jesus is your Savior!	24	110
90	The gift which I give to the Church—I will gather all the good	31	112

1976

YOU MUST BE LITTLE

[Chapter]		[Date]	[Page]
91	A sign of contradiction	Feb. 2	116
92	The perfume of your purity	11	118
93	The perfect consolers	Mar. 7	119
94	Mother of Jesus, and yours—Your true Mother	25	120
95	Your light will shine resplendently	Apr. 3	122
96	Look at my Crucified Son! (H. Tues.)	13	123

97	See if there is a greater sorrow (G. Fri.)	16	124
98	You will be capable of loving	May 3	126
99	Consecrate yourselves to my Immaculate Heart	13	127
100	Follow Me on the path of my Son	28	129
101	Say with Me your "yes"	June 19	130
102	Your necessary witness – The ecclesiastical dress	July 3	131
103	In the spirt of filial surrender – The coldness of desertion	16	133
104	My time	26	134
105	Your difficulties	31	135
106	Only with the Pope	Aug. 7	137
107	Live in Paradise with Me – Do not let yourselves be imprisoned	15	139
108	Your Queen and your Leader	22	141
109	You must be little	Sep. 8	143
110	This is why I speak to you – Little children understand their Mother	25	144
111	Look at your Mother!	Nov. 8	146
112	The time of the purification – Satan is seducing you	20	147
113	What are you afraid of? – In serentiy of spirit	Dec. 4	149
114	I ask the gift of your love	24	150
115	True poverty of spirit	31	152

1977

IN EVERY PART OF THE WORLD

[Chapter]		[Date]	[Page]
116	Walk in my light – It is good which triumphs	Jan. 1	156
117	I will teach you love	13	158
118	You will be completely renewed – You will be more beautiful	15	158
119	I am carrying you in my arms – The action of the Holy Spirit	Feb. 2	161
120	Pure of mind, of heart, of body	11	163
121	In every part of the world	18	165
122	Your martyrdom of the heart	Mar. 10	166
123	The angel of consolation	21	167
124	With Me beneath the Cross (G. Fri.)	Apr. 8	168
125	Do not let yourselves be led astray	23	169
126	My Plan	29	171
127	My battle	May 18	172
128	The snares of my Adversary	July 8	174
129	United in love	14	176

130	Your docility		25	177
131	Enter my garden		29	179
132	Love always!	Aug.	4	181
133	My property		6	181
134	The decisive move		24	183
135	I have been pointing out the way to you	Sep.	8	184
136	It is not given to all	Oct.	1	185
137	The miracle of the sun		13	186
138	Doubts and perplexity		29	187
139	Everything is about to be accomplished	Nov.	5	188
140	The Immaculate One at your side	Dec.	8	189
141	You too beget my Son—They no longer believe		24	190
142	The end of a period		31	192

1978

YOUR PUBLIC MISSION

[Chapter]		[Date]		[Page]
143	It will begin with the Church	Jan.	1	196
144	You can love this way too		6	196
145	Help Me, O sons		21	197
146	You will be immolated in the Temple	Feb.	2	198
147	Only then will you understand—The hour of the Martyrs		10	200
148	You must prepare yourselves now		11	201
149	You will be consoled	Mar.	3	203
150	The hour of darkness (Palm S.)		19	205
151	How much blood!—His blood and yours (G. Fri.)		24	206
152	You will be the witnesses—I will live again in you	Apr.	10	208
153	My hour has come	May	13	209
154	The whole Church is my refuge	June	3	210
155	This immense nation!		12	212
156	Your public mission—The final stage	July	13	213
157	A sign for all!		28	215
158	In the Heart of the Church	Aug.	5	216
159	The death of the Pope		9	218
160	Your new birth	Sep.	8	218
161	The hour of the apostles of light	Oct.	13	220
162	The new Pope, John Paul II		17	221
163	Do not feel you are alone	Nov.	2	222
164	My motherly action		25	223
165	Mother of the Church	Dec.	8	224
166	His second coming		24	226

1979

THE SIGNS OF THE PURIFICATION

[Chapter]		[Date]	[Page]
167	The plan of merciful love – Obey him in everything	Jan. 1	230
168	The first sign: confusion – There is no longer any belief	28	232
169	The second sign: lack of discipline	Feb. 2	234
170	The third sign: division	11	236
171	The fourth sign: persecution	Mar. 3	238
172	Your liberation is near – A new spring	9	240
173	Your interior equilibrium – Filial abandonment	25	242
174	Near my Son and my sons (G. Fri.)	Apr. 13	244
175	The Woman clothed in the sun	May 13	246
176	Jesus in the Eucharist	June 14	247
177	In my Immaculate Heart	23	248
178	In this Cova da Iria	July 1-7	250
179	Your response – Each at his post	29	251
180	The five first Saturdays	Aug. 4	253
181	Faithful, prompt and obedient	22	255
182	An anguished appeal	Sep. 8	257
183	The Angels of the Lord	29	258
184	Your Rosary	Oct. 7	259
185	In the temple of my Heart – Intense recollection	Nov. 21	261
186	The desert will blossom	28	263
187	Look at the heart	Dec. 3	265
188	Mother of all	8	266
189	How great a Light	24	267
190	Your last hour	31	268

1980

YOUR VICTORIOUS MOTHER

[Chapter]		[Date]	[Page]
191	Your victorious Mother	Jan. 1	272
192	A great net of love – Cenacles of prayer	22	273
193	Offer yourself to the glory of God	Feb. 2	275
194	Under my Immaculate mantle	11	276
195	With Jesus in the desert – You will be tested	Mar. 1	277
196	My 'yes' and yours – Withdraw from the clamor	25	280
197	In his greatest abandonment – One has stayed (G. Fri.)	Apr. 4	282
198	Have confidence	24	284

199	The same dimensions as the world	May 8	285
200	The time of battle	13	286
201	A torrent of water	June 14	287
202	The desert where I withdraw	29	289
203	The work of co-redemption	July 13	290
204	Mediatrix of Graces	16	292
205	The powerful weapon	Aug. 8	294
206	My glorified body	15	295
207	The rock of the great division	Sept. 2	297
208	He will come to you as fire	8	298
209	The sufferings of the Church	15	299
210	A great design on this people	Oct. 2	299
211	Do not sin any more	13	300
212	The marvels of love and of light	19	302
213	The way of unity	27	302
214	Mother of the poorest	Nov. 3	304
215	The power of the Gospel	14	305
216	Great mercy	Dec. 8	307
217	About the crib	24	308
218	The greatest cry	31	310

1981

THE LIGHT AND GLORY OF THE LORD

[Chapter]		[Date]	[Page]
219	The only possibility of salvation	Jan. 1	312
220	The light and glory of the Lord	Feb. 2	313
221	I look upon you with pleasure	11	314
222	Mortify your senses	Mar. 4	315
223	Yes, Father	25	317
224	Today the Passion is repeated	Apr. 17	318
225	In have come down from Heaven	May 13	320
226	Come, Holy Spirit	June 7	321
227	This is the hour of my Victory	July 1	322
228	Refuge of sinners	Aug. 15	325
229	Mother of Mercy	Sept. 4	326
230	By the power of the little ones	8	327
231	Mother of All Sorrows	15	328
232	Queen of the Angels	29	329
233	An interior wound	Oct. 13	330
234	Peace will come to you	22	331
235	The communion of Saints	Nov. 1	332

236 The great trial   12   333
237 On the road of perfect love   Dec. 8   334
238 In the cradle of suffering   24   336
239 A gentle and sad voice   31   337

1982

I AM THE MOTHER OF CONSOLATION

[Chapter]   [Date]   [Page]
240 I am the Mother of Consolation   Jan. 1   340
241 The light of love and hope   Feb. 2   341
242 The New Jerusalem   (First Fri.)   Mar. 5   343
243 "Yes" to the Gospel of Jesus   25   344
244 This is how I found my Son   (G. Fri.)   Apr. 9   346
245 Look to the Pope   May 13   347
246 The hour of the Holy Spirit (Pentecost)   30   349
247 In you the Mother is glorified   June 19 350
248 The Secret of my Immaculate Heart   30   351
249 Instruments of my mercy   Aug. 13 353
250 It will be saved   Sept. 8 354
251 A great force of reparation   15   356
252 I am the dawn   Oct. 13 357
253 Obedient, chaste and poor   Nov. 20 358
254 My plan   Dec. 8   360
255 God is with you   24   362
256 Watch in prayer   31   363

1983

OPEN WIDE THE GATES TO CHRIST
(Extraordinary Holy Year of the Redemption)

[Chapter]   [Date]   [Page]
257 Mother of Hope   Jan. 1   368
258 I am asking you for a spiritual childhood   Feb. 2   369
259 Love one another   11   371
260 The path of penance   Mar. 5   372
261 Open wide the gates to Christ   25   375

262	All Is Accomplished (Good Friday)	Apr. 1	377
263	Let Nothing Disturb Your Peace (Easter Sunday)	3	379
264	This Month of May	May 1	380
265	New Heavens and a New Earth (Pentecost)	22	382
266	The Gate of Heaven (Imm. Heart of Mary)	June 11	383
267	Why I Wanted You Here (San Marino)	29	385
268	The Holy Mountain (Our Lady of Mt. Carmel)	July 16	388
269	In the Light of Paradise	Aug. 15	389
270	Mother of the Purification	26	391
271	Ministers of the Redemption (1st Sat.)	Sept. 3	393
272	The Smallest of My Children	8	394
273	I Am Beneath the Cross	15	395
274	The Role of the Angels	29	397
275	The Dragon Will Be Shackled	Oct. 7	399
276	Leader of a Single Cohort	Nov. 1	401
277	Along the Roads of Africa (Presentation)	21	403
278	The Medicine You Need	Dec. 8	404
279	His New Birth	24	405
280	Return to Your Redeemer	31	407

1984

I ASK THE CONSECRATION OF ALL

[Chapter]		[Date]	[Page]
281	Have Courage	Jan. 1	410
282	My Book	21	411
283	My Signs	24	413
284	My Gift to You	28	416
285	The Soul Transpierced	Feb. 2	418
286	Look at My Spouse Joseph	Mar. 19	420
287	I Ask for the Consecration of All	25	422
288	Close to Every Altar (Good Friday)	Apr. 20	425
289	Be Converted	May 13	427
290	The Mystery of My Immaculate Heart	June 30	429
291	Mother of Jesus, The Priest	July 5	430
292	Walk in the Light	Aug. 15	432
293	Mother of Faith	30	433
294	In Cenacle with Me	Sept. 13	435

295	Be My Apostles		20	438
296	Do Battle Beloved Sons		Oct. 24	440
297	My Messages		Nov. 9	442
298	My Urgent Invitation		14	444
299	The Will of God		Dec. 8	446
300	Everything Has Already Been Revealed		24	447
301	The Signs of Your Times		31	449

1985

I AM THE BEGINNING OF THE NEW TIMES

[Chapter]
             [Date]   [Page]

302	I Am the Beginning of the New Times		Jan. 1	454
303	I See Your Littleness		Feb. 2	456
304	My Word		9	457
305	My Purity and Yours		14	460
306	The Fast Which I Ask of You		Mar. 16	464
307	The Hour of a New Agony	(Holy Thurs.)	Apr. 4	466
308	Your Sorrowful Passion	(G. Fri.)	5	468
309	Your Reparation		May 2	469
310	Come, Spirit of Love		26	470
311	Instruments of My Peace		July 5	472
312	Do Not Be Afraid		Aug. 15	475
313	The Hour of Public Witness		Sept. 8	476
314	The Two Cohorts		Oct. 13	478
315	My Path		Nov. 12	479
316	Blessed in Expectation		Dec. 1	480
317	Your Motherly Shepherdess		8	481
318	A Great Silence		24	482
319	Your Prayer with Me		31	483

1986

QUEEN OF PEACE

[Chapter]		[Date]	[Page]
320	Queen of Peace	Jan. 1	486
321	The Way to the Divine Will	Feb. 2	487
322	A Divine Mystery (Holy Thurs.)	Mar. 27	489
323	Why Have You Abandoned Me? (G. Fri.)	28	490
324	Jesus Is Your Peace	30	492
325	Mother of Grace and of Mercy	May 8	493
326	Anchor of Salvation	June 7	495
327	A Spirit of Joy and of Peace	July 4	497
328	Ark of the New Covenant	30	501
329	Climb the Mountain	Aug. 6	503
330	Mother of the Eucharist	8	504
331	You Will Give Peace of Heart	15	509
332	My Heart Is Bleeding	Sept. 6	510
333	My Birth	8	512
334	I Am Forming You to Suffering	15	513
335	With You in the Combat	29	515
336	The Rosary Brings You to Peace	Oct. 7	517
337	The Task Entrusted to the Church	27	519
338	Your Place in Paradise	Nov. 1	520
339	The Way Which Leads You to His Kingdom	23	522
340	My Remedy for Your Illnesses	Dec. 3	523
341	My Candor of Heaven	8	526
342	The Crib at His Glorious Return	24	527
343	And Peace Will Come to You	31	528

CENTERS OF DISTRIBUTION
FOR THE
ENGLISH LANGUAGE EDITION

INTERNATIONAL HEADQUARTERS
ITALY

MOVIMENTO SACERDOTALE MARIANO
Via Mercalli, 23
20.122 Milano, <u>Italy</u>

**UNITED STATES
OF
AMERICA**

THE MARIAN MOVEMENT OF PRIESTS
(National Headquarters)
Fr. Albert G. Roux
St. Francis, Maine 04774-0008

CANADA

THE MARIAN MOVEMENT OF PRIESTS
Rev. Lawrence J. Faye, C.S.B.
1515 Bathurst St.
Toronto, Ontario M5P 3H4

AUSTRALIA, NEW ZEALAND & OCEANIA
THE MARIAN MOVEMENT OF PRIESTS
Rev. Eugene Szondi
P.O. Box 301
Hurstville, N.S.W. 2220, Australia

ENGLAND
THE MARIAN MOVEMENT OF PRIESTS
Rev. Michael J. Gaughran, S.S.C.
890 New Chester Road
Bromborough
Wirral Merseyside
L62 6AT England

GHANA
THE MARIAN MOVEMENT OF PRIESTS
Rev. Albert Kretschmer, S.V.D.
Chancery Office, Box 247
Accra, Ghana, Africa

INDIA
THE MARIAN MOVEMENT OF PRIESTS
Rev. Rosario Stroscio, SDB
Auxilium Parish
8A, Mahendra Roy Lane
Calcutta, 700 046, India

INDONESIA
THE MARIAN MOVEMENT OF PRIESTS
Rev. Viktor M. Parera
8, JLN. Jenderal A. Jani
Sintang-KALBAR
West-Kalemantan, INDONESIA

IRELAND
THE MARIAN MOVEMENT OF PRIESTS
Rev. Michael Maher, S.M.
89 Lr. Leeson St.
Dublin 2
Ireland

KENYA
THE MARIAN MOVEMENT OF PRIESTS
Rev. Desmond O'Sullivan, C.SSp.
P.O. Box 80
Kalo-Machakos, Kenya, Africa

NETHERLANDS ANTILLES
THE MARIAN MOVEMENT OF PRIESTS
Rev. J. Bouman, O.P.
Pastorie Oranjestad
P.O. Box 702
Aruba, N.A.

PHILIPPINES
THE MARIAN MOVEMENT OF PRIESTS
Rev. Lorenzo MA. Guerrero, S.J.
1310 Belen-Perez Paco
P.O. Box 692
Manila, Philippines

SCOTLAND
THE MARIAN MOVEMENT OF PRIESTS
Rev. Benedict O'Keeffe
St. Cadoc's, 24, Fruin Ave.
Newton Mearns, Glasgow
G77 6HA Scotland

SOUTH AFRICA
THE MARIAN MOVEMENT OF PRIESTS
Rev. Ronald Cairns, O.M.I.
Catholic Church Alexandra
P.O. Box 39084, Bramley
2018 Johannesburg, South Africa

SOUTH KOREA
THE MARIAN MOVEMENT OF PRIESTS
Rev. Joseph A. Slaby, M.M.
Seong Dong, P.O. Box 10
Seoul 133, South Korea

SRI LANKA
THE MARIAN MOVEMENT OF PRIESTS
Rev. Theophane Wickramaratne, OSB
Paul VI Centre
Front Street
Colombo, 11, Sri Lanka

TANZANIA
THE MARIAN MOVEMENT OF PRIESTS
Msgr. Second Arbogast, V.G.
Moshi Cathedral
P.O. Box 3041
Moshi, Tanzania, Africa

THAILAND
THE MARIAN MOVEMENT OF PRIESTS
Rev. Marius Bray
Catholic Church
Korat
Pakchong 30130
Thailand, Asia

TRINIDAD
THE MARIAN MOVEMENT OF PRIESTS
Most Rev. Anthony Pantin
Archbishop's House
27 Maraval Road
Port of Spain, Trinidad, West Indies

UGANDA
THE MARIAN MOVEMENT OF PRIESTS
Brother Alphonsus
P.O. Box 25
Kisubi, Uganda, Africa

ZAMBIA
MARIAN MOVEMENT OF PRIESTS
Rev. Edward O'Connor, S.J.
The Catholic Church
P.O. Box 660-199
Monze, Zambia, Africa

CENTERS OF DISTRIBUTION
FOR EDITIONS
IN OTHER LANGUAGES

ARABIC

Rev. P. Antoine Messina
B.P. 23
83.140 Six Fours, France

CHINESE

Rev. Theobald Diederick, OFM
6 Henderson Rd.
Jar iner Lookout
Hong-Kong

Rev. C. Nardon
Catholic Church
335 Ta-Chi
San Min, Taiwan R.O.C.

Padre Cirillo Meacci
Padres Franciscanos
21, Calcado do Paiol
Macao

. . . .

CROATIAN

c/o Rev. Mihajlo Dudas
Radicev Trg. 5
41.000 Zagreb, Yugoslavia

. . . .

FLEMISH-DUTCH

Rev. Sylvester De Munter, OFM
Minderbroederstraat, 5
3.800 Sint Truiden
Belgium

Rev. Dr. Charles Dury, SDB
Arondeusstraat, 9
1063 Amsterdam,
Holland

. . . .

FRENCH

M. l'abbe Briot
19, rue de Robache
88100 Saint-Die
France

R.P. Arthur Delhaye, SDB
Rue Solovaz, 20
4240 Saint-Georges,
Belgium

Rev. Gabriel Parenteau
P.O. Box 8
St. Francis, Maine 04774
U.S.A.

R.P. Jacques Pagnoux
Foyer de Charite
Cap des Biches
C.P. 60
Rufisque-Dakar
Senegal, Africa

Mons. Norbert Rakotondrasoa
Eveque
38100 Antsirabe
Madagascar

M. Oscar Mutanda
B.P. 146
Kinshasa-Limete
Zaire, Africa

Rev. Georges Flieg
Foyer Ste-Marie
Box 995
Port-au-Prince, Haiti

GERMAN

Pater Herman Netter, SLD
Schrutkagasse, 48
1130 Wien
Austria

Dr. Hans Albert Reul
Blumenfeld
7708 Tengen 2,
W. Germany

HUNGARIAN

Rev. R. Melegh
3, Windsor Avenue
Para Hills
South Australia 50096

M.M.P.
St. Emeric Church
1017 N. 17th Street
Milwaukee, WI 53233
U.S.A.

. . . .

ITALIAN

Movimento Sacerdotale Mariano
P. Paolino Potalivo
Madonna dei Sette Dolori
65100 Pescara Colli
Italia

JAPANESE
Hayashi P. John
Catholic Church
Kita 4, Nishi 23, Chuo-Ku
064 Sapporo
Hokkaido, Japan

KOREAN
Rev. Joseph A. Slaby, M.M.
Seong Dong, P.O. Box 10
Seoul 133
So. Korea

LITHUANIAN
Rev. Chester Auglys
2751 West 38th Place
Chicago, IL 60632-1686

MAYLAYALAM
V. Rev. Andrew Fernandez, OCD
St. Joseph Seminary
Vazhapuzha P.O. 683-517
Kerala, S. India

POLISH
Not Available outside Poland

. . . .

PORTUGUESE
Movimiento Sacerdotal Mariano
Casa das Servas Reparadoras
Rua do Coracao de Maria
Cova da Iria, Fatima,
Portugal

Dr. Jose Sebastiano Saba
Rua Hilario Ribeiro 209
Cidade Vargas - CEPO 4319
Sao Paulo,
Brazil

RUMANIAN
P. Pietro Tocamel
Piazza SS Apostoli, 51
00187 Rome, Italy

SLOVENIAN

Rev. Ivan Pojavnik
1 Dolnicarjeva
61.000 Ljubljana,
Yugoslavia

. . . .

SPANISH

Padre Sylvio Venturini, CP
Gaspar Campos, 759
1638 Vicente Lopez
Buenos Aires,
Argentina

Padre Jose Allavena
Santuario de Lourdes
Casilla 2024
Santiago,
Chile

Padre Roberto Hymus, S.F.M.
Padres de Scarboro
Apartado 314
Santo Domingo, D.N.
Dominican Republic

Padare Angelo Cossu
Curico Provincial Somaseos
13 Avenida Y29 Calle, Zona 5
Guatemala City,
Guatemala

Padre James F. Lacey, C.SS.R.
Tacuari y Blas Garay
Casilla Postal 665
Asuncion,
Paraguay

H. Francisco Villescas
Convento San Francisco
Casilla 82
Santa Curz,
Bolivia

Padre Luis Bonilla, SDB
Salesianos CL Suffragio
Apatado Aero 1683
Medellin,
Columbia

Padre Bernabe M.
Loma Novoccidentalde
Pielsinca
San Miguel de los Bancos
Ecuador

Centro Xavier
Prados Providencia
A. Postal 1-133
C.P. 44100
Guadalajara, Jal.
Mexico

Padre Juan Jose Arteaga
Alvarez, SDB
Paseo de la Habana, 208
Madrid, 16,
Spain

Marian Movement of Priests
P.O. Box 8
St. Francis, ME 04774-0008
<u>U.S.A.</u>

Msgr. Pedro J. Ballester
Box 110, Station 6
Ponce, <u>Puerto Rico</u> 00732

TAMIL
Rev. Anthony Xavier
S.H. Sanatorium
Tuticorin-628 002
Tamilnadu, <u>India</u>

UKRANIAN
Collegio S. Giosafat
Passeggiata del Gianicolo
00187 Rome, <u>Italy</u>

VIETNAMESE
MARIAN MOVEMENT OF PRIESTS
P.O. Box 8
St. Francis, Maine 04774-0008
<u>U.S.A.</u>

TABLE OF CONTENTS

Page

Note from the New Spiritual Director ix
Preface xi
Our Lady Speaks to Her Beloved Priests 1

   1973 The Movement Is Now Born 3
   1974 Cenacles of Life with Me 39
   1975 Live in Joy 75
   1976 You Must Be Little 115
   1977 In Every Part of the World 155
   1978 Your Public Mission 195
   1979 The Signs of the Purification 229
   1980 Your Victorious Mother 271
   1981 The Light and Glory of the Lord 311
   1982 I Am the Mother of Consolation 339
   1983 Open Wide the Gates to Christ 367
   1984 I Ask the Consecration of All 409
   1985 I Am the Beginning of the New Times 428
   1986 Queen of Peace 485

Acts of Consecration A1
   For Priests A2
   For Religious and Laity A4
Index B1
Centers of Distribution C1
   International Center (Milan) C2
   English Edition C3
   Other Languages C7